I0012823

Kotlin
Bootstrapped

Learn, Code, and Build Like a Pro

By

Mike Zephalon

Copyright © 2025 by Mike Zephalon.

Book Title: Kotlin Bootstrapped: Learn, Code, and Build Like a Pro

All rights reserved. No part of this publication may be reproduced, transmitted, or distributed in any form or by any means, electronic or mechanical, including photocopying, recording, or any information storage or retrieval system, without the prior written permission of the author or publisher, except in the case of brief quotations used in reviews or scholarly works.

For information regarding permissions, please contact the author at:
mikezephalon@gmail.com

Publisher: Mike Zephalon

Disclaimer:

The author and publisher make no representations or warranties with respect to the accuracy or completeness of the contents of this book and specifically disclaim any implied warranties of merchantability or fitness for any particular purpose.

About Author

Mike Zephalon was born in Toronto, Canada, and developed a passion for technology and programming at an early age. His journey into the world of coding began when he was just a teenager, experimenting with simple scripts and exploring the vast possibilities of web development. Mike pursued his studies at the University of Toronto, where he majored in Computer Science. During his time at university, he became deeply interested in JavaScript, captivated by its versatility and power in building dynamic, interactive web applications.

Over the years, Mike has worked with several tech startups and companies, where he honed his skills as a front-end developer. His dedication to mastering JavaScript and its frameworks has made him a respected voice in the developer community. Through his books and tutorials, Mike aims to empower new and experienced developers alike, helping them unlock the full potential of JavaScript in their projects.

Table of Contents

1. Kotlin Basics

Introduction

Kotlin is a modern programming language that has gained immense popularity since its introduction by JetBrains in 2011. Designed to interoperate seamlessly with Java, Kotlin offers a concise, expressive, and safe syntax, making it a favorite among developers for building Android applications, server-side applications, and more. In this guide, we will explore the fundamentals of Kotlin programming, helping you understand its core concepts and how to get started.

1. What is Kotlin?

Kotlin is a statically typed, general-purpose programming language that runs on the Java Virtual Machine (JVM). It can also be compiled to JavaScript or native code, making it versatile for various platforms. Kotlin is officially supported by Google for Android development and is known for addressing many of Java's shortcomings, such as verbosity and null safety issues.

2. Features of Kotlin

- **Conciseness**: Kotlin reduces boilerplate code, making programs shorter and easier to read.
- **Null Safety**: Kotlin eliminates null pointer exceptions (NPE) by design.
- **Interoperability**: Kotlin works seamlessly with Java codebases, enabling gradual migration.
- **Coroutines**: Kotlin provides built-in support for asynchronous programming with coroutines.
- **Extension Functions**: Developers can extend the functionality of existing classes without modifying their code.

3. Setting Up Kotlin

3.1. Installing Kotlin

To start coding in Kotlin, you need to set up your development environment:

- **IntelliJ IDEA**: JetBrains' IntelliJ IDEA IDE provides first-class support for Kotlin.
- **Android Studio**: For Android development, Kotlin support is built into Android Studio.
- **Command-Line Compiler**: You can install the Kotlin command-line compiler from the official website.

3.2. Writing Your First Kotlin Program

Here's a simple "Hello, World!" program in Kotlin:

```
fun main() {
    println("Hello, World!")
}
```

4. Basic Syntax

4.1. Variables

Kotlin supports two types of variables:

- **Immutable Variables**: Declared using val. Their values cannot be changed once assigned.

```
val name = "John" // Immutable
```

- **Mutable Variables**: Declared using var. Their values can be reassigned.
- var age = 25 // Mutable

age = 26

4.2. Data Types

Kotlin has a rich set of data types, including:

- Numbers: Int, Double, Float, Long, Short, Byte
- Characters: Char
- Booleans: Boolean
- Strings: String

Example:

val number: Int = 42

val isKotlinFun: Boolean = true

val character: Char = 'K'

val message: String = "Hello, Kotlin!"

4.3. Functions

Functions in Kotlin are declared using the fun keyword:

```
fun greet(name: String): String {
    return "Hello, $name!"
}


fun main() {
    println(greet("Alice"))
}
```

Kotlin supports single-expression functions, allowing you to write concise function definitions:

```
fun square(number: Int) = number * number
```

5. Control Flow

5.1. Conditional Statements

Kotlin provides the usual conditional statements like if-else and when.

```
val age = 18
if (age >= 18) {
    println("You are an adult.")
} else {
    println("You are a minor.")
}
```

The when statement is a more powerful alternative to switch in Java:

```kotlin
val day = 3
val dayName = when (day) {
    1 -> "Monday"
    2 -> "Tuesday"
    3 -> "Wednesday"
    else -> "Unknown"
}
println(dayName)
```

5.2. Loops

Kotlin supports for, while, and do-while loops:

```kotlin
for (i in 1..5) {
    println(i)
}
```

```kotlin
var count = 1
while (count <= 5) {
    println(count)
    count++
}
```

6. Null Safety

One of Kotlin's standout features is its null safety mechanism, which prevents null pointer exceptions.

6.1. Nullable Types

By default, variables cannot hold null values. To allow null, you must declare the type as nullable using ?:

```kotlin
var name: String? = null
```

6.2. Safe Calls

To access a nullable variable safely, use the safe call operator ?.:

```kotlin
val length = name?.length // Returns null if name is null
```

6.3. Elvis Operator

The Elvis operator ?: provides a default value if the variable is null:

```kotlin
val length = name?.length ?: 0
```

6.4. Non-Null Assertion

You can force a nullable variable to be treated as non-null using !! (use with caution):

```kotlin
val length = name!!.length
```

7. Classes and Objects

7.1. Declaring Classes

Kotlin classes are concise and require less boilerplate than Java:

```kotlin
class Person(val name: String, var age: Int)
fun main() {
    val person = Person("Alice", 30)
    println("Name: ${person.name}, Age: ${person.age}")
}
```

7.2. Inheritance

Kotlin classes are final by default. To allow inheritance, use the open keyword:

```kotlin
open class Animal {
    open fun sound() {
        println("Some sound")
    }
}

class Dog : Animal() {
    override fun sound() {
        println("Bark")
    }
}

fun main() {
    val dog = Dog()
    dog.sound()
}
```

8. Collections

Kotlin provides a comprehensive collection framework, including lists, sets, and maps.

8.1. Lists

Lists in Kotlin can be mutable or immutable:

```kotlin
val immutableList = listOf(1, 2, 3)
val mutableList = mutableListOf(1, 2, 3)
mutableList.add(4)
```

8.2. Maps

Maps store key-value pairs:

```
val map = mapOf("key1" to "value1", "key2" to "value2")
println(map["key1"])
```

9. Lambdas and Higher-Order Functions

Kotlin treats functions as first-class citizens, enabling support for higher-order functions and lambdas.

9.1. Lambda Expressions

A lambda expression is an anonymous function:

```
val sum = { a: Int, b: Int -> a + b }
println(sum(3, 5))
```

9.2. Higher-Order Functions

Functions that take other functions as parameters or return them are called higher-order functions:

```
fun operate(a: Int, b: Int, operation: (Int, Int) -> Int): Int {
    return operation(a, b)
}
fun main() {
    val result = operate(3, 5) { x, y -> x + y }
    println(result)
}
```

Let's begin

Your Kotlin Development Environment

Welcome to Kotlin Apprentice! In this first chapter, you're going to set up a development environment to let you program in the Kotlin language and work with the sample projects for each chapter in the book.

Then, you'll write your very first Kotlin code and see how to run the code on your machine.

The primary tool that you'll use in this book to create Kotlin projects is **IntelliJ IDEA** from **JetBrains**. JetBrains is also the company behind the Kotlin language itself, so Kotlin development is very tightly integrated into IntelliJ IDEA.

IntelliJ IDEA is an **Integrated Development Environment**, or **IDE**, and is similar to other IDEs such as **Visual Studio** and **Xcode**. IntelliJ IDEA provides the foundation of many other IDEs from JetBrains, including **Android Studio** for Android app development, **PyCharm** for Python programming and **CLion** for C and C++ programming.

You use an IDE to write code in an editor, **compile** the code into a form that can be run on your computer, see output from your program, fix issues in your code and much more! You'll just scratch the surface of the power of IntelliJ IDEA in this chapter, but you'll be setup to work with the code examples throughout the rest of the book.

Getting started with IntelliJ IDEA

You can download IntelliJ IDEA from the JetBrains website. There are both **Community** and **Ultimate** editions of the IDE; you'll just need the Community edition to work with the code in this book. The Community edition is a free download.

Go ahead and download IntelliJ IDEA 2020.3 or later on your platform of choice. There are versions for macOS, Windows and Linux. Follow the installation instructions on the JetBrains site to install IntelliJ IDEA on your machine. Most of the screenshots in this book will be from the macOS version, but the Windows and Linux versions are similar.

Before you first run IntelliJ IDEA, you'll also want to install a **Java Development Kit**, or **JDK**, which will easily let you run Kotlin code on your machine.

Java and the JDK

Kotlin allows you to program on a number of different platforms. The two most prominent platforms are the **Java Virtual Machine**, or **JVM**, and **Android**. See "Kotlin Multiplatform" for more information on all the different platforms that Kotlin runs on.

In many ways, Kotlin was initially created as a modern replacement for the **Java** programming language. Java was created in the 1990's as an early attempt at a **crossplatform** application language, promising a "Write Once, Run Everywhere" approach to software development.

Instead of compiling to native machine code on each platform, Java programs are compiled into a format called **bytecode**. The bytecode runs inside an application on the Java Virtual Machine. The JVM can be thought of as a layer above your actual machine. By running as bytecode on a virtual machine, you are able to share Java code and applications across many types of computer systems.

One of the goals of the Kotlin programming languages is to be 100% **interoperable** with the Java language. This includes Kotlin code being converted to Java-compatible bytecode by the Kotlin compiler, so that the Kotlin code can be run on the JVM.

Most of the code and projects in this book are meant to be run as Kotlin projects on the JVM. In order to do so, you must install the JDK alongside IntelliJ IDEA. The easiest way to get a JDK for your platform is to visit the Oracle website.

You'll want to download and install the latest version of the JDK — at least version 8. The Java software tools go by the name "Java SE," which includes the JDK and also the **Java Runtime Environment**, or **JRE**.

Running IntelliJ IDEA

Once you've installed IntelliJ IDEA and the JDK, follow the normal process of starting the IntelliJ IDEA application on your platform.

If you've installed previous versions of IntelliJ IDEA on the same machine, the installer will likely prompt you to import settings from a previous version. If you've not installed previous versions on the same machine, you'll be prompted to choose a color theme and choose plugins to install into the IDE. You can just choose the default settings and proceed.

You'll then arrive at the **Welcome to IntelliJ IDEA** window.

From the welcome window, you can create new projects, import or open existing projects, check out code from a version control system such as **Git**, run configuration tools and get help on the IDE.

Your first project

Go ahead and choose **New Project** on the welcome screen. You'll see the first of two project configuration screens.

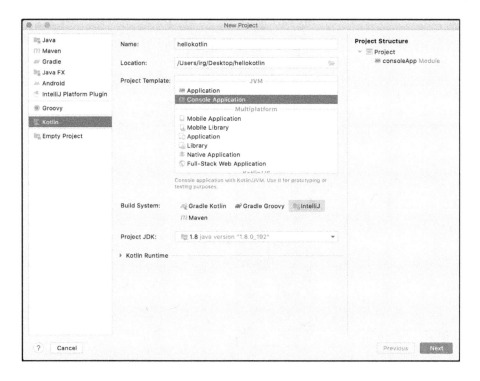

Choose **Kotlin** in the list of options on the left and **Console Application** as the project template. Type in **hellokotlin** as the project name, and choose a project location or accept the default, pick **IntelliJ** as a build system. You also see the **Project JDK**, which should be the JDK version that you installed earlier — or a different JDK version if you have more than one installed on your machine. When you are ready click **Next**.

You'll see the following:

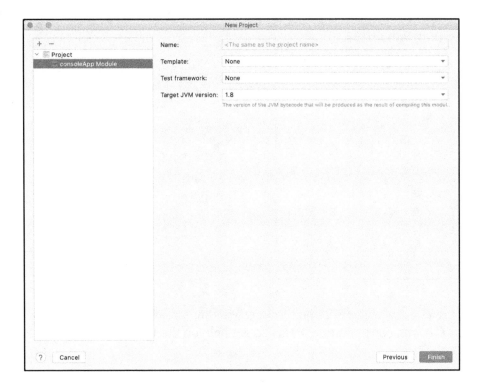

Pick **None** for both template and the test framework, later on, you will use different options for a faster setup of your project. Now click **Finish**.

At this point, IntelliJ IDEA will create and configure the project for you.

When it's finished, you'll arrive at a **Tip of the Day** window, which gives you helpful IntelliJ IDEA tips each time you open the application.

You'll see the following:

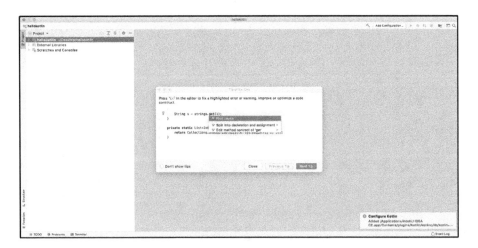

Close the tip window, and check out the **Project** panel on the left of the main IntelliJ IDEA window. The Project panel is where you manage all the files associated with the project, such as your Kotlin source code files, which end with a **.kt** file extension.

Click the arrow next to **hellokotlin** to reveal its contents, and you'll see a **src** folder for the project and its subfolders. Expand the **src** and **main** folders. Right-click on the **kotlin** folder and choose **New ▸ Kotlin File/Class**.

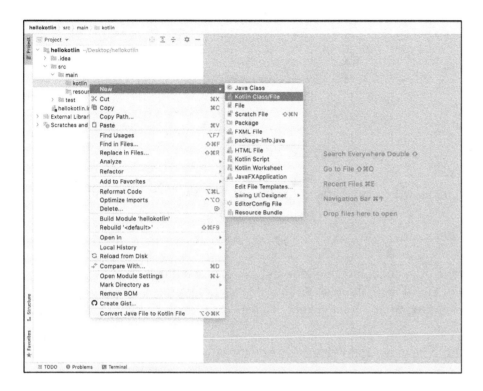

The **New Kotlin File/Class** dialog will open. Enter the name **hello** and double-click **File**.

The file **hello.kt** will then open in the IntelliJ IDEA editor.

The basic layout of the IntelliJ IDEA window contains the Project panel on the left, the **Editor** panel in the middle, and a **Toolbar** in the upper right that you can use to run your code.

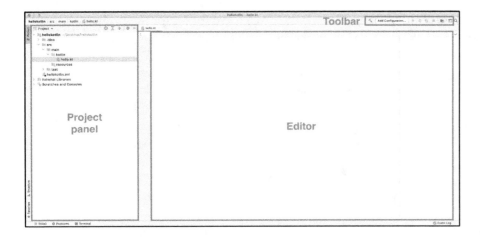

Now that your project is setup and you know the main parts of the IntelliJ IDEA window, it's time to run some Kotlin code!

Hello, Kotlin!

For this first chapter, you'll type some Kotlin code into an editor and run it, without necessarily understanding all the parts of the code. You'll learn more about the code you're typing as you proceed in the book. If you have experience with other programming languages, such as Java, Swift or Python, then the code might look familiar.

In the Editor panel for the file **hello.kt**, type in the following code exactly as written:

fun main() {

  println("Hello, Kotlin!")

}

You've written a single Kotlin **function** named main(), and added a single line of code to the function inside the braces, which then calls another function named println(). You're telling Kotlin to print the text "Hello, Kotlin!" to the screen. You'll learn much more about Kotlin functions later in the book.

There are a few different ways you can run this code, including using the IntelliJ IDEA menu, using the toolbar and using certain keystrokes.

The easiest way to run the code is to click the little green Run/Play button to the left of the main() function in the Editor panel. It may take a moment to show up after you add the code.

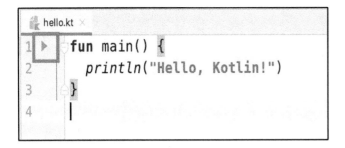

Go ahead and click the green Run button and a menu will open. Choose **Run 'HelloKt'** from the menu.

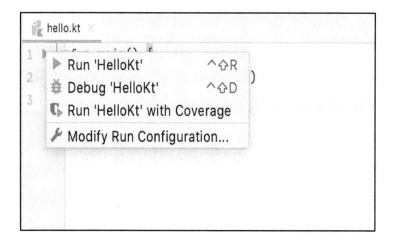

When you do, the Kotlin compiler will parse your code and convert the code to bytecode, and it will run it on your local JVM.

A panel will then open at the bottom of the IntelliJ IDEA window named the **Run** panel, sometimes also called the **console**.

You'll see the program output in the Run panel — in this case, the text that you wanted to show on the screen.

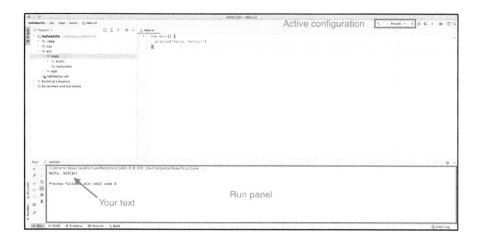

After this first run of the code in your project, you now have an active project **configuration** in the toolbar, and you can run the code by tapping the green Run button in the toolbar.

Nice! You've created your first Kotlin project and run your first Kotlin program!

Kotlin JVM projects

Kotlin JVM projects are just like the one you created in the last section of this chapter. For most of the chapters in the book, the projects look just like that project, with a single main() function in which you can put the Kotlin code you need to run. In certain cases, you may need to add code outside the main() function in the editor, and that will be pointed out when needed.

As you work through these chapters, you can either open the **starter** project for the chapter, which will have an empty main() function to which you can add code, or you can create a new project to work with, as you did in the last section.

In either case, you just enter code as you work your way through the chapter. You press the Run button in IntelliJ IDEA to run the code in the project at any point.

If you choose to create your own projects, you can always open the chapter sample code in a text editor if you want to see the code yourself, in order to address any issues, you have when entering the code. Just open the files that end with the extension **.kt** in a text editor like **Notepad** on Windows or **TextEdit** on macOS.

Try to avoid copy-and-pasting the code from a text editor into IntelliJ IDEA though, since typing in the code yourself helps to solidify your knowledge.

If you choose to open the starter project instead of making your own, do so by clicking **Open** from the **Welcome to IntelliJ IDEA** window, or selecting **File ▸ Open** from the IntelliJ IDEA menu.

You then just need to choose the root folder for the project, e.g., the folder named **starter** for opening the starter project, and click **Open**.

You'll see the following:

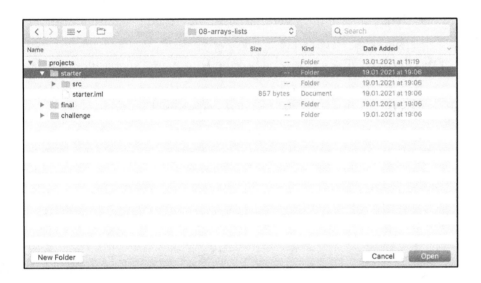

IntelliJ IDEA will then open the project, and you can start entering code as if you had created the project yourself.

When the project opens, you may need to select **View ▸ Tool Windows ▸ Project** to open the Project panel.

You can also click the Project tool button in the upper left of the IntelliJ IDEA window, or press **command-1** on Mac or **Alt-1** on PC to show the Project panel:

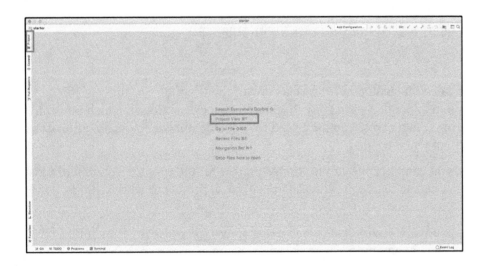

Once the Project panel is open, expand the root project and open up the **kotlin** folder to find the Kotlin source code files for the project:

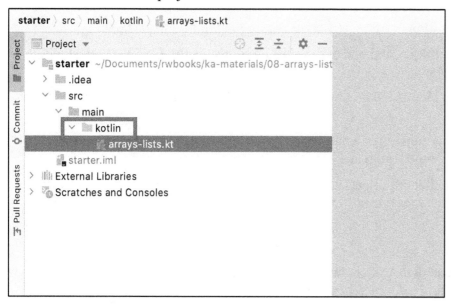

Gradle projects

For a couple of the chapters, the code projects use Gradle, in order to allow pulling an external dependency into the project.

Gradle is a **build system** and **dependency management** tool that is popular within the Java ecosystem. It's an extremely powerful and versatile build tool, and its power goes well beyond our purposes in the book.

Gradle is used as the build system for Android apps built using Android Studio, which, as was mentioned earlier, is based on IntelliJ IDEA.

To open the Gradle projects, you use the exact same steps as for the Kotlin JVM projects. You choose **File ▸ Open** and then navigate to and select the root folder of the project.

IntelliJ IDEA will detect that the project is Gradle-based and then open and configure the project accordingly.

Final projects and challenges

In addition to a starter project, each chapter also has a folder for the **final** project and a folder with solutions to the **challenges** you find at the end of each chapter. You can open the final and challenge projects in the same manner as described above for the starter projects. The challenge projects also contain solutions to **Mini-Exercises** that you come across in the chapters.

Challenges

Challenges are a key part of working through the Kotlin Apprentice. Each chapter contains some challenges at the end of the chapter, and most chapters contain Mini exercises in the text of the chapter. Solving the challenges and mini-exercises will enhance and enforce the knowledge you've learned in each chapter.

As your challenge for this first chapter, make sure you've both run through the process of creating a new Kotlin JVM project, as well as opened an existing project from the final project folder for Chapter. Make sure to run the code in both cases.

Doing so will ensure that you can run the sample code in the rest of the book.

Key points

- **IntelliJ IDEA** is an **Integrated Development Environment** from JetBrains, the creators of the Kotlin language, in which you can write and run Kotlin code.

- IntelliJ IDEA **Community edition** is a free version to use for the projects in the book.

- Kotlin code runs on many platforms, and one of the most prominent is the **Java Virtual Machine**, which will be used for most of the book.

- To build Kotlin projects with IntelliJ IDEA, you need to install the **Java Development Kit**, version 8 or above.

- The IntelliJ IDEA app window consists of a number of panels, the most relevant of which are the **Project** panel, the **Editor** panel, and the **Run** panel.

- The book starter, final and challenge projects can be opened by choosing **File ▸ Open** from the IntelliJ IDEA menu and selecting the root folder of the corresponding project.

Where to go from here?

There's a lot more to explore in IntelliJ IDEA, including debugging, refactoring, code profiling and version control system integration. You can find out more about these features of IntelliJ IDEA in the official JetBrains documentation.

Now that your setup with a development environment, in Chapter 2, "Expression, Variables & Constants," you'll first get a primer on how computers work, and then you'll start writing some real Kotlin code!

Expressions, Variables & Constants

You're going to learn a few basics. You'll learn how code works first. Then, you'll start your adventure into Kotlin by learning some basics such as code comments, arithmetic operations, constants and variables. These are some of the fundamental building blocks of any language, and Kotlin is no different.

First of all, you'll cover the basic workings of computers, because it really pays to have a grounding before you get into more complicated aspects of programming.

How a computer works

You may not believe it when you hear it, but a computer is not very smart on its own. The power of computers is all derived from how they're programmed by people like you and me. If you want to successfully harness the power of a computer — and presumably you do, if you're reading this book — it's important to understand how computers work.

It may also surprise you to learn that computers themselves are rather simple machines. At the heart of a computer is a **Central Processing Unit (CPU)**. This is essentially a math machine. It performs addition, subtraction, and other arithmetical operations on numbers. Everything you see when you operate your computer is all built upon a CPU crunching numbers many millions of times per second. Isn't it amazing what can come from just numbers?

The CPU stores the numbers it acts upon in small memory units called **registers**. The CPU is able to read numbers into registers from the computer's main memory, known as **Random Access Memory (RAM)**. It's also able to write the number stored in a register back into RAM. This allows the CPU to work with large amounts of data that wouldn't all fit in the bank of registers.

Here is a diagram of how this works:

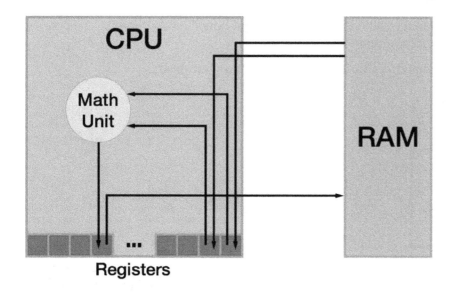

Registers

As the CPU pulls values from RAM into its registers, it uses those values in its math unit and stores the results back in another register.

Each time the CPU makes an addition, a subtraction, a read from RAM or a write to RAM, it's executing a single **instruction**. Each computer program is usually made up of thousands to millions of instructions. A complex computer program such as your operating system, be it iOS, Android, macOS, Windows or Linux (yes, they're computer programs too!), may have many millions of instructions in total.

It's entirely possible to write individual instructions to tell a computer what to do, but for all but the simplest programs, it would be immensely time-consuming and tedious. This is because most computer programs aim to do much more than simple math — computer programs let you surf the internet, manipulate images, and allow you to chat with your friends.

Instead of writing individual instructions, you write **code** in a specific **programming language**, which in your case will be Kotlin. This code is put through a computer program called a **compiler**, which converts the code into instructions the CPU knows how to execute. Each line of code you write will turn into many instructions — some lines could end up being tens of instructions!

In the case of Kotlin, with its origins as a language on the **Java Virtual Machine** or **JVM**, there is an extra layer between the compiler and the OS. The Kotlin compiler creates what is known as **bytecode**, which gets run on the JVM and converted to native code along the way. Kotlin began on the JVM but now it is possible to compile Kotlin directly to native code, as you'll see later in the book.

Representing numbers

As you know by now, numbers are a computer's bread and butter, the fundamental basis of everything it does. Whatever information you send to the compiler will eventually become a number. For example, each character within a block of text is represented by a number. You'll learn more about this in Chapter 3, "Types & Operations," which delves into types including **strings**, the computer term for a block of text.

Images are no exception. In a computer, each image is also represented by a series of numbers. An image is split into many thousands, or even millions, of picture elements called **pixels**, where each pixel is a solid color. If you look closely at your computer screen, you may be able to make out these blocks. That is unless you have a particularly high-resolution display where the pixels are incredibly small! Each of these solid color pixels is usually represented by three numbers: one for the amount of red, one for the amount of green and one for the amount of blue. For example, an entirely red pixel would be 100% red, 0% green and 0% blue.

The numbers the CPU works with are notably different from those you are used to. When you deal with numbers in day-to-day life, you work with them in **base 10**, otherwise known as the **decimal** system.

Having used this numerical system for so long, you intuitively understand how it works. So that you can you can appreciate the CPU's point of view, consider how base 10 works.

The decimal or base 10 number **423** contains **three units**, **two tens** and **four hundreds**:

1000	100	10	1
0	4	2	3

In the base 10 system, each digit of a number can has a value of 0, 1, 2, 3, 4, 5, 6, 7, 8 or 9, giving a total of 10 possible values for each digit. Yep, that's why it's called base 10!

But the true value of each digit depends on its position within the number. Moving from right to left, each digit gets multiplied by an increasing power of 10. So the multiplier for the far-right position is 10 to the power of 0, which is 1. Moving to the left, the next multiplier is 10 to the power of 1, which is 10. Moving again to the left, the next multiplier is 10 to the power of 2, which is 100. And so on.

This means each digit has a value ten times that of the digit to its right. The number **423** is equal to the following:

$$(0 * 1000) + (4 * 100) + (2 * 10) + (3 * 1) = 423$$

Binary numbers

Because you've been trained to operate in base 10, you don't have to think about how to read most numbers — it feels quite natural. But to a computer, base 10 is way too complicated! Computers are simple-minded, remember? They like to work with base 2.

Base 2 is often called **binary**, which you've likely heard of before. It follows that base 2 has only two options for each digit: 0 or 1.

Almost all modern computers use binary because at the physical level, it's easiest to handle only two options for each digit. In digital electronic circuitry, which is mostly what comprises a computer, the presence of an electrical voltage is 1 and the absence is 0 — that's base 2!

Here's a representation of the base 2 number 1101:

8	4	2	1
1	1	0	1

In the base 10 number system, the place values increase by a factor of 10: 1, 10, 100, 1000, etc. In base 2, they increase by a factor of 2: 1, 2, 4, 8, 16, etc. The general rule is to multiply each digit by an increasing power of the base number — in this case, powers of 2 — moving from right to left.

So, the far-right digit represents $(1 * 2^0)$, equal to $(1 * 1)$, which is 1. The next digit to the left represents $(0 * 2^1)$, equal to $(0 * 2)$, which is 0. In the illustration above, you can see the powers of 2 on top of the blocks.

Put another way, every power of 2 either is (1) or isn't (0) present as a component of a binary number. The decimal version of a binary number is the sum of all the powers of 2 that make up that number. So the binary number 1101 is equal to:

$(1 * 8) + (1 * 4) + (0 * 2) + (1 * 1) = 13$

And if you wanted to convert the base 10 number 423 into binary, you would simply need to break down 423 into its component powers of 2. You would wind up with the following:

$(1 * 256) + (1 * 128) + (0 * 64) + (1 * 32) + (0 * 16) + (0 * 8)$

$+ (1 * 4) + (1 * 2) + (1 * 1) = 423$

As you can see by scanning the binary digits in the above equation, the resulting binary number is 110100111. You can prove to yourself that this is equal to 423 by doing the math! The computer term given to each digit of a binary number is a **bit** (a contraction of "binary digit"). Eight bits make up a **byte**. Four bits is called a **nibble**, a play on words that shows even old-school computer scientists had a sense of humour.

A computer's limited memory means it can normally deal with numbers up to a certain length. Each register, for example, is usually 32 or 64 bits in length, which is why we speak of 32-bit and 64-bit CPUs.

Therefore, a 32-bit CPU can handle a maximum base-number of 4,294,967,295, which is the base 2 number 11111111111111111111111111111111. That is 32 ones—count them!

It's possible for a computer to handle numbers that are larger than the CPU maximum, but the calculations have to be split up and managed in a special and longer way, much like the long multiplication you performed in school.

Hexadecimal numbers

As you can imagine, working with binary numbers can become quite tedious, because it can take a long time to write or type them. For this reason, in computer programming, we often use another number format known as **hexadecimal**, or **hex** for short. This is **base 16**.

Of course, there aren't 16 distinct numbers to use for digits; there are only 10. To supplement these, we use the first six letters, **a** through **f**.

They are equivalent to decimal numbers like so:

- a = 10
- b = 11
- c = 12
- d = 13
- e = 14
- f = 15

Here's a base 16 example using the same format as before:

4096	256	16	1
c	0	d	e

Notice first that you can make hexadecimal numbers look like words. That means you can have a little bit of fun.

Now the values of each digit refer to powers of 16. In the same way as before, you can convert this number to decimal like so:

$(12 * 4096) + (0 * 256) + (13 * 16) + (14 * 1) = 49374$

You translate the letters to their decimal equivalents and then perform the usual calculations.

But why bother with this?

Hexadecimal is important because each hexadecimal digit can represent precisely four binary digits. The binary number 1111 is equivalent to hexadecimal f. It follows that you can simply concatenate the binary digits representing each hexadecimal digit, creating a hexadecimal number that is shorter than its binary or decimal equivalents.

For example, consider the number c0de from above:

c = 1100 0 = 0000 d = 1101 e = 1110

c0de = 1100 0000 1101 1110

This turns out to be rather helpful, given how computers use long 32-bit or 64-bit binary numbers. Recall that the longest 32-bit number in decimal is 4,294,967,295. In hexadecimal, it is ffffffff. That's much more compact and clearer.

How code works

Computers have a lot of constraints, and by themselves, they can only do a small number of things. The power that the computer programmer adds, through coding, is putting these small things together, in the right order, to produce something much bigger.

Coding is much like writing a recipe. You assemble ingredients (the data) and give the computer a step-by-step recipe for how to use them.

Here's an example:

Step 1. Load photo from hard drive. Step 2. Resize photo to 400 pixels wide by 300 pixels high. Step 3. Apply sepia filter to photo. Step 4. Print photo.

This is what's known as **pseudo-code**. It isn't written in a valid computer programming language, but it represents the **algorithm** that you want to use. In this case, the algorithm takes a photo, resizes it, applies a filter and then prints it. It's a relatively straightforward algorithm, but it's an algorithm nonetheless!

Kotlin code is just like this: a step-by-step list of instructions for the computer. These instructions will get more complex as you read through this book, but the principle is the same: You are simply telling the computer what to do, one step at a time.

Each programming language is a high-level, pre-defined way of expressing these steps. The compiler knows how to interpret the code you write and convert it into instructions that the CPU can execute.

There are many different programming languages, each with its own advantages and disadvantages. Kotlin is an extremely modern language. It incorporates the strengths of many other languages while ironing out some of their weaknesses. In years to come, programmers will look back on Kotlin as being old and crusty, too. But for now, it's an extremely exciting language because it is quickly evolving.

This has been a brief tour of computer hardware, number representation and code, and how they all work together to create a modern program. That was a lot to cover in one section! Now it's time to learn about the tools you'll use to write in Kotlin as you follow along with this book.

Getting started with Kotlin

Now that you know how computers work, it's time to start writing some Kotlin!

You may wish to follow along with your own IntelliJ IDEA project. Simply create one using the instructions from the first chapter and type in the code as you go.

First up is something that helps you organize your code. Read on!

Code comments

The Kotlin compiler generates bytecode or executable code from your source code. To accomplish this, it uses a detailed set of rules you will learn about in this book. Sometimes these details can obscure the big picture of why you wrote your code a certain way or even what problem you are solving. To prevent this, it's good to document what you wrote so that the next human who passes by will be able to make sense of your work. That next human, after all, may be a future you.

Kotlin, like most other programming languages, allows you to document your code through the use of what are called **comments**. These allow you to write any text directly alongside your code which is ignored by the compiler.

The first way to write a comment is like so:

// This is a comment. It is not executed.

This is a **single line comment**.

You could stack these up like so to allow you to write paragraphs:

// This is also a comment.

// Over multiple lines.

However, there is a better way to write comments which span multiple lines. Like so:

/* This is also a comment.

  Over many..   many...   many lines. */

This is a **multi-line comment**. The start is denoted by /* and the end is denoted by */. Simple!

Kotlin also allows you to nest comments, like so:

/* This is a comment.

 /* And inside it

 is another comment.

 */

Back to the first.

```
*/
```

This might not seem particularly interesting, but it may be if you have seen other programming languages. Many do not allow you to nest comments like this as when it sees the first */ it thinks you are closing the first comment. You should use code comments where necessary to document your code, explain your reasoning, or simply to leave jokes for your colleagues.

Printing out

It's also useful to see the results of what your code is doing. In Kotlin, you can achieve this through the use of the println command. println will output whatever you want to the **console**.

For example, consider the following code:

println("Hello, Kotlin Apprentice reader!")

This will output a nice message to the console, like so:

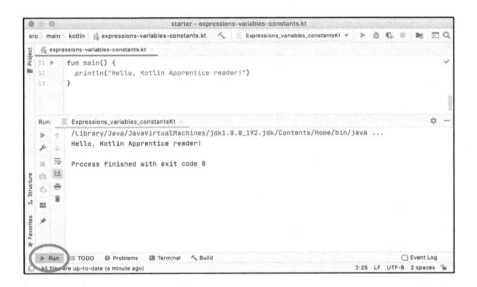

can hide or show the console using the **Run** button at the bottom highlighted with the red oval in the picture above.

Arithmetic operations

When you take one or more pieces of data and turn them into another piece of data, this is known as an **operation**.

The simplest way to understand operations is to think about arithmetic. The addition operation takes two numbers and converts them into the sum of the two numbers. The subtraction operation takes two numbers and converts them into the difference of the two numbers. You'll find simple arithmetic all over your apps; from tallying the number of "likes" on a post, to calculating the correct size and position of a button or a window, numbers are indeed everywhere!

In this section, you'll learn about the various arithmetic operations that Kotlin has to offer by considering how they apply to numbers. In later chapters, you see operations for types other than numbers.

Simple operations

All operations in Kotlin use a symbol known as the **operator** to denote the type of operation they perform. Consider the four arithmetic operations you learned in your early school days: addition, subtraction, multiplication and division.

For these simple operations, Kotlin uses the following operators:

- Add: +
- Subtract: • Multiply: *
- Divide: /

These operators are used like so:

2 + 6

10 - 2

2 * 4

24 / 3

Each of these lines is what is known as an **expression**. An expression has a value. In these cases, all four expressions have the same value: 8. You write the code to perform these arithmetic operations much as you would write it if you were using pen and paper.

In your IDE, you can see the values of these expressions as output in the console

using`println()`

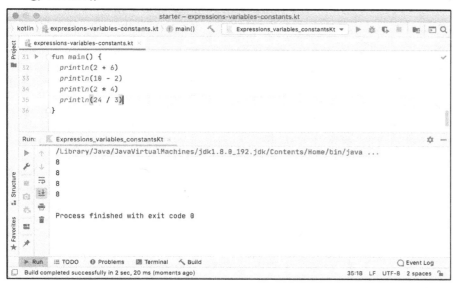

If you want, you can remove the whitespace surrounding the operator:

2+6

You can even mix where you put the whitespace. For example:

2+6   // OK

2 + 6 // OK

2 +6 // OK

2+ 6 // OK

It's often easier to read expressions if you have white space on either side of the operator.

Decimal numbers

All of the operations above have used whole numbers, more formally known as **integers**. However, as you know, not every number is whole.

As an example, consider the following:

22 / 7

This, you may be surprised to know, results in the number 3. This is because if you only use integers in your expression, Kotlin makes the result an integer also. In this case, the result is rounded down to the next integer.

You can tell Kotlin to use decimal numbers by changing it to the following:

22.0 / 7.0

This time, the result is 3.142857142857143 as expected.

The remainder operation

The four operations you've seen so far are easy to understand because you've been doing them for most of your life. Kotlin also has more complex operations you can use, all of them standard mathematical operations, just less common ones. Let's turn to them now.

The first of these is the **remainder** operation, also called the **modulo** operation. In division, the denominator goes into the numerator a whole number of times, plus a remainder. This remainder is exactly what the remainder operation gives. For example, 10 modulo 3 equals 1, because 3 goes into 10 three times, with a remainder of 1.

In Kotlin, the remainder operator is the % symbol, and you use it like so:

28 % 10

In this case, the result equals 8, because 10 goes into 28 twice with a remainder of 8. If you want to compute the same thing using decimal numbers you, do it like so:

28.0 % 10.0

The result is identical to % when there are no decimals, which you can see by printing it out using a **format specifier**:

println("%.0f".format(28.0 % 10.0))

Shift operations

The **Shift left** and **shift right** operations take the binary form of a decimal number and shift the digits left or right, respectively. Then they return the decimal form of the new binary number.

For example, the decimal number 14 in binary, padded to 8 digits, is 00001110. Shifting this left by two places results in 00111000, which is 56 in decimal.

Here's an illustration of what happens during this shift operation:

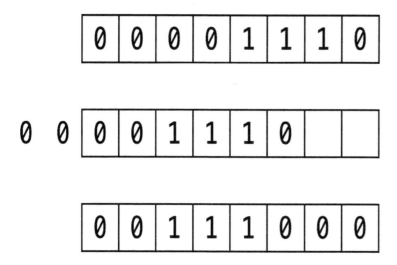

The digits that come in to fill the empty spots on the right become 0. The digits that fall off the end on the left are lost. Shifting right is the same, but the digits move to the right. The Kotlin functions for these two operations are as follows:

- Shift left: shl
- Shift right: shr

These are **infix** functions that you place in between the operands so that the function call looks like an operation. You'll learn more about infix functions later.

Here's an example:

1 shl 3

32 shr 2

Both of these values equal the number 8.

One reason for using shifts is to make multiplying or dividing by powers of two easy. Notice that shifting left by one is the same as multiplying by two, shifting left by two is the same as multiplying by four, and so on. Likewise, shifting right by one is the same as dividing by two, shifting right by two is the same as dividing by four, and so on.

In the old days, code often made use of this trick because shifting bits is much simpler for a CPU to do than complex multiplication and division arithmetic. Therefore, the code was quicker if it used to shift. However, these days, CPUs are much faster and compilers can even convert multiplication and division by powers of two into shifts for you. So, you'll see shifting only for binary twiddling, which you probably won't see unless you become an embedded systems programmer!

Order of operations

Of course, it's likely that when you calculate a value, you'll want to use multiple operators. Here's an example of how to do this in Kotlin:

((8000 / (5 * 10)) - 32) shr (29 % 5)

Note the use of parentheses, which in Kotlin serve two purposes: to make it clear to anyone reading the code — including yourself — what you meant, and to disambiguate.

For example, consider the following:

350 / 5 + 2

Does this equal 72 (350 divided by 5, plus 2) or 50 (350 divided by 7)? Those of you who paid attention in school will be screaming "72!" And you would be right!

Kotlin uses the same reasoning and achieves this through what's known as **operator precedence**. The division operator (/) has a higher precedence than the addition operator (+), so in this example, the code executes the division operation first.

If you wanted Kotlin to do the addition first — that is, to return 50 — then you could use parentheses like so:

350 / (5 + 2)

The precedence rules follow the same that you learned in math at school. Multiply and divide have the same precedence, higher than add and subtract which also have the same precedence.

Math functions

Kotlin also has a vast range of math functions in its **standard library** for you to use when necessary. You never know when you need to pull out some trigonometry, especially when you're a pro at Kotlin and writing those complex games!

To use the following math functions, make sure you have this **import** near the top of your file. Otherwise, IntelliJ IDEA will tell you it can't find these functions.

import kotlin.math.*

For example, consider the following:

sin(45 * PI / 180)

// 0.7071067811865475

 cos(135 * PI / 180) // -0.7071067811865475

These compute the sine and cosine respectively. Notice how both make use of PI which is a constant Kotlin provides us, ready-made with π to as much precision as is possible by the computer.

Then there's this:

sqrt(2.0) // 1.414213562373095

This computes the square root of 2. Did you know that sin(45°) equals 1 over the square root of 2?

Not to mention these would be a shame:

max(5, 10)

// 10

 min(-5, -10)

// -10

These compute the maximum and minimum of two numbers respectively.

If you're particularly adventurous you can even combine these functions like so:

max(sqrt(2.0), PI / 2) // 1.570796326794897

Naming data

At its simplest, computer programming is all about manipulating data. Remember, everything you see on your screen can be reduced to numbers that you send to the CPU. Sometimes you yourself represent and work with this data as various types of numbers, but other times the data comes in more complex forms such as text, images and collections.

In your Kotlin code, you can give each piece of data a name you can use to refer to it later. The name carries with it an associated **type** that denotes what sort of data the name refers to, such as text, numbers, or a date.

You'll learn about some of the basic types in this chapter, and you'll encounter many other types throughout the rest of this book.

Constants

Take a look at this:

val number: Int = 10

This uses the val keyword to declare a constant called number which is of type Int. Then it sets the value of the constant to the number 10.

Note: Thinking back to operators, here's another one. The equals sign, =, is known as the **assignment operator**.

The type Int can store integers. The way you store decimal numbers is like so:

val pi: Double = 3.14159

This is similar to the Int constant, except the name and the type are different. This time, the constant is a Double, a type that can store decimals with high precision.

There's also a type called Float, short for floating point, that stores decimals with lower precision than Double. In fact, Double has about double the precision of Float, which is why it's called Double in the first place. A Float takes up less memory than a Double but generally, memory use for numbers isn't a huge issue and you'll see Double used in most places.

Even though we call an item created with val a "constant," it's more correct to say that the identifier marked with val is what is constant.

Once you've declared a constant, you can't change its data. For example, consider the following code:

val number: Int = 10 number = 0

This code produces an error:

Val cannot be reassigned

In your IDE, you would see the error represented this way:

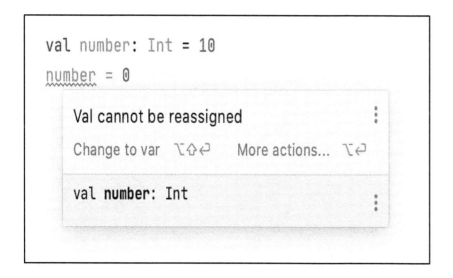

Constants are useful for values that aren't going to change. For example, if you were modeling an airplane and needed to keep track of the total number of seats available, you could use a constant.

You might even use a constant for something like a person's age. Even though their age will change as their birthday comes, you might only be concerned with their age at this particular instant.

In certain situations, for example, at the top level of your code outside of any functions, you can add the const keyword to a val to mark it as a **compile-time constant**:

const val reallyConstant: Int = 42

Values marked with const must initialized with a String or a primitive type such as an Int or Double. You can also use const inside a Kotlin type that you'll learn about in Chapter: "Objects."

Variables

Often you want to change the data behind a name. For example, if you were keeping track of your bank account balance with deposits and withdrawals, you might use a variable rather than a constant.

If your program's data never changed, then it would be a rather boring program! But as you've seen, it's not possible to change the data behind a constant.

When you know you'll need to change some data, you should use a variable to represent that data instead of a constant. You declare a variable in a similar way, like so:

var variableNumber: Int = 42

Only the first part of the statement is different: You declare constants using val, whereas you declare variables using var.

Once you've declared a variable, you're free to change it to whatever you wish, as long as the type remains the same. For example, to change the variable declared above, you could do this:

variableNumber = 0 variableNumber = 1_000_000

To change a variable, you simply assign it a new value.

Note: In Kotlin, you can optionally use underscores to make larger numbers more human-readable. The quantity and placement of the underscores is up to you.

Using meaningful names

Always try to choose meaningful names for your variables and constants. Good names can act as documentation and make your code easy to read. A good name specifically describes the role of variable or constant. Here are some examples of good names:

- personAge
- numberOfPeople
- gradePointAverage

Often a bad name is simply not descriptive enough. Here are some examples of bad names:

- a
- temp
- average

The key is to ensure that you'll understand what the variable or constant refers to when you read it again later. Don't make the mistake of thinking you have an infallible memory! It's common in computer programming to look back at your own code as early as a day or two later and have forgotten what it does. Make it easier for yourself by giving your variables and constants intuitive, precise names.

Also, note how the names above are written. In Kotlin, it is common to **camel case** names. For variables and constants, follow these rules to properly case your names:

- Start with a lowercase letter.

- If the name is made up of multiple words, join them together and start every word other than the first word with an uppercase letter.

- If one of these words is an abbreviation, follow the same pattern as if it was a word (e.g., sourceUrl and urlDescription).

Increment and decrement

A common operation that you will need is to be able to increment or decrement a variable. In Kotlin, this is achieved like so:

var counter: Int = 0

counter += 1 // counter = 1

counter -= 1 // counter = 0

The counter variable begins as 0. The increment sets its value to 1, and then the decrement sets its value back to 0.

These operators are similar to the assignment operator (=), except they also perform an addition or subtraction. They take the current value of the variable, add or subtract the given value and assign the result to the variable.

In other words, the code above is shorthand for the following:

var counter: Int = 0 counter = counter + 1 counter = counter - 1

Similarly, the *= and /= operators do the equivalent for multiplication and division, respectively:

counter = 10

counter *= 3 // same as counter = counter * 3

// counter = 30

counter /= 2 // same as counter = counter / 2 // counter = 15

Mini-exercises

If you haven't been following along with the code in IntelliJ IDEA, now's the time to try some exercises to test yourself!

1. Declare a constant of type Int called myAge and set it to your age.

2. Declare a variable of type Double called averageAge. Initially, set it to your own age. Then, set it to the average of your age and the age of 30.

3. Create a constant called testNumber and initialize it with whatever integer you'd like. Next, create another constant called evenOdd and set it equal to testNumber modulo 2. Now change testNumber to various numbers. What do you notice about evenOdd?

4. Create a variable called answer and initialize it with the value 0. Increment it by 1. Add 10 to it. Multiply it by 10. Then, shift it to the right by 3. After all of these operations, what's the answer?

Challenges

Before moving on, here are some challenges to test your knowledge of variables and constants. You can try the code in IntelliJ IDEA to check your answers. If you get stuck, check out the solutions included in the materials for this chapter.

1. Declare a constant exercises with value 9 and a variable exercise Solved with value 0. Increment this variable every time you solve an exercise (including this one).

2. Given the following code:

age = 16 print(age) age = 30 print(age)

Declare age so that it compiles. Did you use var or val?

3. Consider the following code:

val a: Int = 46 val b: Int = 10

Work out what answer equals when you add the following lines of code:

// 1

val answer1: Int = (a * 100) + b

// 2

val answer2: Int = (a * 100) + (b * 100)

// 3

val answer3: Int = (a * 100) + (b / 10)

4. Add parentheses to the following calculation. The parentheses should show the order in which the operations are performed and should not alter the result of the calculation.

5 * 3 - 4 / 2 * 2

5. Declare two constants a and b of type Double and assign both a value. Calculate the average of a and b and store the result in a constant named average.

6. A temperature expressed in °C can be converted to °F by multiplying by 1.8 then incrementing by 32. In this challenge, do the reverse: convert a temperature from

°F to °C. Declare a constant named fahrenheit of type Double and assign it a value. Calculate the corresponding temperature in °C and store the result in a constant named celcius.

7. Suppose the squares on a chessboard are numbered left to right, top to bottom, with 0 being the top-left square and 63 being the bottom-right square. Rows are numbered top to bottom, 0 to 7. Columns are numbered left to right, 0 to 7. Declare a constant position and assign it a value between 0 and 63. Calculate the corresponding row and column numbers and store the results in constants named row and column.

8. A circle is made up of 2π radians, corresponding with 360 degrees. Declare a constant degrees of type Double and assign it an initial value. Calculate the corresponding angle in radians and store the result in a constant named radians.

9. Declare four constants named x1, y1, x2 and y2 of type Double. These constants represent the two-dimensional coordinates of two points. Calculate the distance between these two points and store the result in a constant named distance.

Key points

- Computers, at their most fundamental level, perform simple mathematics.

- A programming language allows you to write code, which the compiler converts into instructions that the CPU can execute. Kotlin code on the JVM is first converted to bytecode.

- Computers operate on numbers in base 2 form, otherwise known as binary.

- Code comments are denoted by a line starting with // or multiple lines bookended with /* and */.

- Code comments can be used to document your code.

- You can use println to write things to the console area.

- The arithmetic operators are:

Add: +

Subtract: -

Multiply: *

Divide: /

Remainder: %

- Constants and variables give names to data.

- Once you've declared a constant, you can't change its data, but you can change a variable's data at any time.

- Always give variables and constants meaningful names to save yourself and your colleagues headaches later.

- Operators to perform arithmetic and then assign back to the variable:

Add and assign: +=

Subtract and assign: -=

Multiply and assign: *= Divide and assign: /=

Types & Operations

Now that you know how to perform basic operations and manipulate data using operations, it's time to learn more about **types**. Formally, a **type** describes a set of values and the operations that can be performed on them.

You'll learn about handling different types, including strings which allow you to represent text. You'll learn about converting between types and you'll also be introduced to type inference which makes your life as a programmer a lot simpler.

You'll also learn about Pair and Triple, which allow you to make your own types made up of two or three values of any type, respectively.

Finally, you'll learn about the important types Any, Unit, and Nothing.

Type conversion

Sometimes you'll have data in one format and need to convert it to another. The naïve way to attempt this would be like so:

var integer: Int = 100 var decimal: Double = 12.5 integer = decimal

Kotlin will complain if you try to do this and will spit out the following error:

Type mismatch.

Required: Int

Found: Double

Some programming languages aren't as strict and will perform conversions like this automatically. Experience shows this kind of automatic conversion is a source of software bugs and often hurts performance.

Kotlin disallows you from assigning a value of one type to another and avoids these issues.

Remember, computers rely on us programmers to tell them what to do. In Kotlin, that includes being explicit about type conversions. If you want the conversion to happen, you have to say so!

Instead of simply assigning, you need to explicitly say that you want to convert the type. You do it like so:

integer = decimal.toInt()

The assignment now tells Kotlin unequivocally that you want to convert from the original type, Double, to the new type, Int.

Operators with mixed types

So far, you've only seen operators acting independently on integers or doubles. But what if you have an integer that you want to multiply by a double?

You might think you have to do something like this:

val hourlyRate: Double = 19.5 val hoursWorked: Int = 10

val totalCost: Double = hourlyRate * hoursWorked.toDouble()

In this example, hours Worked is explicitly converted to a Double, to match the type of hourly Rate. But it turns out, this is unnecessary. Kotlin will allow you to multiply these values without any conversion, like so:

val totalCost: Double = hourlyRate * hoursWorked

In Kotlin, you can apply the * operator to mixed types. This rule also applies to the other arithmetic operators. Even though hours Worked is an Int, this will not remove the precision of hourly Rate. The result will still be 195.0! Kotlin attempts to be as concise as possible as often as possible and will try to infer the expected behavior when it can. This way you spend less time worrying about types and more time building awesome things!

Type inference

Up to this point in this book, each time you've seen a variable or constant declared it's been accompanied by a type declaration. You may be asking yourself why you need to bother writing the: Int and: Double, since the right-hand side of the assignment is already an Int or a Double. It's redundant, to be sure; your clever brain can see this without too much work.

It turns out the Kotlin compiler can deduce this as well. It doesn't need you to tell it the type all the time — it can figure it out on its own. This is done through a process called **type inference**. Not all programming languages have this, but Kotlin does, and it's a key component of Kotlin's power as a language.

So, you can simply drop the type in most places where you see one.

For example, consider the following constant declaration:

val typeInferredInt = 42

Sometimes it's useful to check the inferred type of a variable or constant. You can do this in IntelliJ by clicking on the variable or constant's name and holding down the **Control** + **Shift** + **P** keys. IntelliJ will display a popover like this:

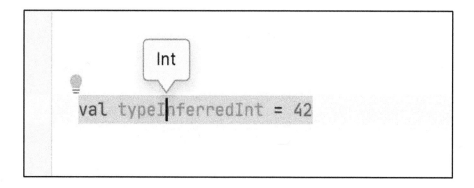

IntelliJ tells you the inferred type by giving you the declaration you would have had to use if there were no type inference. In this case, the type is Int.

It works for other types, too:

val typeInferredDouble = 3.14159

Holding down the **Control** + **Shift** + **P** keys reveal the following:

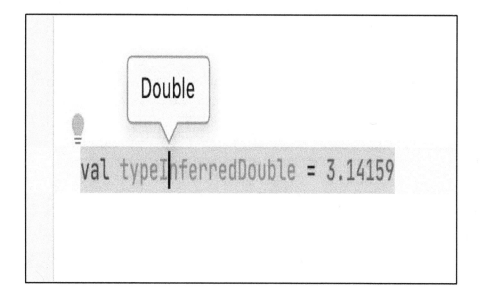

You can see from this that type inference isn't magic. Kotlin is simply doing what your brain does very easily. Programming languages that don't use type inference can often feel verbose, because you need to specify the often-obvious type each time you declare a variable or constant.

Note: In later chapters, you'll learn about more complex types where sometimes Kotlin can't infer the type. That's a pretty rare case though, and you'll see type inference used for most of the code examples in this book — except in cases where you want to highlight the type.

Sometimes you want to define a constant or variable and ensure it's a certain type, even though what you're assigning to it is a different type. You saw earlier how you can convert from one type to another. For example, consider the following:

val wantADouble = 3

Here, Kotlin infers the type of wantADouble as Int. But what if you wanted Double instead? The first thing you could do is the following:

val actuallyDouble = 3.toDouble()

This is like you saw before with type conversion.

Another option would be to not use type inference at all and do the following:

val actuallyDouble: Double = 3.0

Something you may be tempted to try is this:

val actuallyDouble: Double = 3

This is not allowed and results in the compiler giving you the following error: The integer literal does not conform to the expected type Double.

Mini-exercises

1. Create a constant called age1 and set it equal to 42. Create a constant called age2 and set it equal to 21. Check using Control+Shift+P that the type for both has been inferred correctly as Int.

2. Create a constant called avg1 and set it equal to the average of age1 and age2 using the naive operation (age1 + age2) / 2. Use Control+Shift+P to check the type and check the result of avg1. Why is it wrong?

3. Correct the mistake in the above exercise by converting age1 and age2 to type Double in the formula. Use Control+Shift+P to check the type and check the result of avg1. Why is it now correct?

Strings

Numbers are essential in programming, but they aren't the only type of data you need to work with in your apps. Text is also an extremely common data type, such as people's names, their addresses, or even the words of a book. All of these are examples of text that an app might need to handle.

Most computer programming languages store text in a data type called a **string**. This chapter introduces you to strings, first by giving you background on the concept of strings and then by showing you how to use them in Kotlin.

How computers represent strings

Computers think of strings as a collection of individual **characters**. In Chapter of this book, you learned that numbers are the language of CPUs, and all code, in whatever programming language, can be reduced to raw numbers. Strings are no different!

That may sound very strange. How can characters be numbers? At its base, a computer needs to be able to translate a character into the computer's own language, and it does so by assigning each character a different number. This forms a two-way mapping from character to number that is called a **character set**.

When you press a character key on your keyboard, you are actually communicating the number of the character to the computer. Your word processor application converts that number into a picture of the character and finally, presents that picture to you.

Unicode

In isolation, a computer is free to choose whatever character set mapping it likes. If the computer wants the letter **a** to equal the number 10, then so be it. But when computers start talking to each other, they need to use a common character set. If two computers used different character sets, then when one computer transferred a string to the other, they would end up thinking the strings contained different characters.

There have been several standards over the years, but the most modern standard is **Unicode**. It defines the character set mapping that almost all computers use today.

As an example, consider the word **cafe**. The Unicode standard tells us that the letters of this word should be mapped to numbers like so:

c	a	f	e
99	97	102	101

The number associated with each character is called a **code point**. So, in the example above, **c** uses code point 99, **a** uses code points 97, and so on.

Of course, Unicode is not just for the simple Latin characters used in English, such as **c**, **a**, **f** and **e**. It also lets you map characters from languages around the world. The word **cafe**, as you're probably aware, is derived from French, in which it's written as **café**. Unicode maps these characters like so:

c	a	f	é
99	97	102	233

And here's an example using Chinese characters (this, according to Google translate, means "Computer Programming"):

电	脑	编	程
30005	33041	32534	31243

You've probably heard of emojis, which are small pictures you can use in your text.

These pictures are, in fact, just normal characters and are also mapped by Unicode. For example:

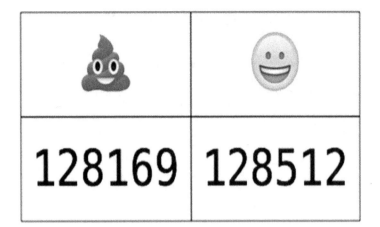

128169	128512

This is only two characters. The code points for these are very large numbers, but each is still only a single code point. The computer considers these as no different than any other two characters.

Note: The word "emoji" comes from Japanese, where "e" means picture and "moji" means character.

Strings in Kotlin

Kotlin, like any good programming language, can work directly with characters and strings. It does so through the data types Char and String, respectively. In this section, you'll learn about these data types and how to work with them.

Characters and strings

The Char data type can store a single character which must be wrapped in single quotes. For example:

val characterA: Char = 'a'

This data type is designed to hold only single characters. The String data type, on the other hand, stores multiple characters, which must be wrapped in double quotes. For example:

val stringDog: String = "Dog"

It's as simple as that! The right-hand side of this expression is what's known as a **string literal**; it's the Kotlin syntax for representing a string.

Of course, type inference applies here as well. If you remove the type in the above declaration, then Kotlin does the right thing and makes the stringDog a String constant:

val stringDog = "Dog" // Inferred to be of type String

Concatenation

You can do much more than create simple strings. Sometimes you need to manipulate a string, and one common way to do so is to combine it with another string.

In Kotlin, you do this in a rather simple way: by using the addition operator. Just as you can add numbers, you can add strings:

var message = "Hello" + " my name is "

val name = "Joe" message += name // "Hello my name is Joe"

You need to declare message as a variable rather than a constant because you want to modify it. You can add string literals together, as in the first line, and you can add string variables or constants together, as in the last line.

It's also possible to add characters directly to a string. This is similar to how you can easily work with numbers if one is an Int and the other is a Double.

To add a character to a string, you do this:

```
val exclamationMark: Char = '!' message += exclamationMark // "Hello my name is Joe!"
```

No need to explicitly convert the Character to a String before you add it to message; Kotlin takes care of that for you!

String templates

You can also build up a string by using **string templates**, which use a special Kotlin syntax that lets you build a string in a way that's easy to read:

```
message = "Hello my name is $name!" // "Hello my name is Joe!"
```

This is much more readable than the example from the previous section. It's an extension of the string literal syntax, whereby you replace certain parts of the string with other values. Simply prepend the value you want to insert with a $ symbol.

This syntax works in the same way to build a string from other data types, such as numbers:

```
val oneThird = 1.0 / 3.0 val oneThirdLongString = "One third is $oneThird as a decimal."
```

Here, you use a Double in the template. At the end of this code, your oneThirdLongString constant will contain the following:

```
One third is 0.3333333333333333 as a decimal.
```

Of course, it would actually take infinite characters to represent one third as a decimal, because it's a repeating decimal. Using string templates with a Double gives you no way to control the precision of the resulting string.

This is an unfortunate consequence of using string templates: they're simple to use, but offers no ability to customize the output.

You can also put expressions inside a string template, by following the $ symbol with a pair of braces that contain the expression:

```
val oneThirdLongString = "One third is ${1.0 / 3.0} as a decimal."
```

The result is just the same as before.

Multi-line strings

Kotlin has a neat way to express strings that contain multiple lines. This can be rather useful when you need to put a very long string in your code.

You do it like so:

```
val bigString = """
  |You can have a string
  |that contains multiple
  |lines
  |by
  |doing this.
  """.trimMargin() println(bigString)
```

The three double-quotes signify that this is a multi-line string. Handily, the first and final new lines do not become part of the string. This makes it more flexible as you don't have to have the three double-quotes on the same line as the string.

In the case above, it will print the following:

You can have a string that contains multiple lines by doing this.

Notice |, also known as the "pipe character", at the start of each line as well as the call to trimMargin(). This prevents the string from having leading spaces, allowing you to format your code with pretty indentation without affecting the output.

Mini-exercises

1. Create a string constant called firstName and initialize it to your first name.

Also create a string constant called lastName and initialize it to your last name.

2. Create a string constant called fullName by adding the firstName and lastName constants together, separated by a space.

3. Using string templates, create a string constant called myDetails that uses the fullName constant to create a string introducing yourself. For example, it could read: "Hello, my name is Joe Howard.".

Pairs and Triples

Sometimes data comes in groups. An example of this is a pair of (x, y) coordinates on a 2D grid. Similarly, a set of coordinates on a 3D grid is comprised of an x-value, a y-value and a z-value. In Kotlin, you can represent such related data in a very simple way through the use of a Pair or Triple.

Other languages use a type named "Tuple" to hold similar combinations of values.

Pair or Triple are types that represent data composed of two or three values of any type. If you want to have more than three values, you use what Kotlin calls a data class, which you will cover in a future chapter.

Sticking with Pair for now, as an example you can define a pair of 2D coordinates where each axis value is an integer, like so:

```
val coordinates: Pair<Int, Int> = Pair(2, 3)
```

The type of coordinates is Pair<Int, Int>. The types of the values within the Pair, in this case Int, are separated by commas and surrounded by <>. The code for creating the Pair is much the same, with each value separated by commas and surrounded by parentheses.

Type inference can infer Pair types too:

```
val coordinatesInferred = Pair(2, 3)
```

You can make this even more concise, which Kotlin loves to do, by using the two operators:

```
val coordinatesWithTo = 2 to 3
```

You could similarly create a Pair of Double values, like so:

```
val coordinatesDoubles = Pair(2.1, 3.5)
// Inferred to be of type Pair<Double, Double>
```

Or you could mix and match the types comprising the pair, like so:

```kotlin
val coordinatesMixed = Pair(2.1, 3)
// Inferred to be of type Pair<Double, Int>
```

And here's how to access the data inside a Pair:

```kotlin
val x1 = coordinates.first val y1 = coordinates.second
```

You can reference each item in the Pair by its position in the pair, starting with first. So, in this example, x1 will equal 2 and y1 will equal 3.

In the previous example, it may not be immediately obvious that the first value is the x-coordinate and the second value is the y-coordinate. This is another demonstration of why it's important to always name your variables in a way that avoids confusion.

Fortunately, Kotlin allows you to use a destructuring declaration on individual parts of a Pair, and you can be explicit about what each part represents. For example:

```kotlin
val (x, y) = coordinates
// x and y both inferred to be of type Int
```

Here, you extract the values from coordinates and assign them to x and y.

Triple works much the same way as Pair, just with three values instead of two.

If you want to access multiple parts of a Triple at the same time, as in the examples above, you can also use a shorthand syntax to make it easier:

```kotlin
val coordinates3D = Triple(2, 3, 1) val (x3, y3, z3) = coordinates3D
```

This declares three new constants, x3, y3 and z3, and assigns each part of the Triple to them in turn. The code is equivalent to the following:

```kotlin
val coordinates3D = Triple(2, 3, 1) val x3 = coordinates3D.first val y3 = coordinates3D.second val z3 = coordinates3D.third
```

If you want to ignore a certain element of a Pair or Triple, you can replace the corresponding part of the declaration with an underscore. For example, if you were performing a 2D calculation and wanted to ignore the z-coordinate of coordinates3D, then you'd write the following:

```kotlin
val (x4, y4, _) = coordinates3D
```

This line of code only declares x4 and y4. The _ is special and simply means you're ignoring this part for now.

Mini-exercises

1. Declare a constant Triple that contains three Int values. Use this to represent a date (month, day, year).

2. Extract the values in the triple into three constants named month, day and year.

3. In one line, read the month and year values into two constants. You'll need to employ the underscore to ignore the day.

4. Since the values inside Pairs and Triples cannot be modified, you will need to extract the values from them, make any modifications you want, and then create a new Pair or Triple. Using the values you extracted in step three, modify the month value and create a new Pair containing the modified month along with the unmodified year.

Number types

Many C-based languages like Java have primitive types that take up a specific number of bytes. For example, in Java, a 32-bit signed primitive number is an int. There is also an object version of an int known as an Integer. You may be wondering why it is necessary to have two types that store the same number type.

Well, primitives require less memory, which means they are better for performance, but they also lack some of the features of Integer. The good news is in Kotlin, you don't have to worry about whether you need to use a primitive type or an object type. Kotlin handles that complexity for you, so all you have to do is use an Int.

You've been using Int to represent whole numbers which are represented using 32 bits. Kotlin provides many more number types that use different amounts of storage. For whole numbers, you can use Byte, Short, and Long. These types consume 1, 2, and 8 bytes of storage respectively. Each of these types use one bit to represent the sign.

Here is a summary of the different integer types and their storage size in bytes. Most of the time you will just want to use an Int. These become useful if your code is interacting with another piece of software that uses one of these more exact sizes or if you need to optimize for storage size.

Type	Minimum value	Maximum value	Storage size
Byte	-128	127	1
Short	-32768	32767	2
Int	-2147483648	2147483647	4
Long	-9223372036854775807	9223372036854775806	8

You've been using Double to represent fractional numbers. Kotlin offers a Float type which has less range and precision than Double, but requires half as much storage. Modern hardware has been optimized for Double so it is the one that you should reach for unless you have good reason not to.

Type	Minimum value	Maximum value	Precision	Storage size
Float	-3.4028235E+38	3.4028235E+38	6 digits	1
Double	-1.797693E+308	1.797693E+308	15 digits	2

Most of the time you will just use Int and Double to represent numbers, but every once in a while, you might encounter the other types. Suppose you need to add together a Short with a Byte and a Long. You can do that like so:

val a: Short = 12 val b: Byte = 120 val c: Int = -100000

val answer = a + b + c // Answer will be an Int

Any, Unit, and Nothing Types

The Any type can be thought of as the mother of all other types (except nullable types, which will be covered in Chapter 7). Every type in Kotlin, whether an Int or a String, is also considered an Any. This is similar to the Object type in Java, which is the root of all types except primitives.

For example, it is perfectly valid Kotlin to declare an Int literal and String literal as Any like so:

val anyNumber: Any = 42 val anyString: Any = "42"

Unit is a special type which only ever represents one value: the Unit object. It is similar to the void type in Java, except it makes working with generics easier. Every function (you will cover functions in Chapter, but for now think of a function as a piece of reusable code) which does not explicitly return a type, e.g., a String, returns Unit.

For example, here is a function that simply adds 2 + 2 and prints the result but does not actually return anything:

```
fun add() {   val result = 2 + 2   println(result)
}
```

The return type Unit is implied, so the above function is the same as this:

```
fun add(): Unit {   val result = 2 + 2   println(result)
}
```

Nothing is a type that is helpful for declaring that a function not only doesn't return anything, but also never completes.

This can occur if a function either causes the program to stop completely by throwing an Exception or if it simply goes on forever without ever finishing.

By way of example, the saddest function ever written:

```
fun doNothingForever(): Nothing {

  while(true) {

  }

}
```

You will cover while loops more in the next chapter, but for now understand that this function will simply run forever without ever returning anything. Welcome to the land of Nothing!

Basic Control Flow

When writing a computer program, you need to be able to tell the computer what to do in different scenarios. For example, a calculator app would need to do one thing if the user tapped the addition button and another thing if the user tapped the subtraction button.

In computer-programming terms, this concept is known as **control flow**. It is so named because the flow of the program is controlled by various methods. In this chapter, you'll learn how to make decisions and repeat tasks in your programs by using syntax to control the flow. You'll also learn about **Booleans**, which represent true and false values, and how you can use these to compare data.

Open up a project in IntelliJ to follow along!

Comparison operators

You've seen a few types now, such as Int, Double and String. Here you'll learn about another type, one that will let you compare values through the **comparison operators**.

When you perform a comparison, such as looking for the greater of two numbers, the answer is either true or false. Kotlin has a data type just for this! It's called a Boolean, after a rather clever man named George

Boole who invented an entire field of mathematics around the concept of true and false.

This is how you use a Boolean in Kotlin:

val yes: Boolean = true val no: Boolean = false

And because of Kotlin's type inference, you can leave off the type annotation:

val yes = true val no = false

A Boolean can only be either true or false, denoted by the keywords true and false. In the code above, you use the keywords to set the state of each constant.

Boolean operators

Booleans are commonly used to compare values. For example, you may have two values and you want to know if they're equal: either they are (true) or they aren't (false).

In Kotlin, you do this using the **equality operator**, which is denoted by ==. Try it out:

val doesOneEqualTwo = (1 == 2)

Kotlin infers that doesOneEqualTwo is a Boolean. Clearly, 1 does not equal 2, and therefore doesOneEqualTwo will be false.

Similarly, you can find out if two values are not equal using the != operator:

val doesOneNotEqualTwo = (1 != 2)

This time, the comparison is true because 1 does not equal 2, so doesOneNotEqualTwo will be true.

The prefix ! operator, also called the **not-operator**, toggles true to false and false to true. Another way to write the above is:

val alsoTrue = !(1 == 2)

Because 1 does not equal 2, (1 == 2) is false, and then ! flips it to true.

Two more operators let you determine if a value is greater than (>) or less than (<) another value. You'll likely know these from mathematics:

val isOneGreaterThanTwo = (1 > 2) val isOneLessThanTwo = (1 < 2)

And it's not rocket science to work out that isOneGreaterThanTwo will equal false and isOneLessThanTwo will equal true.

There's also an operator that lets you test if a value is less than or equal to another value: <=. It's a combination of < and ==, and will therefore return true if the first value is either less than the second value or equal to it.

Similarly, there's an operator that lets you test if a value is greater than or equal to another — you may have guessed that it's >=.

Boolean logic

Each of the examples above tests just one condition. When George Boole invented the Boolean, he had much more planned for it than these humble beginnings. He invented Boolean logic, which lets you combine multiple conditions to form a result.

One way to combine conditions is by using **AND**. When you AND together two Booleans, the result is another Boolean. If both input Booleans are true, then the result is true. Otherwise, the result is false.

In Kotlin, the operator for Boolean AND is &&, used like so:

val and = true && true

In this case, and will be true. If either of the values on the right was false, then and would be false.

Another way to combine conditions is by using **OR**. When you OR together two Booleans, the result is true if either of the input Booleans is true. Only if both input Booleans are false will the result be false.

In Kotlin, the operator for Boolean OR is ||, used like so:

val or = true || false

In this case, or will be true. If both values on the right were false, then or would be false. If both were true, then or would still be true.

In Kotlin, Boolean logic is usually applied to multiple conditions. Maybe you want to determine if two conditions are true; in that case, you'd use AND. If you only care about whether one of two conditions is true, then you'd use OR.

For example, consider the following code:

val andTrue = 1 < 2 && 4 > 3 val andFalse = 1 < 2 && 3 > 4
val orTrue = 1 < 2 || 3 > 4 val orFalse = 1 == 2 || 3 == 4

Each of these tests two separate conditions, combining them with either AND or OR.

It's also possible to use Boolean logic to combine more than two comparisons. For example, you can form a complex comparison like so:

val andOr = (1 < 2 && 3 > 4) || 1 < 4

The parentheses disambiguate the expression. First Kotlin evaluates the subexpression inside the parentheses, and then it evaluates the full expression, following these steps:

(1 < 2 && 3 > 4) || 1 < 4

(true && false) || true

false || true

true

String equality

Sometimes you want to determine if two strings are equal. For example, a children's game of naming an animal in a photo would need to determine if the player answered correctly.

In Kotlin, you can compare strings using the standard equality operator, ==, in exactly the same way as you compare numbers. For example:

val guess = "dog" val dogEqualsCat = guess == "cat"

Here, dogEqualsCat is a Boolean that in this case equals false, because "dog" does not equal "cat". Simple!

Just as with numbers, you can compare not just for equality, but also to determine if one value is greater than or less that another value. For example:

val order = "cat" < "dog"

This syntax checks if one string comes before another alphabetically. In this case, order equals true because "cat" comes before "dog".

The if expression

The first and most common way of controlling the flow of a program is through the use of an **if expression**, which allows the program to do something only if a certain condition is true.

For example, try typing out and running the following:

```
if (2 > 1) {
  println("Yes, 2 is greater than 1.")
}
```

This is a simple if expression. If the condition is true, then the expression will execute the code between the braces. If the condition is false, then the expression won't execute the code between the braces. It's as simple as that!

The term **if expression** is used here instead of **if statement**, since, unlike many other programming languages, a value is returned from the if expression. The value returned is the value of the last expression in the if block.

You are not required to use the returned value or assign it to a variable. You'll see more on returning a value below.

The else expression

You can extend an if expression to provide code to run in case the condition turns out to be false. This is known as the **else clause**. Here's an example:

```
val animal = "Fox"
if (animal == "Cat" || animal == "Dog") {   println("Animal is a house pet.")
} else {
  println("Animal is not a house pet.") }
```

Here, if animal equals either "Cat" or "Dog", then the expression will run the first block of code. If animal does not equal either "Cat" or "Dog", then the expression will run the block inside the else part of the if expression, printing the following to the console:

Animal is not a house pet.

You can also use an if-else expression on one line. Let's take a look at how this can make your code more concise and readable.

If you wanted to determine the minimum and maximum of two variables, you could use if expressions like so:

```
val a = 5 val b = 10
val min: Int if (a < b) {   min = a } else {   min = b
```

```
}
val max: Int if (a > b) {   max = a } else {   max = b
}
```

By now you know how this works, but it's a lot of code. Let's take a look at how we can improve this using the fact that the if-else expression returns a value.

Simply remove the brackets and put it all on one line, like so:
```
val a = 5 val b = 10

val min = if (a < b) a else b val max = if (a > b) a else b
```

In the first example, the condition is a < b. If this is true, the result assigned back to min will be the value of a; if it's false, the result will be the value of b. So min is set to 5. In the second example, max is assigned the value of b, which is 10.

I'm sure you'll agree that's much simpler! This is an example of **idiomatic** code, which means you are writing code in the expected way for a particular programming language. You want to use idioms whenever they make your code clearer, as it not only makes the code better, but it allows other developers familiar with the language to comprehend your code quickly.

Note: Because finding the greater or smaller of two numbers is such a common operation, the Kotlin standard library provides two functions for this purpose: max() and min(). If you were paying attention earlier in the book, then you'll recall you've already seen these.

The else-if expression

But you can go even further than that with if expressions. Sometimes you want to check one condition, then another. This is where **else-if** comes into play, nesting another if clause in the else clause of a previous if clause.

You can use else-if like so:

```
val hourOfDay = 12

val timeOfDay = if (hourOfDay < 6) {
  "Early morning"
} else if (hourOfDay < 12) {
  "Morning"
} else if (hourOfDay < 17) {
  "Afternoon"
} else if (hourOfDay < 20) {
  "Evening"
} else if (hourOfDay < 24) {
  "Late evening"
} else {
  "INVALID HOUR!"
}
```

```
println(timeOfDay)
```

These nested if clauses test multiple conditions one by one until a true condition is found. Only the code associated with that first true condition is executed, regardless of whether subsequent else-if conditions are true. In other words, the order of your conditions matters!

You can add an else clause at the end to handle the case where none of the conditions are true. This else clause is optional if you don't need it; in this example you do need it, to ensure that timeOfDay has a valid value by the time you print it out.

In this example, the if expression takes a number representing an hour of the day and converts it to a string representing the part of the day to which the hour belongs. Working with a 24-hour clock, the conditions are checked in order, one at a time:

- The first check is to see if the hour is less than 6. If so, that means it's early morning.

- If the hour is not less than 6, the expression continues to the first else-if, where it checks the hour to see if it's less than 12.

- Then in turn, as conditions prove false, the expression checks the hour to see if it's less than 17, then less than 20, then less than 24.

- Finally, if the hour is out of range, the expression returns that the value is invalid.

In the code above, the hourOfDay constant is 12. Therefore, the code will print the following:

Afternoon

Notice that even though both the hourOfDay < 20 and hourOfDay < 24 conditions are also true, the expression only executes and returns the first block whose condition is true; in this case, the block with the hourOfDay < 17 condition.

Short circuiting

An important fact about if expressions and the Boolean operators is what happens when there are multiple Boolean conditions separated by ANDs (&&) or ORs (||).

Consider the following code:

```
if (1 > 2 && name == "Matt Galloway") {

  // ...

}
```

The first condition of the if expression, 1 > 2 is false. Therefore, the whole expression cannot ever be true. So Kotlin will not even bother to check the second part of the expression, namely the check of name.

Similarly, consider the following code:

```
if (1 < 2 || name == "Matt Galloway") {

  // ...

}
```

Since 1 < 2 is true, the whole expression must be true as well. Therefore, once again, the check of name is not executed. This will come in handy later on when you start dealing with more complex data types.

Encapsulating variables

if expressions introduce a new concept, **scope**, which is a way to encapsulate variables through the use of braces.

Imagine you want to calculate the fee to charge your client. Here's the deal you've made:

You earn $25 for every hour up to 40 hours, and $50 for every hour thereafter.

Using Kotlin, you can calculate your fee in this way:

```
var hoursWorked = 45
 var price = 0 if (hoursWorked > 40) {
 val hoursOver40 = hoursWorked - 40
 price += hoursOver40 * 50   hoursWorked -= hoursOver40
}
price += hoursWorked * 25
 println(price)
```

This code takes the number of hours and checks if it's over 40. If so, the code calculates the number of hours over 40 and multiplies that by $50, then adds the result to the price. The code then subtracts the number of hours over 40 from the hours worked. It multiplies the remaining hours worked by $25 and adds that to the total price.

In the example above, the result is as follows:

1250

The interesting thing here is the code inside the if expression. There is a declaration of a new constant, hoursOver40, to store the number of hours over 40. Clearly, you can use it inside the if statement.

But what happens if you try to use it at the end of the above code?

```
println(price) println(hoursOver40)
```

This would result in the following error:

Unresolved reference: 'hoursOver40'

This error informs you that you're only allowed to use the hoursOver40 constant within the scope in which it was created.

In this case, the if expression introduced a new scope, so when that scope is finished, you can no longer use the constant.

However, each scope can use variables and constants from its parent scope. In the example above, the scope inside of the if expression uses the price and hours Worked variables, which you created in the parent scope.

Loops

Loops are Kotlin's way of executing code multiple times. In this section, you'll learn about one type of loop: the while loop.

If you know another programming language, you'll find the concepts and maybe even the syntax to be familiar.

While loops

A **while loop** repeats a block of code while a condition is true. You create a while loop this way:

```
while (/* CONDITION */) {
```

```
/* LOOP CODE */
}
```

The loop checks the condition for every iteration. If the condition is true, then the loop executes and moves on to another iteration.

If the condition is false, then the loop stops. Just like if expressions, while loops introduce a scope.

The simplest while loop takes this form:

```
while (true) {

}
```

This is a while loop that never ends because the condition is always true. Of course, you would never write such a while loop, because your program would spin forever! This situation is known as an **infinite loop**, and while it might not cause your program to crash, it will very likely cause your computer to freeze.

Here's a more useful example of a while loop:

```
var sum = 1

while (sum < 1000) {   sum = sum + (sum + 1)

}
```

This code calculates a mathematical sequence, up to the point where the value is greater than 1000.

The loop executes as follows:

- **Before iteration 1:** sum = 1, loop condition = true
- **After iteration 1:** sum = 3, loop condition = true
- **After iteration 2:** sum = 7, loop condition = true
- **After iteration 3:** sum = 15, loop condition = true
- **After iteration 4:** sum = 31, loop condition = true
- **After iteration 5:** sum = 63, loop condition = true
- **After iteration 6:** sum = 127, loop condition = true
- **After iteration 7:** sum = 255, loop condition = true
- **After iteration 8:** sum = 511, loop condition = true
- **After iteration 9:** sum = 1023, loop condition = false

After the ninth iteration, the sum variable is 1023, and therefore the loop condition of sum < 1000 becomes false. At this point, the loop stops.

Repeat-while loops

A variant of the while loop is called the **do-while loop**. It differs from the while loop in that the condition is evaluated at the end of the loop rather than at the beginning.

You construct a do-while loop like this:

```
do {
/* LOOP CODE */
```

} while (/* CONDITION */)

Here's the example from the last section, but using a repeat-while loop:

```
sum = 1
do {
  sum = sum + (sum + 1)
} while (sum < 1000)
```

In this example, the outcome is the same as before. However, that isn't always the case; you might get a different result with a different condition. Consider the following while loop:

```
sum = 1
while (sum < 1) {   sum = sum + (sum + 1)
}
```

Consider the corresponding do-while loop, which uses the same condition:

```
sum = 1
do {
  sum = sum + (sum + 1)
} while (sum < 1)
```

In the case of the regular while loop, the condition sum < 1 is false right from the start. That means the body of the loop won't be reached because the condition is checked at the beginning! The value of sum will equal 1 because the loop won't execute any iterations.

In the case of the do-while loop, sum will equal 3 because the loop executes once and then the condition is checked for the first time.

Breaking out of a loop

Sometimes you want to break out of a loop early. You can do this using the break statement, which immediately stops the execution of the loop and continues on to the code after the loop.

For example, consider the following code:

```
sum = 1
while (true) {   sum = sum + (sum + 1)   if (sum >= 1000) {
    break
  }
}
```

Here, the loop condition is true, so the loop would normally iterate forever. However, the break means the while loop will exit once the sum is greater than or equal to 1000.

You've seen how to write the same loop in different ways, demonstrating that in computer programming, there are often many ways to achieve the same result.

You should choose the method that's easiest to read and conveys your intent in the best way possible. This is an approach you'll internalize with enough time and practice.

Finally, print After X rolls, roll is Y where X is the value of counter and Y is the value of roll. Set the loop condition such that the loop finishes when the first 0 is rolled.

Advanced Control Flow

You learned how to control the flow of execution using the decision-making powers of if expressions and the while loop. In this chapter, you'll continue to learn how to control the flow of execution. You'll learn about another loop known as the for loop.

Loops may not sound very interesting, but they're very common in computer programs. For example, you might have code to download an image from the cloud; with a loop, you could run those multiple times to download your entire photo library. Or if you have a game with multiple computer-controlled characters, you might need a loop to go through each one and make sure it knows what to do next.

You'll also learn about when expressions, which are particularly powerful in Kotlin. They let you inspect a value and decide what to do based on that value. They're incredibly powerful when used with argument matching.

Open of the starter project for this chapter or create a fresh project to get going.

Ranges

Before you dive into the for-loop statement, you need to know about the **range** data types, which let you represent a sequence of countable integers. Let's look at two types of ranges.

First, there's a **closed range**, which you represent like so:

val closedRange = 0..5

The two dots (..) indicate that this range is closed, which means the range goes from 0 to 5 inclusive. That's the numbers (0, 1, 2, 3, 4, 5).

Second, there's a **half-open range**, which you represent like so:

val halfOpenRange = 0 until 5

Here, you replace the two dots with until. Half-open means the range goes from 0 up to, but not including, 5. That's the numbers (0, 1, 2, 3, 4).

Open and half-open ranges created with the .. and until operators are always increasing. In other words, the second number must always be greater than or equal to the first. To create a decreasing range, you can use downTo, which is inclusive:

val decreasingRange = 5 downTo 0

That will include the numbers (5, 4, 3, 2, 1, 0).

Ranges are commonly used in both for loops and when expressions, which means that throughout the rest of the chapter, you'll use ranges as well!

For loops

In the previous chapter you looked at while loops. Now that you know about ranges, it's time to look at another type of loop: The **for loop**. This is probably the most common loop you'll see, and you'll use it to run code a certain number of times.

You construct a for loop like this:

```
for (/* VARIABLE */ in /* RANGE */) {
  /* LOOP CODE */
}
```

The loop begins with the for keyword, followed by a name given to the loop variable (more on that shortly), followed by in, followed by the range to loop through. Here's an example:

```
val count = 10
var sum = 0 for (i in 1..count) {
  sum += i
}
```

In the code above, the for loop iterates through the range 1 to count. At the first iteration, i will equal the first element in the range: 1. Each time around the loop, i will increment until it's equal to count; the loop will execute one final time and then finish.

Note: If you'd used a half-open range, the last iteration would see i equal to count - 1.

Inside the loop, you add i to the sum variable; it runs 10 times to calculate the sequence 1 + 2 + 3 + 4 + 5 + ... all the way up to 10.

Here are the values of the constant i and variable sum for each iteration:

- **Start of iteration 1:** i = 1, sum = 0
- **Start of iteration 2:** i = 2, sum = 1
- **Start of iteration 3:** i = 3, sum = 3
- **Start of iteration 4:** i = 4, sum = 6
- **Start of iteration 5:** i = 5, sum = 10
- **Start of iteration 6:** i = 6, sum = 15
- **Start of iteration 7:** i = 7, sum = 21
- **Start of iteration 8:** i = 8, sum = 28
- **Start of iteration 9:** i = 9, sum = 36
- **Start of iteration 10:** i = 10, sum = 45
- **After iteration 10:** sum = 55

In terms of scope, the i constant is only visible inside the scope of the for loop, which means it's not available outside of the loop.

Repeat loops

Finally, sometimes you only want to loop a certain number of times, and so you don't need to use the loop constant at all. In that case, you can employ a repeat loop, like so:

```
sum = 1 var lastSum = 0 repeat(10) {   val temp = sum   sum += lastSum   lastSum = temp
}
```

Steps in loops

It's also possible to only perform certain iterations in the range. For example, imagine you wanted to compute a sum similar to that of triangle numbers, but only for odd numbers:

```
sum = 0
for (i in 1..count step 2) {
  sum += i
}
```

The previous loop has a step operator in the for-loop statement. The loop will only run through the values that the step falls on. In this case, rather than step through every value in the range, it will step through every other value. As such, i will always be odd because the starting value is 1.

You can even count down in a for loop using downTo. In this case if count is 10 then the loop will iterate through the following values (10, 8, 6, 4, 2).

```
sum = 0
for (i in count downTo 1 step 2) {
  sum += i
}
```

Labeled statements

Sometimes you'd like to skip a loop iteration for a particular case without breaking out of the loop entirely. You can do this with the continue statement, which immediately ends the current iteration of the loop and starts the next iteration. The continue statement gives you a higher level of control, letting you decide where and when you want to skip an iteration.

Take the example of an 8 by 8 grid, where each cell holds a value of the row multiplied by the column. It looks much like a multiplication table, doesn't it?

	0	1	2	3	4	5	6	7
0	0	0	0	0	0	0	0	0
1	0	1	2	3	4	5	6	7
2	0	2	4	6	8	10	12	14
3	0	3	6	9	12	15	18	21
4	0	4	8	12	16	20	24	28
5	0	5	10	15	20	25	30	35
6	0	6	12	18	24	30	36	42
7	0	7	14	21	28	35	42	49

Let's say you wanted to calculate the sum of all cells but exclude all even rows, as shown below:

	0	1	2	3	4	5	6	7
0								
1	0	1	2	3	4	5	6	7
2								
3	0	3	6	9	12	15	18	21
4								
5	0	5	10	15	20	25	30	35
6								
7	0	7	14	21	28	35	42	49

Using a for loop, you can achieve this as follows:

```
sum = 0
for (row in 0 until 8) {   if (row % 2 == 0) {     continue
  }
  for (column in 0 until 8) {     sum += row * column
  }
}
```

When the row modulo 2 equals 0, the row is even. In this case, continue makes the for loop skip to the next row.

The break statement you saw in the last chapter used with while loops also works with for loops, and takes you to the next statement after the for loop. Just like break, continue works with both for loops and while loops.

The second code example will calculate the sum of all cells, excluding those where the column is greater than or equal to the row. To illustrate, it should sum the following cells:

	0	1	2	3	4	5	6	7
0								
1	0							
2	0	2						
3	0	3	6					
4	0	4	8	12				
5	0	5	10	15	20			
6	0	6	12	18	24	30		
7	0	7	14	21	28	35	42	

Using a for loop, you can achieve this as follows:

```
sum = 0
rowLoop@ for (row in 0 until 8) {   columnLoop@ for (column in 0 until 8) {
    if (row == column) {       continue@rowLoop
    }
    sum += row * column
  }
}
```

The previous code block makes use of a **label**, labeling the two loops as rowLoop and columnLoop, respectively. When the row equals the column inside the inner columnLoop, the outer rowLoop will continue.

You can use labeled statements like these with break to break out of a certain loop. Normally, break and continue work on the innermost loop, so you need to use labeled statements if you want to manipulate an outer loop.

When expressions

You can also control flow via the when expression. It executes different code depending on the value of a variable or constant. Here's a when expression that acts on an integer:

```
val number = 10
 when (number) {
  0 -> println("Zero")   else -> println("Non-zero") }
```

In this example, the code will print the following:

Non-zero

The purpose of this when expression is to determine whether or not a number is zero. It will get more complex — I promise!

To handle a specific case, you add the value followed by -> which indicates the code that will execute if the condition is met. Then, you use else to signify what should happen for all other values. Unlike other languages such as Java, there is no need to include a break statement in each branch, as the when expression will only use the first matching branch and then return.

Here's another example:

```
when (number) {
  10 -> println("It's ten!")
}
```

This time you check for 10, in which case, you print a message. Nothing should happen for other values.

Of course, when expressions also work with data types other than integers. Here's an example using a string:

```
val string = "Dog" when (string) {
  "Cat", "Dog" -> println("Animal is a house pet.")   else -> println("Animal is not a house pet.") }
```

This will print the following:

Animal is a house pet.

In this example, you provide two values for the first argument, meaning that if the value is equal to either "Cat" or "Dog", then the statement will execute that branch of the expression.

Returning values

You can also give your when expressions more than one branch. And, due to the fact that when is an expression, you can use it to return a value, just like you can with if expressions. You can also ignore the value if you want to just use when as a statement. A when expression will return the value from the first branch with a matching argument.

If you want to determine the name of the number, you can assign the value with a when expression as follows

```
val numberName = when (number) {
  2 -> "two"
  4 -> "four"
  6 -> "six"
  8 -> "eight"
  10 -> "ten"   else -> {
    println("Unknown number")
    "Unknown"
  }
}
println(numberName) // > ten
```

In the else branch, you've used braces to include an entire block of code in the branch. The last value in the block is returned from the branch, so if number were not in (2, 4, 6, 8, 10) then number Name would have the value "Unknown".

Advanced when expressions

In the previous chapter, you saw an if expression that used multiple else clauses to convert an hour of the day to a string describing that part of the day. You could rewrite that with a when expression, like so:

```
val hourOfDay = 12 val timeOfDay: String
 timeOfDay = when (hourOfDay) {
  0, 1, 2, 3, 4, 5 -> "Early morning"
  6, 7, 8, 9, 10, 11 -> "Morning"
  12, 13, 14, 15, 16 -> "Afternoon"
  17, 18, 19 -> "Evening"
  20, 21, 22, 23 -> "Late evening"
  else -> "INVALID HOUR!"
 }
println(timeOfDay)
```

This code will print the following:

Afternoon

Using when expressions with ranges

Remember ranges? Well, you can use ranges to simplify this when expression. You can rewrite the above code using ranges:

```
timeOfDay = when (hourOfDay) {  in 0..5 -> "Early morning"  in 6..11 -> "Morning"  in 12..16 ->
"Afternoon"  in 17..19 -> "Evening"  in 20..23 -> "Late evening"  else -> "INVALID HOUR!"
 }
```

This is more succinct than writing out each value individually for all branches.

When there are multiple branches, the expression will execute the first one that matches. You'll probably agree that this is more succinct and clearer than using an if expression for this example.

It's slightly more precise as well, because the if expression method didn't address negative numbers, which here are correctly deemed to be invalid.

Using when expressions with conditions

It's also possible to match a branch to a condition based on a property of the value, without any argument being supplied to the when expression. As you can use the modulo operator to determine if an integer is even or odd.

Consider this code:

```
when {
  number % 2 == 0 -> println("Even")
```

```
    else -> println("Odd")
}
```

This will print the following:

Even

The first branch of this when expression uses the == operator, meaning the argument will match only when a certain condition is true.

In this example, you've designed the argument to match if the value is even — that is, if the value modulo 2 equals 0.

Another example of using conditions in when expressions to great effect is as follows:

```
val (x, y, z) = Triple(3, 2, 5)
when {
  x == 0 && y == 0 && z == 0 -> println("Origin")   y == 0 && z == 0 -> println("On the x-axis at x = $x")
  x == 0 && z == 0 -> println("On the y-axis at y = $y")   x == 0 && y == 0 -> println("On the z-axis at z = $z")   else -> println("In space at x = $x, y = $y, z = $z") }
```

Here's what each branch does, in order:

Matches precisely the case where the value is (0, 0, 0). This is the origin of 3D space.

Matches y=0, z=0 and any value of x. This means the coordinate is on the x-axis.

Matches x=0, z=0 and any value of y. This means the coordinate is on the y-axis.
Matches x=0, y=0 and any value of z. This means the coordinate is on the z-axis.

Matches the remainder of coordinates.

The final branch with the else clause is the default; it matches anything, because there are no constraints on any part of the coordinates. Here's an example of a more complex case:

```
when {
  x == y -> println("Along the y = x line.")   y == x * x -> println("Along the y = x^2 line.") }
```

Here, you match the "y equals x" and "y equals x squared" lines. Since there is no argument to the when expression, you do not need an else branch, and the when expression will not execute a branch if there is no matching condition. And those are the basics of when expressions!

Functions

Functions are a core part of many programming languages. Simply put, a function lets you define a block of code that performs a task. Then, whenever your app needs to execute that task, you can run the function instead of having to copy and paste the same code everywhere.

In this chapter, you'll learn how to write your own functions, and see firsthand how Kotlin makes them easy to use.

Function basics

Imagine you have an app that frequently needs to print your name. You can write a function to do this. Try out this code:

```
fun printMyName() {
  println("My name is Joe Howard.")
```

```
}
```

The code above is known as a **function declaration**. You define a function using the fun keyword. After that comes the name of the function, followed by parentheses. You'll learn more about the need for these parentheses in the next section.

After the parentheses comes an opening brace, followed by the code you want to run in the function, followed by a closing brace. With your function defined, you can use it like so:

```
printMyName()
```

This prints out the following:

My name is Joe Howard.

If you suspect that you've already used a function in previous chapters, you're correct! println, which prints the text you give it to the console, is indeed a function. This leads nicely into the next section, in which you'll learn how to pass data to a function and get data back in return.

Function parameters

In the previous example, the function simply prints out a message. That's great, but sometimes you want to **parameterize** your function, which lets the function perform differently depending on the data passed into it via its **parameters**.

As an example, consider the following function:

```
fun printMultipleOfFive(value: Int) {   println("$value * 5 = ${value * 5}")

}
printMultipleOfFive(10)
```

Here, you can see the definition of one parameter inside the parentheses after the function name, named value and of type Int. In any function, the parentheses contain what's known as the **parameter list**. These parentheses are required both when declaring and when invoking the function, even if the parameter list is empty. This function will print out any given multiple of five. In the example, you call the function with an **argument** of 10, so the function prints the following:

```
10 * 5 = 50
```

Note: Take care not to confuse the terms "parameter" and "argument". A function declares its parameters in its parameter list. When you call a function, you provide values as arguments for the function's parameters.

You can take this one step further and make the function more general. With two parameters, the function can print out a multiple of any two values.

```
fun printMultipleOf(multiplier: Int, andValue: Int) {   println("$multiplier * $andValue = ${multiplier * andValue}")
} printMultipleOf(4, 2)
```

There are now two parameters inside the parentheses after the function name: one named multiplier and the other named andValue, both of type Int.

Parameter named arguments

Sometimes it is helpful to use **named arguments** when calling a function to make it easier to understand the purpose of each argument.

```
printMultipleOf(multiplier = 4, andValue = 2)
```

It is now immediately obvious at the call site of the function what purpose the arguments serve. This is especially helpful when a function has several parameters.

Parameter default values

You can also give **default values** to parameters:

```
fun printMultipleOf(multiplier: Int, value: Int = 1) {   println("$multiplier * $value = ${multiplier * value}")
}
 printMultipleOf(4)
```

The difference is the = 1 after the second parameter, which means that if no value is provided for the second parameter, it defaults to 1.

Therefore, this code prints the following:

```
4 * 1 = 4
```

It can be useful to have a default value when you expect a parameter to be one particular value the majority of the time, and it will simplify your code when you call the function.

Return values

All of the functions you've seen so far have performed a simple task: Printing something out. Functions can also return a value. The caller of the function can assign the return value to a variable or constant, or use it directly in an expression.

This means you can use a function to manipulate data. You simply take in data through parameters, manipulate it and then return it. Here's how you define a function that returns a value:

```
fun multiply(number: Int, multiplier: Int): Int {
  return number * multiplier }
```

To declare that a function returns a value, you add a : followed by the type of the return value after the set of parentheses and before the opening brace. In this example, the function returns an Int.

Inside the function, you use a return statement to return the value. In this example, you return the product of the two parameters.

It's also possible to return multiple values through the use of Pairs:

```
fun multiplyAndDivide(number: Int, factor: Int): Pair<Int, Int>
{
  return Pair(number * factor, number / factor)
} val (product, quotient) = multiplyAndDivide(4, 2)
```

This function returns both the product and quotient of the two parameters by returning a Pair containing two Int values.

If a function consists solely of a single expression, you can assign the expression to the function using = while at the same time not using braces, a return type, or a return statement:

```
fun multiplyInferred(number: Int, multiplier: Int) = number * multiplier
```

In such a case, the type of the function return value is inferred to be the type of the expression assigned to the function. In the example, the return type is inferred to be Int since both number and multiplier are Ints.

Parameters as values

Function parameters are constants by default, which means they can't be modified.

To illustrate this point, consider the following code:

```
fun incrementAndPrint(value: Int) {
  value += 1   print(value)
}
```

This results in an error:

Val cannot be reassigned

The parameter value is the equivalent of a constant declared with val and hence cannot be reassigned. Therefore, when the function attempts to increment it, the compiler emits an error.

Usually, you want this behavior. Ideally, a function doesn't alter its parameters. If it did, then you couldn't be sure of the parameters' values and you might make incorrect assumptions in your code, leading to the wrong data.

If you want a function to alter a parameter and return it, you must do so indirectly by declaring a new variable like so:

```
fun incrementAndPrint(value: Int): Int {
  val newValue = value + 1   println(newValue)   return newValue
}
```

Overloading

What if you want more than one function with the same name?

```
fun getValue(value: Int): Int {
  return value + 1
}
  fun getValue(value: String): String {   return "The value is $value" }
```

This is called **overloading** and lets you define similar functions using a single name.

However, the compiler must still be able to tell the difference between these functions within a given scope. Whenever you call a function, it should always be clear which function you're calling.

This is usually achieved through a difference in the parameter list:

- A different number of parameters.
- Different parameter types.

For example, defining two methods like so will result in an error:

```
fun getValue(value: String): String {   return "The value is $value" }
```

```
// Conflicting overloads error fun getValue(value: String): Int {
    return value.length
}
```

The methods above both have the same name, parameter types and number of parameters. Kotlin will not be able to distinguish them!

It's worth noting that overloading should be used with care. Only use overloading for functions that are related and similar in behavior.

Functions as variables

Functions in Kotlin are simply another data type. You can assign them to variables and constants just as you can any other type of value, such as an Int or a String.

To see how this works, consider the following function:

```
fun add(a: Int, b: Int): Int {
  return a + b }
```

This function takes two parameters and returns the sum of their values.

You can assign this function to a variable using the **method reference operator**, ::, like so:

```
var function = ::add
```

Here, the name of the variable is function and its type is inferred as (Int, Int) -> Int from the add function you assigned to it. The function variable is of a function type that takes two Int parameters and returns an Int.

Now you can use the function variable in just the same way you'd use add, like so:

```
function(4, 2)
```

This returns 6.

Now consider the following code:

```
fun subtract(a: Int, b: Int) : Int {
  return a - b }
```

Here, you declare another function that takes two Int parameters and returns an Int. You can set the function variable from before to your new subtract function, because the parameter list and return type of subtract are compatible with the type of the function variable.

```
function = ::subtract function(4, 2)
```

This time, the call to function returns 2.

The fact that you can assign functions to variables comes in handy because it means you can pass functions to other functions. Here's an example of this in action:

```
fun printResult(function: (Int, Int) -> Int, a: Int, b: Int) {
  val result = function(a, b)
  print(result)
} printResult(::add, 4, 2)
```

printResult takes three parameters:

function is of a function type that takes two Int parameters and returns an Int, declared like so: (Int, Int) -> Int.

a is of type Int.

b is of type Int.

printResult calls the passed-in function, passing into it the two Int parameters. Then it prints the result to the console:

6

It's extremely useful to be able to pass functions to other functions, and it can help you write reusable code. Not only can you pass data around to manipulate, but passing functions as parameters also means you can be flexible about what code executes.

Assigning functions to variables and passing functions around as arguments is one aspect of **functional programming**.

The land of no return

There are some functions which are designed to never, ever, return. This may sound confusing, but consider the example of a function that is designed to crash an application. This may sound strange, but if an application is about to work with corrupt data, it's often best to crash rather than continue in an unknown and potentially dangerous state.

Another example of a non-returning function is one which handles an event loop. An event loop is at the heart of every modern application which takes input from the user and displays things on a screen. The event loop services requests coming from the user, then passes these events to the application code, which in turn causes the information to be displayed on the screen. The loop then cycles back and services the next event.

These event loops are often started in an application by calling a function which is known to never return. If you start developing Android apps, think back to this paragraph when you encounter the **main thread**, also known as the **UI thread**.

Kotlin has a way to tell the compiler that a function is known to never return. You set the return type of the function to the Nothing type, indicating that nothing is ever returned from the function.

A crude, but honest, implementation of a function that wouldn't return would be as follows:

```
fun infiniteLoop(): Nothing {
  while (true) {
```

```
    }
}
```

You may be wondering why bother with this special return type. It's useful because by the compiler knowing that the function won't ever return, it can make certain optimizations when generating the code to call the function.

Essentially, the code which calls the function doesn't need to bother doing anything after the function call, because it knows that this function will never end before the application is terminated.

Writing good functions

There are many ways to solve problems with functions. The best (easiest to use and understand) functions do one simple task rather than trying to do many. This makes them easier to mix and match and assemble into more complex behaviors. Good functions also have a well-defined set of inputs that produce the same output every time. This makes them easier to reason about and test in isolation. Keep these rules of-thumb in mind as you create functions.

Before you move on, check out the challenges ahead as you'll need to fully grasp functions before understanding some of the upcoming topics! If you need help when solving them, use the solutions included in the chapter materials for a hint.

Nullability

All the variables and constants you've dealt with so far have had concrete values. When you had a string variable, like var name, it had a string value associated with it, like "Joe Howard". It could have been an empty string, like "", but nevertheless, there was a value to which you could refer.

That's one of the built-in safety features of Kotlin: If the type says Int or String, then there's an actual integer or string there — guaranteed.

This chapter will introduce you to **nullable** types, which allow you to represent not just a value, but also the absence of a value. By the end of this chapter, you'll know why you need nullable types and how to use them safely.

Introducing null

Sometimes, it's useful to be able to represent the absence of a value. Imagine a scenario where you need to refer to a person's identifying information; you want to store the person's name, age and occupation. Name and age are both things that must have a value — everyone has them. But not everyone is employed, so the absence of a value for occupation is something you need to be able to handle.

Without knowing about nullables, this is how you might represent the person's name, age and occupation:

var name = "Joe Howard" var age = 24 var occupation = "Software Developer & Author"

But what if I become unemployed? Maybe I've reached enlightenment and wish to live out the rest of my days on top of a mountain. This is when it would be useful to be able to refer to the absence of a value.

Why couldn't you just use an empty string? You could, but nullable types are a much better solution. Read on to see why.

Sentinel values

A valid value that represents a special condition, such as the absence of a value, is known as a **sentinel value**. That's what your empty string would be in the previous example.

Let's look at another example. Say your code requests something from a server, and you use a variable to store any returned error code:

var errorCode = 0

In the success case, you represent the lack of an error with a zero. That means 0 is a sentinel value. Just like the empty string for occupation, this works, but it's potentially confusing for the programmer. 0 might actually be a valid error code — or could be in the future, if the server changed how it responded. Either way, you can't be completely confident that the server didn't return an error without consulting the documentation. In these two examples, it would be much better if there were a special type that could represent the absence of a value. It would then be explicit when a value exists and when one doesn't.

Null is the name given to the absence of a value, and you're about to see how Kotlin incorporates this concept directly into the language in a rather elegant way. Some other programming languages simply use sentinel values. Some have the concept of a null value, but it is merely a synonym for zero. It is just another sentinel value.

Kotlin introduces a whole new set of types, **nullable types**, that handles the possibility a value could be null. If you're handling a non-null type, then you're guaranteed to have a value and don't need to worry about the existence of a valid value. Similarly, if you are using a nullable type, then you know you must handle the null case. It removes the ambiguity introduced by using sentinel values.

Introducing nullable types

Nullables are Kotlin's solution to the problem of representing both a value and the absence of a value. A nullable is allowed to hold either a value or null.

Think of a nullable as a box: it either contains a value, or it doesn't. When it doesn't contain a value, it's said to contain null. The box itself always exists; it's always there for you to open and look inside.

Nullable box
containing a
value

Nullable box
containing no
value

A String or an Int, on the other hand, doesn't have this box around it. Instead, there's always a value, such as "hello" or 42. Remember, non-null types are guaranteed to have an actual value.

Note: Those of you who've studied physics may be thinking about Schroedinger's cat right now. Nullables are a little bit like that, except it's not a matter of life and death!

You declare a variable of a nullable type by using the following syntax:

var errorCode: Int?

The only difference between this and a standard declaration is the question mark at the end of the type. In this case, errorCode is a "nullable Int". This means the variable itself is like a box containing either an Int or null.

Note: You can add a question mark after any type to create a nullable type. For example, nullable type String? is a nullable String. In other words: a nullable box of type String? holds either a String or null.

Also, note how a nullable type must be made explicit using a type declaration (here : Int?). Nullable types can never be inferred from initialization values, as those values are of a regular, non-null type.

The exception is if you're assigning the value using the result of a function call. If the return type of the function is nullable, the variable will be inferred to be nullable.

Setting the value is simple. You can either set it to an Int, like so:

errorCode = 100

Or you can set it to null, like so:

errorCode = null

This diagram may help you visualize what's happening:

errorCode = 100

errorCode =

The nullable box always exists. When you assign 100 to the variable, you're filling the box with the value. When you assign null to the variable, you're emptying the box.

Take a few minutes to think about this concept. The box analogy will be a big help as you go through the rest of the chapter and begin to use nullables.

Checking for null

It's all well and good that nullables exist, but you may be wondering how you can look inside the box and manipulate the value it contains.

In some limited cases, you can just use the nullable as if it were a non-null type.

Take a look at what happens when you print out the value of a nullable:

var result: Int? = 30 println(result)

This just prints out 30.

To see how a nullable type is different from a non-null type, see what happens if you try to use result in an expression as if it were a normal integer:

println(result + 1)

This code triggers an error:

Operator call corresponds to a dot-qualified call

'result.plus(1)' which is not allowed on a nullable receiver 'result'.

It doesn't work because you're trying to add an integer to a box — not to the value inside the box, but to the box itself. That doesn't make sense!

Not-null assertion operator

The error message gives an indication of the solution: It tells you that the nullable is still inside its box. You need to remove the value from its box. It's like Christmas!

Let's see how that works. Consider the following declarations:

var authorName: String? = "Joe Howard" var authorAge: Int? = 24

There are two different methods you can use to remove these nullables from the box. The first is using the **not-null assertion operator** !!, which you do like so:

val ageAfterBirthday = authorAge!! + 1

println("After their next birthday, author will be

$ageAfterBirthday")

This code prints:

After their next birthday, author will be 25

Great! That's what you'd expect.

The double-exclamation mark after the variable name tells the compiler that you want to look inside the box and take out the value. The result is a value of the nonnull type. This means ageAfterBirthday is of type Int, not Int?.

The use of the word "assertion" and the exclamation marks !! probably conveys a sense of danger to you, and it should. You should use not-null assertions sparingly. To see why, consider what happens when the nullable doesn't contain a value:

authorAge = null

println("After two birthdays, author will be ${authorAge!! + 2}")

This code produces the following runtime error:

Exception in thread "main" kotlin.KotlinNullPointerException

The **null-pointer exception** occurs because the variable contains no value when you try to use it. What's worse is that you get this exception at runtime rather than compile time — which means you'd only notice the exception if you happened to execute this code with some invalid input. Worse yet, if this code were inside an app, the null-pointer exception would cause the app to crash!

How can you play it safe? For that, you'll turn to the second way to get a value out of the nullable.

Smart casts

Under certain conditions, you can check whether a nullable has a value, and if so, you can use the variable as if it were not null:

var nonNullableAuthor: String var nullableAuthor: String?

```
  if (authorName != null) {   nonNullableAuthor = authorName
} else {
  nullableAuthor = authorName }
```

You'll immediately notice that there are no exclamation marks here when using the nullable author Name. Using nullable checks in this way is an example of Kotlin **smart casts**.

If the nullable contains a value, the if expression then executes the first block of code, within which Kotlin will smart cast authorName to a regular non-null String. If the nullable doesn't contain a value, then the if expression executes the else block.

You can see how using smart casts is much safer than not-null assertions, and you should use them whenever a nullable might be null. Not-null assertion is only appropriate when a nullable is guaranteed to contain a value.

Using smart casts for nullables is only helpful if the nullable being checked is not or cannot be changed after the null check occurs. For example, if the nullable is assigned to a var that is not-changed after the smart cast occurs and before usage or is assigned to a val.

Now you know how to safely look inside a nullable and extract its value, if one exists.

Safe calls

Suppose you want to do something with a nullable string other than print it, such as accessing its length. Using a smart cast inside a null check is overkill for such a simple use of the string. If you try to access the length as if the string were not nullable and without a smart cast, you'll get a compiler error:

Only safe (?.) or non-null asserted (!!) calls are allowed on a nullable receiver of type String?

The error tips you off to the solution, which is to use a **safe call** with the ?. operator:

```
var nameLength = authorName?.length println("Author's name has length $nameLength.") // > Author's name has length 10.
```

By using the safe call operator, you're able to access the length property.

Safe calls can be chained:

```
val nameLengthPlus5 = authorName?.length?.plus(5) println("Author's name length plus 5 is $nameLengthPlus5.") // > Author's name length plus 5 is 15.
```

If a safe call is made on a value that is null, the expression stops evaluating the chain and returns null.

Since the result of a safe call can be null, expressions using safe calls on nullables return nullable types. For example, nameLength above is of type Int? and not Int, even though the length property on a string is not-nullable. The type of the entire expression is nullable.

The let() function

The safe call operator provides another way to use smart casts to work with the nonnull value inside a nullable, via the let() function from the standard library:

```
authorName?.let {
  nonNullableAuthor = authorName
}
```

Within a let function call following the safe call operator, the variable becomes nonnullable, so you can access its properties without using the safe call operator:

```
authorName?.let {
  nameLength = authorName.length
}
```

You'll learn more about the syntax used to call the let function, called trailing lambda syntax, in the next section of the book.

Elvis operator

There's another handy way to get a value from a nullable. You use it when you want to get a value out of the nullable no matter what — and in the case of null, you'll use a default value.

Here's how it works:

```
var nullableInt: Int? = 10 var mustHaveResult = nullableInt ?: 0
```

The operator used on the second line ?: is known as the **Elvis operator**, since it resembles a certain rock star when rotated by 90 degrees clockwise.

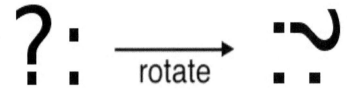

Using the Elvis operator means mustHaveResult will equal either the value inside nullableInt, or 0 if nullableInt contains null. In this example, mustHaveResult is inferred to be of type Int and contains the concrete Int value of 10. The previous code using the Elvis operator is equivalent to the following use of a null check and smart cast, but is more concise:

```
var nullableInt: Int? = 10 var mustHaveResult = if (nullableInt != null) nullableInt else 0
```

Set the nullableInt to null, like so:

```
nullableInt = null mustHaveResult = nullableInt ?: 0
```

Now mustHaveResult equals 0.

Conclusion: Mastering Kotlin Basics for Future-Ready Development

Recap of Kotlin's Strengths

Kotlin has emerged as a powerful, modern programming language that provides developers with a robust toolset for building high-quality, scalable, and efficient applications. From its seamless interoperability with Java to its expressive syntax, Kotlin is designed to boost productivity while minimizing common pitfalls in software development. By focusing on concise code, strong type safety, and built-in null safety, Kotlin addresses many of the challenges developers face with other languages.

Over the course of this journey, we explored the foundational pillars of Kotlin, including variables, data types, functions, control flow, object-oriented programming, and more. These fundamentals serve as the building blocks for advanced Kotlin development, equipping you with the knowledge to tackle real-world challenges.

Kotlin's Role in Modern Development

In the rapidly evolving tech landscape, Kotlin continues to gain prominence, especially in the following domains:

1. **Android Development**: Officially endorsed by Google as the preferred language for Android development, Kotlin's concise syntax and modern features streamline app creation. Tools like Jetpack Compose have made Android development more intuitive, and Kotlin's first-class support further enhances the developer experience.

2. **Server-Side Programming**: Kotlin's compatibility with JVM-based frameworks like Spring Boot has opened doors for server-side development. Its clean syntax and powerful coroutines make it an excellent choice for handling concurrency and scalability in web applications.

3. **Cross-Platform Development**: Kotlin Multiplatform allows developers to write shared business logic across multiple platforms, including Android, iOS, and the web, reducing duplication of effort and enhancing code maintainability.

4. **Data Science**: With libraries like KotlinDL and support for JVM-based data science tools, Kotlin is gradually carving a niche in data analysis and machine learning.

Revisiting Kotlin Basics

Let's revisit the key topics covered in this book:

1. **Variables and Data Types**
   Kotlin introduces a clean distinction between mutable (var) and immutable (val) variables, promoting best practices in immutability and functional programming. Its rich set of data types—such as integers, floats, and strings—combined with type inference, reduces boilerplate code and ensures safer operations.

2. **Null Safety**
   One of Kotlin's standout features is its built-in null safety, eliminating the dreaded null pointer exceptions (NPE). By requiring explicit handling of nullable types with ? and safe calls, Kotlin enforces better coding practices and improves application reliability.

3. **Control Flow**
   Kotlin's control structures, such as if, when, and loops, make it easy to write readable and efficient code. The when expression, in particular, serves as a powerful alternative to traditional switch-case constructs, allowing more expressive conditions.

4. **Functions**
   Functions in Kotlin are first-class citizens, enabling a functional programming paradigm. We explored various types of functions, including standard functions, extension functions, higher-order functions, and lambda expressions, showcasing Kotlin's versatility in function-based programming.

5. **Object-Oriented Programming**
   Kotlin simplifies object-oriented programming with features like classes, objects, inheritance, and interfaces. Its support for sealed classes and data classes allows developers to represent state and behavior concisely, making it ideal for domain modeling.

6. **Collections and Functional Operations**
   Kotlin's rich collection APIs enable effortless manipulation of data structures like lists, sets, and maps. Functional operations like map, filter, and reduce empower developers to write concise and expressive data processing pipelines.

7. **Coroutines**
   A standout feature of Kotlin is its support for coroutines, which simplifies asynchronous programming. With coroutines, developers can write non-blocking code that's easy to read and maintain, making it ideal for modern applications requiring high concurrency.

Why Kotlin Matters for the Future

As technology advances, the importance of versatile and developer-friendly programming languages becomes evident. Kotlin's features align perfectly with the needs of modern software development, providing:

1. **Productivity Boost**
   Kotlin's concise syntax and powerful abstractions reduce development time and errors, enabling developers to focus more on solving complex problems rather than wrestling with verbose syntax.

2. **Reliability**
   By enforcing null safety and type safety, Kotlin prevents common runtime errors, leading to more stable and robust applications.

3. **Community and Ecosystem**
   Kotlin's active and growing community ensures a wealth of resources, libraries, and frameworks to support developers. Its strong integration with existing Java ecosystems ensures a smooth transition for developers migrating from Java.

4. **Versatility**
   Kotlin's adaptability across Android, backend, cross-platform, and even data science applications make it a valuable tool in any developer's arsenal.

Challenges and How to Overcome Them

While Kotlin is a powerful language, adopting it comes with its challenges, particularly for beginners. Some common hurdles include:

1. **Learning Curve**
   Transitioning to Kotlin from Java or other languages can feel overwhelming at first. However, by practicing frequently, leveraging official documentation, and exploring Kotlin's online community, this challenge can be mitigated.

2. **Interoperability Pitfalls**
   Although Kotlin is interoperable with Java, mixing Kotlin and Java code in the same project may introduce complexities. It's essential to understand best practices for interoperability to maintain clean codebases.

3. **Ecosystem Maturity**
   While Kotlin's ecosystem is rapidly maturing, certain areas, like data science libraries, are still catching up to more established languages. However, with Kotlin's increasing popularity, these gaps are likely to close soon.

Taking the Next Steps

Mastering the basics of Kotlin is just the beginning. To truly harness its power, consider exploring the following:

1. **Advanced Topics**
   Delve into advanced Kotlin features like DSLs (Domain-Specific Languages), inline functions, type aliases, annotations, and reflection.

2. **Building Real-World Projects**
   Apply your knowledge by building practical projects, such as Android apps, backend APIs, or cross-platform applications. This hands-on experience will deepen your understanding of Kotlin's capabilities.

3. **Community Engagement**
   Join Kotlin forums, attend meetups, and contribute to open-source Kotlin projects. Engaging with the community will keep you updated on best practices and emerging trends.

4. **Certifications and Courses**
   Enhance your expertise with certifications and advanced Kotlin courses. These credentials can boost your career prospects and demonstrate your proficiency in Kotlin development.

Final Thoughts

Kotlin Basics 2025 has laid a strong foundation for your journey as a Kotlin developer. As you continue to explore the language, remember that the key to mastery lies in consistent practice, curiosity, and a willingness to learn. Kotlin's elegant design and growing ecosystem make it a valuable skill for developers across industries.

Whether you're developing Android apps, server-side applications, or cross-platform solutions, Kotlin equips you with the tools to create efficient, maintainable, and scalable software. By building upon the concepts introduced in this book, you'll be well-prepared to tackle complex challenges and thrive in the ever-evolving world of software development.

2. Lambdas and Collections

Introduction

Kotlin, known for its expressive and concise syntax, offers robust support for functional programming. Central to this paradigm are lambdas and collections, which empower developers to write elegant and efficient code. In this guide, we will explore the core concepts, features, and best practices for using lambdas and collections in Kotlin, ensuring you can harness their full potential in your applications.

1. Understanding Lambdas in Kotlin

A lambda expression is an anonymous function that can be treated as a value. In Kotlin, lambdas play a pivotal role in enabling functional programming constructs.

1.1 Syntax of Lambdas

The basic syntax of a lambda in Kotlin is as follows:

val lambdaName: (InputType) -> ReturnType = { parameter -> expression }

For example:

val square: (Int) -> Int = { number -> number * number }

Here:

- (Int) -> Int indicates that the lambda takes an Int as input and returns an Int.
- { number -> number * number } is the lambda body.

1.2 Simplified Syntax

Kotlin allows for further simplifications:

- **Implicit Parameter it**: If a lambda has a single parameter, you can omit its declaration and use it.
- val square = { number: Int -> number * number }

println(square(5)) // Output: 25

- **Type Inference**: Kotlin can infer parameter and return types in many cases, reducing boilerplate.

1.3 Lambdas as Function Arguments

Kotlin's higher-order functions (functions that take other functions as arguments or return them) make extensive use of lambdas. For example:

val numbers = listOf(1, 2, 3, 4, 5)

val evenNumbers = numbers.filter { it % 2 == 0 }

println(evenNumbers) // Output: [2, 4]

Here, the filter function accepts a lambda that specifies the filtering condition.

1.4 Inline Functions and Lambdas

To reduce runtime overhead, Kotlin provides the inline keyword, which inlines the lambda into the calling code. For example:

inline fun <T> measureTime(block: () -> T): T {

```
    val start = System.currentTimeMillis()
    val result = block()
    println("Time taken: ${System.currentTimeMillis() - start}ms")
    return result
}
```

1.5 Lambda with Receiver

Lambdas with receivers allow you to access the context object (this) inside the lambda, enabling DSL-like constructs. For example:

```
val buildString = buildString {
    append("Hello, ")
    append("Kotlin!")
}
println(buildString) // Output: Hello, Kotlin!
```

2. Collections in Kotlin

Kotlin's standard library provides a rich set of collection types and functions, making it easier to work with data structures like lists, sets, and maps.

2.1 Types of Collections

- **Immutable Collections**: These cannot be modified after their creation. Examples: listOf, setOf, mapOf.
- **Mutable Collections**: These can be modified. Examples: mutableListOf, mutableSetOf, mutableMapOf.

For example:

```
val immutableList = listOf(1, 2, 3)
val mutableList = mutableListOf(1, 2, 3)
mutableList.add(4) // Modifies the list
```

2.2 Common Collection Operations

Kotlin collections support a wide range of operations:

- **Transformation**: map, flatMap
- val doubled = listOf(1, 2, 3).map { it * 2 }

```
println(doubled) // Output: [2, 4, 6]
```

- **Filtering**: filter, filterNot, filterIndexed
- val evenNumbers = listOf(1, 2, 3, 4, 5).filter { it % 2 == 0 }

```
println(evenNumbers) // Output: [2, 4]
```

- **Sorting**: sorted, sortedBy, sortedDescending
- val sorted = listOf(3, 1, 4, 1, 5).sorted()

```kotlin
println(sorted) // Output: [1, 1, 3, 4, 5]
```
- **Aggregation**: reduce, fold
- ```kotlin
  val sum = listOf(1, 2, 3).reduce { acc, num -> acc + num }
  ```
```kotlin
println(sum) // Output: 6
```

2.3 Sequences

Sequences provide a way to perform lazy operations on collections, which can be more efficient for large data sets. For example:

```kotlin
val sequence = sequenceOf(1, 2, 3, 4, 5)

val lazyResult = sequence.filter { it % 2 == 0 }.map { it * 2 }

println(lazyResult.toList()) // Output: [4, 8]
```

2.4 Mutable and Immutable Differences

Understanding mutability in collections is crucial to avoid unintended side effects.

```kotlin
val immutableList = listOf(1, 2, 3)

// immutableList.add(4) // Error: Cannot add to immutable list


val mutableList = mutableListOf(1, 2, 3)

mutableList.add(4) // Works

println(mutableList) // Output: [1, 2, 3, 4]
```

3. Combining Lambdas and Collections

Kotlin's collection functions seamlessly integrate with lambdas, enabling expressive and concise code.

3.1 Functional Style Operations

Common operations like map, filter, and reduce rely on lambdas:

```kotlin
val numbers = listOf(1, 2, 3, 4, 5)

val result = numbers.filter { it % 2 == 0 }.map { it * 2 }

println(result) // Output: [4, 8]
```

3.2 Grouping and Partitioning

- **Grouping**:
- ```kotlin
  val grouped = listOf("apple", "banana", "cherry").groupBy { it.first() }
  ```
```kotlin
println(grouped) // Output: {a=[apple], b=[banana], c=[cherry]}
```
- **Partitioning**:
- ```kotlin
  val (even, odd) = listOf(1, 2, 3, 4, 5).partition { it % 2 == 0 }
  ```
- ```kotlin
  println(even) // Output: [2, 4]
  ```
```kotlin
println(odd) // Output: [1, 3, 5]
```

3.3 Custom Operations

You can combine lambdas to create custom behavior:

```kotlin
val words = listOf("Kotlin", "is", "awesome")
val capitalizedWords = words.map { it.uppercase() }.joinToString(" ")
println(capitalizedWords) // Output: KOTLIN IS AWESOME
```

4. Advanced Topics

4.1 Inline and Crossinline in Lambdas

- **Inline**: Optimizes performance by inlining lambda code.
- **Crossinline**: Prevents non-local returns in lambdas passed to inline functions.

4.2 Creating DSLs with Lambdas

Kotlin's DSL (Domain Specific Language) capabilities leverage lambdas with receivers. For example:

```kotlin
fun html(block: Html.() -> Unit): Html {
    val html = Html()
    html.block()
    return html
}
```

4.3 Performance Considerations

- Use sequence for large data sets to optimize performance.
- Avoid creating unnecessary intermediate collections.
- Inline functions can reduce overhead.

Let's begin,

Introduction to Lambdas

As you might recall from a literal is when you directly write out a value in your code. For example, in Kotlin, you can create literals for basic types such as **String, Int**, and **Boolean**. The highlighted parts of the code below are values that are written as literals.

```kotlin
val string: String = "This is a string"
val integer: Int = 49
val boolean: Boolean = true
```

Listing - Code that includes literals.

Just as you can write literals of Strings, Integers, and Booleans, you can also write a literal of a function!

"Wait," I can hear you say, "we've already been writing functions! How is this any different?" Yes, we've been writing named functions with the **fun** keyword, but we've never defined a function directly in an expression, such as on the right-hand side of an assignment, or directly inside a function call.

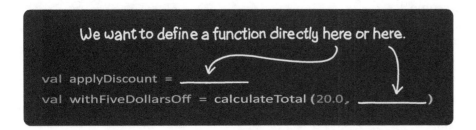

Let's take another look at the **discountFiveDollars()** function from earlier in this chapter. We defined that function and then assigned it to a variable by using a function reference. Here's what it looked like:

```
fun discountFiveDollars(price: Double) = price -5.0
val applyDiscount: (Double) -> Double = ::discountFiveDollars
```

Instead of defining the **discountFiveDollars()** function with the **fun** keyword, we can rewrite it as a **function literal** like this:

```
val applyDiscount: (Double) -> Double ={ price: Double -> price -5.0 }
```
Listing - Code that includes a function literal instead of a function reference.

The highlighted part of the code above is a function literal. In Kotlin, a function literal written like this is called a **lambda**.

Lambdas are functions, just like the ones we've written so far. They're simply expressed differently. To write a lambda:

- Use an opening brace { and a closing brace }.

- Write the parameters *before* the arrow -> and the body *after* the arrow.

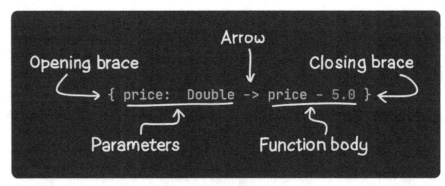

Once you've assigned a lambda to a variable, you can call it using the variable's name.

Traditional Functions vs Lambdas

Both traditional functions and lambdas have parameters and a body, and evaluate to some kind of result. However, unlike traditional functions, the lambda itself does not have a name. Sure, you can choose to assign it to a variable that has a name, but the lambda itself is nameless.

The lambda in Listing indicates that the **price** parameter has a type of **Double**. Most of the time, however,

Kotlin can use its type inference to figure it out. For example, we can rewrite that listing and omit the parameter's type in the lambda:

```
val applyDiscount: (Double) -> Double = {price -> price - 5.0 }
```

Kotlin knows that **price** must be a **Double**, because that's what the type of **applyDiscount** says it must be. Similarly, the result of the lambda has to match.

```
                                  ┌─Parameter Type─┐
val applyDiscount: (Double) -> Double = { price -> price - 5.0 }
                                           ↑           └─Result Type─┘
```

So, lambdas are a concise way of creating a function right in the middle of an expression. Our lambda above is pretty small already, but we can make it even more concise!

The Implicit its parameter

In cases where there's only a single parameter for a lambda, you can omit the parameter name and the arrow. When you do this, Kotlin will automatically make the name of the parameter **it**. Let's rewrite our lambda to take advantage of this:

```
val applyDiscount: (Double) -> Double = {it - 5.0 }
```

The code here is incredibly more concise than the original **discountFiveDollars()** function!

The implicit **it** parameter is used often in Kotlin, especially when the lambda is small, like this one. In cases when the lambda is longer, as we'll see in a moment, it can be a good idea to give the parameter a name explicitly.

In future chapters, we'll also see cases where lambdas are nested inside other lambdas, which is another situation where explicit names are preferred. In many cases, though, the implicit **it** parameter can make your code easier to read.

Assigning a lambda to a variable can be helpful, but things get even more interesting when we start using lambdas with higher-order functions!

Lambdas and Higher-Order Functions

Passing Lambdas as Arguments

As we learned above, higher-order functions are those that have a function as an input (i.e., parameter) or an output (i.e., the result). Here's the code from above, where we used function references to pass functions as arguments to the **calculateTotal()** function:

```
fun calculateTotal (
    initialPrice: Double,
    applyDiscount: (Double) -> Double
): Double {
    // Apply coupon discount
    val priceAfterDiscount = applyDiscount(initialPrice)
    // Apply tax
    val total = priceAfterDiscount * taxMultiplier

    return total
}

fun discountFiveDollars(price: Double): Double = price -5.0
fun discountTenPercent(price: Double): Double = price *0.9
fun noDiscount(price: Double): Double = price

val withFiveDollarsOff = calculateTotal(20.0, ::discountFiveDollars) // $16.35
val withTenPercentOff  = calculateTotal(20.0, ::discountTenPercent)  // $19.62
val fullPrice            calculateTotal(20.0, ::noDiscount)          // $21.80
```

It's easy to call **calculateTotal()** with a lambda instead of a function reference. Let's rewrite the last few lines of the code above to use lambdas. We'll just take the body from each corresponding function and write it as a lambda instead:

val withFiveDollarsOff = calculateTotal(20.0, { price -> price - 5.0 }) // $16.35 val withTenPercentOff = calculateTotal(20.0, { price -> price * 0.9 }) // $19.62 val fullPrice   = calculateTotal(20.0, { price -> price }）   // $21.80

Listing - Replacing the function references from Listing with lambdas.

In cases where function's last parameter is a function type, you can move the lambda argument outside of the parentheses to the right, like this:

val withFiveDollarsOff = calculateTotal(20.0) { price -> price - 5.0 } // $16.35 val withTenPercentOff = calculateTotal(20.0) { price -> price * 0.9 } // $19.62 val fullPrice   = calculateTotal(20.0) { price -> price }   // $21.80

Listing - Placing a lambda argument outside of the parentheses.

We're still sending two arguments to **calculateTotal()**. The first is inside the parentheses, and the second is outside to the right.

In Kotlin, writing the lambda outside of the parentheses like this is called **trailing lambda syntax**. Regardless of whether you put that last lambda argument inside the parentheses or outside, it works exactly the same. Kotlin developers usually prefer trailing lambdas, though.

Trailing lambda syntax is even more fun when the lambda is the only argument that you're passing to the function, because then you can omit the parentheses completely!

For example, here's a higher-order function with a single parameter, which has a function type:

```kotlin
fun printSubtotal(applyDiscount: (Double) -> Double) {
    val result = applyDiscount(20.0)
    val formatted = "$%.2f".format(result)
    println("A $20.00 haircut will cost you$formatted before tax.")
}
```

When calling **printSubtotal()**, no parentheses are needed!

```kotlin
printSubtotal { price -> price -5.0 }
printSubtotal { price -> price *0.9 }
```

Listing - Calling **printSubtotal()** without parentheses.

In addition to using lambdas as arguments, we can also use them as function results!

Returning Lambdas as Function Results

Here's the code from Listing above, where we returned function references:

```kotlin
fun discount(couponCode: String): (Double) -> Double = when (couponCode) {
    "FIVE_BUCKS" -> ::discountFiveDollars
    "TAKE_10"    -> ::discountTenPercent
    else         -> ::noDiscount
}
```

We can very easily replace these function references with lambdas, just as we did for the function arguments in Listing.

```kotlin
fun discount(couponCode: String): (Double) -> Double = when (couponCode) {
    "FIVE_BUCKS" -> { price -> price -5.0 }
    "TAKE_10"    -> { price -> price *0.9 }
    else         -> { price -> price }
}
```

Listing - Returning lambdas from a function.

Lambdas with Multiple Statements

So far, the lambdas that we've used have contained only one simple expression each.

Sometimes you need a lambda that has multiple statements in it. To do this, simply put each statement on a separate line, as you would inside any other function. Unlike a regular function, though, you won't use the return keyword to return your result. Instead, the very last line of the lambda will be the result of the call.

For example, we might want to print some debugging information inside our lambda that calculates the five dollars-off coupon:

```
val withFiveDollarsOff = calculateTotal(20.0) { price ->
    val result = price -5.0
    println("Initial price: $price")
    println("Discounted price: $result")
    result
}
```

Listing - A lambda that has multiple lines of code.

When we've got a lambda that spans multiple lines like this, it's conventional to put the parameters and arrow on the same line as the opening brace, as seen above.

Here's the same code, with some callouts indicating each part.

```
val withFiveDollarsOff = calculateTotal(20.0) { price ->    Parameter and arrow
    val discountedPrice = price - 5.0
    println("Initial price: $price")                        Multiple statements
    println("Discounted price: $discountedPrice")
    discountedPrice                                         Result (no "return" keyword!)
}
```

Before we wrap up this chapter, we've got one more concept to cover!

Closures

Bert's salon is doing great now. Let's take a look at his code, including **calculateTotal()**, **discountForCouponCode()**, and how he ends up calling them to get the total.

```
fun calculateTotal (
    initialPrice: Double,
    applyDiscount: (Double) -> Double
): Double {
    val priceAfterDiscount = applyDiscount(initialPrice) // Apply coupon discount
    val total = priceAfterDiscount * taxMultiplier      // Apply tax

    return total
}

fun discountForCouponCode(couponCode: String): (Double) -> Double = when (couponCode) {
    "FIVE_BUCKS" -> { price -> price -5.0 }
    "TAKE_10"    -> { price -> price *0.9 }
    else         -> { price -> price }
}

val initialPrice = 20.0
val couponDiscount = discountForCouponCode("FIVE_BUCKS")
val total = calculateTotal (initialPrice, couponDiscount)
```

Listing - Putting it all together.

Bert noticed that when he introduces a new coupon, he needs to write another lambda. For example, if he adds a new coupon for nine dollars off, and another one for fifteen percent off, he would need to write a few more lambdas, like this:

```
fun discount(couponCode: String): (Double) -> Double = when (couponCode) {
    "FIVE_BUCKS" -> { price -> price -5.0 }
    "NINE_BUCKS" -> { price -> price -9.0 }
    "TAKE_10"    -> { price -> price *0.9 }
    "TAKE_15"    -> { price -> price *0.85 }
    else         -> { price -> price }
}
```

Listing - Adding more coupon codes.

That's not too bad, actually, but he decided he could make one last small improvement. There are really two main categories of coupons - dollar amount and percentages.

Dollar Amount Coupons

Bert's Snips & Clips

$5 OFF

CODE: FIVE_BUCKS

Bert's Snips & Clips

$9 OFF

CODE: NINE_BUCKS

Percentage Coupons

Bert's Snips & Clips

10% OFF

CODE: TAKE_10

Bert's Snips & Clips

15% OFF

CODE: TAKE_15

He wrote these two functions to match the two categories of coupons that he identified:

```
fun dollarAmountDiscount(dollarsOff: Double): (Double) -> Double =
    { price -> price - dollarsOff }

fun percentageDiscount(percentageOff: Double): (Double) -> Double {
    val multiplier = 1.0 - percentageOff
    return { price -> price * multiplier }
}
```
Listing - Functions that create functions.

It's important to note that these two functions do not calculate the discount themselves. Instead, they create functions that calculate the discount. This is a little easier to see in **percentDiscount()**, where we're using an explicit **return** keyword rather than an expression body.

Another neat thing here is that these lambdas use variables that are defined outside of the lambda body. The first one uses the **amount** variable (a parameter of the wrapping function), and the second uses the **multiplier** variable. When a lambda uses a variable that's defined outside of its body like this, it's sometimes referred to as a **closure**.

Now, creating a new coupon is easy. Instead of writing the lambda inline in **discount()**, Bert can just call either **amountDiscount()** or **percentDiscount()** to create the lambda for him.

```
fun discount(couponCode: String): (Double) -> Double =when (couponCode) {
    "FIVE_BUCKS" -> dollarAmountDiscount(5.0)
    "NINE_BUCKS" -> dollarAmountDiscount(9.0)
    "TAKE_10"        -> percentageDiscount(0.10)
    "TAKE_15"        -> percentageDiscount(0.15)
    else             -> { price -> price }
}
```
Listing - A small improvement to avoid some duplicated code.

Collections: Lists and Sets

Introduction to Lists

Thankfully, there's a much better way! Libby can create a **collection**. Let's start with one of the most common kinds of collections in Kotlin - a **list**. Creating a list is easy - just call **listOf()** with the values that you want, separating them with commas. Let's update Libby's code so that it's using a list.

```
val booksToRead = listOf(
    "Tea with Agatha",
    "Mystery on First Avenue",
    "The Ravine of Sorrows",
    "Among the Aliens",
    "The Kingsford Manor Mystery",
)
```

Listing- Creating a list of strings to represent titles of books.

This code looks pretty similar to Libby's handwritten list. In fact, let's compare the two!

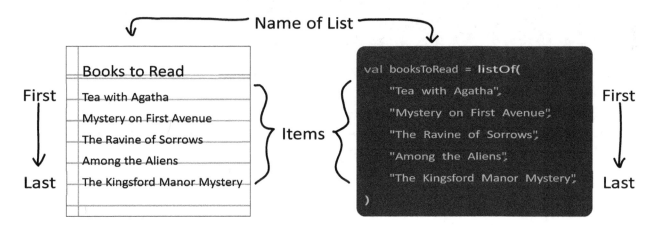

The handwritten list and the Kotlin list have a lot in common:

1.   First, they both have a name. In Kotlin, the name of the variable holding the list is kind of like the name of the list on paper.

2.   Next, both lists have items in them - in this case, the titles of the books. In Kotlin, the items in a list are called **elements**.

3.   Finally, both lists have the titles in a particular order.

In the past, we've used the **println()** function to print out the contents of a variable to the screen. You can also use **println()** with a collection variable.

```
println(booksToRead)
```

Listing- Printing a collection variable to the screen.

When you do this, you'll see its elements in order, like this:

[Tea with Agatha, Mystery on First Avenue, The Ravine of Sorrows, Among the Aliens,
The Kingsford Manor Mystery]

Collections and Types

When working with collections in Kotlin, we have two different types to consider.

1.   The type of the collection we're using.

2.   The type of the elements in the collection.

These two things together determine the overall type of the collection variable. In the case of Listing:

1.   The collection is a **List**.

2.   The type of the elements in the collection is **String**.

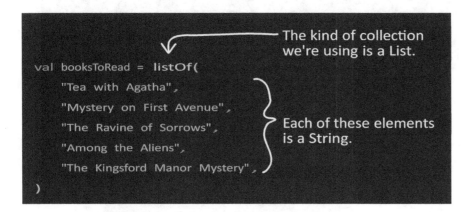

Once you know these two things, you can write the type of a collection variable easily. Just put the type of the collection first, then write the type of the elements second, between a left angle bracket < and a right-angle bracket >. So, the type of **booksToRead** is **List<String>**.

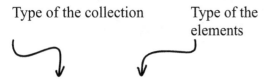

List<String>

Let's rewrite Listing, this time explicitly including the type information for the **booksToRead** collection variable.

```
val booksToRead: List<String> = listOf(
    "Tea with Agatha",
    "Mystery on First Avenue",
    "The Ravine of Sorrows",
    "Among the Aliens",
    "The Kingsford Manor Mystery",
)
```

Listing - Explicitly including the type of a collection variable.

This kind of a type is an instance of a **generic**. We will cover generics in detail in a future chapter. For now, just know how to write the type for a list, in case you need to use it as a function's parameter type or return type.

Adding and Removing an Element

Libby just heard about another great book from her friend, Rebecca! She's ready to add this new title, Beyond the Expanse, to her list. How can she do this?

Of course, she could just add one more argument to the end of **listOf()**. But what about adding the title after the list has already been created?

In Kotlin, once you've already called **listOf()** to create a list, that list can't be changed. You can't add anything to it, and you can't remove anything from it. The fancy word for "change" in programming is **mutate**, so a list that doesn't allow you to add or remove elements is called an **immutable list**.

Even though you can't add or remove elements from a regular Kotlin **List**, you can create a new list by putting the original list together with a new element. To do this, use the **plus operator**. That is, use + to connect the original list with the new item, and assign it to a new variable, like this:

```
val booksToRead = listOf(
    "Tea with Agatha",
    "Mystery on First Avenue",
    "The Ravine of Sorrows",
    "Among the Aliens",
    "The Kingsford Manor Mystery",
)

val newBooksToRead = booksToRead + "Beyond the Expanse"
```

Listing - Creating a new list that combines a list with one new element.

In this code, **booksToRead + "Beyond the Expanse"** is an expression that evaluates to a new **List** instance.

So, by the time this code is done running, we have two collection variables - **booksToRead** and **newBooksToRead**.

This is kind of writing the new list of titles on a second sheet of paper. That way, Libby actually ends up with two lists - the original list and the new list:

Books to Read	New Books to Read
Tea with Agatha	Tea with Agatha
Mystery on First Avenue	Mystery on First Avenue
The Ravine of Sorrows	The Ravine of Sorrows
Among the Aliens	Among the Aliens
The Kingsford Manor Mystery	The Kingsford Manor Mystery
	Beyond the Expanse

As you remember from Chapter, a variable can be declared with either **val** or **var**, and this includes variables that hold a collection. Keep in mind, though, that declaring a collection variable with **var** does not change the fact that the list itself is immutable. In other words, just declaring it with **var** does not make it so that you can add or remove elements. However, **var** does let you assign another immutable list to it.

So, by changing the **booksToRead** variable from **val** to **var**, the new list can be assigned to the existing variable name, like this:

```
var booksToRead = listOf(
    "Tea with Agatha",
    "Mystery on First Avenue",
    "The Ravine of Sorrows",
    "Among the Aliens",
    "The Kingsford Manor Mystery",
)

booksToRead = booksToRead + "Beyond the Expanse"
```

Listing - Reassigning the collection to the existing **booksToRead** *variable.*

This is kind of like trashing the old paper list, and simply giving the new list the same name as the old one.

Libby's list now has six titles in it. Just when she thought she was done updating the list, she heard from Rebecca again. "You know, I read Among the Aliens last week. It really wasn't very good," she said. "You shouldn't bother reading that one."

Libby would like to scratch that one off her list. As you can guess, you can remove an element from a list in a similar way, but instead of the plus operator, use the **minus operator**.

```
var booksToRead = listOf(
    "Tea with Agatha",
    "Mystery on First Avenue",
    "The Ravine of Sorrows",
    "Among the Aliens",
    "The Kingsford Manor Mystery",
)

booksToRead = booksToRead + "Beyond the Expanse"
booksToRead = booksToRead - "Among the Aliens"
```

Listing - Adding and removing an element from a collection.

In fact, those last two lines can be consolidated, like this:

```
booksToRead = booksToRead + "Beyond the Expanse" - "Among the Aliens"
```
Listing - Adding and removing an element from a collection with one assignment.

Now, when Libby does **println(booksToRead)**, she sees this on the screen:

[Tea with Agatha, Mystery on First Avenue, The Ravine of Sorrows,

The Kingsford Manor Mystery, Beyond the Expanse]

"Excellent!" she thought, "My reading list is all up to date!"

List and MutableList

So far, we've been using a regular Kotlin **List**, which doesn't allow changes to it, as we saw above. Instead, we had to create a new list by using a plus or minus operator.

However, Kotlin also provides another kind of list - one that does allow you to change it. Since these lists do allow changes, they're called **mutable lists**, and they have a type of **MutableList**.

When using a mutable list, you can use the **add()** and **remove()** functions to add or remove elements, like this:

```
var booksToRead: MutableList<String> = mutableListOf(
    "Tea with Agatha",
    "Mystery on First Avenue",
    "The Ravine of Sorrows",
    "Among the Aliens",
    "The Kingsford Manor Mystery",
)

booksToRead.add("Beyond the Expanse")
booksToRead.remove("Among the Aliens")
```
Listing - Creating, adding to, and removing from a mutable list.

Using a mutable list is kind of like Libby writing down her paper list with a pencil instead of a pen. She can go in and erase a title, or add another, without using another sheet of paper.

Libby is ready to start reading those books! But in order know which book to start with, she needs to know how to get a single title out of the list.

Books to Read

Tea with Agatha

Mystery on First Avenue

The Ravine of Sorrows

Among the Aliens

The Kingsford Manor Mystery

Beyond the Expanse

Heads Up: Using Plus and Minus Operators with a Mutable List

For what it's worth, you can also use the plus and minus operators on a mutable list, but keep in mind that those expressions evaluate to a regular immutable List, not MutableList. So generally, if you're using a List, use the plus and minus operators, and if you're using a MutableList, use the add() and remove() functions.

Best Practice: List vs Mutable List

MutableList can be convenient, and if you need to add or remove lots of elements, it can also be faster than a regular List. However, similar to the trade-offs of using val versus var, it's often better to stick with things that can't change, because when something can't change, you have guarantees that you wouldn't have otherwise. Sometimes this guarantee is very helpful, and other times it might not be as important. Use whatever is most appropriate for each situation, but by default, go with a regular List.

Getting an Element from a List

First Item

"All right, which title is first on my list?" wondered Libby. She glanced down at her handwritten page. It was easy for her to see which one was first. "Tea with Agatha," she noted. "Now how do I get the first title from the list in Kotlin?"

Books to Read
Tea with Agatha
Mystery on First Avenue
The Ravine of Sorrows
The Kingsford Manor Mystery
Beyond the Expanse

As mentioned earlier, the elements of a list are in a particular order, and that order is very important for getting an individual element out of the list. Here's how it works:

Each element in the list is given a number, called an **index**, based on where it is in the list. The first element has an index of 0, the second has an index of 1, the third has an index of 2, and so on.

It's easy to get an element out of a list once you know its index. Just call the **get()** member function, passing the index as the argument. For example, Libby can get the first element out of the list by calling **get(0)** like this:

```kotlin
val booksToRead = listOf(
    "Tea with Agatha",
    "Mystery on First Avenue",
    "The Ravine of Sorrows",
    "The Kingsford Manor Mystery",
    "Beyond the Expanse"
)


val firstBook = booksToRead.get(0)
println(firstBook) // Tea with Agatha
```

Listing - Using the **get()** function to get a single element out of a collection.

"Great!" said Libby. "Now I can easily get a single title out of the list of books!"

Heads Up: Out-of-Bound Indexes

When you call get(), make sure that the index you give it is for an element that actually exists! In booksToRead, there are five elements, so you could call get() with any number including and between 0 and 4. If you were to call get(86), for example, you would see an error message that says that the index was out of bounds.

For the Nerds: Why Do Indexes Start with Zero?

Kotlin follows the tradition of many other programming languages in that its indexes start with the number 0 instead of 1. One classic data structure for representing a list of values is called an array. In older programming languages, you had to manage the location of your variables and arrays in the computer's memory. A single element of an array took up a certain amount of memory - for example, an integer took up one byte of memory - and an array required a contiguous block of memory. So, if you had an array of integers, they were all physically next to each other in the computer's memory.

If you knew the starting address of the array - that is, the memory address of the first element in the array - you could get any other particular element's memory address by multiplying its index by the size of the individual elements, then adding that to the starting address.

Kotlin doesn't require its developers to manage memory this way, but it does have a few different kinds of lists, each using a different kind of data structure to hold the elements for you behind the scenes. Regardless of whether a particular list uses an array to hold its data, the indexes still always start with zero.
Rather than calling the **get()** function directly, you can use the **indexed access operator** instead, which is written with an opening bracket **[** and a closing bracket **]**, with the index in the middle. The code in the following listing does the exact same thing as the code above.

```
val firstBook = booksToRead[0]
println(firstBook) // Tea with Agatha
```
Listing - Getting a single element out of a collection, using the indexed access operator.

Kotlin developers use the indexed access operator much more than they use the **get()** function, so we'll be using it from now on.

Now, getting an individual item out of the list can be helpful, but collections become especially helpful when we want to do something with each item in the list. Let's see how to do that next!

Loops and Iterations

"Now, I'd like to print out the list of books to the screen," said Libby to herself. "I'll use **println(booksToRead)** for this!" Upon running that code, here's what she saw:

[Tea with Agatha, Mystery on First Avenue, The Ravine of Sorrows,

The Kingsford Manor Mystery, Beyond the Expanse]

"It's nice that I can print out the list so easily, but I'd really like to see the list vertically, like my handwritten list." Here's what she has in mind:

```
Tea with Agatha
Mystery on First Avenue
The Ravine of Sorrows
The Kingsford Manor Mystery
Beyond the Expanse
```

Of course, to achieve this, she could call **println()** on each element one by one, like this:

```
println(booksToRead[0])
println(booksToRead[1])
println(booksToRead[2])
println(booksToRead[3])
println(booksToRead[4])
```

Listing - Printing each element by hand.

However, writing code like this is quite tedious. Plus, it would be easy to make a mistake by printing the elements out of order, or by accidentally printing the same element more than once. In fact, this looks a whole lot like the code back in Listing!

Instead of writing out the same code for each element in the list, what if Kotlin could just go through every element, one by one, and call **println()** on each? Thankfully, this is very easy to do in Kotlin! We can use the **forEach()** function. Here's how it looks.

```
booksToRead.forEach { element ->
    println(element)
}
```

Listing - Using   **forEach()** to print each element.

When Kotlin is running this code, it runs down through   **println(element)** for the first element, then comes back up and runs down it again for the second element, then comes back up and runs down it again for the third element, and so on. By going through this line of code over and over again, it's as if it's looping in circles, like this:

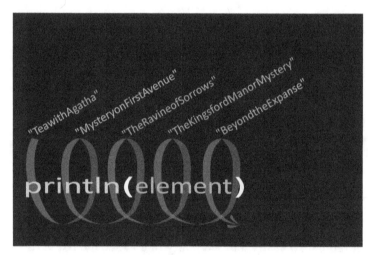

That's why programming languages call this a **loop** - because, for each element in the collection, it cycles back through that code. It's also generally called **iterating**, and each time the code is run, it's called a single **iteration**.

For the Nerds: Using the Term "Loop"

In a lot of the programming texts out there - including the Kotlin documentation - the term "loop" tends to be reserved for traditional programming constructs like for or while, but not used when referring to collection functions like forEach(). Although Kotlin does support these traditional looping constructs, in this book, we'll stick with forEach() and similar functions, which we can put together to do all sorts of cool things, as we'll see later in this chapter.

Since we won't need to distinguish between traditional looping constructs and collection functions, and since those collection functions ultimately use a traditional for loop under the hood anyway, I'll be more liberal with my use of the term "loop."

Let's look a little closer at **forEach()**, to understand why we had to structure the code the way we did. **forEach()** is a member function that exists on collection variables. It's a higher-order function that accepts a lambda. That lambda is the code that you want Kotlin to run "for each" element in the collection.

Here we named the parameter **element**, but you could have named it **title** instead. Alternatively, since this lambda has only a single parameter, you can use the implicit its parameter instead, which makes it nice and concise. In fact, we can put it all on one line:

```
booksToRead.forEach { println(it) }
```
Listing - Using the implicit it parameter with forEach() .

The result in either case is exactly what Libby wanted - the book titles are printed out vertically, just like on her paper notepad!

```
Tea with Agatha
Mystery on First Avenue
The Ravine of Sorrows
The Kingsford Manor Mystery
Beyond the Expanse
```

Collection Operations

Libby is ready to share her list of books with other people who are interested in what she'll be reading, starting with her friend Nolan. However, when she makes a copy of the list for him, she wants to make changes to some of the titles.

"I'd really like to remove the word 'The' from the beginning of each title," thought Libby. "That way, I'll be able to sort it alphabetically, and the titles that begin with 'The' won't clump together."

Mapping Collections: Converting Elements

Sometimes when you create a new collection from an existing one, you also want to convert one or more of the elements in some way. In Libby's case, she wants to remove the word "The" when it appears at the beginning of a title, so that they could be used for sorting.

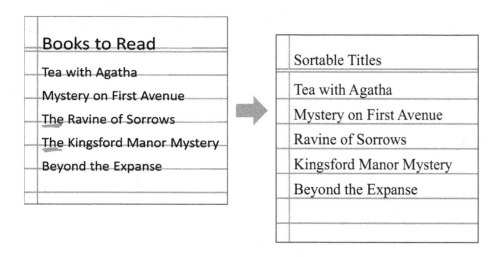

Before doing that conversion on all of the titles, let's start with just one of them. **String** objects have a **removePrefix()** function, which you can use to remove words from the beginning of the string. Here's how you can use it:

```
val sortableTitle ="The Kingsford Manor Mystery".removePrefix("The ")

println(sortableTitle) // Kingsford Manor Mystery
```
Listing - Using **removePrefix()** on a single string.

Perfect! Now all she needs is to apply this **removePrefix()** function to each element in the list!

"Maybe I can use **forEach()**, since I know it operates on each item in the list", thought Libby. She rolled up her sleeves, and cranked out the following code:

```
val sortableTitles: MutableList<String> =mutableListOf()

booksToRead.forEach { title ->
    sortableTitles.add(title.removePrefix("The "))
}

sortableTitles.forEach { println(it) }
```
Listing - Manually creating a list without the word "The" at the beginning of the titles.

"Well, that works," thought Libby. "But it's a little complicated, and it's a lot of code to write…"

The reason this is complicated is that Libby wanted to create a new collection, but **forEach()** doesn't do that. It simply runs the lambda on an existing collection, and then returns Unit.

What she really needs is a collection operation that runs the lambda and includes the result of that lambda as an element in a new collection.

In Kotlin, that collection operation is called **map()**. Here's how Libby can use it to remove the word "The" from the beginning of titles in the new collection:

```
val sortableTitles = booksToRead.map { title ->
    title.removePrefix("The ")
}
```
Listing - Using **map()** to create a list without the word "The" at the beginning of the titles.

This code does the same thing as the previous listing (except that the result is an immutable **List** instead of a **MutableList**).

Like **forEach()**, the map() function calls the lambda once with each element in the list. However, unlike **forEach()**, **map()** will use the result of the lambda on each iteration to build out a new list.

When you print each element of the list, you can see that both The Ravine of Sorrows and The Kingsford Manor Mystery have been updated so that the word "The" is not at the beginning.

```
Tea with Agatha
Mystery on First Avenue
Ravine of Sorrows
Kingsford Manor Mystery
Beyond the Expanse
```

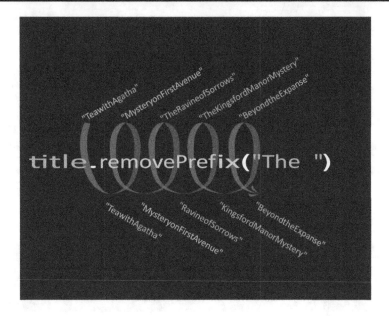

When you print each element of the list, you can see that both The Ravine of Sorrows and The Kingsford Manor Mystery have been updated so that the word "The" is not at the beginning.

Let's take a closer look at the **map()** function:

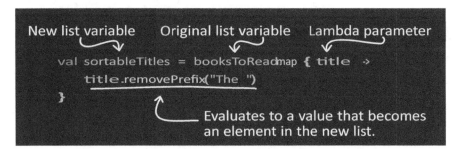

- Similar to **forEach()**, the **map()** function is a higher-order function that takes a lambda.
- That lambda will run once for each element in the list.
- The result of the lambda will be an element in the new collection.
- The **map()** function returns that new collection.

Functions like **forEach()** and **map()** are called **collection operations**, because they're functions that perform some operation on (that is, they do something with) a collection.

"Perfect!" said Libby, "Now that the titles have been changed like I want, maybe I can sort them?"

Sorting Collections

The **forEach()** and **map()** functions are only two of many collection operations in Kotlin. Another one that can be quite helpful is called **sorted()**.

Since the **map()** function returns a collection, Libby can just call **sorted()** immediately after the call to **map()**, like this:

```
val sortedTitles = booksToRead.map { title -> title.removePrefix("The ") }.sorted()
```

Listing - Combining **map()** *with* **sorted()**

When she printed out the elements of **sortedTitles**, she saw the output she was hoping for!

```
Beyond the Expanse
Kingsford Manor Mystery
Mystery on First Avenue
Ravine of Sorrows
Tea with Agatha
```

In order to make things easier to read, each collection operation can go on its own line, like this:

```
val sortedTitles = booksToRead
    .map { title -> title.removePrefix("The ") }
    .sorted()
```

Listing - Formatting multiple collection operations so that they line up.

This code is identical to the previous listing except for the formatting. In other words, all of the letters and punctuation are exactly the same and in the same order - it's only the space between them that's different.

Writing the collection operations vertically like this can be helpful because it makes it easy to scan down the lines to see what collection operations are involved and what order they're in. For example, first the titles are mapped, and then the titles are sorted. For that reason, Kotlin developers often format their code this way.

Filtering Collections: Including and Omitting Elements

Libby is excited! Now she's got a list of books - sorted alphabetically - to share with Nolan.

"I can't wait to see your list of books," said Nolan. "Just remember - I only read mystery novels!"

"Only mysteries…?" repeated Libby. "Okay," she thought to herself, "the final thing I need to do is remove the titles that are not mysteries." She pulled out a sheet from her notepad, and wrote a customized list just for Nolan, omitting any title that is not a mystery.

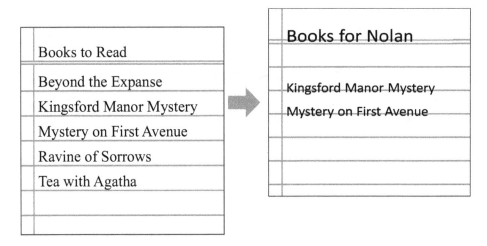

Books to Read	**Books for Nolan**
Beyond the Expanse	
Kingsford Manor Mystery	Kingsford Manor Mystery
Mystery on First Avenue	Mystery on First Avenue
Ravine of Sorrows	
Tea with Agatha	

"How can I do this in Kotlin?" she wondered.

As you probably guessed, Kotlin includes a collection operation that makes this easy, and unsurprisingly, it's called **filter()**.

Just like an air filter that blocks unwanted dust and allergens from getting through to your air conditioner system, a Kotlin list filter blocks elements that you don't want to get through to a new list!

Let's use the **filter()** function to filter down the list of books to just those that have "Mystery" in the title:

```
val booksForNolan = booksToRead
    map { title -> title.removePrefix("The ") }
    sorted()
    filter { title -> title.contains("Mystery") }
```

Listing - Using the **filter()** function to filter out unwanted elements.

The **filter()** function is similar to the **map()** function above - it takes a lambda as an argument, and that lambda will be invoked *once* for each title in the original list. Unlike the **map()** function, however, the lambda for **filter()** must return a **Boolean**. If it returns **true** for an element, then that element is passed into the new collection (i.e., **booksForNolan** in this case). If it returns **false**, then it's omitted from the new collection.

Here's a breakdown of how to use the filter() function:

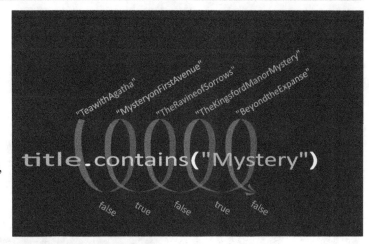

New list variable   Original list variable   Lambda parameter

```
val booksForNolan = booksToRead.filter { title ->
    title.contains("Mystery")
}
```

Determines whether this element is included in the new list.

Printing each element of the list, here's what Libby saw:

```
Kingsford  Manor  Mystery
Mystery  on  First  Avenue
```

"Great," she said. "The list is exactly like I wanted it. It includes only mysteries, and it's sorted properly!"

Collection Operation Chains

Let's look at that code again:

```
val booksForNolan = booksToRead
    map { title -> title.removePrefix("The ") }
    sorted()
    filter { title -> title.contains("Mystery") }
```

Listing - Using **map(), sorted(),** *and* **filter()** - copied from Listing.

In Kotlin, it's common to put multiple collection operations together like this, one after another. When we do this, it's called **chaining** the collection operations - each operation is like one link in the chain. In this code listing, the **map()**, **sorted()**, and **filter()** calls are chained together.

Keep in mind that the operation chain is not mutating a single list. In fact, each of these operations creates a new list. The list that's created by the final operation, **filter()**, is the list that is assigned to the variable **booksForNolan**. The **intermediate lists** - that is, the lists that are created by the collection operations inside the chain - are used by the next operation in the chain, but are not assigned to any variable. It's still important to keep these intermediate lists in mind, though. This next illustration shows the list that's involved at each step in the chain.

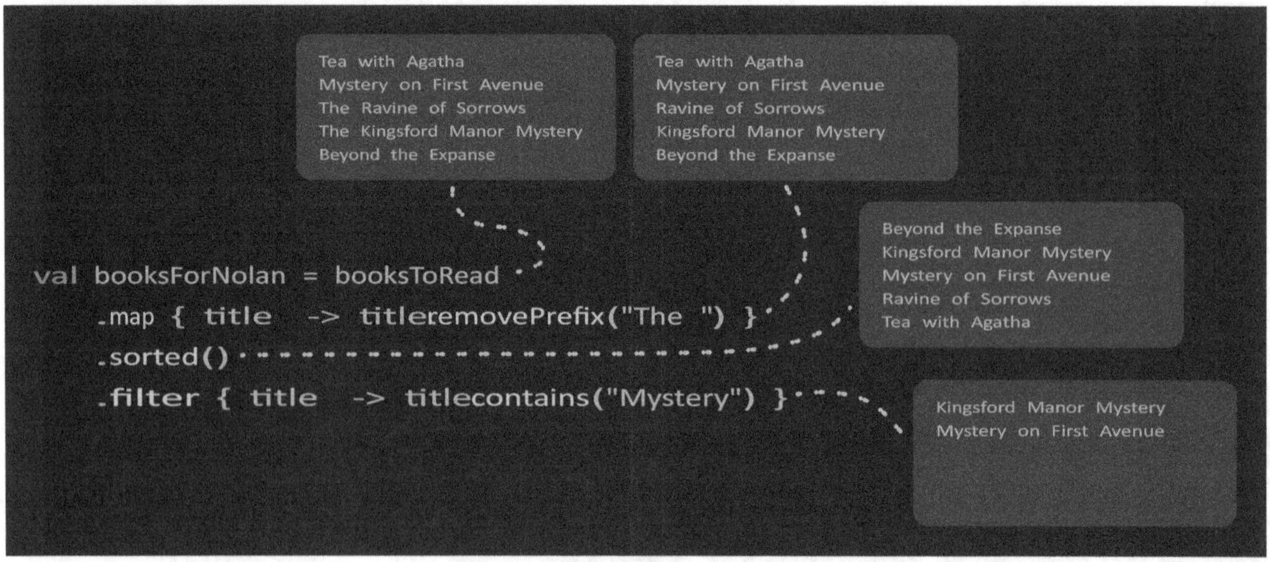

Whenever you've got a collection operation chain like this, it's helpful to consider how many elements are in each intermediate list. For example, the code in Listing has the **filter()** call at the end of the chain. But what if it went at the beginning of the chain instead, like this?

```
val booksForNolan = booksToRead
    filter { title -> title.contains("Mystery") }
    map { title -> title.removePrefix("The ") }
    sorted()
```

Listing - Moving the **filter()** call to the top of the chain.

By doing this, the intermediate list that **filter()** produces would only have two elements, in which case the **map()** function would only need to invoke its lambda twice instead of five times, and **sorted()** would only have two items to sort instead of five. In this example, the final list is the same either way, but Listing is likely to be more efficient than Listing.

Here's an illustration showing the list involved at each step when placing the **filter()** call at the top. Notice that the intermediate lists have fewer elements than they did in the previous illustration.

On a small list like this, it's not a big deal, but on a list that has hundreds or thousands of elements, you could see how this could improve the **performance** of your code - that is, it would run much faster!

Other collection operations

Kotlin has many other collection operations that are easy to use! Just to give you an idea, here are a few others that might be helpful to you.

- **drop(3)** - The new list omits the first 3 elements from the original list.
- **take(5)** - The new list uses only the first 5 elements from the original list.
- **distinct()** - The new list will omit duplicate elements, so that each element is included only once.
- **reversed()** - The new list will have the same elements as the original, but their order will be backwards.

You can see a more complete list of them in the official Kotlin API documentation.

Introduction to Sets

Before we wrap up this chapter, it's worth noting that lists aren't the only kind of collection in Kotlin. Lists are probably the most frequently used, but another helpful collection type is called a **set**. Whereas lists are helpful for ensuring that its elements are in a particular order, sets are helpful for ensuring that each element in it is always unique.

For example, Nolan's favorite mystery author, Slim Chancery, has written three books, and Nolan is proud to say he's got the whole set.

Creating a set in Kotlin is just as easy as creating a list. Simply use **setOf()** or **mutableSetOf()** instead of

listOf() or **mutableListOf()**

```
val booksBySlim: Set<String> = setOf(
    "The Malt Shop Caper",
    "Who is Mrs. W?",
    "At Midnight or Later",
)
```

Listing - Creating a set of strings.

When you add an element to a set that already has that value, the set will remain unchanged.

```
val booksBySlim: MutableSet<String> = mutableSetOf(
    "The Malt Shop Caper",
    "Who is Mrs. W?",
    "At Midnight or Later",
)

booksBySlim.add("The Malt Shop Caper")

println(booksBySlim)
// [The Malt Shop Caper, Who is Mrs. W?, At Midnight or Later]
```

Listing - Adding an element to a set that already contains that element. The set does not include it a second time.

Note that a set does not guarantee the order of its elements when you print them out or use a collection operation on it. It's possible that the elements will be in the same order that you added them, but don't depend on it!

Because sets don't have any particular order to their elements, their elements do not have indexes. For that reason, sets do not even include a **get()** function!

The key takeaway is that:

1.   Lists have elements in a guaranteed order, and can contain duplicates.

2.   Sets have elements in no particular order, and are guaranteed not to contain duplicates.

Also, you can convert a list into a set, or the other way around. Simply use **toSet()** or **toList()**. Just remember that if you convert a list to a set, you'll lose duplicate elements, and the order could possibly be different!

```
val bookList = listOf(
    "The Malt Shop Caper",
    "At Midnight or Later",
    "The Malt Shop Caper",
)

val bookSet = bookListtoSet() // bookSet has two elements
val anotherBookList = bookSettoList() // anotherBookList also has two elements
```

Listing - Converting between lists and sets.

Collections: Maps

The Right Tool for the Job

"You gotta use the right tool for the job." That's what Mr. Andrews taught his young son Jim, who was just starting to learn how to become a handyman like his old man. "When you've got a nail, you need to use a hammer, not a screwdriver."

In order to help Jim pick out the right tool, he sketched out a table of the different hardware and tools in his toolbox.

Hardware	Tool to Use
Nail	Hammer
Hex Nut	Wrench
Hex Bolt	Wrench
Slotted Screw	Slotted Screwdriver
Phillips Screw	Phillips Screwdriver

"Now, with this table, you can easily look up what tool you need. Just scan down the left-hand column for the hardware you need to work with, and then scan across to see the right tool to use."

Which tool should be used with a slotted screw?

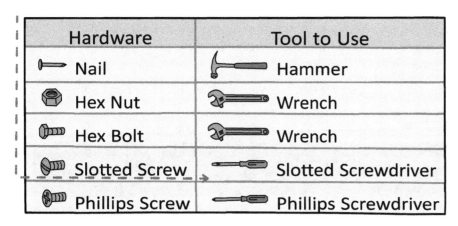

A Slotted Screwdriver!

Tables like this show that there are **associations** between things - a nail is associated with a hammer, a hex nut is associated with a wrench, and so on. In this chapter, we'll build out Kotlin's equivalent of a table like this, but before we do, let's start by creating a single association.

Associating Data

One simple way to associate two values is to use a class called **Pair**. The constructor of this class has two parameters. You can call its constructor with any two objects, regardless of their types. In our case, let's associate two **String** objects - one for a nail, and one for a hammer.

```
val association = Pair("Nail", "Hammer")
```
Listing - Creating a simple association with the **Pair** class.

Pair is a very simple class that has two properties, **first** and **second**, which you can use to get the values back out of it. Below is a UML diagram showing the **Pair** class. The types of **first** and **second** depend on the types of the arguments you give it when calling its constructor, so in this diagram, we will just use **A** and **B** as placeholders for the actual types.

The **first** property will be whatever the first argument was when you called the constructor, and the **second** will be whatever the second argument was.

```
println(association.first)  // Nail
println(association.second) // Hammer
```
Listing - Printing the **first** and second properties of the **Pair**.

Easy, right?

Now, instead of calling the constructor of the **Pair** class, it's sometimes more natural to use a function called **to()**, which will call the **Pair** constructor for you. This function can be called on any object at all. Let's update our code so that it uses the **to()** function.

```
val association = "Nail".to("Hammer")
```
Listing - Creating a **Pair** with the **to** function.

When reading this code, you might say, "When I have a Nail, then I should go **to** a Hammer." Both Listing do the same thing - they create a **Pair** where the left-hand value is assigned to the property called **first** and the right-hand value is assigned to the property called **second**.

The **to()** function also has a special characteristic about it that lets you use it without the punctuation! So, you can also create this same **Pair** like this:

```
val association = "Nail" to "Hammer"

               to
```

Notice that this is the same as Listing above, except that the **.**, the **(**, and the **)** are all missing. When a function lets you call it this way, it's called an **infix function**. We won't see infix functions often, but it's important to know that they exist so that they won't confuse you when you see code like this.

So far, we've used type inference so that we don't have to write out the type of the **association** variable. As with **List** and **Set** in the previous chapter, the type of a **Pair** variable depends on the type of the things that it contains. Since both "Nail" and "Hammer" have type **String**, the type of the **association** variable is **Pair<String, String>**.

Type of the   Type of the first thing second thing

Pair<String, String>

And of course, we can specify the type explicitly like this:

```
val association: Pair<String, String> ="Nail" to "Hammer"
```
Listing- Explicitly specifying the type of the **association** *variable.*

Now that we've successfully made a single association, we can do the same thing for the rest of the tools... and then put them all together into a map!

Map Fundamentals

Let's look at Mr. Andrews' table again.

Hardware	Tool to Use
Nail	Hammer
Hex Nut	Wrench
Hex Bolt	Wrench
Slotted Screw	Slotted Screwdriver
Phillips Screw	Phillips Screwdriver

In Kotlin, a table like this is called a **map**. You might be familiar with maps like street maps and treasure maps, but that's not what we're talking about here.

The term comes from the world of mathematics, where a map defines a correspondence between elements of sets. Similarly, Kotlin maps define an association between each item in the left-hand column, and the corresponding item in the right-hand column.

Before we create our first map, let's cover a few important terms:

- The items in the left-hand column of the table are called **keys**.
- The items in the right-hand column are called **values**.
- The association of a key and a value within a map is called a map **entry**.

There's an important rule to keep in mind - each key in a map is unique. However, the values can be duplicated.

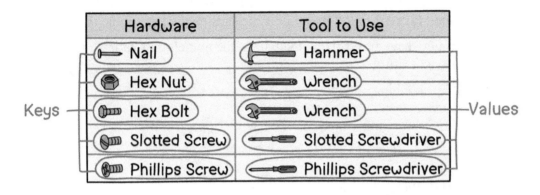

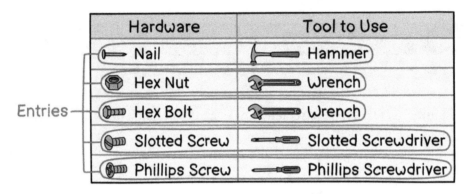

In other words, you cannot have duplicate items in the left-hand column, but it's fine in the right-hand column.

You can see this in the table below, where the left-hand column items are unique, but the wrench appears twice in the right-hand column.

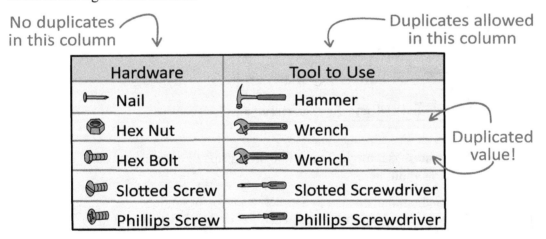

Creating a Map with mapOf()

Now that we understand the main concepts, it's time to create our first map! To do this, we'll use the **mapOf()** function, passing in a **Pair** for each association that we want in the map.

```
val toolbox = mapOf(
    "Nail" to "Hammer",
    "Hex Nut" to "Wrench",
    "Hex Bolt" to "Wrench",
    "Slotted Screw" to "Slotted Screwdriver",
    "Phillips Screw" to "Phillips Screwdriver",
)
```

Listing - Creating a map.

If you read the last chapter, you'll notice that this looks similar to **listOf()** and **setOf()**, except that all of the elements here have two pieces - the key and the value, which are joined together in a **Pair**.

By the way...

Remember - **to** is just another way to create a **Pair**. We could also have created the map like this:

```
val toolbox = mapOf(
    Pair("Nail", "Hammer"),
    Pair("Hex Nut", "Wrench"),
    // ... and so on ...
)
```

You can see the similarities between the Kotlin map and Mr. Andrews' table when you place them side by side:

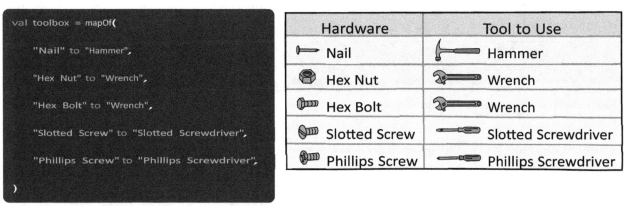

```
val toolbox = mapOf(

    "Nail" to "Hammer",

    "Hex Nut" to "Wrench",

    "Hex Bolt" to "Wrench",

    "Slotted Screw" to "Slotted Screwdriver",

    "Phillips Screw" to "Phillips Screwdriver",

)
```

Hardware	Tool to Use
Nail	Hammer
Hex Nut	Wrench
Hex Bolt	Wrench
Slotted Screw	Slotted Screwdriver
Phillips Screw	Phillips Screwdriver

Just as with lists, sets, and other variables, you can use **println()** to print out the contents of a map.

```
println(toolbox)
```

Listing - Code to print the contents of a map to the screen.

When you print this out, the entries of the map appear between braces. The keys are to the left of the equal signs, and the values are to the right.

{Nail=Hammer, Hex Nut=Wrench, Hex Bolt=Wrench, Slotted Screw=Slotted Screwdriver, Phillips Screw=Phillips Screwdriver}

Just like with **Pair**, the type of a **Map** variable depends on the type of the key and the type of the value.

Type of the Type of the
          key   value

Map<String, String>

So, we could write out the type explicitly like this:

```kotlin
val toolbox: Map<String, String> =mapOf(
    "Nail" to "Hammer",
    "Hex Nut" to "Wrench",
    "Hex Bolt" to "Wrench",
    "Slotted Screw" to "Slotted Screwdriver",
    "Phillips Screw" to "Phillips Screwdriver",
)
```

Listing - Explicitly specifying the type of the **toolbox** *variable.*

Looking Up a Value

The most common thing that you'll need to do with a map is to look up a value. When Jim has a nail, for example, he needs to look up which tool to use. Just as Jim would find the nail in the left-hand column and find the corresponding tool next to it, Kotlin can give you the value when you provide it a key. You can use the **get()** function to do this.

```kotlin
val tool = toolboxget("Nail")
println(tool) // Hammer
```

Listing - Getting a value from a map by the value's corresponding key.

Similar to lists, you can also use the indexed access operator with maps to get a value.

```kotlin
val tool = toolbox['Nail"]
println(tool) // Hammer
```

Listing - Using the indexed access operator to get a value from a map.

If you call **get()** (or use the indexed access operator) with a key that does not exist in the map, it will return a null. This means the **get()** function returns a nullable type rather than a non-nullable type! In Listing, it returns a **String?** rather than a **String**.

You can use the null-safety tools you learned (such as the elvis operator) to get it back to a non-nullable type. Alternatively, you can call **getValue()** instead of **get()**. **getValue()** will return a non-nullable type, but be warned - if you give it a key that does not exist, you'll see an error message and your code will stop running.

```
val tool = toolbox.getValue("Nail")
println(tool) // Hammer

val anotherTool = toolbox.getValue("Wing Nut") // Error at runtime
```
Listing - Using the **getValue()** function to get a value with a non-nullable type.

You can also use **getOrDefault()** to provide a default value if the key doesn't exist. If Mr. Andrews doesn't have a tool for a particular piece of hardware, he'll just need to tighten it by hand!

```
val tool = toolbox.getOrDefault("Hanger Bolt", "Hand")
```
Listing - Using **getOrDefault()** to provide a default value if the key does not exist in the map.

Modifying a Map

As with the other collection types, maps come in two flavors of mutability - **MutableMap** and an immutable **Map**. The mutable variety allows you to change its contents, whereas an immutable map requires you to create a new map instance that you can assign to a new or existing variable.

Let's look at how to change a **MutableMap** first. To start with, we'll need to use **mutableMapOf()** to create the map, instead of just **mapOf()**, which we used back in Listing.

```
val toolbox = mutableMapOf(
    "Nail" to "Hammer",
    "Hex Nut" to "Wrench",
    "Hex Bolt" to "Wrench",
    "Slotted Screw" to "Slotted Screwdriver",
    "Phillips Screw" to "Phillips Screwdriver",
)
```
Listing - Creating a mutable map.

To add a new entry, you can use the **put()** function, where the first argument is the key, and the second argument is the value.

```
toolbox.put("Lumber", "Saw")
```
Listing - Adding a new entry to a mutable map using the **put()** function.

Just like with the **get()** function, though, Kotlin developers typically use the indexed access operator instead of calling the **put()** function directly. The following code accomplishes the same thing as Listing.

```
toolbox["Lumber"] = "Saw"
```
Listing - Adding a new entry to a mutable map using the indexed access operator.

You can also change an existing value exactly the same way. Just provide a key that already exists.

```
toolbox["Hex Bolt"] = "Nut Driver"
```
Listing - Changing an existing value in a mutable map.

Finally, you can remove an entry using the remove() function.

```
Toolbox.remove("Lumber")
```
Listing- Removing an entry from a map.

Note that although you can change a value, you cannot change a key. Instead, you can remove a key and insert a new entry.

```
toolbox.remove("Phillips Screw")
toolbox["Cross Recess Screw"] = "Phillips Screwdriver"
```
Listing - Removing an entry and reinserting it with a new key, to simulate changing a key.

Immutable Maps

As with immutable lists and sets, you can use the plus and minus operators on an immutable map. Remember, doing so will create new map instances, which you'd typically assign to a variable.

The following code demonstrates the same operations as we did above, but on an immutable map. Notice that we use the **var** keyword here so that we can assign each result back to the same **toolbox** variable!

```
var toolbox = mapOf(
    "Nail" to "Hammer",
    "Hex Nut" to "Wrench",
    "Hex Bolt" to "Wrench",
    "Slotted Screw" to "Slotted Screwdriver",
    "Phillips Screw" to "Phillips Screwdriver",
)

// Add an entry
toolbox = toolbox + Pair("Lumber", "Saw")

// Update an entry
toolbox = toolbox + Pair("Hex Bolt", "Nut Driver")

// Remove an entry
toolbox = toolbox - "Lumber"

// Simulate changing a key
toolbox = toolbox - "Phillips Screw"
toolbox = toolbox + Pair("Cross Recess Screw", "Phillips Screwdriver")
```

Listing - Adding, changing, and removing entries by replacing an immutable map.

Map Operations

As with **List** and **Set**, **Map** objects have operations that can be performed on them, and some of them will look very familiar. Let's start with the **forEach()** function.

forEach()

The **forEach()** function is almost identical to the one found on **List** and **Set** objects. It takes a lambda that you can use to do something with each entry in the map. Since maps store entries, the parameter of the lambda will be of type **Map.Entry**.

Map.Entry is very similar to the **Pair** class that we looked at earlier in this chapter - it has two properties on it, but instead of being named **first** and **second**, they're named **key** and **value**.

Map.Entry<K,V>
+ key: K + value: V

Here's how you can use the **forEach()** function on a **Map**.

```
toolbox.forEach { entry ->
    println("Use a ${entry.value} on a ${entry.key}")
}
```

Listing - Using the **forEach()** function on a map.

When you run this code, here's what you'll see.

```
Use a Hammer on a Nail
Use a Wrench on a Hex Nut
Use a Wrench on a Hex Bolt
Use a Slotted Screwdriver on a Slotted Screw
Use a Phillips Screwdriver on a Phillips Screw
```

Because it's so similar to the **forEach()** that you saw in the last chapter, you should be able to identify the main parts. Here they are:

```
Map variable              Lambda parameter

    toolbox.forEach { entry ->
        println("${entry.key} and ${entry.value}")
    }
                              Code to run
                              for each entry
```

Filtering

Similar to lists and sets, you can **filter** a map. Keep in mind that, just as we saw with lists, this function doesn't modify an existing map - it creates a new map instance, so you'll probably want to assign the result to a variable. Let's filter down the toolbox to just screwdrivers.

```
val screwdrivers = toolbox.filter { entry ->
    entry.value.contains("Screwdriver")
}
```

Listing - Using the **filter()** function on a map.

The result is a new **Map** that contains only the screwdrivers.

Hardware	Tool to Use
Nail	Hammer
Hex Nut	Wrench
Hex Bolt	Wrench
Slotted Screw	Slotted Screwdriver
Phillips Screw	Phillips Screwdriver

Hardware	Tool to Use
Slotted Screw	Slotted Screwdriver
Phillips Screw	Phillips Screwdriver

In this case, we filtered on the **value**, but you can just as easily filter by the keys.

```
val screwdrivers = toolbox.filter { entry ->
    entry.key.contains("Screw")
}
```

Listing - Filtering a map based on the entry's key.

Mapping

Yes, you can map a **Map**! Simply use the **mapKeys()** and **mapValues()** functions to convert its keys or values. Just like with the collection operations we looked at in the last chapter, you can create an operation chain. Let's map both keys and values in one chain.

```
val newToolbox = toolbox
    .mapKeys { entry -> entry.key.replace("Hex", "Flange") }
    .mapValues { entry -> entry.value.replace("Wrench", "Ratchet") }
```

Listing 9.23 - Mapping both keys and values of a map.

Hardware	Tool to Use
Nail	Hammer
Hex Nut	Wrench
Hex Bolt	Wrench
Slotted Screw	Slotted Screwdriver
Phillips Screw	Phillips Screwdriver

Hardware	Tool to Use
Nail	Hammer
Flange Nut	Ratchet
Flange Bolt	Ratchet
Slotted Screw	Slotted Screwdriver
Phillips Screw	Phillips Screwdriver

Map objects have many other operations on them, which you can explore in Kotlin's API docs. However, there's one more operation that we'll examine before continuing - **withDefault()**.

Setting Default Values

As we saw earlier, you can use **getOrDefault()** to gracefully handle cases where the key does not exist. However, this can quickly get out of control if you use the same default every time…

val tool = toolbox.getOrDefault("Hanger Bolt", "Hand") val another = toolbox.getOrDefault("Dowel Screw", "Hand") val oneMore = toolbox.getOrDefault("Eye Bolt", "Hand")

Listing - Using **getOrDefault()** can get out of hand when used at every call site.

Instead, you can use an operation called **withDefault()**, which will return a new map based on the original. In this new map, whenever you call **getValue()** with a key that doesn't exist, it will invoke a lambda and return the result. Here's how it looks:

```
toolbox = toolbox.withDefault { key -> "Hand" }
```

Listing - Creating a new map that has a default value.

Now, instead of providing the default every time you try to get a value (as done in Listing 9.24 above), you can just call **getValue()** normally.

This is great, because if you ever wanted to change the default, you could make the change in one spot instead of many!

```
val tool = toolbox.getValue("Hanger Bolt")
val another = toolbox.getValue("Dowel Screw")
val oneMore = toolbox.getValue("Eye Bolt")
```

Listing - Calling **getValue()** instead of **getOrDefault()**, because the new map has a default value.

Keep in mind that this works with **getValue()** but not with **get()** or the indexed access operator, which will continue to return **null** if the key is not found!

Now you know how to create and change maps, get values out of them, and use collection operations on them. But things get really fun when you start using maps in conjunction with other collections! Let's look at that next.

Creating a Map from a List

We've created maps by hand using the **mapOf()** function. It's also possible to create maps that are based on existing list or set collections. With just a few important functions, you can slice and dice your data in many different ways! In order to do this, of course, we will need a list to start with.

Instead of using a simple **String** to represent the tools in Mr. Andrews' toolbox, let's create a class, so that it can hold the name of the tool, its weight in ounces, and the corresponding hardware that it works with.

```
class Tool(
    val name: String,
    val weightInOunces: Int,
    val correspondingHardware: String,
)
```
Listing - Creating a class to hold more information about a tool.

Now, let's create a list of **Tool** objects, so that they include the tools from Mr. Andrews' toolbox.

```
val tools = listOf(
    Tool("Hammer", 14, "Nail"),
    Tool("Wrench", 8, "Hex Nut"),
    Tool("Wrench", 8, "Hex Bolt"),
    Tool("Slotted Screwdriver", 5, "Slotted Screw"),
    Tool("Phillips Screwdriver", 5, "Phillips Screw"),
)
```
Listing - Creating a list of tools.

Now that we have a list, we're ready to create some maps from it!

Associating Properties from a List of Objects

You can use the **associate()** function to create a map from a list of objects. To start with, let's use **associate()** to create a map similar to the one in Listing:

```
val toolbox = tools.associate { tool ->
    tool.correspondingHardware to tool.name
}
```
Listing - Creating a map by associating two properties in the elements of a list.

Hopefully you're starting to feel more comfortable with collection operations at this point. For each element in the list, the **associate()** function will invoke the lambda given to it. The lambda returns a key-value **Pair**, which contains the key and value that you want in the resulting map.

Here's a breakdown of the associate() function.

And here's the effect that it has in Listing:

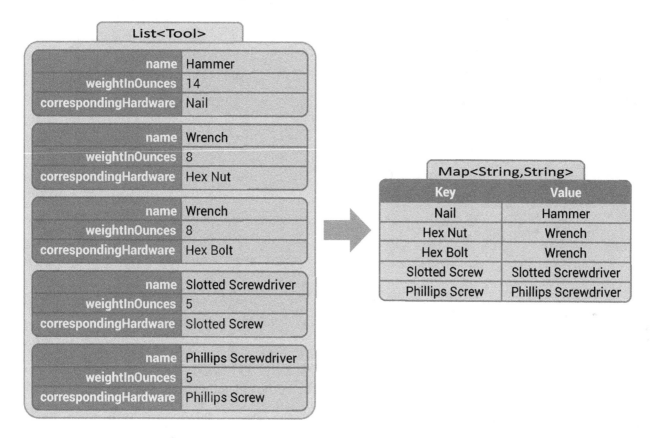

Often, the number of elements in the resulting map will be the same as the number of elements in the original list. In some cases, it could have fewer. Because the keys in a map are all unique, if you try to add a key that already exists, it will overwrite the existing value.

For example, let's reverse the key and value in the lambda in Listing, so that the tool name is the key, and the hardware is the value.

```
val toolbox = toolsassociate { tool ->
    tooname to tool.correspondingHardware
}
```

Listing- Associating the properties in the reverse order from Listing.

The original list has two **Tool** objects with a **name** of **Wrench**, so when **associate()** encounters the first one, it's added to the map, but when it encounters the second, it replaces the first value.

So, the resulting map only includes **Hex Bolt** rather than **Hex Nut**, because of the two, **Hex Bolt** came last.

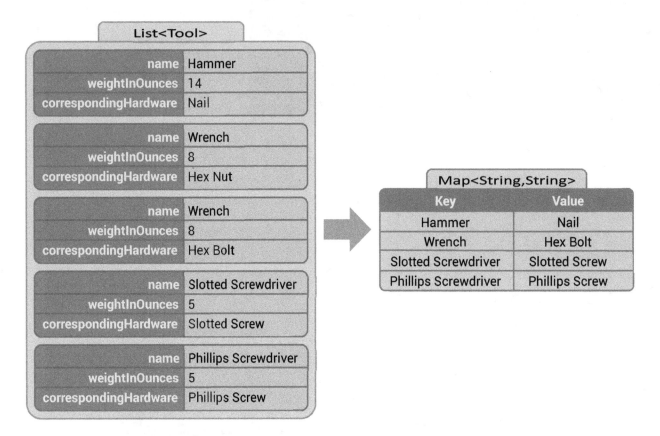

So, in this case, there are fewer entries in the map than elements in the original list. That is, there are only 4 entries in the map, compared with 5 elements in the list.

Other Association Functions

There are a few other variations of the **associate()** function that are good to know. These are especially helpful if you want the original list element to be either the key or the value in the resulting map.

For example, if you want to create a map where the keys are the tool names and the value is the **Tool** object, you can use **associateBy()**. The lambda of this function returns just the key. The original list element itself will be the value.

```
val toolsByName = toolsassociateBy { tool -> toolname }
```
Listing - Calling **associateBy()** to create a map where the original list elements are the map's values.

This has the effect that's depicted in the following illustration.

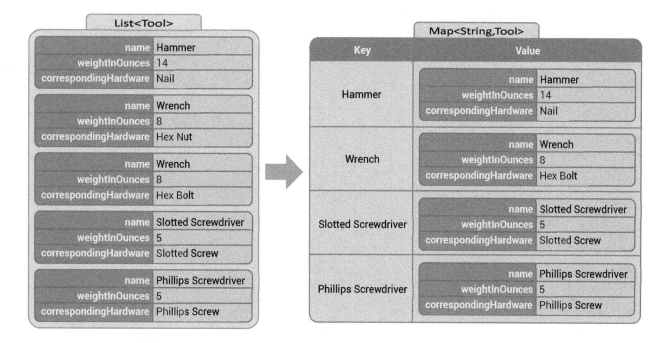

With this map, you can easily get a tool by its name!

```
val hammer = toolsByName["Hammer"]
```

Listing - Getting a **Tool** from a map by its name.

Inversely, if you want to create a map where the keys are the **Tool** object and the value is specified in the lambda, you can use the **associateWith()** function. The lambda of this function returns the value, and the original list element will be the key.

```
val toolWeightInPounds = tools.associateWith { tool ->
    tool.weightInOunces * 0.0625
}
```

Listing - Calling **associateWith()** to create a map where the original list elements are the map's keys.

Map<Tool,Double>		
Key		Value
name: Hammer weightInOunces: 14 correspondingHardware: Nail		0.875
name: Wrench weightInOunces: 8 correspondingHardware: Hex Nut		0.5
name: Wrench weightInOunces: 8 correspondingHardware: Hex Bolt		0.5
name: Slotted Screwdriver weightInOunces: 5 correspondingHardware: Slotted Screw		0.3125
name: Phillips Screwdriver weightInOunces: 5 correspondingHardware: Phillips Screw		0.3125

To get the weight of a hammer, you'd need to have a hammer object already.

```
val hammerWeightInPounds = toolWeightInPounds[hammer]
```

Listing - Using an object as a key.

Grouping List Elements into a Map of Lists

Sometimes when you've got a list, you want to split it up into multiple smaller lists, based on some characteristic. For example, we can take the **tools** list and split it up by weight.

To do this, we can use the **groupBy()** function. This function will run the provided lambda for each element in the list.

Elements for which the lambda returns the same result will be assembled into a list, and inserted into a map.

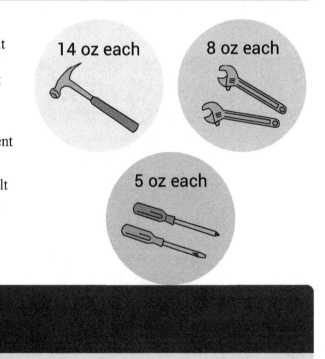

```
val toolsByWeight = toolsgroupBy { tool ->
    tool.weightInOunces
}
```

Listing - Using the **groupBy()** function to group a list of tools by their weight.

The result is a **Map** with one list of tools that weigh 14 ounces, another list of tools that weigh 8 ounces, and a third list of tools that weigh 5 ounces.

The map's key is the weight in ounces, and the map's value is a list of tools that have that weight. This illustration shows the effect that this operation has.

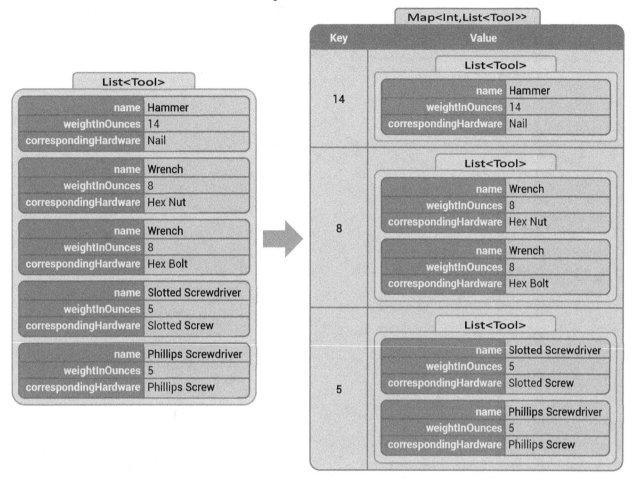

Here's a breakdown of the **groupBy()** function:

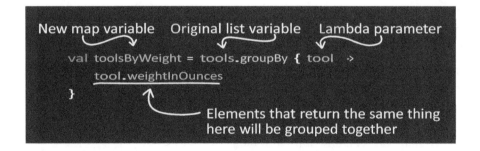

In case you want something other than the original list element in the resulting lists, you can also call this function with a second argument. For that one, give it a lambda that returns whatever you want in the resulting list.

For example, if you only want the names of the tools in those lists, you can do this:

```
val toolNamesByWeight = tool.groupBy(
    { tool -> tool.weightInOunces },
    { tool -> tool.name }
)
```

Listing - Calling the **groupBy()** function with two arguments instead of one.

Here's the effect that this operation has:

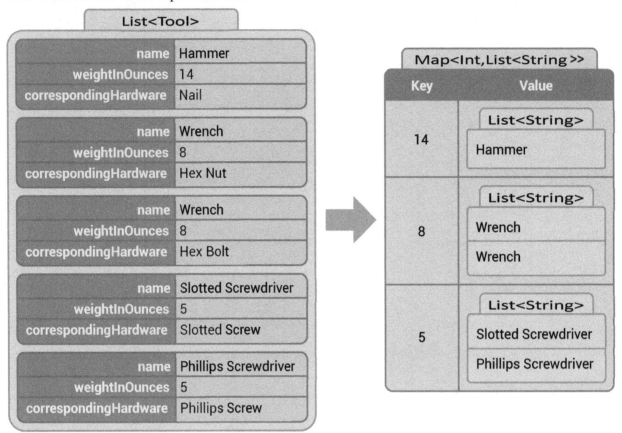

Conclusion: Unleashing the Power of Lambdas and Collections in Kotlin

Kotlin, as a modern programming language, exemplifies the balance between elegance and functionality. The synergy between lambdas and collections represents one of its most powerful and versatile features. Understanding and mastering this relationship is crucial for any developer aiming to write concise, expressive, and efficient Kotlin code. Let us reflect on what we've explored and how these features empower Kotlin developers in building robust and readable applications.

The Essence of Lambdas in Kotlin

Lambdas, or lambda expressions, are essentially anonymous functions. Their compact syntax and inline nature make them an indispensable tool for simplifying code while retaining its clarity. By offering features like implicit parameters (it), trailing lambda syntax, and the ability to access variables from the enclosing scope (closures), Kotlin ensures lambdas are not only syntactically elegant but also contextually powerful.

Key Advantages of Lambdas

1. **Conciseness**: Lambdas drastically reduce boilerplate code. For instance, replacing verbose anonymous classes with a single expression makes the code easier to read and maintain.

2. **Flexibility**: Lambdas, when combined with higher-order functions, allow developers to pass behavior as parameters, enabling dynamic and flexible coding paradigms.

3. **Expressiveness**: With Kotlin's rich functional programming capabilities, lambdas enable developers to write expressive and domain-specific constructs.

These attributes are especially impactful when working with collections, where the real power of lambdas shines.

Collections and Their Functional Transformations

Kotlin collections, encompassing both immutable (List, Set, Map) and mutable variants, offer a plethora of utility functions. These functions leverage lambdas to enable functional-style programming paradigms. The functional transformations on collections include operations like mapping, filtering, reducing, grouping, and partitioning, all of which rely on lambdas to define their behavior succinctly.

Functional Operations and Their Benefits

1. **Mapping**: The map function allows developers to transform a collection by applying a lambda to each element. This is especially useful for scenarios like converting data formats or deriving new values.

2. **Filtering**: With filter and related functions (filterNot, filterIndexed), developers can create subcollections that match specific criteria, enhancing code modularity.

3. **Reducing**: Aggregation operations like reduce, fold, and sumBy use lambdas to combine elements into a single value. This is ideal for scenarios like calculating totals or combining data.

4. **Grouping and Partitioning**: Functions like groupBy and partition allow collections to be categorized or split based on lambda conditions, enabling efficient data organization.

Performance Considerations

While Kotlin's collections and lambdas offer remarkable expressiveness, it's vital to consider performance. Inline functions, sequence transformations, and lazy evaluations help mitigate overhead, particularly for large datasets. Sequences, in particular, are optimized for chaining operations without creating intermediate collections, making them a go-to choice for performance-sensitive tasks.

Real-World Applications

1. Data Processing Pipelines

In applications dealing with large datasets, lambdas and collections form the backbone of data processing pipelines. From filtering and transforming raw data to aggregating results, the functional operations in Kotlin make the code concise, readable, and highly maintainable.

For example, consider processing customer data in an e-commerce application:

```
val customers = listOf(Customer("Alice", 25), Customer("Bob", 30))

val adultNames = customers
    .filter { it.age >= 18 }
    .map { it.name }
```

This succinct pipeline processes the data in a declarative manner, highlighting intent over implementation details.

2. Functional Composition

Kotlin encourages combining lambdas with reusable higher-order functions. This enables modular code design, where small building blocks can be composed to create complex behavior.

For instance, reusable predicates or transformations can simplify workflows:

val isAdult = { customer: Customer -> customer.age >= 18 }

val names = customers.filter(isAdult).map { it.name }

3. Streamlining Asynchronous Tasks

With the rise of coroutines in Kotlin, lambdas have found extensive use in asynchronous programming. Functions like launch and async use lambdas to define background tasks, allowing developers to handle concurrency without compromising readability.

```
GlobalScope.launch {
    val results = async { fetchData() }.await()
    println(results)
}
```

Best Practices for Working with Lambdas and Collections

1. **Prefer Readable Lambdas**: Overly complex lambdas can compromise readability. Keep them concise and use meaningful parameter names where possible. For instance, replace it with descriptive names in multi-line lambdas.

2. **Use Inline Functions**: Inline functions reduce the performance overhead of lambdas by eliminating the need to allocate objects for lambda instances. Kotlin's standard library extensively uses inline functions for collection operations.

3. **Avoid Nesting Excessively**: Deeply nested lambda operations can make code harder to follow. Break down complex transformations into smaller functions or steps to improve maintainability.

4. **Leverage Sequences for Large Data**: When working with large datasets, sequences prevent the creation of intermediate collections, reducing memory overhead and improving performance.

5. **Adopt Immutability**: Favor immutable collections to enhance code safety, avoiding unintended side effects and making concurrent programming easier.

Challenges and Limitations

While Kotlin's lambdas and collections are robust, they are not without challenges:

- **Learning Curve**: For developers transitioning from imperative paradigms, adopting functional programming concepts like lambdas and higher-order functions can be initially daunting.

- **Debugging and Tracing**: Debugging lambda-heavy code can sometimes be challenging due to the abstraction involved.

- **Performance Traps**: While sequences mitigate performance pitfalls, inappropriate use of collections in performance-critical sections can lead to inefficiencies.

By recognizing these challenges, developers can adopt strategies like profiling, refactoring, and adhering to best practices to mitigate them.

The Future of Kotlin's Lambdas and Collections

Kotlin's evolution, particularly with versions like Kotlin 2025, continues to enhance the power of lambdas and collections. Anticipated improvements include:

- **Enhanced Compiler Optimizations**: As Kotlin compilers evolve, we can expect better inlining, reduced bytecode size, and more efficient runtime behavior for lambdas and collections.

- **Interoperability with Multiplatform Projects**: Kotlin's multiplatform support ensures that lambdas and collections work seamlessly across JVM, JavaScript, and native environments, paving the way for reusable code in diverse ecosystems.

- **DSL Development**: Lambdas play a pivotal role in Domain-Specific Languages (DSLs), and Kotlin's ongoing DSL enhancements promise more intuitive and powerful constructs.

Conclusion: A Paradigm Shift in Kotlin Development

The integration of lambdas with collections epitomizes Kotlin's philosophy of combining pragmatism with power. By enabling developers to write code that is both concise and expressive, Kotlin empowers teams to focus on problem-solving rather than boilerplate.

Whether you are filtering data, transforming structures, or building complex pipelines, the interplay of lambdas and collections offers unparalleled flexibility. Mastering these features not only elevates your proficiency in Kotlin but also opens doors to adopting functional programming principles across other paradigms and languages.

As you continue your journey in Kotlin, remember that lambdas and collections are more than just tools—they represent a mindset of simplicity, composability, and elegance. By embracing these principles, you'll not only write better code but also enjoy the process of crafting solutions that are as beautiful as they are effective.

3. Object-Oriented Programming (OOP) Concepts

Introduction

Object-Oriented Programming (OOP) is a paradigm that organizes software design around data, or objects, rather than functions and logic. This approach provides a modular and reusable structure for complex software systems. Kotlin, a modern and statically-typed programming language, embraces OOP principles while also supporting functional programming paradigms. This duality makes Kotlin a highly versatile choice for developers. In this introduction, we will explore OOP concepts as implemented in Kotlin.

Core Concepts of OOP in Kotlin

Kotlin's object-oriented capabilities are centered around the following key principles:

1. **Classes and Objects**
2. **Encapsulation**
3. **Inheritance**
4. **Polymorphism**
5. **Abstraction**

Let's examine each concept in detail.

1. Classes and Objects

In OOP, a class is a blueprint for creating objects. It defines the structure and behaviour of the objects it produces. An object, on the other hand, is an instance of a class.

Defining Classes and Creating Objects in Kotlin

In Kotlin, a class is defined using the class keyword:

```
class Person(val name: String, var age: Int) {
    fun introduce() {
        println("Hi, I am $name and I am $age years old.")
    }
}
fun main() {
    val person = Person("Alice", 25)
    person.introduce()
}
```

Here:

- Person is a class with a primary constructor.
- name and age are properties.
- introduce() is a method that prints a message.

Constructors in Kotlin

Kotlin supports:

1. **Primary Constructor**: Declared in the class header.
2. **Secondary Constructor**: Defined inside the class body for additional initialization.

Example with secondary constructor:

```
class Employee(val id: Int) {
    var name: String = ""
    constructor(id: Int, name: String) : this(id) {
        this.name = name
    }
}
```

Objects in Kotlin

Kotlin allows creating objects directly from classes. It also supports:

- **Object Declarations**: Singleton objects.
- **Companion Objects**: Static-like members within a class.

Example of an object declaration:

```
object DatabaseConfig {
    const val URL = "jdbc:mysql://localhost:3306/mydb"
    fun connect() {
        println("Connecting to database at $URL")
    }
}

fun main() {
    DatabaseConfig.connect()
}
```

2. Encapsulation

Encapsulation restricts direct access to an object's internal state and requires interactions through defined methods. This principle is implemented using access modifiers in Kotlin.

Access Modifiers

Kotlin provides the following visibility modifiers:

1. **Public**: Default; accessible everywhere.
2. **Private**: Accessible only within the containing class.

3. **Protected**: Accessible in the class and its subclasses.
4. **Internal**: Accessible within the same module.

Example:

```
class BankAccount(private var balance: Double) {
    fun deposit(amount: Double) {
        if (amount > 0) balance += amount
    }

    fun withdraw(amount: Double) {
        if (amount > 0 && amount <= balance) balance -= amount
    }

    fun getBalance() = balance
}
```

Here, balance is private, ensuring that it can only be modified through the deposit and withdraw methods.

3. Inheritance

Inheritance allows a class (child) to inherit properties and methods from another class (parent). Kotlin supports single inheritance and provides the open keyword to make a class inheritable.

Defining a Base Class and a Derived Class

```
open class Animal(val name: String) {
    open fun sound() {
        println("$name makes a sound.")
    }
}

class Dog(name: String) : Animal(name) {
    override fun sound() {
        println("$name barks.")
    }
}

fun main() {
    val dog = Dog("Buddy")
    dog.sound()
```

}

In this example:

- Animal is the base class.
- Dog is the derived class.
- The sound method is overridden in the Dog class.

Abstract Classes

Abstract classes cannot be instantiated and may include abstract methods (methods without a body).

```kotlin
abstract class Shape {
    abstract fun area(): Double
}
class Circle(val radius: Double) : Shape() {
    override fun area() = Math.PI * radius * radius
}
```

4. Polymorphism

Polymorphism allows one interface to be used for different underlying forms (data types or classes). Kotlin supports both compile-time (method overloading) and runtime (method overriding) polymorphism.

Method Overloading

```kotlin
class Calculator {
    fun add(a: Int, b: Int) = a + b
    fun add(a: Double, b: Double) = a + b
}
```

Method Overriding

Method overriding occurs when a subclass provides a specific implementation of a method already defined in its superclass.

```kotlin
open class Printer {
    open fun print() {
        println("Printing a document.")
    }
}


class ColorPrinter : Printer() {
    override fun print() {
        println("Printing a color document.")
    }
```

```kotlin
}
```

Polymorphic Behavior

```kotlin
fun main() {
    val printer: Printer = ColorPrinter()
    printer.print() // Prints "Printing a color document."
}
```

5. Abstraction

Abstraction focuses on hiding the implementation details of a class while exposing only essential functionalities. Kotlin achieves abstraction through abstract classes and interfaces.

Interfaces

Interfaces in Kotlin can contain abstract methods as well as method implementations.

```kotlin
interface Vehicle {
    val maxSpeed: Int
    fun drive()

    fun stop() {
        println("The vehicle has stopped.")
    }
}


class Car : Vehicle {
    override val maxSpeed = 240

    override fun drive() {
        println("Driving at speed $maxSpeed km/h")
    }
}


fun main() {
    val car = Car()
    car.drive()
    car.stop()
}
```

Additional OOP Features in Kotlin

Data Classes

Kotlin's data classes simplify the creation of classes intended to store data by auto-generating common methods like toString, equals, and hashCode.

```kotlin
data class User(val id: Int, val name: String)

fun main() {
    val user = User(1, "Alice")
    println(user)
}
```

Sealed Classes

Sealed classes restrict class hierarchies to a defined set of subclasses, making them useful for representing restricted data types.

```kotlin
sealed class Result {
    data class Success(val data: String) : Result()
    data class Error(val message: String) : Result()
}

fun handleResult(result: Result) {
    when (result) {
        is Result.Success -> println("Success: ${result.data}")
        is Result.Error -> println("Error: ${result.message}")
    }
}
```

Delegation

Kotlin supports delegation, enabling a class to delegate its functionality to another class or object.

```kotlin
interface Logger {
    fun log(message: String)
}

class FileLogger : Logger {
    override fun log(message: String) {
        println("Logging to file: $message")
    }
}

class Service(logger: Logger) : Logger by logger
fun main() {
```

```
val logger = FileLogger()
val service = Service(logger)
service.log("Service started.")
}
```

We will discuss the Object-Oriented Programming's (OOP's) concept in Kotlin, where we cover class object, constructor, inheritance, and interfaces.

Objects and Classes in Kotlin

Kotlin supports both functional and OOP. In the previous section, we covered about functions, higher-order functions, and lambdas, representing Kotlin as an available language. This section will learn about the fundamental OOP's ideas that define Kotlin as an OOP language.

Language for Object-Oriented Programming

The fundamental ideas of an OOP language are class and object. These support OOP principles like inheritance, abstraction, and so forth.

Class

Class, like Java, is a blueprint for objects with comparable features. Before creating an object, we must first specify a class, and the class keyword is used to do so.

The class declaration comprises the class name, the class header, and the class body, all enclosed by curly braces.

Syntax:

class class-Name

```
{     // class header    // property
   // member-function
}
```

Class name: Each class has its name.

Class header: Class headers are made up of a class's arguments and constructors.

Class body: The class body is enclosed by curly brackets and comprises member functions and other properties.

The header and class body are optional; if there is nothing between the curly braces, the class body can be removed.

class emptyClass

If we wish to include a constructor, we must include the term constructor right after the class name.

Creating a constructor:

class class-Name constructor(parameters) {

```
   // property
   // member-function
}
```

Kotlin class example:

class employees

```
{
  // properties
  var name: String = ""     var age: Int = 0     var gender: Char = 'D'
  var salary: Double = 0.toDouble()
  //member functions    fun names(){
  }
  fun ages() {
  }
  fun salary(){
  }
}
```

Object

It is an OOP core unit that represents real-world items with state and behaviour. Objects are used to access a class's attributes and member functions. Multiple instances of the same class can create in Kotlin. An item is made up of:

State: It is represented through an object's characteristics. It also reflects an object's attributes.

Behaviour: It is expressed through an object's methods. It also represents an object's interaction with other objects.

Identity: It provides an object with a unique name and allows one thing to communicate with other objects.

Create an object: Using the class reference, we can create an object.

var obj = class-Name()

Accessing a class's properties: We may use an object to access a class's properties. First, use the class reference to build an object and then access the property.

obj.nameOfProperty

Accessing a class member function: We may use the object to access a class member function.

obj.funtionName(parameters)

Kotlin program for creating many objects and accessing the class's properties and member functions:

class employee

```
{// Constructor Declaration of Class
  var name: String = ""     var age: Int = 0     var gender: Char = 'F'     var salary: Double = 0.toDouble()
fun insertValues(n: String, a: Int, g: Char, s:
Double) {      name = n      age = a      gender = g      salary = s
    println("Name of the employee: $name")      println("Age of the employee: $age")
println("Gender: $gender")
```

```kotlin
        println("Salary of the employee: $salary")
    }
    fun insertName(n: String) {        this.name = n
    } }
fun main(args: Array<String>) {     // creating multiple objects     var obj = employee()
    // object 2 of class employee     var obj2 = employee()
    //accessing the member function
    obj.insertValues("Praveen", 5, 'F', 50000.00)


    // accessing the member function     obj2.insertName("Alie")
    // accessing the name property of class
println("The Name of the new employee: ${obj2. name}")
}
```

Nested Class and Inner Class in Kotlin

Nested Class

When a class is declared within another class, it is referred to as a nested class. Because nested classes are static by default, we may access their properties or variables using dot(.) notation without generating an instance of the class.

Syntax:

class outClass {

```
        ............
        // properties of the outer class or a member
function
        class nestClass {              ..........
            // properties of the inner class or
member function
        }
}
```

Note that nested classes cannot access the members of the outer class, but we may access nested class properties from the outer class without generating an object for the nested class.

Program of accessing nested class attributes in Kotlin:

```kotlin
// outer class declaration class outerClass {     var str = "Outer class"
    // nested class declaration     class nestedClass {        val firstName = "Pravi"        val lastName = "Ruhi"
    }
}
fun main(args: Array<String>) {
```

```
    // accessing member of Nested class     print(outerClass.nestedClass().firstName)
    print(" ")
    println(outerClass.nestedClass().lastName)
}
```

To access a nested class's member function in Kotlin, we must first build the nested class's object and then call the member function from it.

Program of accessing nested class member functions in Kotlin:

```
// outer class declaration class outerClass {     var str = "Outer class"
    // nested class declaration     class nestedClass {        var st1 = "Nested class"
        // nested class member function        fun nestfunc(str2: String): String {         var st2 = st1.plus(str2)
            return st2
        }
    }
}
fun main(args: Array<String>) {
    // the creating object of Nested class     val nested = outerClass.nestedClass()
    //the  invoking the nested member function by
passing string
    var result = nested.nestfunc(" The member function
call successful")
println(result)
}
```

In Comparison to Java

When it comes to features and use cases, Kotlin classes are quite close to Java classes but not identical. The Nested class in Kotlin is analogous to a static nested class in Java, whereas Inner class is comparable to a non-static nested class in the Java.

Kotlin	Java
Nested class	Static Nested class
Inner class	Non-Static class

Kotlin Inner Class

The term "inner class" refers to a class that can be declared within another class using the keyword inner. Using the inner class, we may access the outer class property from within the inner class.

class outerClass { ....

```
    // properties of the outer class or member
function
    inner class innerClass {

        ..........

        // properties of the inner class or member function
    }
}
```

In the following program, we attempt to access str from the inner class member function. However, it does not work and generates a compile-time error.

Inner-Class Kotlin Program

```
/ outer class declaration class outerClass {    var str = "Outer class"
    // innerClass declaration without using inner keyword
    class innerClass {       var st1 = "Inner class"       fun nestfunc(): String {
        // it can not access the outer class
property str           var st2 = str          return st2
    }
  } }
// main function
fun main(args: Array<String>) {
    // creating object for inner class
val inner= outerClass().innerClass()    // inner function call using object
println(inner.nestfunc())
}
```

First, put the inner keyword before the inner class. Then, make an instance of the outer class; otherwise, we won't be able to utilize inner classes.

```
// outer class declaration class outerClass {  var str = "Outer class"
    // innerClass declaration with using inner keyword
    inner class innerClass {       var st1 = "Inner class"       fun nestfunc(): String {
        // can access the outer class property str
        var st2 = str           return st2
    }
  } }
// main function
fun main(args: Array<String>) {
    // for inner class creating object
```

```
val inner= outerClass().innerClass()     // using object inner function call
println(inner.nestfunc()+" property accessed
```

successfully from the inner class ")
}

Setters and Getters in Kotlin

Properties are an essential component of every programming language. In Kotlin, we may declare properties in the same way we declare variables. Properties in Kotlin can be specified as changeable using the var keyword or immutable using the var keyword.

Syntax:

var <propertyName>[: <PropertyType>]

[= <property_initializer>]   [<getter>]   [<setter>]

The property initializer, getter, and setter are all optional in this case. If the property type can infer from the initializer, we may also omit it.

The syntax of a read-only or immutable property declaration varies from that of a mutable property declaration in two ways:

It begins with val rather than var.

It does not permit a setter.

fun main(args : Array) {   var x: Int = 0   val y: Int = 1

= 2 // It can be allocated an unlimited

number of times

= 0 // It will never be allocated again
}

In the above code, we attempt to assign a value to "y," but it generates a build time error since it cannot accept the modification.

Setters and Getters

The setter is used to set the value of a variable in Kotlin, while the getter is used to get the discount. Getters and Setters are produced automatically in the code. Let's define a "names" property in the "company" class. "names" has the data type String and will be initialized with a default value.

class company

{
var names: String = "Defaultvalue"
}

The preceding code is identical to the following code:

class company

{
    var names: String = "defaultvalue"   get() = field   // getter   set(value) { field = value }
// setter }

We create an object "c" of the class "company..". When we initialize the "name" property, we provide the setter's argument value, which sets the "field" to value. When we try to access the object's names property, we obtain a field because the code get() = field. Using the dot(.) syntax, we may acquire or set the properties of a class object.

val d = company()

d.names = "Hubtutor"   // access setter println(d.names)   // access getter

Default Setter and Getter Kotlin Program

class company

```
{

   var name: String = ""     get() = field     // getter     set(value) {     // setter

      field = value

   }

}
fun main(args: Array<String>) {     val d = Company()

   d.name = "Hubtutor"  // access setter     println(d.names)     // access getter }
```

Identifiers for Values and Fields

In the preceding program, we have discovered these two identifiers:

Value: Typically, we use the name of the setter parameter as the value, but we can use a different name if we want. The value parameter holds the value to which a property has been allocated. In the above program, we set the property name to d.name = "Hubtutor," and the value parameter holds the value "Hubtutor."

Backing Field (field): It enables saving the property value in memory. When we initialize property with value, the value is written to the property's backing field. The value is allocated to the field in the preceding program, and subsequently, the field is assigned to get ().

Private Modifier

If we want the get method available to the public, we may use the following code:

var names: String = ""   private set

Because of the private modifier near the set accessor, we can only set the name in a method within the class. A method within a class is used in a Kotlin application to set the value.

class company () {

```
var names: String = "abc"
private set

   fun myfunc(n: String) {

      names = n          // we set the name here

   }

}
fun main(args: Array<String>) {     var d = company()

   println("Name of the company is: ${d.names}")

   d.myfunc("Hubtutor")
```

```
    println("Name of the new company is: ${d.names}")
}
```

Explanation: We utilized the private modifier in conjunction with the set in this case. First, create an object of type company() and use $c.name to access the property name. Then, in the function specified within the class, we supply the name "Hubtutor" as a parameter. The name property is updated with the new name, and access is granted once more.

Setter and Getter with Custom Parameters

class registration(email: String, pwd: String, age:

Int, gender: Char) {

```
    var email_id: String = email
        // Custom Getter        get() {
            return field.toLowerCase()
        }
    var password: String = pwd
        // Custom Setter        set(values){
            field = if(values.length > 7) value else throw IllegalArgumentException("Password is small")
        }     var age: Int = age       // Custom Setter       set(values) {
            field = if(values > 18 ) value else throw
IllegalArgumentException("Age must be 18+")
        }
    var gender : Char = gender
        // Custom Setter        set (values){
            field = if(values == 'F') value else throw
IllegalArgumentException("User should be male")
        } }
fun main(args: Array<String>) {       val geek = registration("PRAViRUHi1998@GMAIL.
COM","Hub@123",25,'F')

    println("${hub.email_id}")     geek.email_id = "HUBTUTOR@CAREERS.ORG"
    println("${hub.email_id}")     println("${hub.password}")     println("${hub.age}")
println("${hub.gender}")

    // throw IllegalArgumentException("Passwords is
small")
    geek.password = "abc"
    // throw IllegalArgumentException("Age should be
18+")
```

```
geek.age= 5
// throw IllegalArgumentException("User should be
male")
geek.gender = 'M'        }
```

Class Properties and Custom Accessors in Kotlin

Encapsulation is the fundamental and most crucial concept of a class. It is a property that allows us to combine code and data into a single object. In Java, data is saved in fields, which are typically private. As a result, accessor methods – a getter and a setter – are supplied to allow the data to be accessed by the users of the specified class. Additional logic is implemented in the setter for delivering change notifications and verifying the passed value.

Property

In the case of Java, it is a mixture of accessories and fields. Properties are intended to be first-class language features in Kotlin. These features have taken the place of fields and accessor methods. A class property is declared in the same way as a variable, using the val and var keywords. A var-declared property is mutable and hence changeable.

Creating a class:

class Abcd(val names: String,   val ispassed: Boolean)

Readable Property: Generates a field and a trivial getter

Writable Property: A getter, a setter, and a field

Essentially, the property declaration declares the related accessors (both setter and getter for writable and getter for the readable property). The value is stored in a field.

Let's have a look at how the class is used:

class Abcd(val names: String,   val ispassed: Boolean
)
```
fun main(args: Array<String>) {

    val abcd = Abcd("Bobi",true)    println(abc.names)    println(abc.ispassed)

    /*
    In Java
    Abcd abcd = new Abcd("Bobi",true);    System.out.println(person.getName());
    System.out.println(person.isMarried());
    */
}
```

The constructor in Kotlin can be invoked without the need for a new keyword. Instead of using the getter, the property is directly addressed. The logic is same, but the code is significantly shorter. Setters of mutable properties operate identically.

Customer Accessors

Property accessor implementation on a custom basis:

class Rectanglee(val height: Int, val width: Int)

```
{

   val isSquare: Boolean        get() {

       return height == width

     } }


fun main(args: Array<String>) {


   val rectangle = Rectanglee(42, 44)
println(rectangle.isSquare)
}
```

The property is Square does not require a field to contain the value. It just has a custom getter with the given implementation. The value is calculated each time the property is accessed.

Kotlin Constructor

A constructor is a specific member function called when a class object is formed to initialize variables or attributes. A constructor is required for every class, and if we do not specify one, the compiler will build one for us.

There are two kinds of constructors in Kotlin:

Primary Constructor

Secondary Constructor

In Kotlin, a class can have one primary constructor and more subsidiary constructors. The primary constructor is responsible for initializing the class, whereas the secondary constructor is responsible for initializing the class and introducing some extra logic.

Primary Constructor

After the class name, the constructor keyword is used to initialize the primary constructor in the class header. The arguments in the main constructor are optional.

class Add constructor(val c: Int, val d: Int) {

// code }

The constructor keyword can be omitted if no annotations or access modifiers are supplied.

class Add(val c: Int, val d: Int) {

// code }

Program of primary constructor in Kotlin:

//main function

fun main(args: Array<String>)

{

```kotlin
    val add = Add(6, 8)
    println("The Sum of numbers 6 and 8 is: ${add.c}")
}
//primary constructor
class Add constructor(c: Int,d:Int)
{
    var a = c+d;
}
```

Explanation: When we build the class's object add, the numbers 6 and 8 are sent to the constructor. The constructor arguments a and b are initially set to 6 and 8, respectively.

The total of variables is stored in the local variable a. In the primary function, we use $add.a to access the constructor property.

Primary Constructor with Initializer Block

The primary constructor cannot include any code; however, the initialization code can insert in a separate initializer block preceded by the init keyword.

Kotlin primary constructor program with initializer block:

```kotlin
fun main(args: Array<String>) {
val emp = employees(18118, "Sanik")
}
class employees(emp_id : Int,  emp_name: String) {
    val id: Int    var names: String

    // initializer block
    init {      id = emp_id      names = emp_names

        println("Employees id is: $id")        println("Employees name: $names")
    }
}
```

Explanation: When the object emp is formed for the class employee, the values 18118 and "Sanik" are supplied to the constructor's arguments emp id and emp names. The class id and names declare two attributes.

When an object is created, the initializer block is called, which initializes the attributes and prints to the standard output.

The default value in the primary constructor: We may initialize the constructor parameters with some default values, similar to initializing functions' default values.

In the main constructor of a Kotlin program, the following default values are used:

```kotlin
fun main(args: Array<String>) {
val emp = employees(18118, "Sanik")
```

```kotlin
    // the default value for emp_name will be used
here
    val emp2 = employees(10011)
    //the default values for both parameters because
no arguments passed
    val emp3 = employees()
}
class employees(emp_id : Int = 110,  emp_name: String
= "abcd") {    val id: Int    var name: String

    // initializer block
    init {        id = emp_id        name = emp_name

        print("Employee id is: $id, ")        println("Employee name: $name")
        println()
    }
}
```

Explanation: In this case, we've set the constructor arguments to the default values emp id = 110 and emp name = "abcd."

We gave the values for both arguments when we formed the object emp, which outputs those values.

However, the initializer block utilizes the default values and prints to standard output because we did not give the emp name when we created the object emp2.

Secondary Constructor

As previously stated, Kotlin may have one or more secondary constructors. Secondary constructors allow for variable initialization and the addition of logic to the class. The keyword constructor precedes them.

Program of Kotlin implementation of a secondary constructor:

//main function

```kotlin
fun main(args: Array<String>)
{
    Add(8, 6)
}
//class with one secondary constructor
class Add
{
    constructor(c: Int, d:Int)
    {
```

```kotlin
        var a = c + d
        println("The sum of numbers 8 and 6 is: ${a}")

    }
}
```

The compiler determines which secondary constructor will be invoked based on the parameters received. The above program does not indicate which constructor should be invoked, and the compiler makes the decision.

In a class, there are two secondary constructors in Kotlin:

```kotlin
fun main(args: Array<String>) {
employee(18118, "Sanik")    employee(10011,"Praveen",60000.5)

}
class employee {


    constructor (emp_id : Int, emp_name: String ) {
        var id: Int = emp_id        var name: String = emp_name        print("Employee id is: $id, ")
println("Employee name: $name")

        println()

    }
    constructor (emp_id : Int, emp_name: String,
emp_salary : Double) {        var id: Int = emp_id        var name: String = emp_name        var salary :
Double = emp_salary        print("Employee id is: $id, ")        print("Employee name: $name, ")
println("Employee name: $salary")

    }
}
```

In a class, there are three secondary constructors in Kotlin program:

```kotlin
//main function
fun main(args: Array<String>)

{

  Add(51, 61)

  Add(51, 61, 71)

  Add(51, 61, 71, 81)

}
//class with three secondary constructors
class Add

{

  constructor(c: Int, d: Int)

  {
```

```kotlin
        var a = c + d
        println("Sum of 51, 61 = ${a}")

    }
    constructor(c: Int, d: Int, a: Int)
    {
        var b = c + d + a
        println("Sum of 51, 61, 71 = ${b}")

    }
    constructor(c: Int, d: Int, a: Int, b: Int)
    {
        var e = c + d + a + b
        println("Sum of 51, 61, 71, 81 = ${e}")

    }
}
```

Using one secondary constructor to refer to another: Using this() method, a secondary constructor of the same class can invoke another secondary constructor. In the following program, we called another constructor (a,b,71) since it requires three parameters to be invoked.

Calling one constructor from another in Kotlin:

//main function

```kotlin
fun main(args: Array<String>)
{
    Add(51,61)
} class Add {
    // calling another secondary using this     constructor(c: Int,d:Int) : this(c,d,71) {
        var sumOfTwo = c + d       println("The sum of two numbers 51 and 61 is: $sumOfTwo")    }
    // this executes first
    constructor(c: Int, d: Int,a: Int) {       var sumOfThree = c + d + a
        println("The sum of three numbers 51,61 and 71 is: $sumOfThree")
    }
}
```

Calling the secondary constructor of the parent class from the secondary constructor of the child class: using the super keyword, we may call the parent class's secondary constructor from the child class's secondary constructor. We demonstrated the calling procedure below.

fun main(args: Array<String>) {

Child(18118, "Sanik")

```
}
```

open class Parent {

constructor (emp_id: Int, emp_name: String, emp_

salary: Double) {   var id: Int = emp_id   var name: String = emp_name   var salary : Double = emp_salary   println("Employee id is: $id")   println("Employee name: $name")
println("Employee salary: $salary")

        println()

    }

}

class Child : Parent {   constructor (emp_id : Int, emp_name: String):super(emp_id,emp_name,5000.55){

        var id: Int = emp_id   var name: String = emp_name   println("Employee id is: $id")
println("Employee name: $name")

    }

}

Kotlin Visibility Modifiers

Visibility modifiers are used in Kotlin to limit the accessibility of classes, objects, interfaces, constructors, functions, properties, and their setters. There is no need to make getters visible because they have the same visibility as the property.

In Kotlin, there are four visibility modifiers:

Modifier	Description
Public	Visible everywhere
Private	Visible inside the same class only
Internal	Visible inside the same module
Protected	Visible inside the same class and its subclasses

If no modifier is supplied, it is public by default. Let's go through the modifiers above one by one.

Public Modifier

The default modifier in Kotlin is public. It is the most often used modifier in the language, and there are extra limits on who may view the part being modified. Unlike Java, there is no need to define anything as public in Kotlin – it is the default modifier if no other modifier is declared – public works the same in Kotlin as it does in Java. When the public modifier is applied to top-level items – classes, methods, or variables defined directly within a package – any other code can access them. If the public modifier is applied to a nested element – an inner class or function within a class – then any code that can access the container may also access this element.

```
// by default
public class C {
var int = 20

}
// specified with public modifier
```

```kotlin
public class D {      var int2 = 30    fun display() {

    println("Accessible everywhere")

    }
}
```

Classes C and D are available from anywhere in the code, and the variables int and int2 and the method display() are accessible from everything that can access classes C and D.

Private Modifier

Private modifiers in Kotlin restrict access to code defined inside the same scope. It prevents access to the modifier variable or function from being available outside of the scope. Unlike Java, Kotlin enables several top-level declarations in the same file – a private top-level element in the same file can be accessible by everything else in the same file.

// class C is accessible from the same source file

```kotlin
private class C {
private val int = 20     fun display()

    {

       // we can access int in the same class

       println(int)

       println("Accessing int successful")

    }

}
fun main(args: Array<String>){

    var c = C()    c.display()

    // can not access 'int': it is private in class C

    println(c.int)
}
```

In this case, class C can only access from within the same source file, and the int variable can only be accessed from within class C. When we attempted to access int from outside the class, we met with a compile-time error.

Internal Modifier

The internal modifier is a newly introduced modifier in Kotlin that Java does not support. Internal signifies that it will only be available in the same module; attempting to access the declaration from another module will result in an error. A module is a collection of files that have been built together.

internal class C {

}

public class D {   internal val int = 20   internal fun display() {

    }
}

Class C is only available from inside the same module in this case. Even though class D may be accessed everywhere, the variable int and method display() are only available inside the same module.

Protected Modifier

The protected modifier in Kotlin only enables access to the declaring class and its subclasses. At the top level, the protected modifier cannot be disclosed. We used the derived class's getvalue() function to retrieve the int variable in the following example.

// base class open class C {

// protected variable
protected val int = 20

}
// derived class class D: C() {

    fun getvalue(): Int {

      // accessed from the subclass

     return int

  } }
fun main(args: Array<String>) {

  var a = D()

  println("The value of integer is: "+a.getvalue())
}

Overriding of Protected Modifier

To override the protected variable or function in the derived class, we must mark it with an open keyword. In the following program, we override the int variable.

// base class open class C {

// protected variable   open protected val int = 20

} // derived class class D: C() {   override val int = 30   fun getvalue():Int {

    // accessed from the subclass

   return int

  } }
fun main(args: Array<String>) {

  var a = D()   println("The overridden value of integer is: "+a. getvalue())
}

Constructor Visibility

Constructors are always public by default, but modifiers may adjust their visibility.

class C (name : String) {

// other code }

We must express this explicitly by using the constructor keyword when modifying the visibility.

class C private constructor (name : String) {

// other code

}

Inheritance in Kotlin

One of the most significant aspects of OOP is inheritance. Inheritance allows for code reuse by allowing all of the features of an existing class (base-class) to be inherited by a new class (derived-class). Furthermore, the derived class can add its features.

Syntax:

open class base-Class (x:Int) {

.... }

class derived-Class(x:Int) : base-Class(x) {

.... }

By default, all classes in Kotlin are final. We must apply the open keyword in front of the base class to allow the derived class to inherit from it.

Kotlin inheriting properties and methods from the base class: We inherit all of its properties and functions when we inherit a class. We can utilize the variables and functions from the base class in the derived class and call functions from the derived class object.

```
//base class open class base-Class{
val name = "Hubtutor"

    fun C(){

        println("Base Class")

    }

}
//derived class

class derived-Class: base-Class() {

    fun D() {

        println(name)          //inherit name
property

        println("Derived class")

    }

}
fun main(args: Array<String>) {     val derived = derived-Class()

    derived.C()          // inheriting the  base class
function

    derived.D()          // calling derived class function
}
```

Explanation: There is a base class and a derived class in this case. When we instantiate the derived class, we generate an object, which is then utilized to call the base and derived class functions. The derived.C() function is used to invoke the C() function, which prints "Base Class." The derived.D() method is used to invoke the function D(), which prints the variable name inherited from the base class as well as the "Derived class."

Inheritance Use

Assume a corporation has three employees: a webDeveloper, an iOSDeveloper, and an AndroidDeveloper. They all have certain characteristics in common, such as a name and an age and some unique abilities.

First, we divide the individuals into three classes, and each class has certain common and specific skills.

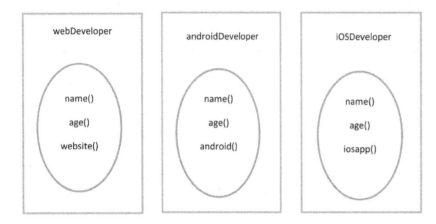

All three developers have the same name and age, but their programming skills are very different. We would be replicating the identical code for each character's name and age in each class.

If we wish to add a salary() function, we must duplicate the code in all three classes. This results in several duplicate copies of code in our program, which will almost certainly result in more complicated and chaotic code.

The work is made more accessible by employing inheritance. We may construct a new base class Employee that contains the features shared by the three original types. These three classes can then inherit common characteristics from the basic class and add their unique features. We can easily add the salary functionality to the Employee class without creating duplicates.

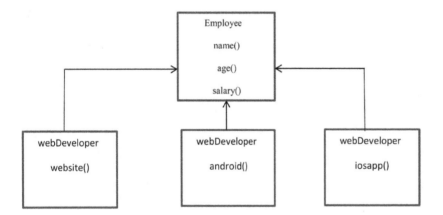

In this case, webDeveloper inherits all of the features from the base class and its feature website(). The same for the other two classes: iosDeveloper and androidDeveloper. It improves the readability and extensibility of our code.

Kotlin inheritance program:

//base-class open class Employees(names: String,age: Int,salary :

```kotlin
Int) {
init {
    println("Name is $names, $age years old and
earning $salary per month. ")
 } }
//derived-class class webDevelopers( names: String,age: Int,salary :
Int): Employees(names, age,salary) {
   fun website() {
      println("website-developer")
      println()
   } }
//derived-class
class androidDeveloper( names: String,age: Int,salary
: Int): Employees(names, age,salary) {
   fun android() {
      println("android app developer")
      println()
   } }
//derived class class iosDevelopers( names: String,age: Int,salary :
Int): Employees(names, age,salary) {
   fun iosapp() {
      println("iOS app developer")
      println()
   } }
//main method
fun main(args: Array<String>) {
   val wd = webDevelopers("Genna", 28, 12000)
   wd.website()
   val ad = androidDevelopers("Gautam", 29,14000)
   ad.android()
   val iosd = iosDevelopers("Praniti", 22,18000)
   iosd.iosapp()
}
```

Explanation: In this case, we have a base class Employees prefixed with the open keyword and includes the common characteristics of the derived classes. The Employee class has a primary constructor that takes three parameters: "name, age, and salary." There are three derived classes: webDevelopers, androidDevelopers, and iosDevelopers, all of which have primary constructors and three variables.

First, we create an object for the webDevelopers class and send the name, age, and salary to the derived class as arguments. It will set the values of the local variables and pass them to the base class. Then, using the object "wd," we execute the member function website(), which publishes the string to standard output.

Similarly, we make objects for the remaining two classes and call their member functions.

Primary Constructor for Kotlin Inheritance

If the derived class has the main constructor, we must initialize the base class constructor using the derived class's arguments. We have two parameters in the base class's primary constructor and three parameters in the derived class in the following program.

```
//base-class
open class Employees(names: String,age: Int) {
    init{
        println("The name of Employee is $name")      println("The Age of an Employee is $age")
    }
}
// derived-class class CEO( names: String, age: Int, salary: Double):
Employees(names,age) {
    init {
        println("The Salary per annum is $salary crore
rupees")
    }
}
fun main(args: Array<String>) {
    CEO("Suniti Pichai", 40, 420.00)
}
```

Explanation: In this case, we instantiate the derived class CEO and supply the parameters name, age, and salary. The derived class's local variables are initialized with the appropriate values, and the variable name and age are sent as arguments to the Employee class.

The employees class outputs the variable names and values to standard output before returning control to the derived class. The derived class then terminates after executing the println() command.

Secondary Constructor for Kotlin Inheritance

If the derived class lacks the main constructor, we must use the super keyword to call the base class's secondary constructor from the derived class's secondary constructor. We must additionally initialize the base class's secondary constructor using the derived class's arguments.

```
//base class open class Employees {
    constructor(names: String,age: Int){      println("The Name of Employee is $name")
println("The Age of Employee is $age")
    }
// derived class class CEO : Employees{    constructor( names: String,age: Int, salary:
```

```
Double): super(names,age) {
    println("The Salary per annum is $salary
million dollars")
  }
}
fun main(args: Array<String>) {
  CEO("Sunidhi Nadela", 49, 220.00)
}
```

Explanation: We instantiate the class CEO and give the argument values to the secondary constructor in this case. It will initialize the local variables and use super to pass them to the base class Employees (name, age).

Overriding Member Functions and Properties

If member function with the same name exists in both the base and derived classes, we may use the override keyword to override the base member function in the derived class, but we must also mark the member function of the base class with the open keyword.

Program of overriding the member function in Kotlin:

// base class open class Animals {

```
open fun run() {
    println("The Animals can run")
  } }
// derived class class Tiger: Animals() {
  override fun run() {     // it overrides the run
method of base class
    println("The Tiger can run very fast")
  }
}
fun main(args: Array<String>) {
  val t = Tiger()
  t.run()
```

Similarly, we may override the base class's property in the derived class.

Program of overriding the member property in Kotlin:

// base class open class Animals {
```
open var name: String = "Dog"     open var speed = "50 km/hr"
  }
// derived class class Tiger: Animals() {     override var name = "Tiger"     override var speed = "120 km/hr"
}
```

```kotlin
fun main(args: Array<String>) {
    val d = Tiger()
    println(d.name+" can run at speed "+d.speed)
}
```

Calling the Superclass Implementation

We can call the base class member methods or attributes from the derived class using the super keyword. We call the base class's property color and method displayCompany() in the super class using the super keyword.

```kotlin
// base class open class Phones() {
var color = "White Gold"    fun displayCompany(name:String) {       println("The Company is: $name")
    } }
// derived class class iphone: Phones() {    fun displayColor(){

    // calling the base class property color        println("Color is: "+super.color)

    // calling the base class member function
    super.displayCompany("Apple")
}
fun main(args: Array<String>) {
    val p = iphone()    p.displayColor()
}
```

Interfaces In Kotlin

Interfaces are Kotlin provided custom types that cannot be instantiated directly. Instead, these describe a type of behaviour that the implementing types must follow. The interface allows us to create a collection of attributes and methods that concrete types must follow and implement.

Interfaces Creating

The interface declaration in Kotlin starts with the interface keyword, then the name of the interface, and finally the curly brackets that contain the interface's members. The distinction is that the members will not have their definition. The conforming types will offer these definitions.

Example:

interface Vehicles()

{   fun start()   fun stop() }

Implementing interfaces: A class or an object can implement an interface. When we implement an interface, the conforming type must define all of its members. The name of the custom-type is followed by colon and the name of the interface to be implemented to implement an interface.

class Car: Vehicles

An example of an interface in Kotlin:

```
interface Vehicles {
fun start()     fun stop()

}


class Car : Vehicles {     override fun start()     {

    println("The Car is started")

  }


  override fun stop()

  {

    println("The Car is stopped")

  } }

 fun main()

{

   val obj = Car()     obj.start()     obj.stop()

}
```

Explanation: The interface vehicle specifies two methods in this application, start() and stop(), which must be overridden. Car implements the interface using class-literal syntax and overrides the two methods using the override keyword. Finally, the main function creates a Car object and calls the two functions.

Default Methods and Default Values

An interface's methods can have default values for its arguments. If a parameter's value is not provided at the function call time, the default value is utilized. Additionally, the methods may have default implementations. When the method is not overridden, they are used.

Example of a default value and default method:

interface FirstInterface {

```
fun add(c: Int, d: Int = 6)

  fun print()

  {

    println("This is a default method defined in

the interface")

  }

}

class InterfaceDemo : FirstInterface {     override fun add(c: Int, d: Int)

  {

    val a = c + d     println("Sum is $a")

  }
```

```
    override fun print()
    {
        super.print()
        println("It has been overridden")
    } }
  fun main()
{
    val obj = InterfaceDemo()    println(obj.add(6))    obj.print()
}
```

Explanation: The FirstInterface in the above program provides two methods: add() and print(). The add() function accepts two arguments, one of which has a default value of 6. A default implementation is also given for the print() function. So, when the class InterfaceDemo implements the interface, it uses the super keyword to override both methods and call the default implementation of print(). In addition, when using the add method in the primary function, only one parameter is needed because the second is set to a default value.

Interface Properties

Interfaces, like methods, can include attributes. However, because the interface doesn't have a state, they cannot be created, and hence there are no underlying fields to keep their values. As a result, the interface's fields are either left abstract or given an implementation.

Example of interface properties:

interface InterfaceProperties {

```
    val c : Int    val d : String        get() = "Helloo"
}

class PropertiesDemo : InterfaceProperties {
    override val c : Int = 6000
    override val d : String = "Property Overridden"
}
  fun main()
{
    val x = PropertiesDemo()
    println(x.c)    println(x.d)
}
```

Explanation: In the above program, InterfaceProperties specifies two properties: a, an integer, and b, which is of type String and has a getter. The class PropertiesDemo implements InterfaceProperties and adds value to the two properties. The method main generates a class object and uses dot-syntax to access its attributes.

Interface Inheritance

In Kotlin, interfaces can inherit from other interfaces. When one interface extends another, it can add its properties and methods, and the implementing type must define all of the properties and methods in both interfaces. An interface can inherit from many interfaces.

An example of interface inheritance:

```
interface Dimensions {
val len : Double    val br : Double

}


interface CalculateParameters : Dimensions {

   fun area()    fun perimeter()

}


class XYZ : CalculateParameters {    override val len : Double       get() = 20.0   override val br : Double
get()= 17.0


   override fun area()

   {

      println("Area is ${len * br}")

   }


   override fun perimeter()

   {

      println("Perimeter is ${2*(len+br)}")

   } }
 fun main()
{

   val obj = XYZ()    obj.area()    obj.perimeter()
}
```

Explanation: The interface Dimensions in the program define two properties: len (length) and br (breadth). The CalculatedParameters interface inherits Dimensions and adds the methods area() and perimeter(). CalculatedParameters are implemented by the class XYZ, which overrides both the properties and methods, then executed in the main function.

Implementation of Multiple Interfaces

Because Kotlin classes follow the idea of single inheritance, each class can inherit just one class, interfaces support multiple inheritances known as multiple conformances in Kotlin. A class implements more than one interface as provided as it defines all of the interface's members.

Example of multiple interface implementation:

interface InterfaceProperties {

```kotlin
    val c : Int    val d : String      get() = "Helloo"
}

interface InterfaceMethods {    fun description()
}

class MultipleInterface : InterfaceProperties,
InterfaceMethods {    override val c : Int      get() = 60

    override fun description()
    {
        println("The Multiple Interfaces implemented")
    }
} fun main()
{
    val obj = MultipleInterface()
    obj.description()
}
```

Explanation: Two interfaces, InterfaceProperties and InterfaceMethods, are specified in the program. The class MultipleInterface implements these interfaces, and the methods are then executed in the main function.

Data Classes in Kotlin

We frequently build classes to store data in them. Few standard functions are often derivable from the data in such classes. This class is known as a data class in Kotlin and is identified as such.

An example of data:

data class Students(val name: String, val roll_no: Int)

The compiler generates the following functions automatically:

toString()

copy()

hashCode()

equals()

Data Class Creation Rules

To maintain consistency, data classes must meet the following requirements:

At least one argument is required for the primary constructor.

All primary constructor arguments must denote with val or var.

Data classes are not allowed to be abstract, open, sealed, or inner.

Data classes may implement only interfaces.

toString()

This function returns a string containing all of the data class's arguments.

First Example:

```
fun main(args: Array<String>)
{
    //declarion of a data class     data class man(val roll: Int,val name:
String,val height:Int)

    //declarion of a variable of the above data
class
    //and initializing values to all parameters

    val man1=man(1,"man",40)

    //print all the details of the data class
    println(man1.toString());
}
```

For the automatically created functions, the compiler only uses the attributes defined inside the primary constructor.

It does not include the properties declared in the body of class.

Second Example:

```
fun main(args: Array<String>)
{
    //declarion of a data class     data class man(val name: String)     {
        //the property declared in class body
        var height: Int = 0;
    }
    //declarion of a variable of the above data
class and
    //initializing values to all parameters

    val man1=man("manisha")
    //class body properties must be assigned
uniquely
    man1.height = 80
```

```
//this method print the details of class that
//are declared in primary constructor
println(man1.toString());


//printing the height of man1    println(man1.height);
}
```

copy()

Sometimes we need to replicate an object and update some of its attributes while keeping the others intact.
The copy() method is utilized in this scenario.

Copy() properties:

It duplicates all of the parameters or members defined in the primary constructor.

If declared, two objects might have the same main parameter values but distinct class body values.

copy() Declaration:

fun copy(name: String = this.a, age: Int = this.b) = user(a, b) where user is a data class: user(String, Int).

Example:

fun main(args: Array<String>)

```
{
   //declaring a data class
   data class man(val name: String, val age: Int)
   {
      //property declared in class body
      var height: Int = 0;
   }

   val man1 = man("manisha",19)

   //copying details of man1 with change in name
of man
   val man2 = man1.copy(name="rahi")

   //copying all details of man1 to man3
   val man3 = man1.copy();

   //declaring heights of individual men
   man1.height=110    man2.height=92    man3.height=130
```

```
    //man1 & man3 have different class body
values,
    //but same parameter values


    //printing info all 3 men    println("${man1} has ${man1.height} cm
height")
    println("${man2} has ${man2.height} cm
height")
    println("${man3} has ${man3.height} cm
height")
}
```

hashCode() and equals()

The hashCode() method returns the object's hash code value.

The equals() function returns true if two objects have identical contents and operate similarly to "==", but differently for Float and Double values.

hashCode() Declaration: open fun hashCode(): Int hashCode() properties:

Two hash codes specified twice on the same object will be equivalent.

If two objects are equal according to the equals() function, the hash codes given will be the same.

```
fun main(args: Array<String>)
{
    //declaring a data class
    data class man(val name: String, val age: Int)

    val man1 = man("manish",19)    val man2 = man1.copy(name="rahi")    val man3 = man1.copy();

    val hash1=man1.hashCode();    val hash2=man2.hashCode();    val hash3=man3.hashCode();

    println(hash1)    println(hash2)    println(hash3)

    //checking equality of these hash codes    println("hash1 == hash 2 ${hash1.equals(hash2)}")
    println("hash2 == hash 3 ${hash2.equals(hash3)}")    println("hash1 == hash 3 ${hash1.equals(hash3)}")
}
```

Explanation: Because man1 and man2 have the same object contents, they are equal and have the same hash code values.

Kotlin Sealed Classes

Kotlin introduces a new type of class that is not seen in Java. These are referred to as sealed classes. As the name implies, sealed classes conform to constrained or bounded class hierarchies. Within a sealed class, a collection of subclasses is defined. It is used when it is known that a type will conform to one of the subclass types in advance. Sealed classes guarantee type safety by limiting the types that can match at compile time rather than runtime.

Declaration of sealed class: sealed class Demo

Simply use the sealed keyword before the class modifier to define a sealed class. Another distinguishing aspect of sealed classes is that their constructors are, by default, private.

Because a sealed class is implicitly abstract, it cannot be instantiated. sealed class Demoo

fun main(args: Array)

```
{
    var d = Demoo()    //compiler error  }
```

Kotlin sealed class program:

```
sealed class Demo {    class C : Demo() {        fun display()
    {
        println("Subclass A of sealed class Demo")
    }
}
    class D : Demo() {        fun display()
    {
        println("Subclass B of sealed class
Demo")
    }
}
} fun main() {
    val obj = Demo.D()    obj.display()


    val obj1 = Demo.C()    obj1.display()
}
```

It should be noted that all subclasses of the sealed class must specify in the same Kotlin file. However, they do not have to be specified within the sealed class; they can be defined where the sealed class is accessible.

Example:

//sealed class with single subclass defined inside

sealed class ABCD { class X: ABCD(){...}

```
}
```

// Another subclass of the sealed class defined

class Y: ABCD() { class Z: ABCD() // This will cause an error.

Sealed class is not visible here

}

Sealed Class with When

Because the kinds to which a sealed class reference can conform are limited, it is most typically used with a when clause. This eliminates the need for the otherwise clause entirely.

Here's an example of a sealed class with a when clause:

// A sealed class with a string property

sealed class Fruits   (val x: String) {

```
   // Two subclasses of sealed class defined within
   class Apple : Fruits("Apple")     class Mango : Fruits("Mango")
}


// A subclass defined outside the sealed class class Pomegranate: Fruits("Pomegranate")


// A function to take in an object of type Fruit
// And to display an appropriate message depending on
the type of Fruit fun display(fruit: Fruits){
   when(fruit)
   {
     is Fruits.Apple -> println("${fruit.x} is good
for iron")
     is Fruits.Mango -> println("${fruit.x} is
yummy")
     is Pomegranate -> println("${fruit.x} is good
for vitamin d")
   }
} fun main()
{
   // Objects of different subclasses created
   val obj = Fruits.Apple()     val obj1 = Fruits.Mango()     val obj2 = Pomegranate()


   // Function called with different objects
   display(obj)     display(obj1)     display(obj2)
}
```

Kotlin Abstract Class

The abstract keyword is used in front of class to declare an abstract class in Kotlin. Because an abstract class cannot instantiate, we cannot create objects.

Declaration of an abstract class:

abstract class class-Name {

   .... }

Remember the following:

We are unable to generate an object for the abstract class.

All variables (properties) and member functions of an abstract class are non-abstract by default. As a result, if we wish to override these members in the child class, we must use the open keyword.

When we declare a member function as abstract, we don't need to annotate it with the open keyword because they are open by default.

A derived class must implement an abstract member function since it doesn't have a body.

As demonstrated below, an abstract class can have both abstract and nonabstract members:

```kotlin
abstract class className(val c: String) {
// Non-Abstract Property
    abstract var d: Int     // Abstract Property


    abstract fun method1()   // Abstract Methods


    fun method2() {        // Non-Abstract Method
        println("Non abstract function")
    }
}
```

Program using both abstract and non-abstract members in an abstract class in Kotlin:

```kotlin
//abstract class
abstract class Employee(val name: String,val experience: Int) {   // Non-Abstract
// Property
    // Abstract Property (Must be overridden by
Subclasses)
    abstract var salary: Double


    // Abstract Methods (Must be implemented by
Subclasses)
    abstract fun dateOfBirth(date:String)


    // Non-Abstract Method     fun employeeDetails() {
        println("Name of the employee: $name")        println("Experience in years: $experience")
println("Annual Salary: $salary")
    } }
```

```kotlin
// derived class class Engineer(name: String,experience: Int) :
Employee(name,experience) {    override var salary = 510000.00    override fun dateOfBirth(date:String){
println("Date of Birth is: $date")
    }
}
fun main(args: Array<String>) {    val eng = Engineer("Praniti",3)    eng.employeeDetails()
    eng.dateOfBirth("03 December 1996")
}
```

Explanation: The Engineer class in the preceding software is derived from the Employee class. For the Engineer class, object eng is created. While creating it, we gave two arguments to the primary constructor. This initializes the Employee class's non-abstract properties name and experience.

The eng object is then used to invoke the employeeDetails() function. It will print the employee's name, experience, and the override wage.

Finally, we use the eng object to call dateOfBirth() and provide the argument date to the primary constructor. It overrides the abstract fun of the Employee class and prints the value of to the standard output.

Using an abstract open member to replace a non-abstract open member: In Kotlin, we may use the override keyword followed by an abstract in the abstract class to override the non-abstract open member function of the open class. We shall accomplish that in the following program.

Program of overriding a non-abstract open function by an abstract class in Kotlin:

```kotlin
open class Livingthing {    open fun breathe() {
    println("All living thing breathe")
    }
}
abstract class Animal : Livingthing() {    override abstract fun breathe()
}
class Dog: Animal(){    override fun breathe() {        println("Dog also breathe")
    }
}
fun main(args: Array<String>){    val lt = Livingthing()    lt.breathe()    val d = Dog()
    d.breathe()
}
```

Multiple Derived Classes

All derived classes can override an abstract member of an abstract class. We override the cal function in three derived classes of calculators in the program.

Program of overriding the abstract method in more than one derived class in Kotlin:

```kotlin
// abstract class abstract class Calculators {
    abstract fun cal(a: Int, b: Int) : Int
}
```

```kotlin
// addition of two numbers class Add : Calculators() {
    override fun cal(a: Int, b: Int): Int {
        return a + b
    } }
// subtraction of two numbers class Sub : Calculators() {
    override fun cal(a: Int, b: Int): Int {
        return a - b
    } }
// multiplication of two numbers class Mul : Calculators() {
    override fun cal(a: Int, b: Int): Int {
        return a * b
    }
}
fun main(args: Array<String>) {    var add: Calculators = Add()    var a1 = add.cal(5, 6)
println("Addition of two numbers $a1")
    var sub: Calculator = Sub()    var a2 = sub.cal(11,6)
    println("Subtraction of two numbers $a2")
    var mul: Calculators = Mul()    var a3 = mul.cal(22,6)
    println("Multiplication of two numbers $a3")
}
```

Enum Classes In Kotlin

It is occasionally necessary for a type to contain just particular values in programming. The idea of enumeration was invented to do this. A named list of constants is an enumeration.

An enum has its specialized type in Kotlin, as it does in many other programming languages, signifying that something has several possible values. Kotlin enums are classes, as opposed to Java enums.

Some key facts to remember regarding enum classes in Kotlin:

Enum constants are more than just collections of constants; they contain attributes, methods, and so forth.

A comma denotes each enum constant function as a single class and instance.

Enums enhance code readability by assigning predefined names to constants.

Constructors cannot use to create an instance of the enum class.

Enums are defined by using the "enum" keyword in front of a class, as seen below:

enum class DAYS{

MONDAY,

TUESDAY,

WEDNESDAY,

THURSDAY,

FRIDAY,

SATURDAY,

SUNDAY

}

Enums Initializing

Enums in Kotlin, like Java enums, can have a constructor. Because enum constants are Enum class objects, they may be initialized by supplying specific values to the primary constructor.

Here's an example of how to assign colors to cards:

enum class Cards(val colors: String) {

```
    Diamond("yellow"),

    Heart("white"),

}
```

We easily access the color of a card by using:

val colors = Cards.Diamond.colors

Enums Properties and Methods

Kotlin enum classes, like those in Java and other programming languages, include various built-in properties and functions that the programmer may utilize. Here are some of the most important approaches and properties.

Properties:

ordinal: This property records the constant's ordinal value, typically a zero-based index.

name: The name of the constant is stored in this attribute.

Methods:

values: This function returns a list of all the enum class's constants.

valueOf(): This function returns the enum constant specified in enum that matches the input string. If the constant is missing from the enum, an IllegalArgumentException is produced.

To show the enum class in Kotlin, consider the following example:

enum class DAY {

```
    MONDAY,

    TUESDAY,

    WEDNESDAY,

    THURSDAY,

    FRIDAY,

    SATURDAY,

    SUNDAY

} fun main()

{
```

```kotlin
    // A simple demonstration of properties and
methods
    for (day in DAY.values()) {
        println("${day.ordinal} = ${day.name}")
    }
    println("${DAY.valueOf(" FRIDAY ")}")
}
```

Properties and Functions of the Enum Class

The enum class in Kotlin provides a new type. This class type has its own set of attributes and methods. The properties can give a default value; however, each constant must declare its value for the property if no default value is provided. Functions are often defined within companion objects so that they do not rely on individual class instances. They can, however, be defined without the use of companion objects.

In Kotlin, an example is used to show properties and functions:

```kotlin
// Property with default value provided enum class DAY(val isWeekend: Boolean = false){
    SUNDAY(true),
    MONDAY,
    TUESDAY,
    WEDNESDAY,
    THURSDAY,
    FRIDAY,
    // Default value overridden
    SATURDAY(true);

    companion object{
        fun today(obj: DAY): Boolean {
            return obj.name.compareTo("SATURDAY") == 0
|| obj.name.compareTo("SUNDAY") == 0
        }
    }}

fun main(){
    // A simple demonstration of properties and
methods
    for(day in DAY.values()) {
        println("${day.ordinal} = ${day.name} and is
weekend ${day.isWeekend}")
    }
```

```kotlin
    val today = DAY.MONDAY;
    println("Is today a weekend ${DAY.today(today)}")
}
```

Enums as Anonymous Classes

Enum constants behave similarly to anonymous classes in that they implement their functions and override the class's abstract functions. The most crucial thing is that each enum constant is overridden.

```kotlin
// enum class defining
enum class Season(var weather: String) {
    Summer("hot"){
        // if not override the function foo() compile
time error
        override fun foo() {                println("The Hot days of a year")
        }    },
    Winter("cold"){      override fun foo() {
        println("The Cold days of a year")
        }    },
    Rainy("moderate"){      override fun foo() {
        println("The Rainy days of a year")
        }
    };
    abstract fun foo()
}
// main function
fun main(args: Array<String>) {
    // calling foo() function override be Summer constant
    Season.Summer.foo()
}
```

Usage of When Expression with Enum Class

When enum classes in Kotlin are paired with the when expression, they have a significant benefit. The advantage is that because enum classes limit the values that a type may take when combined with the when expression and all of the constant definitions are supplied, the necessity for the otherwise clause is avoided. A compiler warning will be generated as a result.

```kotlin
enum class DAY{
    MONDAY,
    TUESDAY,
    WEDNESDAY,
    THURSDAY,
```

```
    FRIDAY,
    SATURDAY
    SUNDAY;
}
    fun main(){    when(DAY.SUNDAY){
        DAY.SUNDAY -> println("Today is Sunday")
        DAY.MONDAY -> println("Today is Monday")
        DAY.TUESDAY -> println("Today is Tuesday")
        DAY.WEDNESDAY -> println("Today is Wednesday")
        DAY.THURSDAY -> println("Today is Thursday")
        DAY.FRIDAY -> println("Today is Friday")
        DAY.SATURDAY -> println("Today is Saturday")
        // Adding an else clause will generate a warning
    }
}
```

Kotlin Extension Function

Kotlin allows the programmer to extend the functionality of existing classes without inheriting them. This is accomplished through the use of a feature called extension. An extension function is a function that is added to an existing class.

To add an extension function to a class, create a new function that is attached to the classname, as demonstrated in the following example:

// A sample class to demonstrate extension functions

class Circle (val radius: Double){

```
    // member function of class    fun area(): Double{
        return Math.PI * radius * radius;
    }
} fun main(){
    // Extension function created for a class Circle
    fun Circle.perimeter(): Double{        return 2*Math.PI*radius;
    }
    // create object for class Circle    val newCircle = Circle(3.6);    // invoke member function
println("The Area of the circle is ${newCircle. area()}")
    //invoke extension function
    println("The Perimeter of the circle is
${newCircle.perimeter()}")
}
```

Explanation: In this case, a new function is attached to the class using dot notation, with the function class Circle.perimeter() and a return type of Double. An object is created to instantiate the class Circle in the primary function, and the function is invoked using the println() statement. When the member function is called, it returns the area of the circle, whereas the extension function delivers the perimeter of the circle.

Extended Library Class Using an Extension Function

Not only may user-defined classes be expanded in Kotlin, but library classes can as well. The extension function may be added to library classes and used in the same manner that it can be introduced to user-defined classes.

The example below shows an extension function created for a userdefined class:

fun main(){

    // Extension function defined for Int type

    fun Int.abs() : Int{

       return if(this < 0) -this else this

    }

println((-6).abs())   println(6.abs())

}

Explanation: We used an extension function to expand the library function in this case. We used an integer value to do the modulus operation. We provided the integer values −6 and 6 and received positive results for both. If the parameter value is less than 0, it returns -(value), and if it is more than 0, it returns the same value.

Extensions Are Resolved Statically

The extension functions are resolved statically, which means that whatever extension function is executed relies entirely on the type of the expression on which it is called, rather than the type resolved on the final execution of the expression at runtime.

The following example will demonstrate the above point:

// Open class created to be inherited open class C(val a:Int, val b:Int){

}

// Class D inherits C class D():A(6, 6){} fun main(){

    // Extension function operate defined for A

    fun C.operate():Int{   return c+d

    }

    // Extension function operate defined for B

    fun D.operate():Int{   return c*d;

    }

    // Function to display static dispatch

    fun display(c: C){   print(c.operate())

    }

    // Calling display function

    display(D())

}

Explanation: If we're familiar with Java or another OOP language, we'll note that class D inherits class A. The parameter supplied to the show method is an instance of class D in the above program. According to the dynamic method dispatch paradigm, the output should be 36, but the extension functions are statically resolved, the operate function is called on type C. As a result, the output is 12.

Nullable Receiver

Extension functions can also be defined using the nullable class type. When the check for null is added inside the extension function, the proper value is returned.

A nullable receiver is an example of an extension function:

```
// A sample class to display name name class ABC(val name: String){
override fun toString(): String {       return "Name is $name"

  } }
 fun main(){

  // An extension function as a nullable receiver

  fun ABC?.output(){       if(this == null){          println("Null")

    }else{

      println(this.toString())

    }

  }

  val x = ABC("Charch")

  // Extension function called using an instance

  x.output()

  // Extension function called on null

  null.output()
}
```

Companion Object Extensions

If a class has a companion object, we may also provide extension methods and attributes for the companion object.

Declaration of companion object:

```
class myClass {

  // the companion object declaration

  companion object {      fun display(){

      println("The Function declared in

companion object")

    }

  }

}
```

```
fun main(args: Array<String>) {    // invoking member function    val ob = myClass.display()
}
```

Like regular member functions of the companion object, extension functions can call with merely the class name as the qualifier.

Example of a companion object extension:

```
class myClass {
companion object {

     //the member function of companion object        fun display(str :String) : String{

        return str

    }

  }

}

   // the extension function of companion object
fun myClass.Companion.abc(){

   println("The Extension function of companion

object")

}
fun main(args: Array<String>) {

   val ob = myClass.display("The Function declared in

companion object")    println(ob)

   // invoking the extension function

   val ob2 = myClass.abc()

}
```

Kotlin Generics

Generics are useful features that enable us to build classes, methods, and properties that are accessible using various data types while maintaining compile-time type safety.

Creating parameterized classes: A generic type is a type-parameterized class or function. We always use angle brackets () to define the type parameter in the program.

The following is the definition of the generic class:

class myClass<D>(text: D) {   var name = text }

To build an instance of such a class, we must provide the following type arguments:

val my : myClass<String> = Myclass<String> ("Hubtutors")

If the parameters can deduct from the constructor arguments, the type arguments can be omitted: val my = myClass("Hubtutors ")

Because Hubtutors has the type String, the compiler figures out that we are discussing myclass<String>.

Advantages of generic:

Avoiding typecasting: There is no need to typecast the object.

Type safety: Generic permits just a single type of object at a time.

Compile-time safety: Generics code is tested for parameterized types at compile time to avoid run time errors.

Generic Usage in Our Program

In the following example, we define a Company class with a single argument and a primary constructor. Now, we try to pass other data types in the Company class object, such as String and Integer. The primary constructor of the Company class accepts string types ("Hubtutors") but gives a compile-time error when an Integer type is passed (15).

class Company (text: String) {

```
var y = text    init{        println(y)
}
}
fun main(args: Array<String>){    var name: Company = Company("Hubtutors")    var rank: Company =
Company(15)// compile time error
}
```

To address the above issue, we may develop a user-defined generic type class that takes many parameters in a single class. The Company type class is a general type class that accepts both Int and String types parameters.

A Kotlin program using generic class:

class Company<D> (text : D){

```
var y = text    init{        println(y)
}
}
fun main(args: Array<String>){
    var name: Company<String> = Company<String>("Geeks
forGeeks")
    var rank: Company<Int> = Company<Int>(16)
}
```

VARIANCE

In contrast to Java, Kotlin makes arrays invariant by default. Generic types, by extension, are invariant in Kotlin. The out and in keywords might help with this. Invariance is the feature that prevents a standard generic function/class that has already been created for a specific data type from accepting or returning another data type. All additional data types are supertypes of Any.

There are two kinds of variation:

Declaration-site variance (using in and out)

Use-site variance: Type projection

The out Keyword

We may utilize the out keyword on the generic type in Kotlin to assign this reference to any of its supertypes. The out value can only be created by the specified class and cannot be consumed:

class OutClass<out D>(val value: D) {

    fun get(): D {   return value

    }

}

We defined an OutClass class above that can return a value of type T. Then, for the reference that is a supertype of it, we may allocate an instance of the OutClass:

val out = OutClass("string") val ref: OutClass<Any> = out

Note: If we did not utilize the out type in the preceding class, the next statement will result in a compiler error.

The in Keyword

We may utilize the in keyword on the generic type to assign it to the reference of its subtype. The in keyword may only use on parameter type that are consumed, not produced:

class InClass<in D> {

    fun toString(value: D): String {   return value.toString()

    } }

In this case, we've declared a toString() method that exclusively accepts D values. Then we may allocate a reference of type Number to its subtype – Int:

val inClassObject: InClass<Number> = InClass() val ref<Int> = inClassObject

Covariance

Covariance states that substituting subtypes is permissible but not supertypes, i.e., the generic function/class may accept subtypes of the data type for which it is already defined, for example, a generic class created for Number can accept Int, while a generic class defined for Int cannot accept Number. This may be implemented in Kotlin by using the out keyword as seen below:

fun main(args: Array<String>) {

    val a: MyClass<Any> = MyClass<Int>()

// Error: Type mismatch

    val b: MyClass<out Any> = MyClass<String>()

// Works since String is a subtype of Any   val c: MyClass<out String> = MyClass<Any>()

// Error since Any is a supertype of String

} class MyClass<D>

We may immediately allow covariance by appending the out keyword to the declaration site. The following code works perfectly.

fun main(args: Array<String>) {

      val b: MyClass<Any> = MyClass<String>()

// Compiles without error

} class MyClass<out D>

Contra covariance

It is used to replace a supertype value in the subtypes, i.e., the generic function or class may accept supertypes of the data type it is already defined. For example, a generic class defined for Number cannot take Int, while a generic class defined for Int may accept Number. In Kotlin, it is accomplished using the in keyword as follows:

fun main(args: Array<String>) {

    var x: Container<Dog> = Container<Animal>()

//compiles without error

    var y: Container<Animal> = Container<Dog>()

//gives compilation error

}

open class Animal class Dog : Animal() class Container<in D>

Type Projections

It is feasible to copy all the members of an array of some type into an array of Any type, but for the compiler to compile our code, we must annotate the input argument with the out keyword. As a result, the compiler concludes that the input argument can be a subtype of the Any type.

Kotlin program for copying array elements into another:

fun copy(from: Array<out Any>, to: Array<Any>) {

```
assert(from.size == to.size)

// copying (from) array to (to) array

for (c in from.indices)      to[c] = from[c]

// printing elements of array in which copied

for (c in to.indices) {    println(to[c])

}
```

}

fun main(args :Array<String>) {   val ints: Array<Int> = arrayOf(1, 2, 3,4)   val any :Array<Any> = Array<Any>(4) { "" }

```
copy(ints, any)
```

}

Star Projections

When we don't know what sort of value we're looking for and merely want to print all the items of an array, we use the star(*) projection.

Program of using star projections in Kotlin:

// star projection in array fun printArray(array: Array<*>) {
array.forEach { print(it) }

}

```
fun main(args :Array<String>) {    val name  = arrayOf("Good","for","Good")
   printArray(name)
}
```

Conclusion to Object-Oriented Programming (OOP)

Object-Oriented Programming (OOP) has remained a cornerstone of software development, and Kotlin's seamless integration of OOP principles ensures that developers can leverage this paradigm to build robust, modular, and maintainable applications. As we explore the advancements in Kotlin 2025, the language's adherence to OOP fundamentals while embracing functional programming paradigms demonstrates its versatility and modernity.

Embracing Core OOP Principles in Kotlin

Kotlin's design makes it a powerful tool for implementing OOP concepts. By adhering to the four fundamental principles—encapsulation, inheritance, polymorphism, and abstraction—Kotlin empowers developers to build applications with clarity and structure. Let's revisit how these principles are implemented and their relevance in the Kotlin ecosystem.

1. **Encapsulation**, a core tenet of OOP, promotes data hiding and controlled access. Kotlin supports this through visibility modifiers like private, protected, internal, and public. The use of properties and backing fields allows developers to encapsulate the internal workings of classes while providing clean interfaces for interaction.

With Kotlin's advancements in 2025, tools such as the enhanced @JvmRecord annotation further streamline encapsulation for interoperability with Java. This ensures that encapsulated objects can seamlessly communicate across platforms while retaining data integrity.

2. **Inheritance** Kotlin's inheritance model encourages code reuse and extends functionality through the open keyword, which prevents accidental inheritance by requiring explicit permission. Abstract classes and interfaces remain integral to designing reusable and scalable architectures.

Recent updates in Kotlin 2025, such as support for sealed interface hierarchies and the expanded functionality of data classes, enhance inheritance by enabling developers to create more structured and expressive hierarchies. These features ensure that inherited structures remain predictable and cohesive.

3. **Polymorphism** Kotlin's polymorphism capabilities provide flexibility in method overriding and function behavior customization. The use of override ensures explicit intention, reducing errors and improving code readability. Developers can leverage polymorphic constructs to implement behaviors that adapt to various contexts dynamically.

In 2025, Kotlin's refined support for default interface methods and extension functions furthers polymorphism's applicability. These improvements make it easier to introduce behavior changes without disrupting existing codebases, enhancing adaptability and future-proofing applications.

4. **Abstraction** Kotlin supports abstraction through abstract classes and interfaces, allowing developers to define blueprints for complex systems. By separating implementation details from behavior, abstraction fosters modularity and reusability.

With the addition of context receivers in Kotlin 2025, abstraction has reached new heights. These receivers simplify the creation of domain-specific languages (DSLs) and context-sensitive operations, allowing developers to create concise and intuitive abstractions tailored to their needs.

Kotlin's Evolution: Balancing OOP and Functional Programming

One of Kotlin's standout qualities is its ability to harmonize OOP with functional programming paradigms. This balance empowers developers to choose the approach that best suits their problem domain. Kotlin's rich support for higher-order functions, immutability, and lambdas complements its OOP features, enabling developers to write expressive and concise code.

In 2025, Kotlin's enhancements to inline classes and functional constructs solidify its reputation as a modern programming language. Developers can effortlessly combine object-oriented design with functional techniques, such as immutability and composition, to create hybrid solutions that optimize performance, maintainability, and readability.

Kotlin-Specific OOP Enhancements

Kotlin distinguishes itself from traditional OOP languages like Java through innovative features that simplify and modernize object-oriented design. Let's explore some key enhancements that contribute to Kotlin's OOP capabilities in 2025:

1. **Data Classes** Kotlin's data classes continue to be a hallmark feature, automating the generation of boilerplate code for toString(), hashCode(), and equals(). In 2025, data classes support value-based equality for collections, making them even more versatile for domain modeling and data manipulation.

2. **Sealed Classes and Interfaces** Sealed classes and interfaces enforce exhaustive type checking, making them invaluable for designing state machines and complex hierarchies. The enhanced sealed interface support in 2025 further expands their utility, ensuring exhaustive handling even in deeply nested hierarchies.

3. **Delegation** Kotlin's delegation mechanisms, such as by keyword for property delegation and delegation patterns for interfaces, simplify code reuse without inheritance. These features, combined with the introduction of improved compiler optimizations in 2025, ensure that delegation remains lightweight and efficient.

4. **Extension Functions and Properties** Extension functions and properties exemplify Kotlin's ability to extend class functionality without altering the source code. They are particularly useful for adding utility methods to existing classes in a non-intrusive manner. Kotlin 2025's enhanced context receivers further empower developers to create context-aware extensions, broadening their applicability.

5. **Smart Casts and Null Safety** Kotlin's null safety and smart cast mechanisms reduce runtime errors and improve code clarity. Features like non-nullable types and the ?. operator simplify handling nullable references, aligning with OOP's goal of creating robust and predictable codebases.

6. **Coroutines Integration with OOP** Kotlin's coroutine model seamlessly integrates with OOP principles, enabling developers to build asynchronous and non-blocking systems. Features like structured concurrency and coroutine scopes align with OOP design patterns, ensuring that asynchronous behavior remains manageable and cohesive.

Real-World Applications of OOP in Kotlin

Kotlin's OOP capabilities are leveraged across various domains, from Android development to server-side applications and beyond. Let's explore a few real-world scenarios where Kotlin's OOP features shine:

1. **Android Development** Kotlin has become the de facto language for Android development, thanks to its modern syntax and OOP-friendly features. Developers can design reusable components, such as custom views and fragments, using OOP principles. Tools like Jetpack Compose further enhance this experience by integrating declarative programming with OOP constructs.

2. **Backend Development** Frameworks like Ktor and Spring Boot make full use of Kotlin's OOP capabilities. Developers can design modular services, define domain-specific abstractions, and implement polymorphic behaviors to handle complex business logic.

3. **Game Development** Kotlin's OOP features are well-suited for game development, where encapsulation and polymorphism play a critical role in managing game states, entities, and behaviors. Libraries like libGDX demonstrate Kotlin's versatility in this domain.

4. **Enterprise Applications** In enterprise software, OOP principles are essential for designing maintainable systems. Kotlin's interoperability with Java ensures that developers can migrate legacy systems to Kotlin incrementally while preserving OOP structures.

Best Practices for OOP in Kotlin

To fully harness Kotlin's OOP potential, developers should adhere to the following best practices:

1. **Leverage Sealed Classes for Domain Modeling** Use sealed classes and interfaces to model finite hierarchies, ensuring exhaustive type checking and reducing runtime errors.

2. **Minimize Boilerplate with Delegation** Replace boilerplate code with delegation patterns where applicable, promoting code reuse and clarity.

3. **Adopt Immutability** Design classes with immutability in mind, especially for data classes and domain models. This aligns with functional programming principles and reduces side effects.

4. **Follow Single Responsibility Principle (SRP)** Ensure that classes and methods have a single responsibility. This enhances modularity and makes testing and maintenance easier.

5. **Use Extension Functions Wisely** Avoid cluttering the global namespace with unnecessary extension functions. Restrict their usage to specific use cases where they provide clear value.

6. **Optimize Coroutine Usage** Combine coroutines with OOP constructs thoughtfully to create scalable and responsive applications without sacrificing clarity.

Final Thoughts

Kotlin 2025 solidifies its position as a modern, versatile language that embraces the best of OOP and functional programming. Its seamless integration of OOP principles allows developers to design applications that are not only robust and maintainable but also adaptable to evolving requirements. By leveraging features such as encapsulation, inheritance, polymorphism, and abstraction, alongside Kotlin-specific enhancements like data classes, sealed hierarchies, and delegation, developers can build systems that stand the test of time.

As Kotlin continues to evolve, its commitment to innovation ensures that OOP will remain a central paradigm for application development. Kotlin's ability to harmonize traditional programming principles with cutting-edge features positions it as an indispensable tool for developers seeking to build future-proof solutions. By embracing Kotlin's OOP capabilities and best practices, developers can craft software that is both elegant and efficient, setting new standards for quality and performance in the digital age.

4. Error, Exception Handling, and Extensions Explained

Introduction

Error and exception handling is a fundamental aspect of writing robust and resilient applications. Kotlin, being a modern programming language, provides a structured and developer-friendly approach to handle errors and exceptions, ensuring that your applications are both reliable and maintainable.

1. What Are Exceptions?

Exceptions represent unexpected or erroneous conditions that disrupt the normal flow of a program. For example, trying to divide a number by zero or accessing an array index that is out of bounds results in exceptions.

In Kotlin, exceptions are similar to Java and are represented as objects of the Throwable class or its subclasses. The two primary types of exceptions are:

- **Checked Exceptions**: These are exceptions that the compiler forces you to handle. Kotlin does not have checked exceptions like Java, which means you are not required to explicitly catch or declare them.

- **Unchecked Exceptions**: These exceptions occur at runtime and are not checked by the compiler.

2. Exception Hierarchy in Kotlin

Kotlin's exception hierarchy is based on Java's:

- **Throwable**: The root of the hierarchy.

    - **Error**: Represents serious issues that applications should not attempt to catch (e.g., OutOfMemoryError).

    - **Exception**: Represents conditions that applications might want to catch (e.g., NullPointerException, IllegalArgumentException).

3. Handling Exceptions

Kotlin provides a try-catch-finally block to handle exceptions. Here's how it works:

```kotlin
fun main() {
  try {
    val result = 10 / 0
    println(result)
  } catch (e: ArithmeticException) {
    println("Caught an exception: ${e.message}")
  } finally {
    println("This block is always executed")
  }
}
```

- **try**: Contains the code that might throw an exception.

- **catch**: Handles specific exceptions.
- **finally**: Optional block that executes regardless of whether an exception was thrown or not.

4. Throwing Exceptions

You can throw exceptions using the throw keyword:

```
fun validateInput(input: Int) {
   if (input < 0) {
      throw IllegalArgumentException("Input must be non-negative")
   }
}
```

5. The try Expression

In Kotlin, try is an expression, meaning it can return a value:

```
val result = try {
   "123".toInt()
} catch (e: NumberFormatException) {
   null
}
println(result) // Prints: 123 or null if the conversion fails
```

6. Custom Exceptions

You can define custom exception classes by extending Exception or Throwable:

```
class CustomException(message: String) : Exception(message)
```

7. Best Practices

- Use exceptions only for exceptional conditions.
- Avoid overusing try-catch blocks.
- Prefer null-safety and Kotlin's type system to prevent common errors.
- Log exceptions for debugging and analysis.

Extension Functions and Properties in Kotlin

Kotlin's extension functions and properties are powerful features that allow developers to add functionality to existing classes without modifying their source code. This promotes clean, concise, and reusable code.

1. What Are Extension Functions?

An extension function is a function that can be called as if it were a member of a class, even though it is defined outside the class. Extension functions do not modify the original class; instead, they operate on instances of the class.

2. Defining an Extension Function

To define an extension function, use the following syntax:

```
fun <ClassName>.<FunctionName>(parameters): ReturnType {
    // Function body
}
```

Example:

```
fun String.addExclamation(): String {
    return this + "!"
}
```

```
fun main() {
    val message = "Hello, Kotlin"
    println(message.addExclamation()) // Output: Hello, Kotlin!
}
```

- this refers to the instance on which the extension function is called.
- The extension function addExclamation is now available for all String objects.

3. Extension Functions with Nullable Receivers

Extension functions can also be defined for nullable types:

```
fun String?.isNullOrEmpty(): Boolean {
    return this == null || this.isEmpty()
}
```

```
fun main() {
    val str: String? = null
    println(str.isNullOrEmpty()) // Output: true
}
```

4. Overriding and Extension Functions

Extension functions cannot be overridden. If a member function and an extension function have the same name, the member function takes precedence:

```
class Sample {
    fun display() = "Member Function"
}
```

```
fun Sample.display() = "Extension Function"
```

```
fun main() {
    val sample = Sample()
    println(sample.display()) // Output: Member Function
}
```

5. Extension Properties

Extension properties allow you to add properties to existing classes. Unlike regular properties, they cannot hold state and must have a getter (and optionally a setter):

```
val String.wordCount: Int
    get() = this.split(" ").size
```

```
fun main() {
    val text = "Kotlin is awesome"
    println(text.wordCount) // Output: 3
}
```

6. Common Use Cases for Extension Functions and Properties

- Adding utility functions for classes from external libraries.
- Enhancing readability and reducing boilerplate code.
- Creating DSLs (Domain-Specific Languages).

Example:

```
fun List<Int>.average(): Double {
    return if (this.isEmpty()) 0.0 else this.sum().toDouble() / this.size
}
```

```
fun main() {
    val numbers = listOf(1, 2, 3, 4, 5)
    println(numbers.average()) // Output: 3.0
}
```

7. Limitations of Extensions

- Extensions do not modify the original class; they only appear as additional functionality.
- Extension functions are statically resolved, meaning they depend on the type of the reference at compile time.

8. Extension Functions in Companion Objects

Extensions can also be defined for companion objects:

```
class MyClass {

    companion object {}

}


fun MyClass.Companion.printMessage() {

    println("Hello from Companion Object")

}


fun main() {

    MyClass.printMessage() // Output: Hello from Companion Object

}
```

9. Best Practices for Extensions

- Use extensions for utility and helper functions.
- Avoid adding too many extensions to a single class to prevent clutter.
- Document extension functions for better readability.

Let's begin,

This chapter considers exception and error handling and how it is implemented in Kotlin. The chapter first introduces the object-oriented model of exception handling as well as how to define custom exceptions and exception chaining. The chapter then explores the functional approach to exception handling in Kotlin.

Errors and Exceptions

When something goes wrong in a computer program someone needs to know about it. One way of informing other parts of a program (and potentially those running a program) is by generating an error object and propagating that through the code until either something handles the error and sorts thing out or the point at which the program is entered is found.

If the error propagates out of the program, then the user who ran the program needs to know that something has gone wrong. Typically, they are notified of a problem via a short report on the error that occurred and a stack trace of where that error can be found. The stack trace shows the sequence of calls (both functions and member functions) that were invoked up until the point at which the error occurred.

You may have seen these yourself when writing your own programs. For example, the following program will cause an exception to be generated as it is not possible to convert the string "42a" into an integer:

package com.jjh.exp.basic

fun main() { **val** numberString = "42a" println(numberString.toInt())

}

When we run this program we obtain a stack trace in the output console of your program, such as that displayed within the IntelliJ IDE. This is because the exception is not handled by the program and instead it has propagated out of the program and a stack trace of the code that was called is presented. Note the line numbers are included which helps with debugging the problem.

```
Run:    ThrowingAnExceptionKt
 ►   ↑   Exception in thread "main" java.lang.NumberFormatException Create breakpoint : For input string: "42a"
 ⚙   ↓       at java.base/java.lang.NumberFormatException.forInputString(NumberFormatException.java:68)
 ⊠   ⬚       at java.base/java.lang.Integer.parseInt(Integer.java:652)
 ⊡   ⬚       at java.base/java.lang.Integer.parseInt(Integer.java:770)
 ⌂   ⬚       at com.jjh.exp.basic.ThrowingAnExceptionKt.main(ThrowingAnException.kt:5)
     ⬚       at com.jjh.exp.basic.ThrowingAnExceptionKt.main(ThrowingAnException.kt)
```

What is an Exception?

In Kotlin, almost everything is an instance of some type including integers, strings, booleans and indeed Exceptions and Errors. In Kotlin the Exception/Error types are defined in a class hierarchy with the root of this hierarchy being the kotlin.Throwable type.

All built-in errors and exceptions eventually extend from the kotlin.Throwable type.

The Throwable class has two subclasses: Error and Exception. • Errorsareexceptionsgeneratedatruntimefromwhichitisunlikelythataprogram can recover (such as out of memory errors).

- Whereas Exceptions are issues that your program should be able to deal with (such as attempting to read from the wrong file).

- A third type of exception is a RuntimeException. RuntimeExceptions represents bugs in your code and should not occur.

Part of the class hierarchy is shown below:

What is an Exception?

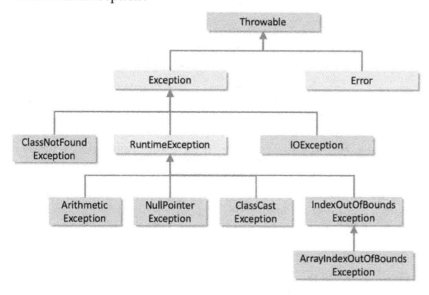

The above diagram illustrates the class hierarchy for some of the common types of errors and exceptions in Kotlin.

When an exception occurs, this is known as raising an exception and when it is passed to other code to handle the error or exception this is known as throwing an exception. The code which receives and handles the error exception is described as having caught the exception. These are terms that will hopefully become more obvious as this chapter progresses.

As stated above all exceptions inherit from kotlin.Throwable.

On the JVM runtime these are actually a set of typealiases that map the Kotlin types to the underlying Java (JVM) runtime exceptions, for example:

- kotlin.Throwable maps to java.lang.Throwable
- kotlin.Exception maps to java.lang.Exception
- kotlin.NullPointerExceptionmapstojava.lang.NullPointerException.

What Is Exception Handling?

An exception moves the flow of control from one place to another. In most situations, this is because a problem occurs which cannot be handled locally but that can be handled in another part of the system.

The problem is usually some sort of error (such as dividing by zero), although it can be any problem (for example, identifying that the postcode specified with an address does not match). The purpose of an exception, therefore, is to handle an error condition when it happens at runtime.

It is worth considering why you should wish to handle an exception; after all the system does not allow an error to go unnoticed. For example, if we try to divide by zero, then the system generates an error for you. However, in general we do not want programs to fail or crash in an uncontrolled manner. We can therefore use exceptions to identify that an issue has occurred and to determine how to correct it, for example we might request that the user correct the mistake and rerun the calculation.

The following table illustrates terminology typically used with exception/error handling in Kotlin.

Exception	An error which is generated at runtime
Raising an exception	Generating a new exception
Throwing an exception	Triggering a generated exception
Handling an exception	Processing code that deals with the error
Handler	The code that deals with the error (referred to as the catch block or exception handler)

Different types of error produce different types of exception. For example, if the error is caused by trying to divide an integer by zero then the exception generated might be an Arithmetic Exception.

The actual type of exception is represented by exception instances and can be caught and processed by exception handlers. Each handler can deal with exceptions associated with its class of error or exception (and its subclasses).

An exception is instantiated when it is thrown. The system searches back up the execution stack (the set of functions or member functions that have been invoked in reverse order) until it finds a handler which can deal with the exception. The associated handler then processes the exception. This may involve performing some remedial action or terminating the current execution in a controlled manner. In some cases, it may be possible to restart executing the code.

As a handler can only deal with an exception of a specified class (or subclass), an exception may pass through a number of handlers blocks before it finds one that can process it.

```
try

    val result = 5 /0

catch NullPointerException

catch IllegalArgumentException

catch ArithmeticException
```

The above figure illustrates a situation in which an exception is generated due to a divide by zero issue. This exception is called an Arithmetic Exception.

What Is Exception Handling?

This exception is thrown when the integer 5 is divided by 0 and is passed up the execution stack where it encounters a catch exception handler defined for an NullPointerException. This handler cannot handle the Arithmetic Exception as it is a different type and so it is passed to the next catch block. It then encounters a catch exception handler for an Illegal Argument Exception. Again, it cannot deal with an Arithmetic Exception and the exception is passed to the final catch exception handler which can handle the Arithmetic Exception. This handler then processes the exception.

Handling an Exception

You can catch an exception by implementing the try catch construct. This construct is broken into three parts:

- try block. The try block indicates the code which is to be monitored for the exceptions listed in the catch expressions.

- catch clauses. You can use one or more optional catch clause to indicate what to do when certain classes of exception/error occur (e.g. resolve the problem or generate a warning message). There can be any number of catch clauses in sequence checking for different types of error/exceptions.

- finallyclause. The optional finally clause runs after the try block exits(whether or not this is due to an exception being thrown). You can use it to clean up any resources, close files, etc.

This language construct may at first seem confusing, however once you have worked with it for a while you will find it less daunting.

As an example, consider the following function which divides a number by zero; this will throw the ZeroDivisionError when it is run for any number:

fun runcalc(x: Int){ x / 0 }

If we now call this function, we will get the exception stack trace in the standard output:

fun main() { runcalc(5) }

This is shown below:

```
/Library/Java/JavaVirtualMachines/jdk-14.0.1.jdk/Contents/Home/bin/java ...
Exception in thread "main" java.lang.ArithmeticException Create breakpoint : / by zero
    at com.jjh.exp.basic.BasicExceptionHandlingKt.runcalc(BasicExceptionHandling.kt:4)
    at com.jjh.exp.basic.BasicExceptionHandlingKt.main(BasicExceptionHandling.kt:8)
    at com.jjh.exp.basic.BasicExceptionHandlingKt.main(BasicExceptionHandling.kt)
```

However, we can handle this by wrapping the call to runcalc within a try block and providing a catch clause. The syntax for the try-catch construct is:

try {

<code to monitor>

} **catch**(<variabe-name>: <type of exception to monitor for>) {

<code to call if exception is found> }

A concrete example of this is given below for a try block that will be used to monitor a call to runcalc:

fun main() { **try** { runcalc(5)

} **catch**(exp: ArithmeticException) { println("Opps")

}
}

which now results in the string 'Oops' being printed out instead of the exception stack trace:

```
/Library/Java/JavaVirtualMachines/jdk-14.0.1.jdk/Contents/Home/bin/java ...
Opps
```

This is because when runcalc is called the '/' operator throws the Arithmetic Exception which is passed back to the calling code which has an catch clause specifying this type of exception. This catches the exception and runs the associated code block which in this case prints out the string 'Oops'.

If we want to log the error and allow the program to proceed we can use the printStackTrace() member function, for example:

fun main() { **try** { runcalc(5)

} **catch**(exp: ArithmeticException) { println("Opps") exp.printStackTrace()

}

}

In fact, we don't have to be as precise as this; the catch clause can be given the class of exception to look for and it will match any exception that is of that exception type or is an instance of a subclass of the exception. We therefore can also write:

fun main() { **try** { runcalc(5)

} **catch**(exp: Exception) { println("Opps") exp.printStackTrace()

}
}

The Exception class is a grandparent of the Arithmetic Exception thus any Arithmetic Exception instance is also a type of Exception and thus the catch block matches the exception passed to it. This means that you can write one catch clause and that clause can handle a whole range of exceptions.

Multiple Catch Blocks

If you don't want to have a common block of code handling your exceptions, you can define different behaviours for different types of exception. This is done by having a series of catch clauses; each monitoring a different type of exception:

fun main() { **try** { runcalc(5)

} **catch** (exp: NullPointerException) { println("NullPointerException")

} **catch** (exp: IllegalArgumentException) { println("IllegalArgumentException")

} **catch** (exp: ArithmeticException) { println("ArithmeticException")

} **catch** (e: Exception) { println("Duh!")

} }

In this case the first catch monitors for a NullPointerException but the other catches monitor for other types of exception. Thus, the second catch monitors for Illegal Argument Exception, the third for the Arithmetic Exception etc.

Note that the catch(e: Exception) is the last catch clause in the list. This is because Null PointerException, Illegal Argument Exception and Arithmetic Exception are all eventual subclasses of Exception and thus this clause would catch any of these types of exception. As only one catch block is allowed to run; if this catch handler came fist the other catch handers would never ever be run.

Accessing the Exception Object

It is possible to gain access to the exception instance being caught by the catch clause as it is available within the catch handler code block. You can name this parameter whatever you like, however names such as e, exp, ex is commonly used. For example:

fun main() { **try** { runcalc(5)

} **catch**(exp: Exception) { println("Opps") println(exp) println(exp.message) exp.printStackTrace()

} }

Which produces:

```
/Library/Java/JavaVirtualMachines/jdk-14.0.1.jdk/Contents/Home/bin/java ...
Opps
java.lang.ArithmeticException: / by zero
/ by zero
java.lang.ArithmeticException Create breakpoint : / by zero
    at com.jjh.exp.basic.BasicExceptionHandlingKt.runcalc(BasicExceptionHandling.kt:6)
    at com.jjh.exp.basic.BasicExceptionHandling3Kt.main(BasicExceptionHandling3.kt:5)
    at com.jjh.exp.basic.BasicExceptionHandling3Kt.main(BasicExceptionHandling3.kt)
```

Jumping to Exception Handlers

One of the interesting features of exception handling in Kotlin is that when an Error or an Exception is raised it is immediately thrown to the exception handlers (the catch blocks). Any statements that follow the point at which the exception is raised are not run. This means that a function or member function may be terminated early and further statements in the calling code will not be run.

As an example, consider the following code. This code defines a function divide(Int, Int) that divides two integers returning the result. Note that function logs entry and exit from the function.

The divide() function is called from within a try statement of the main() function. Notice that there is a println() statement each side of the call to divide(Int, Int). There is also a handler for the Arithmetic Exception.

```
fun divide(x: Int, y: Int): Int { println("entering divide($x, $y)") val result = x / y
println("exiting divide $result")
return result
}
fun main() { println("Starting") try { println("Before the call to divide") val result = divide(6,2)
println("After the call to divide: $result")
} catch (exp: ArithmeticException) { println("Opps")
}
println("Done") }
```

When we run this program, the output is Starting

Before the call to divide entering divide(6, 2) exiting divide 3

After the call to divide: 3 Done

In this example we have run every statement with the exception of the catch clause as the Arithmetic Exception was not thrown.

If we now change the call to divide(Int, Int) such that we pass in 6 and 0 we will throw the ArithmeticException.

```
fun main() { println("Starting") try {
println("Before the call to divide") val result = divide(6,0)
println("After the call to divide: $result")
} catch (exp: ArithmeticException) { println("Opps")
} println("Done")
}
```

Now the output is:

Starting

Before the call to divide entering divide(6, 0)

Opps

Done

The difference is that the second println statement in divide(Int, Int) has not been run; instead after printing 'entering divide(6, 0)' and then raising the error we have jumped strait to the catch clause and run the println statement in the associated exception handling block of code.

This is partly why the term throwing is used with respect to error and exception handling; because the error or exception is raised in one place and thrown to the point where it is handled, or it is thrown out of the application if no catch clause is found to handle the error/exception.

The Finally Clause

An optional finally clause can also be provided with the try statement. This clause is the last clause in the construct and must come after any catch classes.

It is used for code that you want to run whether an exception occurred or not. For example, see the following program:

```
fun main() { println("Starting") try {

println("Before the call to divide") val result = divide(6,2)

println("After the call to divide: $result")

} catch (exp: ArithmeticException) { println("Opps") } finally { println("Always runs")

} println("Done")

}
```

The try block will run, if no error is thrown then the finally code will run, we will therefore have as output:

Starting

Before the call to divide entering divide(6, 2) exiting divide 3

After the call to divide: 3

Always runs

Done

If however we pass in 6 and 0 to divide(Int, Int):

```
fun main() { println("Starting") try {

println("Before the call to divide") val result = divide(6,0)

println("After the call to divide: $result")

} catch (exp: ArithmeticException) { println("Opps") } finally { println("Always runs")

} println("Done")

}
```

We will now cause an exception to be thrown in the divide(Int, Int) function which means that the try block will execute, then the Arithmetic Exception will be thrown, it will be handled by the catch clause and then the finally clause will run. The output is now:

Starting

Before the call to divide entering divide(6, 0)

Opps

Always runs

Done

As you can see in both cases the finally clause is executed.

The finally clause can be very useful for general housekeeping type activities such as shutting down or closing any resources that your code might be using, even if an error has occurred.

Throwing an Exception

An error or exception is thrown using the keyword throw. The syntax of this is

throw <Exception/Error type to throw>()

For example:

```
fun functionBang() { println("entering functionBang") throw RuntimeException("Bang!") println("exiting
functionBang")

}
```

In the above function the second statement in the function body will create a new instance of the Runtime Exception class and then throw it allowing it to be caught by any exception handlers that have been defined.

We can handle this exception by writing a try block with an catch clause for the Runtime Exception class. For example:

```
fun main() { try {

functionBang()

} catch (exp: RuntimeException) { println(exp.message)

} }
```

This generates the output:

entering function Bang Bang!

Throwing an Exception

You can also re-throw an error or an exception; this can be useful if you merely want to note that an error has occurred and then re-throw it so that it can be handled further up in your application. To do this you use the throw keyword and the parameter used to hold the exception for the catch block. For example:

```
fun main() { try {

functionBang()

} catch (exp: RuntimeException) { println(exp.message) throw exp

} }
```

This will re throw the Runtime Exception caught by the catch clause. However, in this case there is nothing to handle the exception and therefore it propagates out of the program causing the program to terminate and generate an exception stack trace:

entering function Bang Bang!

Exception in thread "main" java.lang.RuntimeException: Bang! at

com.jjh.exp.raise.RaisingAnExceptionKt.functionBang(RaisingAnExc eption.kt:5)

at

com.jjh.exp.raise.RaisingAnExceptionKt.main(RaisingAnException.k t:11)

at

com.jjh.exp.raise.RaisingAnExceptionKt.main(RaisingAnException.k t)

Try Catch as an Expression

In Kotlin most statements are actually expressions that return a value. The try-catch finally expression is no different. You can assign the value returned by the try{} block (or the catch{} block if an error occurs) to a value.

For example, the following listing instantiates the class Rational and stores that instance into the val result unless an exception is thrown.

If an exception is thrown then if the exception is of type RuntimeException then a default Rational instance is returned by the catch block.

Thus, the val result with either have an instance created from within the try block or an instance created within the catch block:

```
class Rational(val numerator: Int, d: Int) {
val denominator: Int init {
if (d == 0)
throw RuntimeException(
"Denominator cannot be Zero")
denominator = d
} override fun toString()=
"Rational($numerator, $denominator)"
} fun main() { val result = try {
Rational(5, 0)
} catch (exp: RuntimeException) {
Rational(5, 1)
} println(result)
}
```

The output from this is:

Rational(numerator=5, denominator=1)

However, care should be taken when using the try-catch expression with a finally block. The finally block is optional but when present runs after the try block and if an exception occurs it also runs after any catch block has run. For example:

```
val result = try { throw RuntimeException("oops") } catch (e: RuntimeException) {
3
} catch (e: Throwable) {
0
} finally {
2
} println("result1: $result1")
```

The question here is what is the value of result? It will either be the value returned from the try block if there is no exception or it will be the value returned from the catch block.

Try Catch as an Expression

Notice that although the finally block is executed any value returned from that block will be ignored. Thus the output generated for the above code is:

result1: 3

One common idiom or pattern used with try-catch expressions is that they can represent the whole body of a function or member function. This ensures that the try expression encapsulates all the functionality in the function block. For example:

```
fun func() = try {
```

Rational(5, 0)

} **catch** (exp: RuntimeException) {

Rational(5, 1) }

Defining a Custom Exception

You can define your own exception types, which can give you more control over what happens in particular circumstances. To define an exception, you create a subclass of the Exception class or one of its subclasses.

For example, to define a InvalidAgeException, we can extend the Exception class and generate an appropriate message: **class** InvalidAgeException(**val** invalidAge: Int, message: String)**:** Exception(message)

This class can be used to explicitly represent an issue when an age is set on a Person which is not within the acceptable age range.

We can use this with the class Person that we defined earlier in the book; this version of the Person class defined age as a property and attempted to validate that an appropriate age was being set. We can modify this class so that if the value being used for age is less than zero or greater than 120 then we will throw an InvalidAgeException. For example:

```
class Person(val name: String, _age: Int) {

var age: Int = 0 private set(value) {

if (value < 0 || value > 120) { throw InvalidAgeException(value,

"Age must be between 0 and 120")

} else { field = value

}

} init {

age = _age

}

}
```

Note that the age set() function now throws an InvalidAgeException, so if we write:

```
fun main() {

try {

val p1 = Person("Adam", -1) println(p1)

} catch (exp: InvalidAgeException) { println(exp.invalidAge) println(exp.message) println(exp)

} }
```

When this code runs and we try and create an instance of the Person class with an age of -1 the set() function for the age property will throw the InvalidAgeException passing in information to help any exception handler determine the issue with the data and what that data was.

When the above code runs, we will see:

-1

Age must be between 0 and 120 com.jjh.exp.people.InvalidAgeException: Age must be between 0 and 120

Chaining Exceptions

A feature that can be useful when creating your own exceptions is to chain them to a generic underlying exception. This can be useful when a generic exception is thrown, for example, by some library or by the Kotlin system itself, and you want to convert it into a more meaningful application exception.

For example, let us say that we want to create an exception to represent a specific issue with the parameters passed to a function divide(), but we don't want to use the generic Arithmetic Exception, instead we want to use our own DivideByYWhenZeroException. This new exception could be defined as: **class** DivideByYWhenZeroException(

message: String = "", cause: Throwable? = **null**): Exception(message, cause)

This exception is defined to handle an underlying cause. The cause is defined as a nullable Throwable type (which means that it can be used with any type of Exception or Error). It is then passed up to the parent class exception along with the message. Notice that the cause is optional as we have provided a default value null.

And we can use it in a function divide(): **fun** divide(x: Int, y: Int): Int {

try {

return x / y

} **catch** (exp: ArithmeticException) { **throw** DivideByYWhenZeroException("Divide by Zero", exp)

}

}

We have used the throws keyword when we are instantiating the DivideByYWhenZeroException and passed in the original exception in to the constructor as an argument. This chains our exception to the original exception that indicates the underlying problem.

We can now call the divide() function as shown below:

fun main() { divide(6, 0)

}

This produces a stack trace as given below:

Exception in thread "main"

chained.DivideByYWhenZeroException: Divide by Zero at

chained.ChainedExceptionExampleKt.divide(ChainedExceptionExam ple.kt:12) at

chained.ChainedExceptionExampleKt.main(ChainedExceptionExampl e.kt:17) at

chained.ChainedExceptionExampleKt.main(ChainedExceptionExampl e.kt)

Caused by: **java.lang.ArithmeticException: / by zero**

at

chained.ChainedExceptionExampleKt.divide(ChainedExceptionExam ple.kt:10)

... 2 more

As can be seen you get information about both the (application specific) DivideByYWhenZeroException and the original Arithmetic Exception—the two are linked together.

Nesting Exception Handlers

It is also possible to nest one trycatch expression or statement inside another.

As a handler can only deal with an exception of a specified class (or subclass), an exception may pass through a number of handlers blocks before it finds one that can process it.

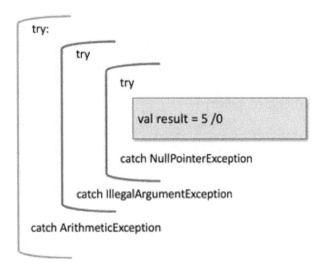

The above figure illustrates a situation in which an ArithemticException is generated due to a divide by zero issue. The exception is thrown when the integer 5 is divided by 0 and is passed up the execution stack where it encounters an exception handler defined for an NullPointerException. This handler cannot handle the ArithmeticException as it is a different type and so it is passed further up the execution stack. It then encounters a handler for an IllegalArgumentException. Again, it cannot deal with a ArithmeticException and the exception is passed further up the execution stack until it finds a handler defined for the Arithmetic Exception. This handler then processes the exception.

This example is illustrated in code below:

fun main() { **try** { **try** { **try** { println("In here") val result = 5 / 0

} **catch** (exp: NullPointerException) { println("Its an NullPointerException") }

} **catch** (ire: IllegalArgumentException) { println("Its an IllegalArgumentException") }

} **catch** (ae: ArithmeticException) { println("Its an ArithmeticException") ae.printStackTrace()

} }

Limitations of Try-Catch

For those of you who are familiar with exception handling in other languages such as Java, C# etc. you will see that Kotlin's try-catch-finally construct is very similar. However, it is not without its drawbacks. The need to work with some resources (such as database connections or connections to a file) in multiple places can result in some awkward programming solutions. In general, there are three key problems with this approach:

• The syntax results in scoping issues leading to unnecessarily complicated constructs as well as the need to nest try-catch block within either the try, catch or finally part of the top-level construct! For example, to open a network connection you might write something like:

  Var connection: Connection? = null **try** {

connection =

// … Use the connection

} catch (exp: ConnectionException) {

// … Log the error occurred when opening the connection } **finally** { **try** {

connection.?close()

} **catch** (expo: Exception) {

// … Log the exception caused when closing the connection } }

- It forces developers to use vars for local variables as in the above code connection must be accessible in at least two different code blocks. This goes against the general approach of using vals in Kotlin programs.

- Multi-threaded code can be difficult to deal with using the try-catch-finally construct. For example, how should you react to an exception which occurs in a separate thread but which impacts the data being accessed? In fact, the try-catch-finally construct primarily assumes that the exception is handled in the current execution thread (that is the exception is completely handled within the thread in which it occurred). This is not ideal for a concurrent program and seems at odds with the coroutine model implemented by Kotlin (see later in this book for chapters on Kotlin coroutines).

It can also be argued that the try-catch-finally approach is not particularly functional and is more procedural in nature. As Kotlin is a hybrid language this is not necessarily an issue in its own right, but it does highlight that alternative approaches can be developed based on the functional programming model.

Functional Exception Handling

Kotlin 1.3 added a new type of run scope function called runCatching{}. This scope function supports functional style exception handling.

It also introduce the kotlin.Result type which encapsulates whether the runCatching{} block was successful or not.

Using runCatching{}

To use the runCatching{} scope function all you have to do is embed the code to be monitored within the body of the runCatching block, for example:

runCatching {

"32".toInt() **}**

This scope function will attempt to convert the String "32" to an Integer. The scope function runCatcing{} will return a result representing success or failure of the block of code.

That is, runCatching{} allows the behaviour defined within the scope block to execute. It then generates a result which is a discriminated union that encapsulates:

- a successful outcome representing a value generated by the runCatching{} block or

- a failure which holds a reference to the Throwable instance (the exception) that caused the code to fail.

It is possible to check the result instance to identify whether it represents a success or failure using the isSuccess and isFailure properties.

For example:

fun main() { **val** result1 = **runCatching** {

"32".toInt()

}

println(result1) println(rresult11.isSuccess) **val** result2 = **runCatching** {

```
"32a".toInt()
}
```

println(result2) println(result2.isFailure)

```
}
```

This example attempts to convert a String to an integer for the val result1 and the val result2. The String used for result1 can be converted to an Int (the integer 32) but the String used for result2 cannot be converted into an integer (as it contains the character 'a'). Thus, the first expression should succeed, but the second should fail. The output of this program is:

Success(32) true

Failure(java.lang.NumberFormatException: For input string:

"32a") true

As you can see from this the value held in r1 is a Success type but the value held in r2 is a Failure type. The Failure also contains information about the problem that occurred and the value associated with it.

Accessing the Failure Exception

To access the exception associated with the Failure you can use the exceptionOrNull() member function, for example:

val result2 = runCatching {

```
"32a".toInt()
}
```

println(r2) println(r2.isFailure) println(r2.exceptionOrNull())

The output from this block of code is:

Failure(java.lang.NumberFormatException: For input string:

"32a") true

java.lang.NumberFormatException: For input string: "32a"

Accessing the Successful Value

To obtain the value held in the Result if it is successful there are a set of getter style member functions available:

- getOrDefault(<defaultValue>) Returns the encapsulated value if this instance represents success or the defaultValue if it is failure.

- GetOrElse{<onFailure function>} Returns the encapsulated value if this instance represents success or the result of the onFailure function for the encapsulated Throwable exception if it is failure.

- getOrNull() Returns the value generated or null.

- getOrThrow() Returns the encapsulated value if this instance represents success or re-throws the encapsulated Throwable exception if it is failure.

Examples of each of these getter member functions are given below:

val result0 = **runCatching** {

"32".toInt() }.**getOrDefault**(-1) println("result0 $result0") **val** result1 = **runCatching** {

```
"32a".toInt() }.getOrElse { println(it)
0 }
```

```
println("result1 $result1") val result2 = runCatching {
"32a".toInt() } getOrNull() println("result2 $result2") val result3 = runCatching {
"32a".toInt() }.getOrThrow() println("result3: $result3")
```

The output from this code block is:

result0 32 java.lang.NumberFormatException: For input string: "32a" result1 0 result2 null

Exception in thread "main" java.lang.NumberFormatException: For input string: "32a"

at

java.base/java.lang.NumberFormatException.forInputString(NumberFormatException.java:68)

at java.base/java.lang.Integer.parseInt(Integer.java:652) at java.base/java.lang.Integer.parseInt(Integer.java:770) at exp.func.FunctionalStyleExceptionHandlingAppKt.main

Treating Result as a Container

Result is actually a type of container and therefore it is also possible to apply higher order functions such as map and filter to the result generated by runCatching{}, for example:

runCatching { "32".toInt() } **.map** { println(**it**) }

runCatching { "32a".toInt() } **.map** { println(**it**) }

In this case the map function is being applied to the result instance. The result either contains a value if it is a success or it contains a Throwable (which is not considered to be a value returned by the block). As such map will be applied to a successful result but will have no effect of there if an exception thrown. The result generated by this code snippet is thus just:

32

This comes for the first runCatching{}block. The second runCatching{} block generates an exception and there is therefore no successful result to apply map to. This approach is fine if you are not interested in the exception and just want to do something if everything goes ok. However, in many situations you want to at least log the fact that an exception happened and may want to take some remedial action.

Recovery Operations

The recover{} operation can be used to handle an exception situation and recover from it. It can therefore be combined with map to provide some exception handling behaviour followed by the map operation. This is an approach favoured by many in the functional programming community.

For example:

runCatching { "32a".toInt() } **.recover** { **it**.printStackTrace()

-1

}

.map { println(**it**) }

In this case we are mimicking the try-catch behaviour where the catch behaviour provides an alternative value to use. Thus, in this case, if the String to be converted to an Int cannot be represented as an Int we will default to the value -1 however we are also logging the exception so that it does not fail silently.

The output from this code is therefore:

java.lang.NumberFormatException: For input string: "32a"

at

java.base/java.lang.NumberFormatException.forInputString(NumberF ormatException.java:68)

at java.base/java.lang.Integer.parseInt(Integer.java:652) at
java.base/java.lang.Integer.parseInt(Integer.java:770) at

.exp.func.FunctionalStyleExceptionHandlingAppKt.main(FunctionalStyleExceptionHandlingApp.kt:47)

at

exp.func.FunctionalStyleExceptionHandlingAppKt.main(FunctionalStyleExceptionHandlingApp.kt)

-1

Providing Explicit OnFailure and OnSuccess Behaviour

In many situations developers want to one thing if the code works successful but do a different thing if it fails. This may be because there is no obvious recovery step. For example, if an error occurs while trying to connect to a server then there may not be a way to recover from that if the server is unavailable.

To support this scenario kotlin.Result provide the onFailure{} and onSuccess{} functions. These higher order functions take a function that is run depending on whether the kotlin.Result represents a success or failure scenario. These functions can be chained together for the result instance.

The order in which the functions are chained together is not significant and as such they can be chained to getter using result.onSuccess{}.onFailure{} or result.OnFailure{}.onSuccess{}.

Within both function blocks the variable it is used to represent the information supplied. For the onFailure{} block it represents the exception that was thrown. In the onSuccess{} block it represents the result generated by the runCatching{} block.

An example of using onSuccess and onFailure is given below:

runCatching {

"32a".toInt()

}.onFailure { when (it) { is NumberFormatException -> { print("Oops - number wasn't formatted correctly: ") println(**it**.message)

} is Exception -> { println("some other exception") **it**.printStackTrace()

} else -> throw **it**

}

}.onSuccess {

println("All went well") println(**it**) **}**

The onSuccess block will print out a message and the value generated.

The onFailure block will use a when expression to check the type of the exception. Depending upon the exception type, different message is printed out. If the issue is not a NumberFormatException or any type of Exception (it must then be an Error) it is thrown out of the runCatching{}.onFailure{].onSuccess{} chain.

The output from this code is:

Oops - number wasn't formatted correctly: For input string: "32a"

This is quiet a common functional style of exception handling.

Exercises

This exercise involves adding error handling support to the Current Account class.

In the Current Account class, it should not be possible to withdraw or deposit a negative amount.

Define an exception/error class called Amount Exception. The Amount Exception should take the account involved and an error message as parameters.

Next update the deposit() and withdraw() member functions on the Account and Current Account classes to throw an Amount Exception if the amount supplied is negative. You should be able to test this using:

try {

acc1.deposit(-1.0)

} **catch** (exp: AmountException) { exp.printStackTrace() }

This should result in the exception stack trace being printed out, for example:

fintech.accounts.AmountException: Cannot deposit negative amounts

at

fintech.accounts.AbstractAccount.deposit(AbstractAccount.kt:71)

at fintech.main.MainKt.main(Main.kt:23) at fintech.main.MainKt.main(Main.kt)

Next modify the class such that if an attempt is made to withdraw money which will take the balance below the overdraft limit threshold a Balance Exception is thrown. This is again an application specific or custom exception that you can define.

The Balance Exception should hold information on the account that generated the error.

This means that you can refactor the withdraw() member function in the Current Account so that it does not print a message out to the user and it does not return a default zero transaction. Instead, it throws the Balance Exception which is a more explicit representation of the situation. The Balance Exception can take the same message string as was previously printed out, for example: **if** (amount < 0) {

throw AmountException("Cannot deposit negative amounts")

}

Test your code by creating instances of Current Account and taking the balance below the overdraft limit.

You should see something similar to:

Exception in thread "main" fintech.accounts.BalanceException:

Withdrawal would exceed your overdraft limit at

fintech.accounts.CurrentAccount.withdraw(AbstractAccount.kt:101)

at fintech.main.MainKt.main(Main.kt:23) at fintech.main.MainKt.main(Main.kt)

Write code that will use try and catch blocks to catch the exception you have defined.

You should be able to add the following to your test application: **try** {

println("balance: ${acc1.balance}") acc1.withdraw(300.00)

print("balance: ${acc1.balance}")

} **catch** (exp: BalanceException) { println("Handling Exception") println("Problem occurred on account: ${exp.acc}") }

The output from this is:

Handling Exception

Problem occurred on account: CurrentAccount('123', 'Customer(name=John, address=10 High Street, email=john@gmail.com)', 21.17) - overdraft -100.0

Extension Functions and Properties

Introduction

In this chapter we will look at both Extension Functions and Extension Properties as well as Infix Extension Operators.

Such extensions are extensions to existing types either to provide additional functionality, to meet some library or framework requirements or just to make the type they are applied to easy to use in Kotlin.

Extensions

Kotlin provides the ability to extend a type with new behaviour without having to modify that type or inherit from the type or to wrap that type etc. This is done via special declarations called extensions.

This means that in Kotlin a type such as a class can have its behaviour and data extended even when:

- The type is closed or final and thus cannot normally be extended.

- When you do not have access to the source code and thus cannot change the type. • The additional functionality or data is only required in one or a small number of situations and you do not wish to pollute the interface for the type in the general case.

- You want to extend the behaviour or data of a built-in type without modifying that type.

Extensions can provide these additional features (sometimes also known as the pimp my type design pattern).

There are three types of extension:

- extension functions that add functionality,

- extension properties that add data,

- infix extension operators that add additional named operators.

Each of these will be discussed in the remainder of this chapter.

Extension Functions

An extension function is a member function defined outside the scope of a type. It is defined using the syntax: **fun** <Type>.<Extension Function Name>() { … function body … } Or using the shorthand form:

fun <Type>.<Extension Function Name>() = expression

Forexample,toaddadditionalbehaviourtothebuilt-inclosed/final classString we can write:

fun String.hasLength(len: Int) = this.length == len

fun String.mult(len: Int): String { var result: String = "" for (i in 0..len) { result += this

} return result }

This add the member functions hasLength(Int) and mult(Int) to the class String.

We can now use this new functionality in our own programs:

```
fun main() {
val s = "John"
println("s.hasLength(4): ${s.hasLength(4)}") println("-".mult(25))
}
```

The output from this is:

s.hasLength(4): true -------------------------

It therefore appears that the String class supports this behaviour. Of course, if you look at the documentation for the class String you will not find these member functions listed. Indeed if you do not define these extension functions in your own code you will find that the above main() function will not even compile.

This illustrates the way in which extension functions add behaviour to an existing type.

Extension Properties

An extension property is a property defined outside the scope of a type. An extension property is defined using the syntax:

Val <Type>.<Extension Property Name> get() { ... function body ... }

And for a var it can be defined as:

Var <Type>.<Extension Property Name> get() { ... function body ... } set(value) { ... function body ... }

For example, to add additional properties to the built in closed/final class String we can write: **val String.size** get() = this.length

This will define a new property size on the class String. The read-only (val) property size has a get() function that uses the length property already defined on the class String to generate the size of the String.

We can therefore now write:

```
fun main() { val s = "John" println("s.size: ${s.size}")
} This generates the output:
```

s.size: 4

It is also possible to define a read–write property, however the set() function cannot introduce a backing field for the property; it is therefore necessary to access existing properties or handle the state in some other way. For example, given the class Person:

```
class Person(var name: String = "",
val age: Int = 0) {
override fun toString() = "Person($name, $age)"
}
```

We can define a read–write extension property that uses the existing var name property to get and set the property tag:

```
Var Person.tag get() = name
set(value) { name = value }
```

We can now use this new read–write tag property in our applications as an alias for the name property:

```
fun main() {
val p = Person("John", 21) println(p.tag)
p.tag = "Bob" println("p: $p")
}
```

The output generated by this program is:

```
John p: Person(Bob, 21)
```

Infix Extension Operators

It is also possible to add named infix extension operators. These are infix operators that are defined outside the scope of a given type using the syntax:

```
infix fun <Type>.<operator name>() {
… operator function body … }
```

For example, to add a new named infix operator to the closed class String we could write:

```
infix fun String.m(len: Int): String { var result: String = "" for (i in 0..len) { result += this
} return result
}
```

This adds a new operator 'm' to the class String (which represents the ability to multiple the string a specific number of times).

We can now use this in our own applications as shown below:

```
fun main() {
// Infix operator example println("-" m 25) // same as println("-".m(25))
}
```

Not that this illustrates that the infix operator extension function can be called using traditional member function syntax or using operator syntax.

The output from the above program is:

```
--------------------------

--------------------------
```

Extensions Scope

It is possible to encapsulate extensions within a class or an object. In this case the extension is only available within the scope of the class or the object. This limits the availability of the extension but also limits the extent to which the interface to the type is polluted by the extensions within the code.

To define an extension function for the class String which is limited to the class MyClass you can define new member level functions that follow the synt:ax. **class** <classname> { **fun** <TypeToExtend>.<function-name>() { … function body … } }

For example:

```kotlin
class MyClass {

// Extension function for a String // But only accessible from within class fun String.rev(): String { return this.reversed()

}

fun printMe(s: String) { println(s.rev())

} }
```

The extension function rev for the class String is only accessible from within the class MyClass. Thus the member function printMe() can access rev() on a String but code outside of the class cannot. We can do a similar thing with objects, for example:

```kotlin
object MyObject { fun String.rev(): String { return this.reversed()

}

fun printMe(s: String) { println(s.rev())

} }
```

Conclusion to Error & Exception Handling, and Extension Functions & Properties

Error and Exception Handling

Error and exception handling are critical components of modern application development, and Kotlin provides a robust framework to manage these effectively. By leveraging Kotlin's features, developers can ensure that their applications are resilient, maintainable, and less prone to unforeseen runtime failures.

Kotlin's try-catch-finally structure forms the backbone of its exception handling mechanism. By encapsulating risky operations within try blocks and handling exceptions in corresponding catch blocks, developers can ensure proper handling of runtime anomalies without crashing the application. Moreover, the optional finally block offers a clean way to perform resource cleanup, making code more reliable and organized. For instance, file operations and database connections can be gracefully terminated, avoiding resource leaks.

One of the standout features of Kotlin is its null safety, which significantly reduces the occurrence of NullPointerException (NPE). With nullable types and the Elvis operator (?:), Kotlin empowers developers to handle potential nullability issues upfront, promoting safer and more predictable code. Combined with the let function and safe call operator (?.), Kotlin's null safety tools ensure that developers can work with nullable values elegantly without cluttering their code with verbose null checks.

Kotlin also provides the ability to create custom exceptions using user-defined exception classes. By extending the Exception class, developers can model domain-specific error scenarios, making debugging and error tracking more intuitive. These custom exceptions allow for more granular handling of errors that are specific to the application's context.

Another significant feature is Kotlin's support for functional error handling via the Result type. By encapsulating success and failure states in a single construct, Result enables developers to handle operations in a functional and expressive manner. This approach not only makes error handling more declarative but also reduces the reliance on traditional exception mechanisms, improving performance and readability.

Coroutine exception handling is another powerful capability of Kotlin. Since coroutines are a cornerstone of asynchronous programming in Kotlin, managing exceptions within coroutines is essential. Kotlin's Coroutine Exception Handler provides a structured way to handle uncaught exceptions, ensuring that coroutine-based code is robust and resilient to errors. Additionally, structured concurrency ensures that errors within child coroutines do not propagate silently, enabling developers to maintain better control over their asynchronous workflows.

To sum up, Kotlin's error and exception handling mechanisms provide a comprehensive toolkit for managing runtime anomalies. By combining traditional exception handling, functional constructs like Result, and coroutine-specific tools, Kotlin equips developers with the means to write safer, more reliable code. This focus on safety and expressiveness is a testament to Kotlin's commitment to enhancing developer productivity and application quality.

Extension Functions and Properties

Kotlin's extension functions and properties represent one of its most innovative and practical features, enabling developers to add new functionality to existing classes without altering their source code. This capability is a cornerstone of Kotlin's design philosophy, promoting extensibility, readability, and maintainability.

Extension Functions

Extension functions allow developers to augment classes with new behaviors while keeping the original class definition intact. By using the fun keyword followed by the receiver type, developers can add functionality to existing classes in a seamless manner. For example, adding a utility function to format a String or calculating the square of an Int can be done effortlessly through extension functions:

```
fun Int.square(): Int = this * this
```

```
fun String.capitalizeWords(): String = this.split(" ").joinToString(" ") { it.capitalize() }
```

These extensions enhance code readability and usability by allowing operations to be invoked directly on the target objects, resulting in a more natural syntax. This approach reduces the need for utility classes and global helper methods, keeping the codebase cleaner and more modular.

One of the most significant advantages of extension functions is their ability to work seamlessly with third-party libraries. Developers can augment library classes with custom functionality without modifying the original library code. This feature is particularly useful in scenarios where developers need to adapt third-party APIs to their specific use cases.

Kotlin's extension functions are also instrumental in building domain-specific languages (DSLs). By defining intuitive and expressive extensions, developers can create DSLs that cater to specific business requirements, making the code more self-explanatory and aligned with the domain.

Extension Properties

Extension properties complement extension functions by allowing developers to define additional properties for existing classes. These properties are essentially getter (and optionally setter) methods defined in an extension context. For example, developers can create a computed property to calculate the area of a rectangle or a read-only property to format a Date:

```
val Int.isEven: Boolean
    get() = this % 2 == 0
```

```
val String.wordCount: Int
    get() = this.split(" ").size
```

Extension properties follow the same principles as extension functions, allowing for seamless augmentation of existing classes without modifying their original structure. By using these properties, developers can encapsulate logic in a concise and reusable manner, improving code clarity and maintainability.

Limitations of Extensions

While extension functions and properties are powerful, they come with certain limitations that developers must be aware of. Extensions cannot override existing methods or properties, ensuring that they do not inadvertently alter the original behavior of the classes. This restriction safeguards the integrity of the underlying class implementations.

Additionally, extensions are statically resolved, meaning that their behavior is determined at compile-time based on the declared type of the receiver. This static resolution can lead to unexpected behavior when dealing with polymorphism. Developers need to exercise caution when using extensions with inheritance hierarchies to avoid confusion.

Best Practices for Extensions

To maximize the benefits of extension functions and properties, developers should adhere to the following best practices:

1. **Contextual Relevance:** Extensions should be used to add functionality that is contextually relevant to the receiver type. Avoid adding unrelated or out-of-scope extensions that can confuse other developers.

2. **Keep Extensions Minimal:** Extensions should be concise and focused. Overloading classes with too many extensions can lead to clutter and reduced readability.

3. **Avoid Name Collisions:** Use descriptive names for extensions to prevent name collisions with existing methods or other extensions.

4. **Document Extensions:** Clearly document the purpose and usage of extensions, especially when they are part of shared libraries or APIs.

5. **Use Extensions Judiciously:** While extensions are a powerful tool, they should not be overused. Evaluate whether an extension is the most appropriate solution for a given problem.

Real-World Applications

Extension functions and properties find wide application in various domains, from utility functions and API customization to DSL design and framework development. For example:

- **Android Development:** Adding custom behaviors to View classes, such as View.gone() and View.visible(), enhances UI management.

- **Web Development:** Simplifying API interactions with custom extensions for HttpClient or JSON parsing libraries.

- **Testing Frameworks:** Creating extensions for test assertions to improve test readability and maintainability.

Conclusion

Error and exception handling, along with extension functions and properties, are indispensable features of Kotlin that elevate its status as a modern, developer-friendly language. The former ensures robust and resilient applications by providing comprehensive mechanisms to handle runtime anomalies. The latter promotes extensibility and code reuse, enabling developers to write cleaner, more expressive, and maintainable code.

Together, these features embody Kotlin's philosophy of safety, expressiveness, and simplicity. By embracing these capabilities, developers can build applications that are not only functional but also elegant and future-proof. As Kotlin continues to evolve, its commitment to empowering developers with innovative tools and constructs reaffirms its position as a leading language for modern software development.

5. Coroutines and Concurrency

Introduction

In this chapter we will introduce Kotlin coroutines. We will first discuss asynchronous programming/concurrency in computer programs. We will then consider threading which is the underlying mechanism used to support concurrency in programs running on the JVM including Kotlin. We will then discuss why threading is too low a level for many applications and introduce Coroutines as the Kotlin higher level solution to concurrency.

In the realm of modern software development, efficient handling of concurrent tasks is crucial for building responsive and scalable applications. Kotlin, a versatile programming language known for its conciseness and interoperability with Java, introduces a powerful feature called coroutines. Coroutines simplify asynchronous programming by providing a structured way to write non-blocking code that looks like traditional sequential code.

What are Coroutines?

Coroutines in Kotlin are lightweight threads that enable developers to write asynchronous code sequentially. Unlike traditional threads, coroutines are not bound to any particular thread, making them highly efficient for concurrency tasks. They allow developers to execute long-running tasks asynchronously without blocking the main thread, thereby improving the responsiveness of applications.

Key Concepts of Coroutines:

1. **Coroutine Builders**: Kotlin provides several coroutine builders like launch, async, and runBlocking to create and manage coroutines.

2. **Coroutine Context and Dispatchers**: Coroutines execute within a CoroutineContext, which defines the coroutine's behavior, such as which thread or thread pool it runs on. Dispatchers facilitate switching between different threads or thread pools.

3. **Suspending Functions**: Suspending functions are the building blocks of coroutines. They can be paused and resumed later without blocking the thread, using suspend keyword.

4. **Coroutine Scope**: Defines the lifecycle of coroutines and manages their cancellation when they are no longer needed.

Concurrency in Kotlin

Concurrency in Kotlin revolves around the effective use of coroutines to achieve parallelism and responsiveness in applications. Kotlin provides robust support for concurrent programming through its coroutine-based approach.

Practical Applications of Coroutines and Concurrency:

1. **Asynchronous Operations**: Coroutines are ideal for handling asynchronous operations such as network requests, database queries, and file I/O without blocking the main thread.

2. **Parallelism**: Using async and await, coroutines can execute multiple tasks concurrently, aggregating results efficiently.

3. **UI Thread Management**: Coroutines help manage background tasks while keeping the UI thread responsive by offloading heavy computations.

4. **Reactive Programming**: Kotlin coroutines integrate well with reactive programming libraries like RxJava and Kotlin Flow, enabling reactive streams of data.

Getting Started with Coroutines

To begin using coroutines in Kotlin, you typically:

- **Import the necessary libraries**: Add Kotlin coroutines dependencies to your project.
- **Define suspending functions**: Create functions that perform asynchronous operations using the suspend keyword.
- **Launch coroutines**: Use coroutine builders like launch or async to execute suspending functions concurrently.

Advanced Concepts

Coroutine Channels:

Coroutine channels facilitate communication and data transfer between coroutines in a structured manner, akin to reactive streams.

Coroutine Context and Dispatchers:

Understanding different dispatchers (Dispatchers.Default, Dispatchers.IO, Dispatchers.Main, etc.) helps optimize coroutine execution based on specific tasks and resource requirements.

Coroutine Scopes and Structured Concurrency:

Managing coroutine lifecycles and ensuring structured concurrency prevents leaks and unintended behavior.

Best Practices

- **Use structured concurrency**: Always launch coroutines within a defined scope to manage their lifecycle and ensure proper cancellation.
- **Avoid blocking operations**: Leverage suspending functions and appropriate dispatchers to keep coroutines non-blocking.
- **Error Handling**: Use try/catch blocks within coroutines to handle exceptions gracefully and prevent application crashes.

Concurrency

Concurrency is defined by the dictionary as. two or more events or circumstances happening or existing at the same time.

In Computer Science concurrency refers to the ability of different parts or units of a program, algorithm or problem to be executed at the same time, potentially on multiple processors or multiple cores.

Here a processor refers to the central processing unit (or CPU) of a computer while core refers to the idea that a CPU chip can have multiple cores or processors on it.

Originally a CPU chip had a single core. That is the CPU chip had a single processing unit on it. However, over time, to increase computer performance hardware manufacturers added additional cores or processing units to chips. Thus, a dual-core CPU chip has two processing units while a quad-core CPU chip has four processing units. This means that as far as the operating system of the computer is concerned, it has multiple CPUs on which it can run programs.

Running processing at the same time, on multiple CPUs, can substantially improve the overall performance of an application.

For example, let us assume that we have a program that will call three independent functions, these functions are:

Make a backup of the current data held by the program, print the data currently held by the program, run an animation using the current data.

Let us assume that these functions run sequentially, with the following timings:

The backup function takes 13 s, the print function takes 15 s, the animation function takes 10 s.

This would result in a total of 38 s to perform all three operations. This is illustrated graphically below:

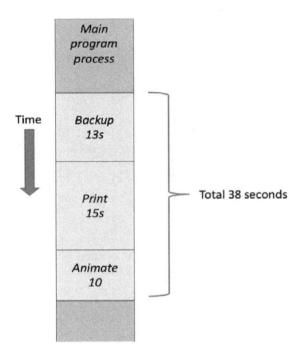

However, the three functions are all completely independent of each other. That is, they do not rely on each other for any results or behaviour; they do not need one of the other functions to complete before they can complete etc. Thus, we can run each function concurrently.

If the underlying operating system and program language being used support multiple processes, then we can potentially run each function in a separate process at the same time and obtain a significant speed up in overall execution time.

If the application starts all three functions at the same time, then the maximum time before the main process can continue will be 15 s, as that is the time taken by the longest function to execute. However, the main program may be able to continue as soon as all three functions are started as it also does not depend on the results from any of the functions; thus, the delay may be negligible (although there will typically be some small delay as each process is set up). This is shown graphically below:

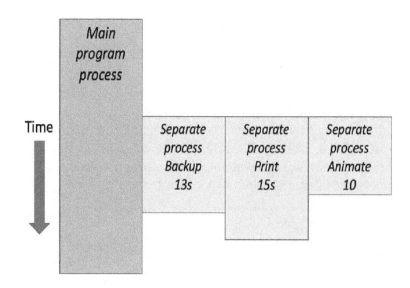

Parallelism

A distinction its often made in Computer Science between concurrency and parallelism.

In concurrency, separate independent tasks are performed potentially at the same time.

In parallelism, a large complex task is broken down into a set of subtasks. The subtasks represent part of the overall problem. Each subtask can be executed at the same time. Typically, it is necessary to combine the results of the subtasks together to generate an overall result. These subtasks are also very similar if not functionally exactly the same (although in general each subtask invocation will have been supplied with different data/parameters).

Thus, parallelism is when multiple copies of the same functionality are run at the same time, but on different data.

Some examples of where parallelism can be applied include:

A web search engine. Such a system may look at many, many web pages. Each time it does so it must send a request to the appropriate web site, receive the result and process the data obtained. These steps are the same whether it is the BBC web site, Microsoft's web site or the web site of Cambridge University. Thus, the requests can be run sequentially or in parallel.

Image Processing. A large image may be broken down into slices so that each slice can be analysed in parallel.

Threads

For any JVM language, including Kotlin, the Thread class represents an activity that is run in a separate thread of execution within a single process. These threads of execution are lightweight, pre-emptive execution threads. A thread is a lightweight process because it does not possess its own address space and it is not treated as a separate entity by the host operating system; it is not a separate operating system process.

Instead, it exists within a single machine process using the same address space as other threads.

Threads are a very well-established technology; however, they provide fairly low-level concurrency features.

The Problems with Threads

There are several issues associated with the direct use of Threads to implement concurrency, including:

Threads represent a low-level API for concurrency.

Threads are expensive in terms of CPU and System overheads.

Threads are expensive to create, schedule and destroy.

A thread may spend a lot of time waiting for Input/Output actions.

A thread may spend a lot of time waiting for results produced by other treads. Even when threads are run natively by the operating system, there are issues such as: in practice the number of threads that can run at the same time (concurrently) is limited by the number of CPUs/cores available, if your program requires more threads than there are cores then some form of scheduler is required to coordinate the execution of the threads on the cores.

Coroutines are a Kotlin specific, lighter weight alternative to the JVM based Threading model. They are an abstraction layer on top of threads and thus at runtime it is still threads that execute the coroutine code for you. However, this is now done in an efficient manner, with the reuse of threads via a pool of reusable threads (referred to as a Thread Pool) and by sharing threads between coroutines.

A Thread can be shared between coroutines whenever a coroutine needs to wait for some reason (for example for some input/output operations need to be performed). This means that rather than blocking a Thread during such waits, other coroutines can make used of the Thread instead. This means coroutines use Threads in a much more efficient manner than would be the case just from directly executing behaviour within an individual Thread.

To summarise the Coroutine to Thread relationship we can say:

coroutines are assigned to threads. The thread will then execute the coroutine for you.

When an active coroutine is suspended, for example when waiting for input/output operations such as waiting for a database system to respond, then:

The state of the coroutine is saved by the Kotlin runtime.

The coroutine is removed from the Thread that is executing it.

Another coroutine can then be assigned to the Thread.

When the original coroutine is resumed, it is assigned to the next free thread which may be a different Thread from that previously executing it.

In this way a limited number of threads can support a larger number of coroutines.

If you are confused by all this think of coroutines as a task that can be performed by a thread, however a thread can switch between tasks if the task is waiting for something to happen.

Working with Coroutines

Adding Coroutine Library Dependencies

Coroutines are not by default apart of the Kotlin environment, as such it is necessary to add the Kotlin Coroutine library to your project. In IntelliJ IDE you can do this by adding the coroutines library directly to your project (see the IntelliJ documentation for more details as this may change between versions—https://www.jetbrains.com/help/idea/library.html).

Once you have done this you can start to use the Coroutine library in your code.

Implementing a Coroutine

Coroutines can be defined using a implicit lambda function or as a named function that is marked with the keyword suspend.

A suspend(ing) function is one that can be run by the Kotlin coroutine execution/runtime but that can be suspended (without suspending the underlying thread) and can be resumed at a later point in time when the reason for its suspension has been met (for example if the coroutine is waiting for some response from a RESTful service or a database management system etc.).

This means that when we run a coroutine we need to launch that coroutine via the coroutine runtime and provide either a lambda or a suspending function.

Launching Coroutines

To use the coroutines library in Kotlin you will need to import seam or all of the contents of the kotlin.coroutines package. In the following program we import three elements from this package, the Global Scope, the delay function and the launch function, for example:

```
import kotlinx.coroutines.GlobalScope
import kotlinx.coroutines.delay
import kotlinx.coroutines.launch
```

To start a coroutine we need to launch it, this can be done using the coroutine builder GlobalScope.launch{}. This allows a coroutine to be started on a separate thread (to the main application). We will return to the term scope with respect to coroutines below.

The GlobalScope.launch{} launcher implements a fire and forget policy that will start an asynchronous task/coroutine which will run to completion. That is there is no result returned to the main thread in which the application runs nor is there any interaction between the task and the main application hence the term fire (off the task) and forget (about it in the main program).

The following program launches a simple coroutine using a lambda function passed to the launch member function (using the trailing lambda syntax). The coroutine prints out a message and then sleeps for 5,000 ms using the delay() function. This function delays/sleeps a coroutine for a given amount of time without blocking the underlying thread and resumes the coroutine after a specified time (potentially in another thread):

```kotlin
import kotlinx.coroutines.GlobalScope
import kotlinx.coroutines.delay
import kotlinx.coroutines.launch

fun main() {

    println("Main -> Launching fire-and-forget task")

    GlobalScope.launch {
        println("coroutine ---> Starting Task")
        delay(5000)
        println("coroutine ---> Done Task")
    }
    println("-------------------------------")
    println("Main -> After launching coroutine")
    println("Main -> Waiting for task - press enter to
continue:")
    readLine()
    println("-------------------------------")
    println("Main -> Done")
}
```

The main() function prints out a message after the coroutine is launched and then asks the user for input so that the main program does not terminate. This is necessary as the launcher runs the coroutine in a background thread. On the JVM, programs automatically terminate when there are no more foreground threads to execute, as this coroutine runs in the background this is not sufficient to stop the program terminating, thus we cause the main application thread (which is a foreground thread) to wait for user input. The output from this coroutine program is:

```
Main -> Launching fire-and-forget task
-------------------------------
Main -> After launching coroutine
Main -> Waiting for task - press enter to continue:
coroutine ---> Starting Task
coroutine ---> Done Task


-------------------------------
Main -> Done
```

Note that the output from the main application thread (the lines prefixed with 'Main ->' are intertwined with the output from the coroutine running in the background thread.

Suspending Functions

We can define a named function to run as the coroutine task by prefixing the function definition with the keyword suspend. For example:

```
import kotlinx.coroutines.delay

suspend fun executeSlowTask() {
        println("Starting Task")
        delay(5000)
        println("Done Task")
}
```

Such a function is known as a suspending function. A suspending function may suspend the execution of the current coroutine without blocking the underlying thread.

This means that the executeSlowTask() function can cause a coroutine to be suspended when it reaches the delay() function. The function can then cause the coroutine to resume when the delay is completed. Of course, the thread that is initially executing the coroutine may or may not be the same thread as is used to resume the coroutine.

The following code illustrates how the executeSlowTask() suspending function can be run within a coroutine using the GloabalScope.launch{} launcher.

```
import kotlinx.coroutines.GlobalScope
import kotlinx.coroutines.launch

fun main() {

    println("Main -> Launching fire-and-forget task")

    GlobalScope.launch {
        executeSlowTask()
    }
    println("--------------------------------")
    println("Main -> After launching coroutine")
    println("Main -> Waiting for task - press enter to

continue:")
    readLine()
    println("--------------------------------")
    println("Main -> Done")
}
```

The output from this second version of the program is given below:

```
Main -> Launching fire-and-forget task
---------------------------------
Main -> After launching coroutine
Main -> Waiting for task - press enter to continue:
executeSlowTask -> Starting Task
executeSlowTask ->Done Task


---------------------------------
Main -> Done
```

As before you can see that the output from the main application (running in the main Thread) is interspersed with the output from the suspending function executeSlowTask() running in a background thread.

Running Multiple Concurrent Coroutines

It is possible to run multiple coroutines concurrently. This can be done by launching each coroutine independently, for example:

```
GlobalScope.launch { executeSlowTask1() }
GlobalScope.launch { executeSlowTask2() }
GlobalScope.launch { executeSlowTask3() }
```

This would cause the three slow tasks to run concurrently.

Coroutine Scope

When a coroutine is launched, it is actually launched within the context of a coroutine scope.

In the examples presented in the previous sections we have been using the GlobalScope. This means that the lifetime of the coroutine being launched is limited only by the lifetime of the whole application. That is the scope of the coroutine, in terms of where and how long it can execute, is the same as the top level (or global) application.

Custom Coroutine Scope

There are other alternatives to the global scope for coroutines. One option is to create a custom   scope. This allows an application to manage a group of coroutines together. For example, the application can then cancel all coroutines with the same scope in one go if required.

Custom scopes are built on top of a Coroutine Dispatcher. A Coroutine Dispatcher is the part of the coroutine runtime that handles how coroutines are executed and is discussed in the next section.

A new custom scope can be created by instantiating a Coroutine Scope instance and passing in a suitable dispatcher, for example:

```
val customScope = CoroutineScope(Dispatchers.Main)
```

This can then be used with the launch() function, to launch a coroutine within a specific scope, for example:

```
val customScope = CoroutineScope(Dispatchers.Main)
customScope.launch {
    executeSlowTask()
}
```

Coroutine Dispatchers

Coroutine Dispatches handle how coroutines are run (dispatched). That is, they handle how coroutines are assigned to JVM Threads. They also handle how coroutines are suspended (which stops them running and unloads them from a particular thread) and how they are resumed (how they are reassigned to an available thread).

There are three built-in dispatchers:

Dispatchers.Default This is the default dispatcher and is intended primarily for CPU intensive tasks. Dispatchers.IO This is the dispatcher that is recommended for network, disk, database or other IO operations.

Dispatchers.Main (Android specific) This is the dispatcher used to run coroutines on the main Android thread. This is significant as it allows a coroutine to make changes to UI components within an Android application.

Coroutine Builders/Launchers

Coroutine Builders/Launchers are used to dispatch (start) a coroutine within a particular scope.

There are several built-in coroutine builders/launchers including:

launch{} starts a coroutine that does not return a result. It is sometimes referred to as a fire and forget coroutine. It can be used to launch a lambda or suspending function from within a normal function.

async{} allows the caller thread to wait for a result generated by another coroutine using await() function. It can only be called from within another suspending function. It returns a Deferred < T > instance – which promises to return a result. The result must be returned from the invoked coroutine using return@async.

withContext{} allows a coroutine to be launched with a different dispatcher context from that used by the parent coroutine. For example, to switch from the Default Dispatcher to the IO dispatcher.

coroutineScope{} used to allow multiple coroutines to be launched in parallel and for some behaviour to execute once all coroutines complete. It can only be launched from within a suspend function. If one (child) coroutine fails then all the coroutines fail.

supervisorScope{} this is similar to coroutineScope{}, but failure of a child coroutine does not cause all child coroutines to fail.

runBlocking{} starts a coroutine and blocks the current thread. This is usually only used for testing. withTimeout(millseconds){} runs the associated coroutine. However, the launched coroutine must complete within the specified time.

An example of a coroutine that returns a result using the async{} launcher and the GloabalScope is given below:

```
suspend fun executeSlowTaskWithResultAsync(): Deferred<Int> =
    GlobalScope.async {
        println("executeSlowTaskWithResultAsync --> Starting
Task")
        delay(5000)
        println("executeSlowTaskWithResultAsync --> Done Task")
        return@async 42
    }
```

Note that the return type of the GlobalScope.async{} is Deferred < Int > in the above suspending function. This is used as the return result for the whole function and indicates that this function will return a result asynchronously. It also indicates that the deferred result will be an Int. It then uses return@async to return the integer 42.

This suspending function can be invoked from the main application as shown below:

```
fun main() {
    println("Main -> Launching deferred result task")
    GlobalScope.launch {
        val result = executeSlowTaskWithResultAsync().await()
        println("coroutine --> result: $result")
    }
    println("Main -> After launching coroutine")
    println("Main -> Waiting for task - press enter to
continue:")
    readLine()
    println("Main -> Done")
}
```

The output from this program is:

```
Main -> Launching deferred result task
Main -> After launching coroutine
Main -> Waiting for task - press enter to continue:
executeSlowTaskWithResultAsync --> Starting Task
executeSlowTaskWithResultAsync --> Done Task
coroutine --> result: 42

Main -> Done
```

As you can see from this the result is returned from the executeSlowTaskWithResult() suspending function. The main launcher waits for this result using the await() member function of a suspending function.

As an example of the withContext{} launcher the following code illustrates running a coroutine using a different dispatcher:

```
suspend fun performTask() {
    println("Task 1: ${Thread.currentThread().name}")
}
```

```
suspend fun startWork() {
    println("startWork")
    withContext(Dispatchers.IO){performTask2()}
    println("end startWork")

}
```

Coroutine Jobs

Each call to a launcher such as launch{}, async{} etc. returns a Job instance. These jobs are instances of the kotlinx.coroutines.Job class. Jobs can be used to track and manage the lifecycle of coroutines. In turn calls to coroutines within a coroutine result in child jobs.

Once you have a reference to a coroutine job you can cancel a job. If the associated coroutine has children then you can also cancel child jobs.

The status of the associated coroutine can also be obtained from a job using Boolean properties such as isActive, isCompleted and isCancelled.

There are also a range of member functions defined for jobs including:

invokeOnCompletion{} this is used to provide behaviour to run when job completed, join() which suspends the current coroutine until the receiver coroutine completes,

cancel(CalcellationException?) which cancels a job, cancelChildren() which cancels child jobs of a receiver job, cancelAndJoin() cancel the receiving coroutine and wait for it to complete before continuing.

The following program illustrate some of these ideas. It creates a new coroutine using the

GlobalScope.launch{} launcher and stores the resulting job reference in the val job. It then uses this job to check to see if it is still active, whether it has completed, has it been cancelled and whether it has any child jobs or not. It also registers a callback lambda to be invoked when the job completes:

```
import kotlinx.coroutines.GlobalScope
import kotlinx.coroutines.launch

fun main() {
    println("Launching fire-and-forget task")
    val job = GlobalScope.launch {
        executeSlowTask()
    }
    println("After launching coroutine")
    println("job.isActive: ${job.isActive}")
    println("job.isCompleted: ${job.isCompleted}")
    println("job.isCancelled: ${job.isCancelled}")
    println("job.children.count(): ${job.children.count()}")
    job.invokeOnCompletion { println("I am Completed") }

        println("Waiting for task - press enter to continue:")
        readLine()
        println("Done")
}
```

The output from this program is:

```
Launching fire-and-forget task
After launching coroutine
job.isActive: true
job.isCompleted: false
job.isCancelled: false
executeSlowTask -> Starting Task
job.children.count(): 0
Waiting for task - press enter to continue:
executeSlowTask ->Done Task
I am Completed

Done
```

As can be seen from this output the job is still active, has not been completed or cancelled, has zero child jobs etc. It also calls the on-completion callback after the task completes.

Exercise

In this exercise you will create a suspending function and run several coroutines concurrently. Create a suspending function called printer() that takes three parameters:

a message to be printed out, a maximum value to use for a period to sleep, the number of times that the message should be printed.

Within the function create a loop that iterates the number of times indicated by the third parameter. Within the loop.

generate a random number from 0 to the max period specified and then sleep for that period of time. You can use the Random.nextLong(0, sleep) function for this,

once the sleep period has finished print out the message passed into the function, then loop again until this has been repeated the number of times specified by the final parameter.

Next run the printer() function with various different parameters. Each execution of the suspending function printer() should be launched independently using the Global Scope.

An example program to concurrently run the printer() function five times is given below:

```
import kotlin.random.Random
import kotlinx.coroutines.delay
import kotlinx.coroutines.GlobalScope
import kotlinx.coroutines.launch

fun main() {
    println("Main -> Launching fire-and-forget tasks")
    GlobalScope.launch { printer("A", 100, 10) }
    GlobalScope.launch { printer("B", 200, 5) }
    GlobalScope.launch { printer("C", 50, 15) }
    GlobalScope.launch { printer("D", 30, 7) }
    GlobalScope.launch { printer("E", 75, 12) }
    println("--------------------------------")
    println("Main -> After launching coroutine")
    println("Main -> Waiting for task - press enter to
continue:")
    readLine()
    println("--------------------------------")
    println("Main -> Done")
}
```

An example of the sort of output this could generate is given below:

```
1.  Main -> Launching fire-and-forget tasks
2.  --------------------------------
3.  Main -> After launching coroutine
4.  Main -> Waiting for task - press enter to continue:
5.  C, B, E, D, A, D, A, C, A, D, C, D, C, D, C, E, C, D, A, D,
    E, C, E, C, A, C, B, A, E, E, E, C, C, A, E, E, A, C, B, E,
    C, A, E, C, E, A, C, B, B,
6.  --------------------------------
7.  Main -> Done
```

Coroutine Channel Communications

However, in many situations one coroutine needs to communication with one or more other coroutines. For example, one coroutine may be a producer of data and another coroutine (or coroutines) may be a consumer of that data.

In this chapter we will consider how channels provide for communications between coroutines, look at how multiple coroutines can send data to a channel and how multiple coroutines can receive data from channels. We will conclude by looking at buffered channels.

Coroutine Channels

Coroutine Channels provide for communications between coroutines. This differs from the use of deferred values between coroutines. A deferred value is a promise from one coroutine to another to supply a value at some point in the future. A channel allows for the transfer of a stream of data between two or more cooperating coroutines.

The idea behind channels is illustrated below:

To enable two coroutines to communicate you need to create a shared channel, have at least one coroutine that must send some data to the channel, have at least one other coroutine that must receive that data.

The terms send and receive above relate to the functions defined on a Channel. That is Channels have a suspending send   function and a suspending receive   function. This means that several coroutines can use channels to pass data to each other in a non-blocking fashion. Thus, you can have multiple senders and multiple receivers.

For example, to send data to a channel:

```
channel.send(data)
```

And to receive data from a channel:

```
val data = channel.receive()
```

It is also possible to close a channel to indicate that there will be no more data sent. A channel can be closed using the close() member function:

```
channel.close()
```

There are four types of channels, and they differ in the number of values they can hold at a time. These four are:

Rendezvous Channel used to coordinate the send and receive of messages.

Buffered Channel provides a predefined buffer that allows several messages to be sent before the channel blocks while waiting for receives to handle those messages.

Unlimited Buffered Channel provides for an unlimited size buffer so any number of messages can be sent without blocking the sending coroutine.

Conflated Channel When using this channel type, the most recent value overwrites any previous values sent but not yet received.

Examples of each of these types of channels will be given in the remainder of this section.

Note to use challenge we need to import the appropriate type form the kotlinx.coroutines.channels package.

Rendezvous Channel

A rendezvous channel is used to allow two or more coroutines to coordinate the sending and receiving of data. With a rendezvous channel the:

Sending coroutine suspends until a receiver coroutine invokes receive on the channel, consuming coroutine suspends until a producer coroutine invokes send on the channel.

A rendezvous channel does not have a buffer so only one value can be sent at a time.

A rendezvous channel is created using the default Channel constructor with no arguments, for example:

val channel = Channel<Int>()

Note that the Channel is a generic type and thus the type of data handled by the channel is specified when it is created. In the above example we are creating a channel that can handle integers, if we wanted to create a channel that could handle Strings then we would write:

val channel = Channel<String>()

An example of a program that creates a shared rendezvous channel used by two coroutines is given below.

```kotlin
import kotlinx.coroutines.GlobalScope
import kotlinx.coroutines.channels.Channel
import kotlinx.coroutines.delay
import kotlinx.coroutines.launch

fun main() {
    val channel = Channel<Int>() // Shared rendezvous Channel

    suspend fun sendDataToChannelTask() {
        repeat(3) {
            delay(100)
            println("Sending ---> $it")
            channel.send(it)
        }
    }

    suspend fun receiveDataFromChannelTask() {
        repeat(3) {
            println("Receiving ---> ${channel.receive()}")
        }
    }

    println("Main -> Launching rendezvous channel task")
    GlobalScope.launch { sendDataToChannelTask() }
    GlobalScope.launch { receiveDataFromChannelTask() }
    println("Main -> After launching coroutines")
    println("Main -> Waiting for tasks - press Enter to
Terminate:")
    readLine()
    channel.close()
    println("Main -> Done")
}
```

In the above program you can see the two functions:

sendDataToChannelTask() which is a suspending function that publishes three values with a 100 ms delay between each.

receiveDataFromChannelTask() which is a suspending function that receives each value but is blocked until a value is available.

The main() function launches both functions as coroutines and then waits for user input before terminating.

The output generated by this program is:

```
Main -> Launching rendezvous channel task
Main -> After launching coroutines
Main -> Waiting for tasks - press Enter to Terminate:
Sending ---> 0
Receiving ---> 0
Sending ---> 1
Receiving ---> 1
Sending ---> 2
Receiving ---> 2

Main -> Done
```

As can be seen from the output the sending and receiving coroutines coordinate their sending and receiving actions. That is, the receiving coroutine blocks until the sending coroutine publishes some data.

Buffered Channel

The Buffered Channel is a channel type that has a predefined buffer. The buffer size is specified when the Channel is created. For example, to create a Channel that can handle Int's and has a buffer of 10 integers you can write:

```
val channel = Channel<Int>(10)
```

This means that the publishing coroutine can send 10 integers to the channel before the send operation will block that coroutine.

A modified version of the program shown in the previous section is given below. It differs in three ways:

The channel created is now a shared buffered channel with a buffer of size 2.

The receiveDataFromChannelTask() suspending function has an initial delay of 50 ms before it enters a while loop that will allow it to continue processing data while there is data available.

Inside the wile loop of the receiveDataFromChannelTask() suspending function a further delay of 100 ms has been used to ensure that the receiver has to wait between reads. This means that the sending coroutine will always run ahead of the receiving coroutine and thus the sender will be able to send up to 2 values into the buffered channel before it is blocked.

```kotlin
import kotlinx.coroutines.GlobalScope
import kotlinx.coroutines.channels.Channel
import kotlinx.coroutines.delay
import kotlinx.coroutines.launch

fun main() {
    val channel = Channel<Int>(2) // Shared Buffered Channel

    suspend fun sendDataToChannelTask() {
        repeat(5) {
            delay(50)
            println("Sending ---> $it")
            channel.send(it)
        }
    }

    suspend fun receiveDataFromChannelTask() {
        delay(500)
        while (true) {
            delay(100)
            println("Receiving ---> ${channel.receive()}")
        }
    }

    println("Main -> Launching Buffered channel task")
    GlobalScope.launch { sendDataToChannelTask() }
    GlobalScope.launch { receiveDataFromChannelTask() }
    println("Main -> After launching coroutines")
    println("Main -> Waiting for tasks - press Enter to
Terminate:")
    readLine()
    channel.close()
    println("Main -> Done")
}
```

The output from this program is:

```
Main -> Launching Buffered channel task
Main -> After launching coroutines
Main -> Waiting for tasks - press Enter to Terminate:
Sending ---> 0
Sending ---> 1
Sending ---> 2
Receiving ---> 0
Sending ---> 3
Receiving ---> 1
Sending ---> 4
Receiving ---> 2
Receiving ---> 3
Receiving ---> 4

Main -> Done
```

Looking at the output it is possible to see that when the sending coroutine send the 3rd value into the channel that it is blocked. It must then wait for the receiving coroutine to receive a value before it can send another value. This behaviour is repeated until the sending coroutine has sent all its values. The receiver can then read the remaining values held in the buffer.

Unlimited Buffered Channel

An unlimited buffered channel has an unlimited buffer size. Therefore, any number of messages can be sent without blocking the sending coroutine. The receiving coroutine will receive buffered data when it is ready to process that data.

The unlimited buffered channel may generate an OutOfMemoryError as the unlimited size of the buffer will allow it to fill up all available memory within the application runtime.

An Unlimited Buffered Channel is created by providing UNLIMITED as the constructor parameter when instantiating a Channel. For example:

```
import kotlinx.coroutines.channels.Channel.Factory.UNLIMITED

val channel = Channel<Int>(UNLIMITED)
```

If the previous program is modified merely by changing the channel to be the above and the program is rerun then the output generated is now:

```
Main -> Launching Unlimited channel task
Main -> After launching coroutines
Main -> Waiting for tasks - press Enter to Terminate:
Sending ---> 0
Sending ---> 1
Sending ---> 2
Sending ---> 3
Sending ---> 4
Receiving ---> 0
Receiving ---> 1
Receiving ---> 2
Receiving ---> 3
Receiving ---> 4

Main -> Done
```

As you can see from this the sending coroutine publishes all its data to the unlimited buffered channel before the receiver even starts processing that data.

Conflated Channel

A Conflated Channel will conflate published but as yet un read values. That is, the most recently written value overrides the previously written values that have not yet been received (read) by any coroutines. Thus:

they send member function of the channel never suspends, the receive member function receives only the latest value.

To create a Conflated Channel, you create a Channel and pass in the CONFLATED value to the constructor:

```
import kotlinx.coroutines.channels.Channel.Factory.CONFLATED

val channel = Channel<Int>(CONFLATED)
```

If we now modify the preceding program by changing the channel declaration to that used above and rerun it, then the output generated is:

```
Main -> Launching rendezvous channel task
Main -> After launching coroutines
Main -> Waiting for tasks - press Enter to Terminate:
Sending ---> 0
Sending ---> 1
Sending ---> 2
Sending ---> 3
Sending ---> 4
Receiving ---> 4
```

Notice how the only value received by the consuming coroutine is the value 4. This is the last value published before the producer coroutine finishes.

Multiple Senders and Receivers

The examples presented so far all show a single sending coroutine and a single receiver coroutine; however, it is possible to have multiple senders and multiple receivers.

Multiple Coroutine Channel Senders

There can be multiple senders to a channel. The values sent are processed in the order they are sent from the various different coroutines using that channel. The values will be received by the receiver in the time order that they were sent (no matter which sending coroutine published that data).

A simple program illustrating the use of two coroutines that publish data to a common rendezvous channel with one receiver is given below:

```kotlin
import kotlinx.coroutines.GlobalScope
import kotlinx.coroutines.channels.Channel
import kotlinx.coroutines.delay
import kotlinx.coroutines.launch

fun main() {

    suspend fun sendMessage(tag: String,
                            channel: Channel<String>,
                            message: String,
                            time: Long) {
        repeat (5) {
            delay(time)
            println("$tag sending --> $message")
            channel.send(message)
        }
    }

    suspend fun receiveMessage(channel: Channel<String>) {
        while (true) {
            println("Receiver --> ${channel.receive()}")
        }
    }
```

```
    println("Main -> Multiple senders and one receiver")
    val msgChannel = Channel<String>()
    GlobalScope.launch { sendMessage("Sender1",
                                     msgChannel,
                                     "Welcome",
                                     300L) }
    GlobalScope.launch { sendMessage("Sender2",
                                     msgChannel,
                                     "Hello",
                                     150L) }
    GlobalScope.launch { receiveMessage(msgChannel) }

    println("Main -> After launching coroutines")
    println("Main -> Waiting for task - press enter to
continue:")
    readLine()
    msgChannel.close()
    println("Main -> Done")
}
```

This program generates the output:

```
Main -> Multiple senders and one receiver
Main -> After launching coroutines
Main -> Waiting for task - press enter to continue:
Sender2 sending --> Hello
Receiver --> Hello
Sender1 sending --> Welcome
Receiver --> Welcome
Sender2 sending --> Hello
Receiver --> Hello
Sender2 sending --> Hello
Receiver --> Hello
Sender1 sending --> Welcome
Receiver --> Welcome
Sender2 sending --> Hello
Receiver --> Hello
Sender2 sending --> Hello
Receiver --> Hello
Sender1 sending --> Welcome
Receiver --> Welcome
Sender1 sending --> Welcome
Receiver --> Welcome
Sender1 sending --> Welcome
Receiver --> Welcome

Main -> Done
```

As you can see the output intermixes Sender1 and Sender2 with the delay used for Sender1 double that used for Sender2.

Multiple Coroutine Channel Receivers

Just as there can be multiple sending coroutines there can be multiple receiving coroutines. In this scenario when the single sending coroutine publishes data to the channel, if there is an available receiving coroutine then that coroutine receives the data. Once the data has been consumed it is removed from the data stream.

Thus, only one receiving coroutine will receive each data item.

A simple program using multiple receiver coroutines is presented below:

```
import kotlinx.coroutines.GlobalScope
import kotlinx.coroutines.channels.Channel
import kotlinx.coroutines.delay
import kotlinx.coroutines.launch
import java.util.*

fun main() {

    suspend fun sendMessage(channel: Channel<String>,
                            message: String,
                            time: Long) {
        repeat(5) {
            delay(time)
            val messageToSend = "$message + ${Date()}"
            println("Sender sending --> $messageToSend")
            channel.send(messageToSend)
        }
    }

    suspend fun receiveMessage(tag: String,
                               channel: Channel<String>,
                               time: Long) {
        while (true) {
            delay(time)
            println("$tag --> ${channel.receive()}")
        }
    }
    println("Main -> Single sender and multiple receivers")
    val msgChannel = Channel<String>()

    // Launch Single sending coroutine
    GlobalScope.launch {
        sendMessage(msgChannel, "Welcome", 1000L)
    }

    // Launch multiple receiver coroutines
    GlobalScope.launch { receiveMessage("Receiver1",
                                        msgChannel,
                                        1000L) }
    GlobalScope.launch { receiveMessage("Receiver2",
                                        msgChannel,
                                        1500L) }

    println("Main -> After launching coroutines")
    println("Main -> Waiting for tasks - press enter to
continue:")
    readLine()
    msgChannel.close()
    println("Main -> Done")

}
```

The output from this program is:

```
Main -> Single sender and multiple receivers
Main -> After launching coroutines
Main -> Waiting for tasks - press enter to continue:
Sender sending --> Welcome + Wed Feb 03 15:01:57 GMT 2021
Receiver1 --> Welcome + Wed Feb 03 15:01:57 GMT 2021
Sender sending --> Welcome + Wed Feb 03 15:01:58 GMT 2021
Receiver2 --> Welcome + Wed Feb 03 15:01:58 GMT 2021
Sender sending --> Welcome + Wed Feb 03 15:01:59 GMT 2021
Receiver1 --> Welcome + Wed Feb 03 15:01:59 GMT 2021
Sender sending --> Welcome + Wed Feb 03 15:02:00 GMT 2021
Receiver2 --> Welcome + Wed Feb 03 15:02:00 GMT 2021
Sender sending --> Welcome + Wed Feb 03 15:02:01 GMT 2021
Receiver1 --> Welcome + Wed Feb 03 15:02:01 GMT 2021

Main -> Done
```

As you can see the data sent by the Sender coroutine is received in turn by either Receiver1 or Receiver2.

Pipelines

Pipelines are a design pattern where one coroutine produces a set of values and another coroutines consume those values, does some processing on the values, and then sends the modified values onto another channel. The idea behind a pipeline is illustrated by the following diagram:

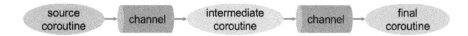

In this diagram an initial source coroutine sends data to a first channel. Another coroutine then receives that data, processes it in some way and then sends the results onto a new channel. The second channel then passes the data onto the final coroutine that consumes the results.

Depending upon the type of channels used, the final coroutine can be the controlling coroutine that determines how data is sent through the pipeline. For example, if both intermediate channels are rendezvous channels, then it is only when the final coroutine consumes the data that the next data item can be sent through the whole pipeline.

A simple example application that implements the two-channel pipeline illustrated above is given below.

In this pipeline an initial source numberGenerator() coroutine generates a series of integer numbers. These numbers are sent to channel1. Another coroutine running the doubler() suspending function receives data from channel1, doubles the number and sends it onto channel2. Finally a third coroutine running the printer() suspending function receives the number from channel2 and prints it out.

```kotlin
import kotlinx.coroutines.GlobalScope
import kotlinx.coroutines.channels.Channel
import kotlinx.coroutines.delay
import kotlinx.coroutines.launch

fun main() {

    suspend fun numberGenerator(channel: Channel<Int>,
                                time: Long) {
        repeat (5) {
            delay(time)
            println("numberGenerator sending --> $it")
            channel.send(it)
        }
    }

    suspend fun doubler(inputChannel: Channel<Int>,
                        outputChannel: Channel<Int>) {

        while (true) {
            val num = inputChannel.receive()
            println("doubler received --> $num")
            val newNum = num * 2
            println("doubler sending --> $newNum")
            outputChannel.send(newNum)
        }
    }

    suspend fun printer(channel: Channel<Int>) {
        while (true) {
            println("printer received --> ${channel.receive()}")
        }
    }

    // Set up channels
    val channel1 = Channel<Int>()
    val channel2 = Channel<Int>()

    // Launch the coroutines
    GlobalScope.launch {numberGenerator(channel1, 150L) }
    GlobalScope.launch { doubler(channel1, channel2) }
    GlobalScope.launch { printer(channel2) }

    // Wait for coroutines to complete
    println("Main -> After launching coroutines")
    println(
        "Main -> Waiting for task - press enter to continue:")
    readLine()
    channel1.close()
    channel2.close()
    println("Main -> Done")

}
```

The output from this is:

```
Main -> After launching coroutines
Main -> Waiting for task - press enter to continue:
numberGenerator sending --> 0
doubler received --> 0
doubler sending --> 0
printer received --> 0
numberGenerator sending --> 1
doubler received --> 1
```

```
doubler sending --> 2
printer received --> 2
numberGenerator sending --> 2
doubler received --> 2
doubler sending --> 4
printer received --> 4
numberGenerator sending --> 3
doubler received --> 3
doubler sending --> 6
printer received --> 6
numberGenerator sending --> 4
doubler received --> 4
doubler sending --> 8
printer received --> 8

Main -> Done
```

From this output you can see that • the numbers are initially published by the numberGenerator() suspending function, they are received and processed by the doubler() suspending function and finally received (and printed) by the printer() suspending function.

This is a common enough pattern that there is a simpler way to set up the different channels. This can be done by defining the suspending functions as extensions of the Coroutine Scope object. Thus, functions are defined using the syntax:

Such a function is not marked as being suspending but will be expected to return a Receive Channel. This is handled via the produce{} function which is used to wrap up the behaviour of the function. The produce{} function launches a new coroutine to produce a stream of values by sending them to a channel and returns a reference to the coroutine as a Receive Channel. Within the lambda passed to the produce{} function calls to send will automatically send the data items to the Receiver Channel return from produce.

An example of using this style of pipelining is given below:

```
import kotlinx.coroutines.CoroutineScope
import kotlinx.coroutines.GlobalScope
import kotlinx.coroutines.channels.ReceiveChannel
import kotlinx.coroutines.channels.produce
import kotlinx.coroutines.delay
import kotlinx.coroutines.launch
```

```kotlin
fun main() {

    fun CoroutineScope.numberGenerator(): ReceiveChannel<Int> =
      produce<Int> {
        var i = 0
        while (true) {
            delay(150L)
            println("numberGenerator sending --> $i")
            send(i)
            i++
        }
      }

    fun CoroutineScope.doubler(channel: ReceiveChannel<Int>):
ReceiveChannel<Int> =
      produce {
        while (true) {
            val num = channel.receive()
            println("doubler received --> $num")
            val newNum = num * 2
            println("doubler sending --> $newNum")
            send(newNum)
        }
      }

    GlobalScope.launch {
        // produces integers from 1 and on
        val numberChannel = numberGenerator()
        // doubles integers received from number channel
        // and resends
        val doublerChannel = doubler(numberChannel)

        // Receiver used to print final results
        repeat (4) {
            println("receiving --> ${doublerChannel.receive()}")
        }
    }

    println("Main -> After launching coroutines")
    println("Main -> Waiting for task - press enter to
continue:")
    readLine()
    println("Main -> Done")

}
```

The output from this is:

```
Main -> After launching coroutines
Main -> Waiting for task - press enter to continue:
numberGenerator sending --> 0
doubler received --> 0
doubler sending --> 0
receiving --> 0
numberGenerator sending --> 1
doubler received --> 1
doubler sending --> 2
receiving --> 2
numberGenerator sending --> 2
doubler received --> 2
doubler sending --> 4
receiving --> 4
numberGenerator sending --> 3
doubler received --> 3
doubler sending --> 6
receiving --> 6
numberGenerator sending --> 4
doubler received --> 4
doubler sending --> 8
receiving --> 8
numberGenerator sending --> 5

Main -> Done
```

In this exercise you will create three suspending functions; one suspending function will publish data to a channel and two other receivers will handle that data when emitted by the channel.

The channel (called msgChannel) will handle strings, it can therefore be defined as:

```
val msgChannel = Channel<String>()
```

Each publishing suspending function and the two receivers will all be launched independently.

The publishing suspending function should take the channel to use, and a timeout to be used between each value being published. The strings to be published should be held in an array of Strings such as:

```
val messages = arrayOf("Hello", "Welcome", "G'day", "Bonjour", "Ola")
```

The suspending function should randomly select a message to be published from the above array.

Two types of receivers should be implemented. One should be a suspending function that will receive a published message and print it. Between each receive it should sleep (delay) for a given amount of time. The parameters to this function shod be the channel to be used for communications and the delay to use as a Long.

The other receiver should be a lambda function that is defined within the launcher itself. A sample of what the main() function might look like for this exercise is given below:

```kotlin
fun main() {

    println("Main -> Single sender and multiple receivers")
    val msgChannel = Channel<String>()

    // Launch Single sending coroutine
    GlobalScope.launch {
        sendMessageOfTheDay(msgChannel, 1000L)
    }

    GlobalScope.launch { receiveMessage(msgChannel, 1000L) }
    GlobalScope.launch {
        while (true) {
            println("\t\treceiving --> ${msgChannel.receive()}")
        }
    }

    println("--------------------------------")
    println("Main -> After launching coroutines")
    println("Main -> Waiting for tasks - press enter to
continue:")
    readLine()
    msgChannel.close()
    println("--------------------------------")
    println("Main -> Done")

}
```

The output from this sample program might look like:

```
Main -> Single sender and multiple receivers
--------------------------------
Main -> After launching coroutines
Main -> Waiting for tasks - press enter to continue:
  Sender sending --> Bonjour + Tue Apr 27 14:45:09 BST 2021
        receiving --> Bonjour + Tue Apr 27 14:45:09 BST 2021
  Sender sending --> Hello + Tue Apr 27 14:45:10 BST 2021

        receiveMessage --> Hello + Tue Apr 27 14:45:10 BST 2021
  Sender sending --> Bonjour + Tue Apr 27 14:45:11 BST 2021
        receiving --> Bonjour + Tue Apr 27 14:45:11 BST 2021
  Sender sending --> Ola + Tue Apr 27 14:45:12 BST 2021
        receiving --> Ola + Tue Apr 27 14:45:12 BST 2021
  Sender sending --> G'day + Tue Apr 27 14:45:13 BST 2021
        receiveMessage --> G'day + Tue Apr 27 14:45:13 BST 2021


--------------------------------
Main -> Done
```

Concurrency

You've most likely heard of Moore's Law. In 1965, Gordon Moore noticed that the number of transistors that could be fit on a circuit board per square inch had doubled every year since their invention. Moore's Law was the name given to the belief that this would continue, albeit every 18 months. So far, this has been remarkably correct. The upshot is that computers are getting faster and smaller, and they use less power; one example is the ubiquity of mobile phones.

However, nothing lasts forever. The exponential growth in the context of processing power is already tailing off. If we are unable to continually make systems work faster by increasing raw speed, we must look for an alternative.

One such alternative is to split programs into parts that could run concurrently and then use multiple processors. Together, a collection of slower chips can perform as fast as one faster chip as long as the programs are able to parallelize their code to take advantage. A collection of chips on a single CPU is referred to as a multicore processor.

Structuring programs that allow them to be run concurrently requires new approaches and techniques. Many of the ideas that underpin concurrency are not new and have been around since the 1970s. What's new is that modern languages allow us to use these ideas more easily than we can in lower-level languages.

Concurrency is such a large subject that an entire book can be dedicated to it, so this chapter focuses on a few key fundamentals. This chapter will cover the following topics:

Threading

Synchronization and monitors

Concurrency primitives

Asynchronous and non-blocking techniques

Threads

A thread is one of the most basic building blocks of concurrent code. It is a part of a program that can execute threads concurrently to the rest of the code. Each thread can share resources, such as memory and file handles. In a system that allows threading, each process is divided into one or more threads. If the program was not written to use multiple threads and run concurrently, then it is called a **single thread process**.

In a single CPU system, multiple threads are interleaved, with each thread receiving a small amount of time called a **quantum**. This is called **time slicing** and happens so quickly that to the user, it appears as if the threads are running in parallel. For example, one thread might be updating a file while another is redrawing a window on the screen. To the user, they appear in parallel but may only be running sequentially. It is the same principle that is applied to running processes using the operating system scheduler.

When a thread expires, it's referred to as a time slice; when complete, the thread scheduler switches the thread with another one. This is called a **thread-context-switch** and is analogous to the context switch that the processes undergo. A thread context switch is more lightweight than a full process switch. This is because threads share many resources, and thus they have the data that needs to be saved and swapped out.

Concurrency is a general term that means two tasks are active and making progress at the same time, whereas parallelism is a stricter term that means two tasks are both executing at a particular instant. The two are often used interchangeably, but true parallelism is the goal of concurrent programming.

On a JVM, each Thread object has an associated state. A thread only has one state at a particular time. These states are listed in the following table:

State	Description
NEW	The thread has been created but not yet started.
RUNNABLE	A thread in this state is running from the point of view of the JVM. This does not necessarily mean it is executing the programming, as it may be waiting for a resource from the operating system, such as a time slice from the processor.
BLOCKED	A thread that is waiting to take ownership of a resource called monitor.

WAITING	A thread that has entered a waiting state. In this state, the thread will not be awakened until it has been notified by some other thread.
TIMED_WAITING	This is the same as WAITING, except that the thread here will exit the waiting state after a period of time has passed, if it has not already been notified.
TERMINATED	A thread that has exited.

Blocking

A thread that is running is consuming CPU resources. If a running thread is unable to make progress, it means it is consuming resources that could ideally be allocated to another thread that is ready to make meaningful use of the resource. An example would be a thread that is reading data from a network. A wireless network could be as much as 1,000 to 10,000 times slower than reading from the RAM; therefore, the majority of the time, the thread will simply be waiting for the network to deliver data.

In a naive threading implementation, the thread would keep looping, checking for the presence of more bytes until the operation is completed or checking whether the thread has expired its time slice. This is an example of busy-waiting, where although a thread is technically busy (using CPU time), it is not doing anything useful.

In a JVM, we are able to indicate that a thread is currently unable to progress and thus take it out of the set of threads that are eligible for scheduling. This is called blocking a thread. The advantage now is that when a thread is blocked, the thread scheduler knows to skip it, and so the thread won't waste CPU time busy-waiting.

Many I/O operations in the standard library perform the blocking operation, for example, InputStream.read(), Thread.sleep(time), or ServerSocket.accept().

Creating a thread

Kotlin has an extension function to make the process of creating a thread very easy. This top-level function, as part of the Kotlin standard library, is simply called **thread**. It accepts a function literal to execute as well as several named parameters to control the setup of the thread:

```
thread(start = true, name = "mythread") {
  while (true) {
    println("Hello, I am running on a thread")
  }
}
```

In the preceding example, we created a named thread that will begin executing immediately. If we want to delay the execution of a thread until sometime in the future, we can store a handle in the thread instance and then call start:

```
val t = thread(start = false, name = "mythread") {
  while (true) {
    println("Hello, I am running on a thread sometime later")
  }
}
```

```
t.start()
```

If you do not name a thread, it will have the default name supplied by the JVM.

Stopping a thread

A thread will naturally stop once the function literal is returned. To pre-emptively stop a thread, we should not use the stop function available on the Thread class. This has been a deprecated method for many years. Instead, we should use a condition that we could loop on; alternatively, if your thread invokes blocking functions, use an interrupt and then allow the function to return.

For the former, we declare a property, say a var named running, which we set to true. Then, allow this variable to be mutated by whichever code needs to stop the thread. We must ensure that the thread regularly checks the state of this variable; otherwise, the thread might get into a state where it would never stop:

```
class StoppableTask: Runnable {      @Volatile var running = true

    override fun run() {

      thread {        while (running) {

        println("Hello, I am running on a thread until I am stopped")

      }

      }

    }

}
```

An important point to mention here is the use of the @Volatile annotation on the state variable. This is crucial to ensuring that the state of the variable is propagated between threads. Without the volatile annotation, outside threads may set the variable to false; however, a running thread may not see the change. This is part of the **Java Memory Model (JMM)**, which is out of the scope of this book. But if you are interested, an Internet search for JMM will get you enough material to have a good understanding.

If we have a thread that invokes blocking calls, then using a running variable alone will not work as the thread may be blocked when we set running to false. Consider the following example of a producer and consumer:

```
class ProducerTask(val queue: BlockingQueue<Int>) {

    @Volatile var running = true      private val random = Random()

    fun run() {      while (running) {

      Thread.sleep(1000)          queue.put(random.nextInt())

      }

    }

}    class ConsumerTask(val queue: BlockingQueue<Int>) {      @Volatile var running = true

    fun run() {        while (running) {        val element = queue.take()

      println("I am processing element $element")

      }

    }

}
```

The producer and consumer both share a queue. This queue is an instance of BlockingQueue, which offers blocking functions for getting and putting values into the queue — take() and put(), respectively. If there are no elements to take from the queue, the thread will be blocked until one is available. Notice the thread sleep on the producer, which is designed to slow the producer down. This is an example of slow-producer fast consumer.

To start the example, we create instances of the tasks and begin the execution of multiple consumers and a single producer, each on their own thread:

```
val queue = LinkedBlockingQueue<Int>()    val consumerTasks = (1..6).map { ConsumerTask(queue) }
val producerTask = ProducerTask(queue)
```

```
val consumerThreads = consumerTasks.map { thread { it.run() } }    val producerThread = thread {
producerTask.run() }
consumerTasks.forEach { it.running = false }    producerTask.running = false
```

At some point in the future, we may decide to shut down the producer and the consumer. We will do this using a control variable:

```
consumerTasks.forEach { it.running = false }    producerTask.running = false
```

Now let's imagine that one of our consumers was in the following state: it had called take, but the queue was empty and now it is in the blocking state. Since the producer is now shut down, it will never receive an item and so it will stay blocked. Because it stays blocked, it will never check for the control variable and so our program will never exit normally.

Note that in this example, this problem only affects the consumer and not the producer because the producer only ever blocks for a limited period of time and so will always wake up to check the control variable.

Thread interrupts

To avoid these issues, we must perform an interrupt on the thread. An interrupt is a way of forcing a thread that is currently blocked to wake up and continue. It literally interrupts the thread. When this happens, the blocking function will throw an exception

Interrupted Exception, which must be handled. Interrupted Exception is your way of knowing that the thread was interrupted.

Let's change our consumer to use interrupts:

```
class InterruptableConsumerTask(val queue: BlockingQueue<Int>) : Runnable {
  override fun run() {
    try {
      while (!Thread.interrupted()) {        val element = queue.take()
        println("I am processing element $element")
      }
    } catch (e: InterruptedException) {
      // shutting down
    }
  }
}
```

As you can see, the loop is now enclosed in a try...catch block; if caught, this allows the run function to return normally, ending the thread. Notice that the infinite while loop has become a while statement with a condition as well. The Thread.interrupted() condition checks to see whether the thread has been interrupted since the last time the function was invoked. This is required because if the thread was not currently blocked in take(), when the interrupt had occurred, then no exception would be thrown and we would not be able to exit. This is very important when using interrupts to handle both cases.

To perform an interrupt, we call interrupt on an instance of Thread. Therefore, our shutdown code needs to operate on the thread instances themselves and not the tasks:

```
val queue = LinkedBlockingDeque<Int>()

val consumerTasks = (1..6).map {        InterruptableConsumerTask(queue)

}

val producerTask = ProducerTask(queue)

val consumerThreads = consumerTasks.map {

  thread { it.run() }

}

val producerThread = thread { producerTask.run() }

consumerThreads.forEach { it.interrupt() }     producerTask.running = false
```

Notice that for the producer, we don't perform interrupt as the control variables work fine.

CPU-bound versus I/O-bound

One common piece of terminology in the threading world is the concept of CPU-bound and I/O-bound computations. This simply means that a particular task is dominated by either the use of CPU or I/O, irrespective of whether it is a network, file, or whatever else. For example, a CPU-bound computation is the one where you could calculate the digits of Pi. An example of an I/O-bound computation is the one where you could download files from the Internet and save them locally.

In the first example, we can make progress as fast as the CPU can process the math operations. In the second example, we can only make progress as fast as the network can supply us with bytes. The latter case would be much slower.

The concept is important when deciding how to split up executions into threads. Let's say we had a thread pool of eight threads and we allocated this pool to both our CPU- and I/Obounded computations.

If this is the case, then it is possible we could have a situation where we could have all the eight threads blocked on a slow network to deliver bytes while the Pi calculation would make no progress despite the CPU being idle.

A common solution to this is to have two thread pools. Have one for CPU-bound operations, which might have its size limited to the number of CPU cores. And have another pool for IO-bound operations, which would typically be larger since these threads would often be in the blocked state, waiting on data.

Deadlocks and livelocks

When a thread cannot continue because it requires some resource that another thread has ownership of, it blocks waiting for that resource. The thread that owns that resource in turn requires something the first thread owns and so it blocks the initial one. Neither can make progress, and this is called a **deadlock**.

If the resource is preemptable, then the operating system or virtual machine can take the lock away from one of the threads and then another thread will be able to grab it; with this, progress would be made eventually. This is not a deadlock. Also, the resources in question must not be shareable, otherwise both threads could simply acquire the lock at the same time, which would also not be a deadlock.

One way to avoid a deadlock is to ensure that threads request the ownership of a resource in the same order. If we have threads t1 and t2 and they both require r1 and r2, then if they always request lock(r1) followed by lock(r2), it is impossible to get into a situation where one thread has r1 and another thread has r2. This is because the thread that gets the ownership of r1 will block the other thread from requesting r2 until it itself has r1.

A livelock is a situation where threads are able to change their state but ultimately make no progress. For example, if we had code to detect when a deadlock had occurred, one that forced both the threads to release the locks, we could get into a situation where the threads would continually re-request the locks in the same order as before, going back to the deadlock state. Although the threads are moving between blocked and running and seem to be doing something, they would ultimately not make any progress to complete their computations.

It is important to consider deadlocks and livelocks when writing concurrent code to ensure program correctness and performance. This is especially true since these kinds of bugs can sometimes only appear when running on certain systems and under certain conditions, so it might appear that the code is correct when what it really doing is harboring a subtle bug.

Dining philosophers' problem

The dining philosopher's problem is a classic in computer science. The problem was initially stated by Edsger Dijkstra, famous for many contributions to software development. It is often used to show how synchronization issues can result in a deadlock and that coming up with a solution is not always simple.

The problem in its current form is stated like this. Imagine a table of five philosophers, each sitting in front of a bowl of spaghetti. Placed between each philosopher is a fork, so each one of them has access to two forks, one on either side of him or her. A philosopher can think, eat, and move between these states at random. In order to eat, he or she must hold both of their forks at the same time, but each fork can only be used by one philosopher at any time. If a fork is not available — it is being held by another philosopher — then that philosopher will wait until it is free, holding the other fork as soon as it becomes available. It is assumed that the bowl would never empty and that the philosophers will always be hungry.

To show that the obvious solution results in a deadlock, consider the following erroneous solution:

Each philosopher should:

Think for a random period of time

Try to acquire the left fork, blocking until it is available

Try to acquire the right fork, blocking until it is available

Eat for a random period of time

Release both the forks

Repeat

This is erroneous because it is easy to get into a state where every philosopher has acquired their left forks, which means no philosopher can then acquire their right fork (because every right fork is another philosopher's left fork).

The problem can further be used as an example of a livelock. Imagine we enhance our first solution with an extra rule: if the process of acquiring a fork is blocked for more than a minute, all the forks should be dropped and the procedure should be restarted. Then no deadlock is possible, as the system can always make progress (from being blocked back to running). However, it is also possible that all the philosophers would acquire and drop the forks at the same time, meaning they would continually move back to the blocking state.

Executors

Creating a thread manually is fine when we want a single thread to do some work, perhaps a long-lived thread or a very simple one-off task that would run concurrently. However, when we want to run many different tasks concurrently while sharing limited CPU time, track the process of tasks in an easy way, or simply want to abstract how each task will run, we can turn to ExecutorService; this is commonly called an **executor** as well. An executor is part of the standard Java library.

An executor is a more generic interface with a single function run(). An ExecutorService is a more fully featured interface and is usually the abstraction used. It is common for people to use the term executor when referring to either.

An ExecutorService is simply an object that executes submitted tasks while allowing us to control the life cycle of the executor, that is, rejecting new tasks or interrupting already running tasks. Executors also allow us to abstract the mechanism of allocating threads to tasks. For example, we may have an executor with a fixed number of threads or an executor that creates a new thread for each submitted task. Any task that is not currently executing will be queued up internally in the executor.

Executors work with two main interfaces. The first, Runnable, is the most generic and used interface when we just want to wrap some code to be able to run in an executor. The second, Callable, adds a return value for when the task is completed. Since both of these are single-abstract-method interfaces, we can just pass in a function literal in Kotlin.

The Java standard library comes with several built-in executors, created from helper methods in Executors, that allow you to create custom executors very easily. The most

common executors used are Executors.newSingleThreadExecutor(), which creates an executor that will process a single task at a time, and

Executors.newFixedThreadPool(n), which creates an executor with an internal pool of threads running up to n tasks concurrently.

Let's see how to handle the life cycle of an executor:

```
val executor = Executors.newFixedThreadPool(4)

for (k in 1..10) {     executor.submit {

println("Processing element $k on thread

${Thread.currentThread()}")

    }
}
```

In this example, we created a thread pool of four threads and then submitted ten tasks. Each task should print out the ID of the thread it ran on. The static method Thread.currentThread() just returns the thread that the code is currently executing on. The output should look something like the following:

```
Processing element 2 on thread Thread[pool-1-thread-2,5,main]

Processing element 5 on thread Thread[pool-1-thread-2,5,main]

Processing element 1 on thread Thread[pool-1-thread-1,5,main]

Processing element 7 on thread Thread[pool-1-thread-1,5,main]

Processing element 8 on thread Thread[pool-1-thread-1,5,main]

Processing element 9 on thread Thread[pool-1-thread-1,5,main]

Processing element 10 on thread Thread[pool-1-thread-1,5,main]

Processing element 3 on thread Thread[pool-1-thread-3,5,main]

Processing element 4 on thread Thread[pool-1-thread-4,5,main]

Processing element 6 on thread Thread[pool-1-thread-2,5,main]
```

It wouldn't be in exactly the same order, as the output is non-deterministic; this shows how the different tasks are being interleaved:

executor.shutdown()   executor.awaitTermination(1, TimeUnit.MINUTES)

Once we are finished with the example, we call shutdown() so that further tasks could be rejected and then use await(), which would block the program until the executor has finished executing all the tasks. If we want to cancel running tasks, then we could use the shutdownNow() function on the executor, which will reject further tasks and interrupt running tasks before they are returned.

Race conditions

A race condition is another type of concurrency bug that occurs when two or more threads access shared data and try to change it at the same time. This means a situation where the output of a piece of logic requires that interleaved code is run in a particular order — an order that cannot be guaranteed.

A classic example is of a bank account, where one thread is crediting the account and another is debiting the account. An account operation requires us to retrieve the value, update it, and set it back, which means the ordering of these instructions can interleave with each other.

For example, assume an account starts with $100. Then, we want to credit $50 and debit $100. One possible ordering of the instructions can be something like this:

<credit thread>	<account balance>	<debit thread>
	start value = 100	
get current balance = 100		
		get current balance = 100
set new balance = 100 + 50		
	Updated = 150	
		set new balance = 100 – 100
	Updated = 0	

As you can see, our customer has lost their deposit! (They might not be as concerned if they had lost the withdrawal.)

The actual ordering can differ each time we run it. This is because if each thread were running on a separate processor, then the timings would never be exactly in sync. And if the threads were running on the same core, then we could never be quite sure how far each thread would get before a context switch is occurred.

One of the particular issues with race conditions is that by their very nature, they may not be apparent immediately. That is to say they are non-deterministic. A machine used for development will have different processing speeds than a server, and this, or the number of concurrent users, may be enough to trigger a race condition that you don't see in development.

Monitors

In a JVM, all instances have what is known as a **monitor**. A monitor can be thought of as a special token, which only one thread is allowed to own at any particular moment. Any thread can request the monitor for any instance, in which case they will either receive it or block it until they make the request. Once a thread has ownership of a particular monitor, it is said to hold the monitor.

To request the monitor, we use the synchronized function, which in Kotlin is a standard library function rather than a built-in feature as in Java. This function accepts two parameters: the first being the object whose monitor we wish to own and the second a function literal, which will be executed once we are assigned the monitor. Refer to the following code:

```
val obj = Any()     synchronized(obj) {
println("I hold the monitor for $obj")     }
```

If we examine the bytecode for this, we would see that the monitor is being acquired (monitor enter) and released (monitor exit):

```
0: new
3: dup
4: invokespecial
7: astore_0
9: aload_0
10: monitorenter
13: getstatic
16: astore_2
17: aload_0
18: monitorexit
19: aload_2
20: goto
23: astore_2
24: aload_0
25: monitorexit
26: aload_2
27: athrow
28: pop
29: return
```

Any code that is executed when inside the monitor is guaranteed to complete (either normally or by throwing an exception) before the monitor is released and before any other thread takes ownership of that monitor. The code that we run when we hold a monitor is referred to as a critical section.

When a thread reaches a synchronized call for a monitor that is already held by another thread, it is placed in a set of waiting threads. Once the holding thread gives up the monitor, one of the waiting threads is chosen. There is no guaranteed ordering as to which the waiting thread will acquire the monitor, that is, the thread that arrives first does not have any priority over the one that arrives at the end.

The main use of a synchronized block is to ensure only one thread can mutate shared variables at the same time. If we were to revisit our bank account example and this time update it to use synchronization on some common instance, we would see a difference in the interleaving of the code:

<credit thread>	<account balance>	<debit thread>
	start value = 100	
request monitor for account		
		request monitor for account
monitor acquired		
get current balance = 100		
set new balance = 100 + 50		
	updated = 150	
monitor released		
		monitor acquired
		get current balance = 150
		set new balance = 150 + 50
	updated = 200	
		monitor released

To be clear, synchronization as a technique only works if the threads are requesting the monitor for the same exact instance. Every instance of a class has its own monitor, so there is no benefit of having two threads request the monitor of different instances of the same class. This is a common cause of errors made by beginners.

Synchronization is somewhat of a blunt concurrency technique. This is because it is typically used to synchronize over a relatively large set of instructions that are blocking other threads for a long time. As we seek to achieve greater throughput in concurrent code, we should try to minimize the amount of time we are in a critical section of code.

Locks

An alternative to synchronization is to use one of the lock implementations provided in the java.util.concurrent.locks package. Typically, the implementation is ReentrantLock. A reentrant lock is one that allows the current owner of the lock to request the lock again without causing a deadlock. This simplifies code which uses recursion or passes the lock to other functions.

Although locks and synchronization have very similar uses, in that they both restrict access to a block of code, the lock interface is more powerful. For example, a lock allows us to attempt to acquire ownership and then back off if it is not successful; however, a synchronized call will only block.

In the following example, if we do not get the lock immediately, we continue. The return value of the tryLock() function indicates whether the lock was acquired or not:

```
val lock = ReentrantLock()      if (lock.tryLock()) {        println("I have the lock")
lock.unlock()
    } else {
    println("I do not have the lock")      }
```

Remember to always release a lock after using it. A lock can also block, but it allows you to interrupt:

```
    val lock = ReentrantLock()
    try {
    lock.lockInterruptibly()      println("I have the lock")
    lock.unlock()
    } catch (e: InterruptedException) {      println("I was interrupted")
    }
```

Kotlin provides an extension function that allows us to use the lock and have it automatically released:

```
    val lock = ReentrantLock()
    lock.withLock {
    println("I have the lock")
}
```

Another advantage is that a lock allows us to enforce fair ordering, which ensures that no particular thread will starve while waiting for the lock. This is done by allocating the lock to the thread that has been waiting for the longest period of time, but this can have a performance penalty, especially on highly contended locks.

Contention is the term given to how much demand there is for a lock or monitor. A high amount of contention means many threads are competing for the same lock at the same time.

Read-write locks

A more sophisticated type of lock provided by the standard library is ReadWriteLock. This is a specialized lock aimed at problems involving groups of readers and writers. Imagine a program that reads data from a file and sometimes updates that file. It is perfectly safe for multiple threads to be reading from the file at once but only as long as no one is modifying the file. In addition, only one writer should be writing at any time.

To accomplish this, the read-write lock has two locks: a read lock and a write lock. The read lock can be requested by multiple threads. The write lock can only be held by a single thread. If the read lock is being held, then the write lock cannot be acquired. Once the write lock has been acquired, no other threads can acquire it or a read lock until the write lock has been released.

The basic design of a read-write lock should also take into account whether a second reader requesting a read lock should take preference over a waiting writer. To explain, imagine that the first thread holds the read lock and the second thread then requests the write lock. While the second thread is waiting for the first reader to finish, another reader could come in and request the read lock. Should it be allocated then? It could be since having multiple readers is fine, but what if this happens indefinitely? The writer will definitely starve then.

To avoid this, we can create the read-write lock in fair mode. Similar to the standard lock implementation, when in fair mode, the writer who has been waiting for the longest period of time will be allocated the writer lock. And if a reader has been waiting for the longest period of time, then all the waiting readers are given the read lock at the same time.

Semaphores

The semaphore was again invented by our old friend Edsger Dijkstra. Although these days, with higher level programming languages, the humble semaphore may not be used as much as it was, it is still useful to understand how it works and why it is useful. This is because semaphores are often used as the basis for higher level abstractions.

A semaphore is a mechanism to keep a count of the number of resources and allow the counter to be changed in a thread-safe manner: either request resources or return them, with the additional ability to optionally wait until the requested number of resources are available. In the original design, the operation to request a resource was called **p** and the operation to return a resource was called **v**. The letters come from the original Dutch terms, Dijkstra being Dutch. In other languages, the terms are often called up and down or signal and wait.

The Java standard library exposes a semaphore implementation in the java.util.concurrent.Semaphore class. In Java terms, the count is called the number of **permits**; p or up is called **acquire** and v or down is called **release**.

The advantage of a semaphore is not only that they can be safely used from multiple threads at once without running into a race condition, but that any thread waiting on an acquire operation will be blocked, avoiding the need to spin lock and waste CPU time.

A spin lock is a type of lock where a thread repeatedly tests a condition until it is true. Since the thread is active, it is consuming CPU time without making process. This is an example of the so-called **busy-waiting** process and is an inferior solution to correctly block a thread.

A special case of the semaphore is the so-called binary semaphore, which only contains a single resource and so has the states 0 and 1 or unlocked and locked. These can be used to implement a lock or restrict access to a resource to a single consumer at any moment.

The bounded buffer problem

The **bounded buffer** (or producer-consumer) problem is a classic in concurrency. The problem to be solved is this: having a producer who would generate items to be put into a fixed size buffer and a consumer who would read these items. The producer should not try to generate items if the buffer is full, and the consumer should not try to read items if the buffer is empty.

An initial naive attempt, without the use of concurrency primitives, may be something like the following:

```
val buffer = mutableListOf<Int>()    val maxSize = 8

(1..2).forEach {        thread {
```

```
        val random = Random()      while (true) {
        if (buffer.size < maxSize)            buffer.plus(random.nextInt())
        }
      }
    }
    (1..2).forEach {      thread {      while (true) {      if (buffer.size > 0) {      val item =
buffer.remove(0)          println("Consumed item $item")
        }
      }
    }
  }
```

There is a shared buffer with two producers and two consumers each accessing it. The producers and consumers respectively check whether there is space to produce an item or an item to consume. They do this by just checking the size of the list. The problem with this solution is that we are spin locking, waiting for an item each time. If the buffer is empty, the consumer threads will continue to just check the condition, wasting CPU time.

So, we need another implementation. Since we have a number of slots in the buffer, it seems that semaphores are a good fit. This is due to their ability to hold a count. The idea behind the next iteration is that we have two semaphores: one containing the number of empty slots and another containing the number of filled slots. A producer will wait for an empty slot before producing an item, after which it will increase the number of filled slots. The consumer will wait for a filled slot before consuming an item; after this, it will increase the number of empty slots:

```
val emptyCount = Semaphore(8)    val fillCount = Semaphore(0)    val buffer = mutableSetOf<Int>()
thread {
    val random = Random()      while (true) {      emptyCount.acquire()      buffer.plus(random.nextInt())
    fillCount.release()
    }
}
    thread {      while (true) {      fillCount.acquire()      val item = buffer.remove(0)
println("Consumed item $item")
    emptyCount.release()
    }
}
```

This is certainly an improvement and avoids spin locking. However, since multiple threads can still access the list concurrently, the list could be modified by different threads at the same time. We can see this through a table of instructions showing one possible interleaving of instructions:

<producer 1>	<list>	<producer 2>

	size = 6	
request empty slot		
		request empty slot
empty slot acquired		
		empty slot acquired
set slot 7 to "x"		
	size = 7	
		set slot 7 to "y"
	size = 7	

This is an issue because of the fact that multiple threads will be mutating the list internally at the same time. Updating a list is not atomic and requires several instructions, which themselves are subject to race conditions.

An operation is said to be atomic if it appears to the rest of the system as if it is one single operation and any intermediate state is never visible outside of the thread.

Therefore, the safe solution is to further limit access to the list to a single thread at a time, and we can do this by introducing mutex:

```
val emptyCount = Semaphore(8)    val fillCount = Semaphore(0)    val mutex = Semaphore(1)    val buffer
= mutableSetOf<Int>()

   thread {

   val random = Random()    while (true) {    emptyCount.acquire()    mutex.acquire()

     buffer.plus(random.nextInt())

     mutex.release()    fillCount.release()

   }

   }    thread {    while (true) {    fillCount.acquire()    mutex.acquire()    val item =
buffer.remove(0)

     mutex.release()

     println("Consumed item $item")

     emptyCount.release()

   }

   }
```

In the final iteration, we've added a mutex acquire and release around each mutation of the buffer. This solution is now thread-safe.

Concurrent collections

As discovered in the section on race conditions, multiple threads accessing shared data can result in an inconsistent state. As we further saw in the section on monitors and locking, writing thread-safe code for updating collections can be tricky. Luckily, the Java standard library has solved many of these problems for us. In Java 1.5 (or version 5) onward, the standard library comes with a large number of concurrency primitives and concurrent collections.

The following several sections will cover some of these primitives, with this chapter on collections specifically and the next three on other non-collection primitives.

A concurrent collection is the term given to collections that are thread-safe and specifically designed for use in multithreaded code. They are less performant than a normal collection would be in a single thread environment, but more performant than wrapping normal collections in synchronized blocks (which was the pre-Java 1.5 solution).

ConcurrentHashMap

The first such collection is java.util.concurrent.ConcurrentHashMap and is possibly the most used of all the concurrent collections. As the name implies, this is an implementation of the Map interface that is thread-safe. The issue with a normal map is that two threads may both try to put an element into the map, one overwriting the other if their keys both hash to the same value. The other, less obvious, issue is that if the map reaches the capacity of putting the first thread, then it will perform a resize operation, which will involve rehashing each element into a new bucket. While this is going on, the put operation from the second thread can be lost.

A concurrent hash map avoids these issues. It maintains a set of locks, and each lock is used to restrict access to a stripe of the map. This way, multiple updates can occur at the same time safely, reducing the amount of code that has to be performed serially. Additionally, a get() operation does not require a lock at all, and it will return the result of the latest completed update.

A blocking queue

A blocking queue is another well-trodden collection. It is an extension of the java.util.Queue interface to support thread-safe blocking operations. It defines an operation called take(), which will block until the queue is non-empty, and put(), which will block until there is capacity in the queue to accept the item. If multiple threads perform the block action on the same operation, say three threads trying to take an item and one becomes available, only one thread will succeed and the others will safely continue to block.

There are two implementations in the Java standard library. The first implementation java.util.concurrent.ArrayListBlockingQueue is backed by an Array implementation. The second java.util.concurrent.LinkedBlockingQueue is backed by LinkedList. Each offers trade-offs of course, the latter being particularly useful as it uses two locks internally, one for the head of the list and one for the tail.

Using a blocking queue would dramatically simplify our earlier, bounded buffer problem. Let's rework that problem using LinkedBlockingQueue so we can see the difference:

```
val buffer = LinkedBlockingQueue<Int>()

  thread {

   val random = Random()     while (true) {

    buffer.put(random.nextInt())

   }
```

```
    }
    thread {      while (true) {        val item = buffer.take(0)
println("Consumed item $item")
    }
}
```

As you can see, all the concurrency-related complication has been taken away for us. We can use the queue as if we were in a single threaded environment:
13.7.x

Atomic variables

Quite often, we will find ourselves wanting a single value that we can atomically update between threads. A collection seems overkill for that purpose and probably slower than a special purpose primitive. he standard library provides such primitives in the java.util.concurrent.atomic package.

There are different implementations for each basic type, plus one for object references. For example, AtomicLong contains a long counter and provides operations to retrieve the current value or update the value in a thread safe manner. A typical use case is a counter shared between threads, perhaps as an increasing ID generator:

```
val counter = AtomicLong(0)
(1..8).forEach {      thread {        while (true) {
    val id = counter.incrementAndGet()        println("Creating item with id $id")
  }
 }
}
```

If you are using JDK 1.8 or higher, they ship with a primitive called **LongAdder** and **DoubleAdder**, which are even more efficient for summing values, with the drawback of being eventually consistent.

The AtomicReference class is similar, but rather than a number, it allows any reference type. It is useful for allowing multiple threads to share a single object and allow them all to update the object safely. One such use case is lazy initialization between threads. The initial value is null and then each thread can check for null, and if found, update to a proper value:

```
val ref = AtomicReference<Connection>()
(1..8).forEach {      thread {
  ref.compareAndSet(null, openConnection())
  val conn = ref.get()
 }
}
```

Now only one thread would call the openConnection() function. And it would occur lazily the first time a thread is executed.

CountDownLatch

The CountDownLatch object is a very useful concurrency primitive that has existed in Java since version 1.5 (or version 5, depending on which Java numbering scheme you prefer). The basic idea of the latch is that it allows one or more threads to block until the latch is released. You can imagine that the naming comes from the latch we see on a gate — once the latch is opened, the sheep behind the gate can escape. So similarly, the threads are queued up behind the gate, and once the latch is released, the threads are allowed to move through.

A latch is initialized with a count, and the countDown() method can be used to decrement the count. Once the count hits zero, any threads waiting on the latch are unblocked. A thread can block the latch using the await method; in fact, any number of threads can block the latch and they will all be released at the same time.

Any thread calling countDown is free to continue. Only threads calling await are blocked. Also note that any thread can call countDown multiple times, which is often the case when we have many tasks that are processed by several threads in turn.

Latches have many uses. We briefly mentioned one in Chapter 11, Testing in Kotlin, when we showed that latches are a useful tool for testing asynchronous functions. Recall that we wanted to prevent assertions from being executed until the asynchronous code that they depended on had finished executing.

Another canonical use of latches is to prevent some main thread from proceeding until worker threads are utilized. Let's say we have an application that needs to download and process multiple feeds before sending a notification via a queue. We want to multithread the processing of the feeds, especially since they are CPU-bound and we happen to be running on a multicore processor. The final notification should only be sent once all the feeds are processed. We don't know in advance which feeds will complete first or in what order. Since the order is unspecified, we can't rely on the logic that the last feed started will be the last feed to complete.

This is an example of the workpile pattern. The feeds to be processed can be imagined as a pile of tasks and a thread can take a task from this pile. Just like if you had a to-do list and each one was represented by a post it notes. You would pick up the top post and do whatever needs to be done before moving on to the next one. This is how the workpile pattern works.

We will model our tasks as a function called processFeed, which accepts a Feed object that describes the feed to be processed. The implementation of this function is not important for this example:

```
fun processFeed(feed: Feed): Unit {     println("Processing feed ${feed.name}")    }
```

We will assume we are somehow given a list of feeds, perhaps we could read them from a database. Each feed in turn will be submitted to an Executor. Our Executor will happen to be a cached thread pool:

```
val executor = Executors.newCachedThreadPool()
```

Finally, we'll need a function to send across the notification once all the feeds are completed:

```
fun sendNotification(): Unit {     println("Sending notification")
}
```

So far, we've multithreaded the processing of each feed. But how do we now make sure the send Notification function is only invoked once all the feeds are complete. The first thought might be to use a counter and have each feed task update the counter as it finishes. However, how do we wait for the counter? Again, naively, we could simply spin lock on the counter until it hits the required number.

A better solution would be to block the thread until it is ready. This is where the countdown latch comes into play. If we create a latch with the count set to the number of feeds and have each task count it down before it finishes, we can then have the main thread wait on the latch. Here is the full example:

```
fun processFeed(feed: Feed): Unit {     println("Processing feed ${feed.name}")    }
fun sendNotification(): Unit {     println("Sending notification")    }
```

```kotlin
val feeds = listOf(
    Feed("Great Vegetable Store",
"http://www.greatvegstore.co.uk/items.xml"),
    Feed("Super Food Shop", "http://www.superfoodshop.com/products.csv")
)    val latch = CountDownLatch(feeds.size)
val executor = Executors.newCachedThreadPool()
for (feed in feeds) {    executor.submit {        processFeed(feed)        latch.countDown()
    }
}
latch.await()
println("All feeds completed")    sendNotification()
```

Now the main thread will block at the latch.await line and consume no more CPU time until it is ready to proceed past the latch.

Cyclic Barrier

Another concurrency primitive along the lines of the countdown latch is CyclicBarrier, which allows multiple threads to wait until they all reach the required point. The common use for a barrier is when you have a set of threads that must perform some logic and then wait until everyone is ready before moving on.

Let's imagine we are writing a system that copies a file at multiple places. We don't want to start the next file until the first one has been successfully written out at all places. Each task is running on a separate thread that writes out to a single location. An implementation for this use case may decide to run multiple tasks on multiple threads, each task taking care of one particular output location. Each task can then wait on the barrier so that the next file is started only once they are all complete.

First, let's define a task that will repeatedly copy a file and then wait on a barrier:

```kotlin
class CopyTask(val dir: Path, val paths: List<Path>, val barrier: CyclicBarrier) : Runnable {
    override fun run() {        for (path in paths) {        val dest = dir.resolve(path)
        Files.copy(path, dest, StandardCopyOption.REPLACE_EXISTING)
        barrier.await()
    }
    }
}
```

Next, set up an executor and submit the tasks for each of the output locations:

```kotlin
fun copyUsingBarrier(inputFiles: List<Path>, outputDirectories: List<Path>) {
    val executor = Executors.newFixedThreadPool(outputDirectories.size)        val barrier =
CyclicBarrier(outputDirectories.size)
    for (dir in outputDirectories) {
    executor.submit {
        CopyTask(dir, inputFiles, barrier)
```

```
        }
    }
}
```

As you can see, one of the advantages of a barrier is that it can be reused. Each time it is released, it is ready to be used again. We could also use a countdown latch here, but we'd have to create a new one each time and then we have the issue of sharing the new instance.

Non-blocking I/O and asynchronous programming

Throughout this chapter, we focused on threads as the main instrument of concurrency. As crucial as they are, as the number of threads increases, the marginal benefit decreases. The more threads exist, the more time is spent on context switching between them. Ideally, we would want to be in a situation where we have one thread per CPU core, avoiding context switching entirely. This is somewhat of an impossible goal, but we can reduce the number of threads in use significantly.

Imagine a problem where we want to download ten feeds from a supplier's website. Once these are downloaded, we want to write them out to our database. One solution would be to create ten threads and have each thread read a single feed.

As each thread waits for more data to become available, it blocks. As the threads block or as their time slice expires, the system will context switch between the threads. If we were to scale out this system to a thousand feeds, that's a lot of switching, when the bulk of the time will still be spent waiting on the network.

A better solution might be to have the I/O system inform us when the data is made available, then we could allocate a thread to process that data. For us to be notified, we must provide a function that the I/O system knows to run when ready, and that function or block is commonly referred to as a callback. This is the idea behind non-blocking I/O. Java introduced non-blocking I/O in the 1.4 edition of the JDK.

If you were to use non-blocking I/O to download all the feeds from our supplier, we would have provided multiple callbacks. Since we have no idea about the order they will execute — this would be determined by the order in which they finish downloading, and some may be much larger than others — this kind of programming is referred to as **asynchronous programming**.

Asynchronous programming doesn't only work on I/O. It may be the case that we have a callback on a thread that runs once we finish a CPU-bound operation. For example, calculate the Pi to one hundred thousand places and then run a completion callback.

While this technique is very powerful, it can also result in what is known as **callback hell**. This is where we have multiple levels of nested callbacks, as each callback triggers a further operation:

```
fun persistOrder(order: Order, callback: (String) -> Unit): Unit = ...    fun chargeCard(card: Card, callback:
(Boolean) -> Unit): Unit = ...    fun printInvoice(order: Order, callback: (Unit) -> Unit): Unit = ...
persistOrder(order, {

    println("Order has been saved; charging card")

    chargeCard(order.card, { result ->

    if (result) {

      println("Order has been charged; printing invoice")

      printInvoice(order, {

        println("Invoice has been printed")

      })
```

```
    }
  })
})
```

As you can see, this code has three levels of callbacks. In the extreme case, this could be in dozens. While this is very efficient, as each further operation will only run once the previous one is completed and won't block any resources while waiting, it does result in somewhat unreadable code.

Futures

Imagine we want to submit tasks to an executor, but we want to know when they would be complete. One way would be to pass some kind of variable into each task, which we could interrogate to check on the status. However, this would require us to manage the volatility of that variable, and potentially spin locking to check on it.

A better solution would be some kind of structure that would represent a computation that hasn't yet completed. This structure would allow us to get the return value once it is completed, queue up an operation to run on it once it was ready, or block until it is finished. This kind of structure is called a **future**. The naming comes from the fact that it represents a value that will be available sometime in the future. (Futures are sometimes called promises in other languages, although in languages such as Scala, a promise and a future are different but related structures.)

We'd need the support of ExecutorService to return a future when we submit a task. To do this, we need to use the Callable interface rather than Runnable:

```
val executor = Executors.newFixedThreadPool(4)

val future: Future<Double> = executor.submit(Callable<Double> {

Math.sqrt(15.64)

  })
```

The basic Future returned here offers functions to test whether it has been completed and to get the value, blocking the calling thread until it is ready.

The real power, however, lies in the CompletableFuture abstraction. This enhanced future supports asynchronous operations and so operates via callbacks rather than explicitly blocking the thread. To create such a future, use the static methods defined on the class, which optionally accept an executor:

```
val executor = Executors.newFixedThreadPool(4)

val future = CompletableFuture.supplyAsync(Supplier { Math.sqrt(15.64) }, executor)
```

With this future, we can now attach a callback:

```
future.thenApply {

println("The square root has been calculated")     }
```

Callbacks can be chained so that the results of one future could be fed into another future. If we revisit the order-processing example from earlier, it can be rewritten as such:

```
fun persistOrder(order: Order): String = TODO()
fun chargeCard(card: Card): Boolean = TODO()
fun printInvoice(order: Order): Unit = TODO()

  CompletableFuture.supplyAsync {

    persistOrder(order)     }.thenApply { id ->
```

```
    println("Order has been saved; id is $id")
    chargeCard(order.card)     }.thenApply { result ->
  if (result) {
  println("Order has been charged; printing invoice")
  printInvoice(order)
  }
  }
```

This is more readable and avoids the many nested levels of callbacks in the case of an ordered series of callbacks. Futures can also be executed together with the results merged back into a single future. Imagine we decided that we wanted to persist the order, charge the card, and print the invoice simultaneously:

```
fun persistOrder(order: Order): CompletableFuture<String> = TODO()
fun chargeCard(card: Card): CompletableFuture<Boolean> = TODO()
fun printInvoice(order: Order): CompletableFuture<Unit> = TODO()
CompletableFuture.allOf(     persistOrder(order),     chargeCard(order.card),     printInvoice(order)
).thenApply {
println("Order is saved, charged and printed")     }
```

The CompletableFuture has many more functions, such as accepting the first completed value of multiple futures, mapping of results, and handling errors.

Conclusion: The Transformative Impact of Coroutines and Concurrency

In the world of programming, where responsiveness, scalability, and resource efficiency are key drivers of success, Kotlin's coroutines have emerged as a game-changing feature. They have fundamentally redefined how developers approach concurrency and asynchronous programming, offering a seamless, efficient, and intuitive alternative to traditional techniques. Let us revisit the critical aspects of Kotlin's coroutines and concurrency, examining how they transform programming practices and empower developers to build better applications.

Revisiting the Challenges of Concurrency

Before the introduction of coroutines, managing concurrency was a complex and error-prone process. Traditional threading models—whether using Java's Thread class, thread pools, or ExecutorService—were not only heavyweight but also fraught with challenges:

- **Resource Intensive**: Threads consume significant memory, making it impractical to create and manage thousands of threads simultaneously.

- **Thread Synchronization**: Managing shared resources between threads often led to race conditions, deadlocks, and complex debugging scenarios.

- **Callback Hell**: Asynchronous programming using callbacks often resulted in deeply nested, hard-to-read code, making maintenance and error handling cumbersome.

- **Limited Scalability**: Applications with high levels of concurrency required careful tuning and optimization of thread pools to avoid bottlenecks and overhead.

Kotlin's coroutines address these issues by offering a lightweight, structured, and intuitive approach to concurrency, which we will summarize and evaluate in detail.

Key Strengths of Coroutines

1. **Lightweight and Efficient**
   Coroutines are not bound to a specific thread. Unlike traditional threads, they are lightweight and managed by the Kotlin runtime. This allows thousands or even millions of coroutines to run concurrently within the same application without consuming excessive memory or CPU resources.

   o **Thread-Saving**: Coroutines suspend their execution without blocking the underlying thread, freeing it for other tasks.

   o **Better Resource Utilization**: By avoiding thread blocking, coroutines reduce overhead and ensure efficient use of system resources.

2. **Simplified Asynchronous Programming**
   Writing asynchronous code using coroutines feels like writing synchronous code. This significantly improves code readability and maintainability.

   o **Suspending Functions**: The suspend keyword makes it easy to create functions that can pause and resume, allowing developers to avoid deeply nested callback chains.

   o **Sequential Flow**: With constructs like launch and async, developers can express complex asynchronous workflows as a sequence of straightforward instructions.

3. **Structured Concurrency**
   Kotlin emphasizes structured concurrency, which ties coroutines to specific scopes. This ensures that coroutines are launched in a structured and predictable manner, simplifying lifecycle management and preventing memory leaks.

   o **Scopes and Lifecycle**: The use of CoroutineScope helps define the lifecycle of coroutines and ensures that they are canceled when no longer needed. For instance, in Android development, tying coroutines to a ViewModelScope ensures they are automatically canceled when the view is destroyed.

   o **Error Propagation**: Errors in coroutines are automatically propagated to their parent scope, ensuring that exceptions are handled gracefully.

4. **Integration with Dispatchers**
   Dispatchers determine the thread or thread pool on which a coroutine runs. By providing built-in dispatchers like Dispatchers.Main, Dispatchers.IO, and Dispatchers.Default, Kotlin allows developers to choose the most appropriate thread for their tasks.

   o **Main-Safe Operations**: Dispatchers ensure that tasks like updating the UI run on the main thread, while background operations such as network requests execute on IO-optimized threads.

   o **Custom Dispatchers**: Advanced developers can create custom dispatchers to optimize performance further, especially in applications with specialized threading requirements.

Impact on Modern Application Development

The versatility of Kotlin's coroutines has far-reaching implications across different domains of software development:

1. **Mobile Development (Android)**
   Kotlin has become the de facto standard for Android development, and coroutines play a pivotal role in this ecosystem. By replacing the older AsyncTask and Java thread-based APIs, coroutines enable developers to write cleaner and more efficient code for tasks such as:

   o Fetching data from a remote server.

   o Performing database queries using Room.

o Running complex computations in the background while ensuring the UI remains responsive.

2. **Server-Side Development**
   On the server side, frameworks like Ktor leverage coroutines to handle high levels of concurrency. Tasks like handling thousands of simultaneous HTTP requests are simplified through coroutines' non-blocking nature. This has significant implications for building scalable and performant web applications.

3. **Game Development**
   In game development, where frame rate consistency is crucial, coroutines are used to handle time-consuming tasks like asset loading and physics calculations. By running these tasks off the main thread, developers can ensure smooth gameplay experiences.

4. **Data-Intensive Applications**
   Coroutines are particularly useful in big data processing and machine learning applications, where tasks such as data retrieval, preprocessing, and model training can be parallelized effectively.

5. **Reactive Programming**
   With Kotlin Flow, coroutines integrate seamlessly into reactive programming paradigms. This enables developers to work with streams of asynchronous data in a declarative manner, making it easier to build reactive systems.

Challenges and Limitations

While coroutines offer many advantages, they are not without challenges:

1. **Learning Curve**: Developers transitioning from traditional threading models may need time to understand coroutine concepts such as suspending functions, contexts, and scopes.

2. **Overuse of GlobalScope**: Using GlobalScope improperly can lead to memory leaks and unexpected behavior, as coroutines launched in this scope are not tied to any lifecycle.

3. **Debugging Complexity**: Although tools like IntelliJ IDEA and Android Studio have improved coroutine debugging, tracing coroutine execution and understanding suspensions can still be challenging for newcomers.

4. **Mismanagement of Context Switching**: Excessive or improper use of context switching can lead to performance bottlenecks.

Best Practices for Leveraging Coroutines

To fully harness the power of coroutines, developers should follow these best practices:

1. **Adopt Structured Concurrency**: Always launch coroutines within a well-defined scope, such as CoroutineScope or lifecycle-aware scopes like ViewModelScope.

2. **Use Appropriate Dispatchers**: Assign tasks to the most suitable dispatcher. For example, use Dispatchers.IO for database queries and Dispatchers.Default for CPU-intensive computations.

3. **Minimize Blocking Calls**: Avoid blocking operations within coroutines, as they defeat the purpose of asynchronous programming.

4. **Handle Exceptions Gracefully**: Use coroutine exception handlers and structured try-catch blocks to ensure robust error handling.

5. **Leverage Kotlin Flow**: Use Kotlin Flow for handling streams of data asynchronously, especially when working with real-time data or event-driven systems.

Looking Ahead: The Future of Coroutines in Kotlin

As we move into 2025 and beyond, Kotlin's coroutine framework continues to evolve, addressing emerging challenges and introducing new features to enhance developer productivity.

- **Improved Debugging**: Enhanced IDE support and runtime tools are making coroutine debugging more intuitive.

- **Performance Optimizations**: Ongoing refinements to the coroutine library are improving performance, particularly for high-throughput applications.

- **Wider Adoption**: As Kotlin continues to expand beyond Android into domains like backend development, data science, and multi-platform projects, coroutines are becoming a standard tool in developers' toolkits.

- **Deeper Integration**: Coroutines are being increasingly integrated with other Kotlin features, such as Jetpack Compose for Android UI development and Kotlin Multiplatform for cross-platform projects.

Final Thoughts

Kotlin's coroutines and concurrency model represent a paradigm shift in how developers approach asynchronous programming. By offering a concise, intuitive, and high-performance alternative to traditional concurrency techniques, coroutines empower developers to build responsive and scalable applications with ease.

The structured nature of coroutines not only simplifies lifecycle management but also fosters better coding practices. Whether it's handling network requests on Android, building high-performance servers, or processing data streams, coroutines adapt effortlessly to diverse use cases.

As you continue to explore and master coroutines in Kotlin, you'll find yourself equipped to tackle complex programming challenges with confidence and efficiency. Kotlin's coroutines aren't just a tool—they're a new way of thinking about programming, making the impossible possible and the difficult easy. Embracing this modern approach to concurrency is the key to staying ahead in the fast-evolving world of software development.

6. Kotlin Domain-Specific Languages (DSLs)

Introduction

Kotlin, the modern programming language from JetBrains, is renowned for its conciseness, safety, and expressiveness. Among its most powerful features is its ability to create Domain-Specific Languages (DSLs). Kotlin's syntax and language features allow developers to craft concise and readable DSLs that solve domain-specific problems effectively. This document introduces Kotlin DSLs, explores their purpose, and provides insights into their design and usage in 2025.

What Are DSLs?

A **Domain-Specific Language (DSL)** is a specialized language designed to express solutions in a specific domain effectively. Unlike general-purpose programming languages (e.g., Kotlin, Java, Python), DSLs are tailored for a particular set of tasks, making them intuitive for domain experts.

Types of DSLs

External DSLs: These are standalone languages with their own syntax and grammar, often requiring custom parsers and interpreters. Examples include SQL and regular expressions.

Internal DSLs: These are built within a host language by leveraging its syntax and features. Kotlin DSLs fall into this category, using Kotlin's expressive syntax to create highly readable constructs.

Benefits of DSLs

Improved readability: DSLs are designed to mimic the natural language or domain-specific terminology, making them more understandable.

Reduced boilerplate: With a focus on the specific problem, DSLs eliminate unnecessary code.

Increased productivity: Domain experts can collaborate more effectively with developers by using DSLs tailored to their needs.

Kotlin's Strengths for DSLs

Kotlin's syntax and features make it ideal for designing internal DSLs. Key aspects include:

Lambda Expressions with Receivers:

Kotlin's lambdas with receivers allow for scoped execution, enabling concise and intuitive syntax.

Example:

```
fun buildString(action: StringBuilder.() -> Unit): String {
    val stringBuilder = StringBuilder()
    stringBuilder.action()
    return stringBuilder.toString()
}

val message = buildString {
    append("Hello, ")
    append("World!")
```

```
    }
```

println(message) // Outputs: Hello, World!

Extension Functions:

By adding functions to existing classes, Kotlin enables seamless integration of DSL constructs without modifying existing code.

Named Arguments and Default Parameters:

These features allow functions to resemble natural language constructs, enhancing readability.

Operator Overloading:

Operators like +, [], and invoke can be redefined, allowing intuitive DSL expressions.

Immutable Collections and Builders:

Kotlin's apply, also, and other scoping functions simplify the creation of immutable DSL-like structures.

String Interpolation:

Simplifies embedding variables within strings, useful for DSLs like templating systems.

Destructuring Declarations:

Helps create concise and meaningful constructs in DSLs that manipulate complex data structures.

Building Blocks of Kotlin DSLs

To construct effective DSLs in Kotlin, you need a combination of techniques and tools. Below is a detailed breakdown of the essential building blocks.

Lambdas with Receivers

Lambdas with receivers are the cornerstone of Kotlin DSLs. They allow you to execute code in the context of a specific object, effectively making its members accessible without explicit qualifiers.

Example: HTML Builder

```
class HTML {

private val elements = mutableListOf<String>()


fun body(content: BODY.() -> Unit) {

val body = BODY().apply(content)

elements.add("<body>\n${body.render()}\n</body>")

}


fun render(): String = elements.joinToString("\n")

}


class BODY {

private val elements = mutableListOf<String>()
```

```kotlin
fun h1(text: String) { elements.add("<h1>$text</h1>") }
fun p(text: String) { elements.add("<p>$text</p>") }

fun render(): String = elements.joinToString("\n")
}

fun html(init: HTML.() -> Unit): String {
val html = HTML().apply(init)
return "<html>\n${html.render()}\n</html>"
}

val page = html {
body {
h1("Welcome to Kotlin DSLs!")
p("This is an example of a DSL for HTML.")
}
}

println(page)
```

Output:

```
<html>
<body>
<h1>Welcome to Kotlin DSLs!</h1>
<p>This is an example of a DSL for HTML.</p>
</body>
</html>
```

Extension Functions

Extension functions allow you to add new functionality to existing classes. In DSLs, they make expressions more concise and natural.

Example: SQL Query Builder

```kotlin
class Query {
private val selectColumns = mutableListOf<String>()
private var fromTable: String = ""

fun select(vararg columns: String) {
selectColumns.addAll(columns)
```

```kotlin
}

fun from(table: String) {
fromTable = table
}

fun build(): String {
return "SELECT ${selectColumns.joinToString(", ")} FROM $fromTable"
}
}

fun query(init: Query.() -> Unit): String {
val query = Query().apply(init)
return query.build()
}

val sql = query {
select("id", "name", "age")
from("users")
}
println(sql) // Outputs: SELECT id, name, age FROM users
```

Custom Operators

Operator overloading can make DSLs feel like natural language constructs.

Example: Arithmetic Expressions

```kotlin
class Expression(private val value: Int) {
operator fun plus(other: Expression) = Expression(this.value + other.value)
operator fun times(other: Expression) = Expression(this.value * other.value)

override fun toString(): String = value.toString()
}

fun expr(block: () -> Expression): Expression = block()

val result = expr {
Expression(5) + Expression(3) * Expression(2)
```

```
}
println(result) // Outputs: 11
```

Type-Safe Builders

Kotlin's ability to enforce type safety in builders is another strength that prevents misuse and runtime errors.

Example: Config Builder

```
class Config {
var host: String = ""
var port: Int = 0

fun build(): String = "Connecting to $host on port $port"
}

fun config(init: Config.() -> Unit): Config {
return Config().apply(init)
}

val serverConfig = config {
host = "localhost"
port = 8080
}
println(serverConfig.build()) // Outputs: Connecting to localhost on port 8080
```

Inline Functions

Using inline functions reduces the runtime overhead of lambdas, making DSLs more efficient.

Annotations for Customization

Annotations like @DslMarker prevent scope conflicts in nested DSLs.

Example:

```
@DslMarker
annotation class HtmlDsl

@HtmlDsl
class HTML {
private val elements = mutableListOf<String>()
fun body(init: BODY.() -> Unit) {
elements.add(BODY().apply(init).render())
```

```kotlin
}
fun render() = elements.joinToString("\n")

}


@HtmlDsl
class BODY {
private val elements = mutableListOf<String>()
fun p(text: String) { elements.add("<p>$text</p>") }
fun render() = elements.joinToString("\n")

}
```

Practical Use Cases of Kotlin DSLs

Build Tools:

Kotlin is widely used in build systems like Gradle. Gradle's Kotlin DSL allows developers to write build scripts in Kotlin instead of Groovy.

Example:

```kotlin
plugins {
    kotlin("jvm") version "1.9.10"
}


repositories {
    mavenCentral()
}


dependencies {
    implementation("org.jetbrains.kotlin:kotlin-stdlib")
}
```

Configuration Management:

Tools like Kubernetes or Spring use YAML or XML, but Kotlin DSLs provide type safety and code completion for configuration management.

Testing Frameworks:

Kotlin DSLs are used in frameworks like Kotest to define test cases concisely.

Example:

```kotlin
class StringSpecTest : StringSpec({
    "length of Hello should be 5" {
        "Hello".length shouldBe 5
    }
```

```
})
```

UI Development:

Jetpack Compose utilizes Kotlin DSLs for declarative UI design.

Game Development:

Kotlin DSLs simplify the creation of game engines and mechanics.

Infrastructure as Code (IaC):

Libraries like Kotlin DSL for Terraform enable managing cloud resources with type safety.

Best Practices for Kotlin DSLs

Keep it Simple: Avoid over-engineering. A DSL should be easy to learn and use.

Use @DslMarker: Prevent scope conflicts in nested DSLs.

Leverage Type Safety: Ensure DSL users cannot misuse the API.

Provide Documentation: Include examples and usage instructions.

Optimize for Performance: Use inline functions and avoid unnecessary object creation.

Test Extensively: Ensure your DSL works as expected in all scenarios.

Let's begin,

In the intricate tapestry of "Kotlin Programming: Concise, Expressive, and Powerful," the module on Kotlin DSLs emerges as a gateway to a world of unparalleled expressiveness and succinctness. Domain-Specific Languages (DSLs) are a paradigm that empowers developers to craft specialized languages tailored to specific problem domains. This module becomes a beacon for developers seeking not only to master the syntax of Kotlin but also to harness its capabilities for building DSLs that elegantly encapsulate complex tasks. From understanding the principles of DSL design to practical implementation techniques, this module equips developers with the skills to wield the full power of Kotlin DSLs in their projects.

Demystifying DSLs: A Conceptual Exploration

The module commences with a conceptual exploration, demystifying the nature and purpose of DSLs. Readers delve into the foundations of DSL design, understanding how these specialized languages provide a higher level of abstraction, enhancing code readability and maintainability. Practical insights into when and why to employ DSLs set the stage for a journey that transcends traditional programming paradigms, offering a fresh perspective on problem-solving through expressive and purpose-built languages.

Building Blocks of Kotlin DSLs: Understanding the Syntax

The heart of the module lies in unraveling the syntax and building blocks that constitute Kotlin DSLs. Developers gain insights into how Kotlin's expressive syntax and language features, such as extension functions, infix notation, and lambda expressions, form the backbone of DSL construction. Through illustrative examples, readers discover the elegance with which Kotlin allows the creation of DSLs that feel natural and concise, aligning closely with the problem domain they aim to address.

Type-Safe Builders: Crafting Declarative DSLs with Precision

Type-safe builders stand out as a pivotal concept within the realm of Kotlin DSLs. This segment of the module delves into the principles of type-safe builders, where the compiler assists in enforcing correctness and adherence to the DSL's structure. Developers witness how Kotlin's type system facilitates the creation of DSLs that not only provide concise and readable syntax but also offer robust compile-time safety, reducing the likelihood of runtime errors and enhancing overall code quality.

Embedding DSLs in Kotlin: Seamless Integration and Interoperability

Kotlin's versatility extends beyond its primary role as a general-purpose programming language. This module explores how developers can seamlessly embed DSLs within Kotlin codebases, allowing for a fluid integration of specialized languages into larger projects. Emphasis is placed on the interoperability of DSLs with existing Kotlin constructs, showcasing how DSLs can coexist harmoniously with conventional programming paradigms, providing developers with a flexible toolkit for addressing diverse challenges.

Practical DSL Implementation: From Concept to Execution

Transitioning from theory to practice, the module guides developers through the practical implementation of DSLs. Readers gain hands-on experience in designing DSLs for specific use cases, witnessing the iterative process of refining language constructs to align with the desired expressive outcomes. Real-world examples illustrate how DSLs can simplify complex tasks, enabling developers to create readable and domain-specific abstractions that resonate with the natural language of the problem domain.

DSLs for Configurations, Testing, and Beyond: Real-World Applications

The module extends its exploration by showcasing real-world applications of Kotlin DSLs. Whether crafting configuration files, designing expressive testing frameworks, or addressing other domain-specific needs, readers discover how Kotlin DSLs provide a powerful toolset for solving a myriad of problems. Through diverse examples, developers gain inspiration and practical insights into the versatility of DSLs in enhancing the expressiveness and maintainability of their Kotlin projects.

The "Kotlin DSLs (Domain-Specific Languages)" module serves as a beacon for developers seeking to elevate their Kotlin programming skills to the next level. By demystifying the conceptual foundations, exploring the syntax and building blocks, and guiding developers through practical implementation, this module empowers readers to master the art of crafting expressive, purpose-built languages that seamlessly integrate with Kotlin, marking a transformative step in their journey toward more concise, expressive, and powerful software development.

Understanding DSLs

Domain-Specific Languages (DSLs) are a powerful concept in Kotlin that allows developers to create concise and expressive syntax tailored to a specific problem domain. DSLs provide a higher-level abstraction, making code more readable and expressive. In Kotlin, the language's flexibility and features, such as extension functions, infix notation, and lambdas, make it particularly well-suited for building DSLs that closely align with the problem space.

Declarative Syntax with Builders

One common use case for DSLs in Kotlin is the creation of declarative syntax using builders. Builders allow developers to design APIs that read like a natural language, enhancing code readability. Consider the following example of a DSL for HTML construction:

```kotlin
class HTML { private val elements = mutableListOf<HTMLElement>()

fun head(init: Head.() -> Unit) { val head = Head() head.init() elements.add(head)

}

fun body(init: Body.() -> Unit) { val body = Body() body.init() elements.add(body)

}
```

```kotlin
override fun toString(): String { return elements.joinToString("\n")

}

}

class Head { private val headElements = mutableListOf<String>()

fun title(text: String) { headElements.add("<title>$text</title>")

}

override fun toString(): String { return headElements.joinToString("\n", "<head>", "</head>") }

}

class Body { private val bodyElements = mutableListOf<String>()

fun p(text: String) { bodyElements.add("<p>$text</p>")

}

override fun toString(): String { return bodyElements.joinToString("\n", "<body>", "</body>") }

}

fun main() { val html = HTML().apply {

head { title("DSLs in Kotlin")

} body { p("Domain-Specific Languages (DSLs) provide a concise syntax.") p("Kotlin's flexibility allows for expressive DSL creation.") }

}

println(html)
}
```

In this example, the HTML class represents an HTML document, and the head and body functions serve as builders for the corresponding sections. The apply function is used to create an instance of HTML and build the document using the DSL. This results in a clean and declarative syntax for constructing HTML.

Type-Safe Configuration with DSLs

DSLs in Kotlin can also be used for type-safe configuration. This is particularly useful in scenarios where configurations involve multiple properties with specific types and constraints. Let's explore a DSL for configuring a network client:

```kotlin
class NetworkConfig { var baseUrl: String = ""

var timeout: Int = 0

}

class NetworkClient { var baseUrl: String = "" var timeout: Int = 0

fun configure(init: NetworkConfig.() -> Unit) { val config = NetworkConfig().apply(init) baseUrl = config.baseUrl timeout = config.timeout

}

}

fun main() { val networkClient = NetworkClient().apply { configure { baseUrl = "https://api.example.com" timeout = 5000

}
```

```
}
println("Configured base URL: ${networkClient.baseUrl}") println("Configured timeout:
${networkClient.timeout} milliseconds") }
```

In this example, the NetworkConfig class defines configuration properties, and the NetworkClient class provides a configure function that takes a lambda with a NetworkConfig receiver. This allows for a typesafe and structured way to configure the network client.

Understanding DSLs in Kotlin opens up avenues for creating expressive and concise syntax tailored to specific domains. Whether building declarative syntax with builders or ensuring type-safe configuration, DSLs in Kotlin empower developers to design APIs that are both elegant and efficient for specific problem spaces.

Creating DSLs in Kotlin

Building Domain-Specific Languages (DSLs) in Kotlin involves leveraging the language's expressive features to create a syntax that closely aligns with a specific problem domain. Kotlin's concise syntax, support for lambdas, and extension functions make it well-suited for designing DSLs that enhance code readability and maintainability. Let's explore the process of creating DSLs in Kotlin with examples that showcase various techniques and patterns.

Extension Functions for DSL-Like Syntax

One fundamental approach to creating DSLs in Kotlin is using extension functions to provide a DSL-like syntax. This involves extending existing classes or types with functions that mimic a domain-specific language. Consider the following example of a DSL for configuring a database connection:

```
class DatabaseConfig { var host: String = "" var port: Int = 0 var username: String = ""

var password: String = ""

}
fun DatabaseConfig.connect(init: DatabaseConfig.() -> Unit) {

init()

}
fun main() { val databaseConfig = DatabaseConfig().apply { connect { host = "localhost" port = 3306
username = "user" password = "password"

}
}
println("Configured host: ${databaseConfig.host}") println("Configured port: ${databaseConfig.port}")
println("Configured username: ${databaseConfig.username}") println("Configured password:
${databaseConfig.password}") }
```

In this example, the connect extension function is defined on the DatabaseConfig class, creating a DSLlike syntax for configuring a database connection. The apply function is then used to initialize the configuration using the DSL.

Lambda Receivers for Scoped DSLs

Kotlin's support for lambda receivers is a powerful feature when creating DSLs. This allows for a more scoped and structured DSL design. Let's explore a DSL for defining HTTP routes:

```
class HttpServer { private val routes = mutableListOf<Route>()
```

```kotlin
fun route(path: String, init: Route.() -> Unit) { val route = Route(path).apply(init) routes.add(route)
}

fun start() { println("Server started with the following routes:") routes.forEach { println(it) }
}

}

class Route(val path: String) { private val handlers = mutableListOf<() -> Unit>()

fun get(handler: () -> Unit) { handlers.add(handler)
}

override fun toString(): String { return "Route(path=$path, handlers=${handlers.size})" }
}

fun main() { val server = HttpServer().apply { route("/home") { get { println("Handling GET request for /home")
}
}

route("/api") { get { println("Handling GET request for /api")
}
}

start()
}
}
```

In this example, the HttpServer class provides a route function with a lambda receiver, allowing for a scoped DSL when defining routes. The Route class, also with a lambda receiver, enables the addition of HTTP handlers within the context of a specific route.

Type-Safe DSLs with Lambdas

Creating type-safe DSLs ensures that the DSL enforces specific constraints and types. This is achieved by using lambdas with receiver types. Consider the following DSL for configuring a logging framework:

```kotlin
class LoggerConfig { var level: LogLevel = LogLevel.INFO

var fileName: String = ""

} enum class LogLevel { INFO, DEBUG, ERROR }

fun configureLogger(init: LoggerConfig.() -> Unit): LoggerConfig { val loggerConfig = LoggerConfig().apply(init) validateConfiguration(loggerConfig) return loggerConfig
}

fun validateConfiguration(config: LoggerConfig) { require(config.level != LogLevel.ERROR || config.fileName.isNotBlank()) { "Error: File name must be specified for ERROR log level." }
}

fun main() { val loggerConfig = configureLogger { level = LogLevel.ERROR fileName = "error.log"
}

println("Logger configured with level: ${loggerConfig.level}, fileName: ${loggerConfig.fileName}") }
```

In this example, the configureLogger function takes a lambda with a receiver of type LoggerConfig, enforcing a type-safe DSL. The validateConfiguration function ensures that the configuration adheres to specific constraints.

Creating DSLs in Kotlin is a powerful tool for improving code expressiveness and readability. Whether through extension functions, lambda receivers, or type-safe DSLs, Kotlin provides a flexible and intuitive environment for designing languages that cater to specific problem domains. These DSLs contribute to more maintainable and concise code, enhancing the overall developer experience.

Building Type-Safe DSLs

Creating type-safe DSLs in Kotlin involves designing domain-specific languages that not only provide a concise and expressive syntax but also ensure compile-time safety. Kotlin's rich type system, combined with features like lambda receivers and extension functions, allows developers to build DSLs that enforce constraints, prevent misuse, and provide a seamless development experience. This section explores the principles and techniques behind building type-safe DSLs in Kotlin.

Leveraging Lambda Receivers for Type-Safety

One key aspect of building type-safe DSLs in Kotlin is leveraging lambda receivers. Lambda receivers allow developers to define the context in which DSL expressions are executed, enabling the DSL to capture the intended types and constraints. Consider the following example of a DSL for configuring a custom authorization system:

```
class AuthorizationConfig { var allowedRoles: Set<String> = emptySet() var maxAttempts: Int = 3

}

fun authorizationConfig(init: AuthorizationConfig.() -> Unit): AuthorizationConfig { val config =
AuthorizationConfig().apply(init) validateAuthorizationConfig(config) return config

}

fun validateAuthorizationConfig(config: AuthorizationConfig) { require(config.maxAttempts > 0) { "Max
attempts must be greater than 0." }

}

fun main() { val authConfig = authorizationConfig { allowedRoles = setOf("admin", "user")

maxAttempts = 5

}

println("Authorization configuration: $authConfig") }
```

In this example, the authorizationConfig function takes a lambda with a receiver of type AuthorizationConfig. The lambda receiver allows developers to configure the authorization settings within a scoped context. The validateAuthorizationConfig function ensures that the configuration adheres to specific constraints, providing compile-time safety.

Using Extension Functions for Fluent APIs

Extension functions are another powerful tool for building type-safe DSLs in Kotlin. They allow developers to extend existing types with DSL-like syntax, creating fluent APIs that read like natural language. Let's explore a DSL for defining validation rules for user input:

```
class ValidationRuleBuilder { private val rules = mutableListOf<ValidationRule>()

fun minLength(length: Int) { rules.add(MinLengthRule(length))
```

```kotlin
}
fun maxLength(length: Int) { rules.add(MaxLengthRule(length))
}
fun build(): List<ValidationRule> { return rules
}
}

data class User(val username: String, val email: String)
fun validateUser(user: User, init: ValidationRuleBuilder.() -> Unit): List<ValidationRule> { val builder =
ValidationRuleBuilder().apply(init) return builder.build()
}
interface ValidationRule { fun validate(value: String): Boolean
}
class MinLengthRule(private val minLength: Int) : ValidationRule { override fun validate(value: String):
Boolean = value.length >= minLength
}
class MaxLengthRule(private val maxLength: Int) : ValidationRule { override fun validate(value: String):
Boolean = value.length <= maxLength
}
fun main() { val user = User("john_doe", "john@example.com")
val validationRules = validateUser(user) { minLength(5) maxLength(15)
}
println("Validation rules for user: $validationRules")
}
```

In this example, the ValidationRuleBuilder class uses extension functions to add DSL-like methods for defining validation rules. The validateUser function takes a lambda with a receiver of type

ValidationRuleBuilder, allowing developers to specify validation rules in a fluent and type-safe manner.

Creating DSLs with Contextual Abstractions

Building type-safe DSLs often involves creating contextual abstractions that encapsulate the DSL's functionality and enforce type constraints. Consider a DSL for defining database queries:

```kotlin
data class Query(val tableName: String, val conditions: List<Condition>)

sealed class Condition { data class Equal(val field: String, val value: Any) : Condition() data class
GreaterThan(val field: String, val value: Any) : Condition()
}
class QueryBuilder(private val tableName: String) { private val conditions = mutableListOf<Condition>()
infix fun String.eq(value: Any) { conditions.add(Condition.Equal(this, value))
}
infix fun String.gt(value: Any) { conditions.add(Condition.GreaterThan(this, value))
}
```

```kotlin
fun build(): Query { return Query(tableName, conditions)

}

}

fun select(tableName: String, init: QueryBuilder.() -> Unit): Query { val builder =
QueryBuilder(tableName).apply(init)

return builder.build()

}

fun main() { val query = select("users") {

"name" eq "John"

"age" gt 25

}

println("Generated query: $query") }
```

In this example, the QueryBuilder class provides extension functions that serve as DSL elements for defining conditions. The select function then takes a lambda with a receiver of type QueryBuilder, allowing developers to construct queries in a type-safe manner.

Building type-safe DSLs in Kotlin involves a thoughtful combination of lambda receivers, extension functions, and contextual abstractions. These techniques empower developers to design expressive and enforceable DSLs that enhance code readability, catch errors at compile time, and provide a smooth and intuitive developer experience.

Real-world DSL Examples

The true power of Domain-Specific Languages (DSLs) in Kotlin becomes evident when examining real-world examples that leverage the language's expressive features to create concise and purpose-built syntax. In this section, we explore practical DSL implementations that highlight the versatility and impact of DSLs in real-world scenarios, from configuring libraries to defining UI layouts.

DSLs for Configuring Libraries

DSLs are often employed to configure and customize the behavior of libraries in a succinct and readable manner. A notable example is the Gradle build system, where Kotlin DSL is commonly used for project configuration. Let's consider a simplified DSL for configuring a fictional networking library:

```kotlin
class NetworkingConfig {

var baseUrl: String = "" var timeout: Int = 0

var maxRetries: Int = 3

}

fun configureNetworking(init: NetworkingConfig.() -> Unit): NetworkingConfig { val config =
NetworkingConfig().apply(init) validateNetworkingConfig(config)

return config

}

fun validateNetworkingConfig(config: NetworkingConfig) { require(config.maxRetries > 0) { "Max retries
must be greater than 0." }

}
```

```kotlin
fun main() { val networkConfig = configureNetworking { baseUrl = "https://api.example.com" timeout =
5000 maxRetries = 5

}

println("Configured base URL: ${networkConfig.baseUrl}") println("Configured timeout:
${networkConfig.timeout} milliseconds") println("Configured max retries: ${networkConfig.maxRetries}")
}
```

This DSL allows developers to configure a networking library in a concise and type-safe manner. The configureNetworking function takes a lambda with a receiver of type NetworkingConfig, enforcing type safety and providing a clear structure for configuring the library.

DSLs for UI Layouts

DSLs are prevalent in frameworks that deal with UI layout construction, providing a declarative syntax for defining complex UI structures. In the Android development ecosystem, Kotlin DSLs are frequently used with libraries like Anko to create UI layouts. Here's a simplified example:

```kotlin
import org.jetbrains.anko.*

class MainActivity : AppCompatActivity() { override fun onCreate(savedInstanceState: Bundle?) {
super.onCreate(savedInstanceState)

verticalLayout { padding = dip(16)

textView("Hello, Kotlin DSL!") { textSize = sp(20).toFloat()

}

button("Click Me") { setOnClickListener { toast("Button clicked!")

}

}

}

}

}
```

In this Android activity, the verticalLayout function from the Anko library is used as a DSL element to define a vertical layout. Within this layout, a textView and a button are declared with their respective properties and event listeners. This results in a concise and readable representation of the UI structure.

DSLs for Database Querying

DSLs are also valuable in the context of database querying, providing a domain-specific syntax for interacting with databases. An example using Exposed, a Kotlin SQL library, illustrates this:

```kotlin
import org.jetbrains.exposed.dao.IntIdTable import org.jetbrains.exposed.sql.* data class User(val id: Int,
val name: String) object Users : IntIdTable() {

val name = varchar("name", 255)

}

fun main() {

Database.connect("jdbc:h2:mem:test;DB_CLOSE_DELAY=-1;", driver = "org.h2.Driver", user = "sa",
password = "")

transaction {
```

```
SchemaUtils.create(Users)

Users.insert { it[name] = "John Doe"

}

val users = Users.selectAll().map { User(it[Users.id].value, it[Users.name]) }

println("Users in the database: $users")

}

}
```

In this example, the DSL-like syntax of Exposed is used to define a table (Users) and perform database operations. The transaction function encapsulates the database transaction, and the DSL-like functions make database interactions expressive and readable.

These real-world examples demonstrate the versatility and practicality of DSLs in Kotlin. Whether configuring libraries, defining UI layouts, or interacting with databases, DSLs provide a powerful mechanism for expressing intent in a domain-specific manner, resulting in more readable, maintainable, and error-resistant code.

Conclusion: Kotlin Domain-Specific Languages (DSLs)

A Recap of Kotlin DSLs

Kotlin Domain-Specific Languages (DSLs) have revolutionized how developers express intent, streamline logic, and craft elegant, concise, and intuitive APIs. DSLs leverage Kotlin's powerful language features—such as lambdas with receivers, extension functions, type-safe builders, and operator overloading—to enable developers to write expressive, readable, and maintainable code.

Over the years, DSLs have been pivotal in making complex software constructs more accessible. They empower developers to build APIs that closely align with the problem domain, allowing both technical and non-technical stakeholders to interact with code effortlessly. Kotlin's continued evolution has solidified its position as the go-to language for creating robust, type-safe DSLs, and 2025 promises even greater potential in this space.

The Benefits of Kotlin DSLs

1. **Readability and Expressiveness:** Kotlin DSLs turn verbose code into clean, natural syntax. They enable the creation of fluent interfaces that often read like human language. This readability reduces the cognitive load for developers and improves collaboration across teams.

2. **Type Safety:** Kotlin's strong static type system ensures that DSLs are inherently type-safe, reducing runtime errors and providing instant feedback during development. This is particularly beneficial for designing DSLs in critical domains such as finance, healthcare, or infrastructure automation.

3. **Declarative Style:** DSLs promote a declarative programming style, focusing on "what to do" rather than "how to do it." This abstraction allows developers to focus on the problem domain without being bogged down by implementation details.

4. **Customization and Flexibility:** With Kotlin DSLs, developers can create highly customized, domain-specific syntax that adapts to the specific needs of their use case. Whether building an internal API or creating tools for external users, DSLs allow fine-grained control over the developer experience.

5. **Wide Adoption Across Industries:** Kotlin DSLs have been widely adopted in areas like build tools (Gradle), server-side development (Ktor), and infrastructure (Terraform Kotlin DSL). Their applicability in diverse domains speaks volumes about their versatility and power.

Challenges in DSL Design and Implementation

Despite their advantages, creating effective DSLs is not without challenges:

1. **Steep Learning Curve for Beginners:** While DSLs simplify usage for end-users, designing DSLs requires an in-depth understanding of Kotlin's advanced features. Developers must master lambdas, scoping functions, and other constructs to build efficient DSLs.

2. **Over-Engineering Risks:** Inappropriate or excessive use of DSLs can lead to over-engineered solutions, making the code harder to debug and maintain.

3. **Performance Considerations:** Though Kotlin DSLs provide a great developer experience, there is potential for performance trade-offs due to the abstractions introduced.

4. **Tooling and IDE Support:** Although Kotlin IDEs like IntelliJ IDEA provide excellent support for DSLs, there can still be limitations, especially for custom DSLs. Features like auto-completion, error highlighting, and debugging might not always work seamlessly for complex DSLs.

Best Practices for Building Kotlin DSLs

To fully leverage Kotlin DSLs while mitigating their challenges, the following best practices are essential:

1. **Define a Clear Problem Domain:** Understand the domain and scope of your DSL. Ensure that the DSL serves a specific purpose and is not overly generalized.

2. **Prioritize Simplicity and Readability:** The primary goal of a DSL is to simplify code for its end-users. Avoid introducing complexity or clever constructs that could confuse users.

3. **Use Type Safety Wisely:** Take advantage of Kotlin's type-safe builders and extension functions to ensure your DSL enforces correct usage patterns while minimizing runtime errors.

4. **Test Rigorously:** DSLs are often used in critical areas where correctness is paramount. Write comprehensive tests for your DSL, ensuring all edge cases are covered.

5. **Document Extensively:** Provide clear, concise documentation and examples for your DSL. This makes it easier for others to understand and adopt your API.

Emerging Trends in Kotlin DSLs (2025)

In 2025, several trends are shaping the landscape of Kotlin DSLs:

1. **AI-Driven DSL Design:** The integration of AI tools in IDEs is helping developers design DSLs more efficiently by suggesting syntax, patterns, and optimizations based on machine learning models.

2. **Cloud-Native DSLs:** With the rise of serverless computing and Kubernetes, Kotlin DSLs are increasingly being used to define cloud infrastructure declaratively, enabling easier management and deployment.

3. **Interoperability with Other Languages:** Kotlin's ability to interoperate with Java, JavaScript, and native code makes it easier to integrate Kotlin DSLs into multi-language ecosystems.

4. **Improved Tooling:** Continued advancements in IntelliJ IDEA and other IDEs are enhancing developer productivity, making it easier to design, debug, and use Kotlin DSLs.

5. **Focus on Accessibility:** DSLs are being designed with a broader audience in mind, including non-developers. Visual editors and simplified syntax are making DSLs more accessible to domain experts with minimal coding knowledge.

Real-World Applications of Kotlin DSLs

The impact of Kotlin DSLs extends across industries and domains:

1. **Build and Configuration Tools:** Tools like Gradle have set the gold standard for Kotlin DSLs, providing a more expressive alternative to XML-based configurations.

2. **Web Development:** Frameworks like Ktor leverage Kotlin DSLs to create intuitive, type-safe APIs for building web applications.

3. **Infrastructure as Code (IaC):** Tools like Terraform Kotlin DSL allow developers to define infrastructure in Kotlin, combining the power of DSLs with the flexibility of a general-purpose language.

4. **Data Science and Machine Learning:** Kotlin DSLs are increasingly being used to define workflows and pipelines in data science, enabling researchers to focus on their domain without delving into boilerplate code.

5. **Testing and Automation:** Testing frameworks like KotlinTest (now Kotest) showcase how DSLs can make test definitions more expressive and readable.

The Future of Kotlin DSLs

The future of Kotlin DSLs lies in their ability to further abstract complex systems while remaining flexible and powerful. The following advancements are anticipated in the coming years:

1. **Greater AI Integration:** AI-driven tools will simplify DSL creation and optimize their usage, making DSLs more intuitive for developers and end-users.

2. **Enhanced Declarative APIs:** As the software industry moves toward declarative paradigms, Kotlin DSLs will play a pivotal role in simplifying configurations, workflows, and processes.

3. **Seamless Multiplatform Support:** Kotlin's multiplatform capabilities will allow DSLs to target various platforms (JVM, JavaScript, and native) with minimal effort, enabling developers to write once and deploy everywhere.

4. **Cross-Domain Applications:** DSLs will extend beyond traditional software development, finding applications in fields like education, entertainment, and digital content creation.

5. **Standardization and Interoperability:** Efforts to standardize DSLs and improve their interoperability will make it easier for organizations to adopt and integrate them into their workflows.

Final Thoughts

Kotlin DSLs represent a powerful paradigm shift in software development. By enabling developers to create highly readable, expressive, and type-safe APIs, they bridge the gap between technical and domain expertise. The journey of Kotlin DSLs from their foundational use in build tools to their application in cloud-native development, testing, and data science—has demonstrated their versatility and potential.

As we look ahead, Kotlin DSLs will continue to evolve, pushing the boundaries of what is possible in software development. With a growing community, enhanced tooling, and a focus on accessibility, Kotlin DSLs will empower developers to craft solutions that are not only elegant and efficient but also transformative for their respective domains. By embracing best practices and leveraging emerging trends, developers can harness the full power of Kotlin DSLs to build the next generation of software.

7. Generics, Annotations and reflection

Introduction

Kotlin, being a modern and versatile programming language, brings a host of powerful features that empower developers to write clean, concise, and efficient code. Among these features, generics, annotations, and reflection play a pivotal role in making the language highly adaptable and extensible. This document provides a detailed introduction to these topics, offering insights into their syntax, use cases, and best practices.

Generics in Kotlin

Generics enable developers to write reusable and type-safe code. They allow classes, interfaces, and functions to operate on different types while ensuring type safety at compile time.

Why Generics?

Generics solve common programming problems such as:

- Avoiding code duplication by creating reusable components.
- Ensuring type safety to prevent runtime type-casting errors.
- Enhancing code readability and maintainability.

Declaring Generics

Kotlin generics are defined using angle brackets (<>) with type parameters.

Generic Classes

```kotlin
class Box<T>(var value: T)
fun main() {
    val intBox = Box(123)
    val stringBox = Box("Hello")
    println(intBox.value) // Outputs: 123
    println(stringBox.value) // Outputs: Hello
}
```

Here, T is a type parameter that can be replaced with any concrete type.

Generic Functions

```kotlin
fun <T> printValue(value: T) {
    println(value)
}


fun main() {
    printValue(42)      // Prints: 42
    printValue("Kotlin") // Prints: Kotlin
```

```
}
```

Variance in Generics

Variance determines how subtyping between more complex types relates to subtyping between their component types.

Invariance

Kotlin generics are invariant by default.

```
fun copy(from: List<Any>, to: MutableList<Any>) {
    to.addAll(from)
}
```

```
val ints: List<Int> = listOf(1, 2, 3)
val anyList: MutableList<Any> = mutableListOf()
// copy(ints, anyList) // Compilation error
```

Covariance

Covariance is denoted by the out keyword, making the type parameter usable only as a return type or producer.

```
interface Producer<out T> {
    fun produce(): T
}
```

```
val stringProducer: Producer<String> = object : Producer<String> {
    override fun produce() = "Kotlin"
}
val anyProducer: Producer<Any> = stringProducer // Allowed due to covariance
```

Contravariance

Contravariance is denoted by the in keyword, making the type parameter usable only as a consumer.

```
interface Consumer<in T> {
    fun consume(item: T)
}
```

```
val anyConsumer: Consumer<Any> = object : Consumer<Any> {
    override fun consume(item: Any) {
        println(item)
    }
}
```

```kotlin
val stringConsumer: Consumer<String> = anyConsumer // Allowed due to contravariance
```

Type Erasure

At runtime, generic type information is erased due to type erasure. To retain type information, Kotlin provides reified type parameters in inline functions.

```kotlin
inline fun <reified T> isTypeMatch(value: Any): Boolean {
    return value is T
}


fun main() {
    println(isTypeMatch<String>("Kotlin")) // Prints: true
    println(isTypeMatch<Int>("Kotlin"))    // Prints: false
}
```

Annotations in Kotlin

Annotations provide metadata about the code to the compiler and runtime. They are used to influence code behavior or supply additional information for tools and libraries.

Declaring Annotations

Annotations are defined using the @ symbol.

Standard Annotations

Kotlin includes several built-in annotations, such as:

- @Deprecated: Marks code as deprecated.
- @JvmStatic: Exposes Kotlin static methods to Java.
- @Test: Used for marking test functions.

Custom Annotations

You can create custom annotations using the annotation keyword.

```kotlin
@Target(AnnotationTarget.FUNCTION)
@Retention(AnnotationRetention.RUNTIME)
annotation class LogExecution


@LogExecution
fun performTask() {
    println("Task performed")
}
```

Annotation Parameters

Annotations can have parameters to provide additional metadata.

```
annotation class Info(val author: String, val version: Int)


@Info(author = "Mike", version = 1)
class MyClass
```

Annotation Targets

Annotations can be applied to specific elements using @Target.

- AnnotationTarget.CLASS
- AnnotationTarget.FUNCTION
- AnnotationTarget.VALUE_PARAMETER

Annotation Retention

@Retention defines whether annotations are accessible at runtime, compile-time, or in the bytecode.

- Retention.SOURCE
- Retention.BINARY
- Retention.RUNTIME

Reflection in Kotlin

Reflection allows a program to introspect or modify its behavior at runtime. Kotlin provides reflection capabilities through the kotlin.reflect package.

Why Reflection?

Reflection is used for:

- Accessing class metadata.
- Inspecting and modifying properties and methods at runtime.
- Building libraries and frameworks like dependency injection tools.

Basic Reflection in Kotlin

Accessing Class Metadata

The ::class keyword retrieves the class metadata.

```
fun main() {
    val clazz = String::class
    println(clazz.simpleName) // Outputs: String
}
```

Inspecting Properties and Functions

Reflection allows access to properties and functions at runtime.

```
class Person(val name: String, var age: Int)
```

```kotlin
fun main() {
    val person = Person("Alice", 30)
    val kClass = person::class

    // Access properties
    kClass.members.filterIsInstance<KProperty<*>>().forEach {
        println("Property: ${it.name}")
    }

    // Access functions
    kClass.members.filterIsInstance<KFunction<*>>().forEach {
        println("Function: ${it.name}")
    }
}
```

Calling Functions Dynamically

Kotlin allows invoking methods dynamically using reflection.

```kotlin
class Calculator {
    fun add(a: Int, b: Int): Int = a + b
}
```

```kotlin
fun main() {
    val calculator = Calculator()
    val kFunction = calculator::class.members.find { it.name == "add" } as KFunction<*>
    val result = kFunction.call(calculator, 5, 10)
    println(result) // Outputs: 15
}
```

Reflection with Annotations

Reflection can inspect annotations at runtime.

```kotlin
@Info(author = "Mike", version = 1)
class AnnotatedClass
```

```kotlin
fun main() {
    val kClass = AnnotatedClass::class
    val annotation = kClass.annotations.find { it is Info } as Info
    println("Author: ${annotation.author}, Version: ${annotation.version}")
```

}

Best Practices

- Use reflection sparingly as it can impact performance.
- Prefer compile-time solutions over runtime reflection when possible.
- Ensure proper documentation for custom annotations.

Let's begin,

Generics

You've already seen a few code examples that use generics in this book. The basic concepts of declaring and using generic classes and functions in Kotlin are similar to Java, so the earlier examples should have been clear without a detailed explanation. In this chapter, we'll return to some of the examples and look at them in more detail.

We'll then go deeper into the topic of generics and explore new concepts introduced in Kotlin, such as reified type parameters and declaration-site variance. These concepts may be novel to you, but don't worry; the chapter covers them thoroughly.

Reified type parameters allow you to refer at run time to the specific types used as type arguments in an inline function call. (For normal classes or functions, this isn't possible because type arguments are erased at run time.)

Declaration-site variance lets you specify whether a generic type with a type argument is a subtype or a supertype of another generic type with the same base type and a different type argument. For example, it regulates whether it's possible to pass arguments of type List<Int> to functions expecting List<Any>.

Use-site variance achieves the same goal for a specific use of a generic type and, therefore, accomplishes the same task as Java's wildcards.

Let's discuss these topics in details, starting with generic type parameters in general.

Creating types with type arguments: Generic type parameters

Generics allow you to define types that have type parameters. When an instance of such a type is created, type parameters are substituted with specific types called type arguments. For example, if you have a variable of type

List, it's useful to know what kind of things are stored in that list. The type parameter lets you specify exactly that —instead of "This variable holds a list," you can say something like "This variable holds a list of strings." Kotlin's syntax for saying "a list of strings" looks the same as in Java: List<String> . You can also declare multiple type parameters for a class. For example, the Map class has type parameters for the key type and the value type: class Map<K, V> . We can instantiate it with specific arguments: Map<String, Person> . So far, everything looks exactly as it does in Java.

Just as with types in general, type arguments can often be inferred by the Kotlin compiler:

val authors = listOf("Sveta", "Seb", "Dima", "Roman")

Because all values passed to the listOf function are strings, the compiler infers that you're creating a List<String> (your IDE can help you visualize this; see figure).

```
val authors : List<String> = listOf("Sveta", "Seb", "Dima", "Roman")
```

Figure Optional inlay hints in IntelliJ IDEA and Android Studio help visualize inferred generic types.

On the other hand, if you need to create an empty list, there's nothing from which to infer the type argument, so you need to specify it explicitly. In the case of creating a list, you have a choice between specifying the type as part of the variable declaration and specifying a type argument for the function that creates a list. The following example shows how this is done:

val readers: MutableList<String> = mutableListOf()

val readers = mutableListOf<String>()

These declarations are equivalent. Note that collection-creation functions are covered in section.

There are no raw types in Kotlin

Unlike Java, Kotlin always requires type arguments to be either specified explicitly or inferred by the compiler. Because generics were only added to Java in version 1.5, it had to maintain compatibility with code written for older versions, so it allows you to use a generic type without type arguments—a so-called raw type. For example, in Java, you can declare a variable of type ArrayList without specifying what kind of things it contains:

List aList = new ArrayList();

Because Kotlin has had generics from the beginning, it doesn't support raw types, and the type arguments must always be defined. If your program receives a variable with a raw type from Java code, it's treated as having a generic parameter of type Any! —a platform type, as you've gotten to know them in section.

Functions and properties that work with generic types

If you're going to write a function that works with a list and you want it to work with any list (a generic one), not a list of elements of a specific type, you need to write a generic function. A generic function has type parameters of its own. These type parameters must be replaced with the specific type arguments on each function invocation.

Most of the library functions working with collections are generic. For example, let's look at the slice function declaration, shown in figure. This function returns a list containing only elements at indices in the specified range.

Type parameter declaration

```
fun <T> List<T>.slice(indices: IntRange): List<T>
```

The type parameter is used in receiver and return types.

Figure: The generic function slice has the type parameter T, allowing it to work with lists of arbitrary elements. This type parameter is used both in the receiver type of the extension function, and the return type of the function.

The function's type parameter T is used in the receiver type and the return type; both of them are List<T>. When you call such a function on a specific list, you can specify the type argument explicitly. But in almost all cases you don't need to because the compiler infers it, as shown next.

Listing Calling a generic function

fun main() {

```
val letters = ('a'..'z').toList()    println(letters.slice<Char>(0..2))    ❶
// [a, b, c]    println(letters.slice(10..13))        ❷
// [k, l, m, n]
}
```

❶ Specifies the type argument explicitly

❷ the compiler infers that T is Char here.

The result type of both of these calls is List<Char>. The compiler substitutes the inferred type Char for T in the function return type List<T>.

In section, you saw the declaration of the filter function, which takes a parameter of the function type (T) -> Boolean. It had the following signature:

```
fun <T> List<T>.filter(predicate: (T) -> Boolean): List<T>
```

Let's see how you can apply it to the readers and authors variables from the previous examples.

Listing Calling a generic higher-order function

```
fun main() {    val authors = listOf("Sveta", "Seb", "Roman", "Dima")    val readers =
mutableListOf<String>("Seb", "Hadi")    println(readers.filter { it !in authors })

   // [Hadi]
}
```

You can declare type parameters on methods of classes or interfaces, top-level functions, and extension functions. In the last case, the type parameter can be used in the types of the receiver and the parameters, as in listings: the type parameter T is part of the receiver type List<T> , and it's used in the parameter function type (T) -> Boolean as well.

You can also declare generic extension properties using the same syntax. For example, here's an extension property that returns the penultimate element in a list—that is, the element before the last one:

```
val <T> List<T>.penultimate: T            ❶    get() = this[size - 2]
 fun main() {    println(listOf(1, 2, 3, 4).penultimate)  ❷
   // 3
}
```

❶ This generic extension property can be called on a list of any kind.

❷ the type parameter T is inferred to be Int in this invocation.

You can't declare a generic non-extension property

Regular (non-extension) properties can't have type parameters. It's not possible to store multiple values of different types in a property of a class; therefore, declaring a generic non-extension property doesn't make sense. If you try to do that, the compiler reports an error:

```
val <T> x: T = TODO()
```

// Error: type parameter of a property must be used in its receiver type

Now, let's recap how you can declare generic classes.

Generic classes are declared with the angle bracket syntax

Just as in Java, you declare a Kotlin generic class or interface by putting angle brackets after the class name and the type parameters inside the angle brackets. Once you do that, you can use the type parameters in the body of the class, just like any other types. Let's look at how a basic interface like List, as you know it from the standard library, could be declared in Kotlin. To simplify it, we've omitted the majority of the methods:

```
interface List<T> {          ❶    operator fun get(index: Int): T   ❷    // ...
}
```

❶ The List interface defines a type parameter T.

❷ T can be used as a regular type in an interface or a class.

Later, in section, when we get to the topic of variance, you'll improve on this example and see how List is declared in the Kotlin standard library.

If your class extends a generic class (or implements a generic interface), you must provide a type argument for the generic parameter of the base type. It can be either a specific type or another type parameter:

```
class StringList: List<String> {          ❶
override fun get(index: Int): String = TODO()  ❷    // . . .
}
class ArrayList<T> : List<T> {                 ❸
override fun gct(index: Int): T − TODO()     // ...
}
```

❶ This class implements List, providing a specific type argument: String.

❷ Note how String is used instead of T.

❸ Now, the generic type parameter T of ArrayList is a type argument for List.

The StringList class is declared to contain only String elements, so it uses String as the type argument of the base type. Any function from the subclass substitutes this proper type instead of T. That means, instead of fun get(Int): T , you have a signature fun get(Int): String .

A class can even refer to itself as a type argument. Classes implementing the Comparable interface are the classic example of this pattern. Any comparable element must define how to compare it with objects of the same type:

```
interface Comparable<T> {    fun compareTo(other: T): Int
} class String : Comparable<String> {    override fun compareTo(other: String): Int = TODO() }
```

The class implements the generic Comparable interface, providing the type String for the type parameter.

So far, generics look similar to those in Java. We'll talk about the differences later in the chapter, in sections. Now, let's discuss another concept that works similar to Java: the one that allows you to write useful functions for working with comparable items.

Restricting the type a generic class or function can use: Type parameter constraints

Type parameter constraints let you restrict the types that can be used as type arguments for a class or function. For example, consider a function that calculates the sum of elements in a list. It can be used on a List<Int> or a List<Double> , but not, for example, a List<String> . To express this, you can define a type parameter constraint that specifies that the type parameter of sum must be a number.

When you specify a type as an upper bound constraint for a type parameter of a generic type, the corresponding type arguments in specific instantiations of the generic type must be either the specified type or its subtypes. (For now, you can think of subtype as a synonym for subclass. Section will highlight the difference.)

To specify a constraint, you put a colon after the type parameter name, followed by the type that's the upper bound for the type parameter. In Java, you use the keyword extends to express the same concept: <T extends Number> T sum(List<T> list).

Type parameter

```
fun <T : Number> List<T>.sum(): T
```

Upper bound

Figure Constraints are defined by specifying an upper bound after a type parameter. In this case, the sum function is constrained to lists of a type whose upper bound is Number.

This function invocation is allowed because the actual type argument (Int in the following example) extends the abstract class Number, a superclass of all classes representing numeric values, from the Kotlin standard library:

fun main() {   println(listOf(1, 2, 3).sum())

   // 6 }

Once you've specified a bound for a type parameter T, you can use values of type T as values of its upper bound.

For example, you can invoke methods defined in the class used as the bound:

fun <T : Number> oneHalf(value: T): Double { ❶   return value.toDouble() / 2.0   ❷
} fun main() {   println(oneHalf(3))

   // 1.5

}

❶ Specifies Number as the type parameter upper bound

❷ Invokes a method defined in the Number class

In the rare case when you need to specify multiple constraints on a type parameter, you use a slightly different syntax. For example, the following listing is a generic way to ensure that the given CharSequence has a period at the end. In this case, you specify that the type used as a type argument must implement both the CharSequence and Appendable interfaces. This means both the operation accessing the data (endsWith) as well as the operation modifying it (append) can be used with values of that type. One class that implements both CharSequence and Appendable is the StringBuilder class, which represents a mutable sequence of characters (you briefly encountered StringBuilder in section).

Listing Specifying multiple constraints for a type parameter

```
fun <T> ensureTrailingPeriod(seq: T)
    where T : CharSequence, T : Appendable {    ❶    if (!seq.endsWith('.')) {    ❷
seq.append('.')                    ❸
    }
} fun main() {    val helloWorld = StringBuilder("Hello World")    ensureTrailingPeriod(helloWorld)
println(helloWorld)    //Hello World.
}
```

❶ List of type parameter constraints

❷ Calls an extension function defined for the CharSequence interface

❸ Calls the method from the Appendable interface

Next, we'll discuss another case when type parameter constraints are common: when you want to declare a non-null type parameter.

Excluding nullable type arguments by explicitly marking type parameters as non-null

If you declare a generic class or function, any type arguments, including nullable ones, can be substituted for its type parameters. In effect, a type parameter with no upper bound specified will have the upper bound of Any? . Consider the following example:

```
class Processor<T> {    fun process(value: T) {    value?.hashCode()    ❶
    }
}
```

❶ value is nullable, so you have to use a safe call.

In the process function, the parameter value is nullable, even though T isn't marked with a question mark.

This is the case because specific instantiations of the Processor class can use a nullable type for T —there are no constraints to forbid the type T to be nullable (e.g., String?):

```
val nullableStringProcessor = Processor<String?>()    ❶    nullableStringProcessor.process(null)    ❷
```

❶ String?, which is a nullable type, is substituted for T.

❷ This code compiles fine, having null as the value argument.

If you want to guarantee that a non-null type will always be substituted for a type parameter, you can achieve this by specifying a constraint. If you don't have any restrictions other than nullability, you can use Any as the upper bound, replacing the default Any?:

```
class Processor<T : Any> {    ❶    fun process(value: T) {    value.hashCode()    ❷
    }
}
```

❶ Specifying a non-null upper bound

❷ The value of type T is now non-null.

The <T : Any> constraint ensures that the T type will always be a non-nullable type. The code Processor<String?> won't be accepted by the compiler because the type argument String? isn't a subtype of Any (it's a subtype of Any? , which is a less specific type):

val nullableStringProcessor = Processor<String?>()

// Error: Type argument is not within its bounds: should be subtype of 'Any'

Note that you can make a type parameter non-null by specifying any non-null type as an upper bound, not only the type Any.

Marking generic types as "definitely non-nullable" when interoperating with Java

A special case worth pointing out is when implementing generic interfaces from Java that are annotated with nullability annotations as you've gotten to know them in section. For example, this generic JBox interface restricts the put method to only be called with a non-null parameter of type T. Note that the interface itself doesn't make such constraints on the type T in general, allowing other methods like putIfNotNull to accept nullable values:

```java
import org.jetbrains.annotations.NotNull;

public interface JBox<T> {
  /**
  *     Puts a non-null value into the box.
  */    void put(@NotNull T t);


  /**
  *     Puts a value into the box if it is not null, * doesn't do anything for null values.
  */    void putIfNotNull(T t);
}
```

With the syntax you have seen so far, you couldn't directly convert this constraint to Kotlin code. If a Kotlin implementation specifies the non-null constraint for the generic type via T: Any, nullable values can't be used with the implementation at all anymore—which would differ from the constraint given by the Java interface:

```kotlin
class KBox<T : Any>: JBox<T> {          ❶    override fun put(t: T) { /* ... */ }    override fun
putIfNotNull(t: T) { /* Problem! */ }   ❷ }
```

❶ Because the generic type T was already constrained to be non-nullable here ...

❷ ... you can no longer relax this constraint for a function that expects a nullable parameter.

Now, T is non-nullable everywhere in the KBox implementation—not only in the put method.

To address this, Kotlin provides a way of marking a type as definitely non-nullable at its use site (rather than at the place where the generic parameter is first defined). Syntactically, it is expressed as T & Any (a form you may recognize from the notation of intersection types in other languages):

```
class KBox<T>: JBox<T> {    override fun put(t: T & Any) { /* ... */ }    override fun putIfNotNull(t: T) {
/* ... */ }

}
```

Using definitely non-nullable types, you can now express the same nullability constraints defined in the Java code in Kotlin.

So far, we've covered the basics of generics—the topics that are most similar to Java. Now, let's discuss another concept that may be somewhat familiar if you're a Java developer: how generics behave at run time.

Generics at run time: Erased and reified type parameters

From an implementation perspective, generics on the Java virtual machine (JVM) are normally implemented through type erasure. This means the type arguments of an instance of a generic class aren't preserved at run time. In this section, we'll discuss the practical implications of type erasure for Kotlin, and how you can get around its limitations by declaring a function as inline. You can declare an inline function so that its type arguments aren't erased (or, in Kotlin terms, are reified). We'll discuss reified type parameters in detail and look at examples when they're useful.

Limitations to finding type information of a generic class at run time: Type checks and casts

Kotlin's generics are erased at run time. This means an instance of a generic class doesn't carry information about the type arguments used to create that instance. For example, if you create a List<String> and put a bunch of strings into it, at run time, you'll only be able to see that it's a List (an effect that you can also see in Java). It's not possible to identify which type of elements the list was intended to contain. (Of course, you can get an element and check its type, but that won't give you any guarantees because other elements may have different types.) Consider what happens with these two lists when you run the code (shown in figure):

```
val list1: List<String> = listOf("a", "b") val list2: List<Int> = listOf(1, 2, 3)
```

Even though the compiler sees two distinct types for the lists, at execution time, they look exactly the same (see figure). Despite that, you can normally be sure a List<String> contains only strings and a List<Int> contains only integers because the compiler knows the type arguments and ensures only elements of the correct type are stored in each list. (You can deceive the compiler through type casts or by using Java raw types to access the list, but you need to make a special effort to do that.)

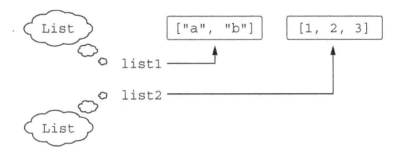

Figure At run time, you don't know whether list1 and list2 were declared as lists of strings or integers.

Each of them is just List. This introduces additional constraints to working with type arguments.

Let's talk next about the constraints that go with erasing the type information. Because type arguments aren't stored, you can't check them—for example, you can't check whether a list is a list of strings rather than other objects. As a general rule, it's not possible to use types with type arguments in is checks. This can prove to be a hurdle when you want to create a function that should exhibit different behavior based on the type argument of its parameter.

For example, you might have a function readNumbersOrWords , which, depending on the user input, either returns a List<String> or List<Int> . Trying to discern between the list of numbers and words via is checks inside the printList function doesn't compile:

```
fun readNumbersOrWords(): List<Any> {    val input = readln()    val words: List<String> =
input.split(",")    val numbers: List<Int> = words.mapNotNull { it.toIntOrNull() }    return
numbers.ifEmpty { words }

} fun printList(l: List<Any>) {    when(l) {

    is List<String> -> println("Strings: $l")  ❶       is List<Int> -> println("Integers: $l")   ❶

  }

} fun main() {    val list = readNumbersOrWords()    printList(list)

}
```

❶ Error: Cannot check for an instance of erased type

Even though it's perfectly possible to find out at run time that value is a List, you can't tell whether it's a list of strings, persons, or something else: that information has been erased. Note that erasing generic type information has its benefits: the overall amount of memory used by your application is smaller because less type information needs to be saved in memory.

As we stated earlier, Kotlin doesn't let you use a generic type without specifying type arguments. Thus, you may wonder how to check that the value is a list, rather than a set or another object. You can do that by using the special star-projection syntax:

```
if (value is List<*>) { /* ... */ }
```

Effectively, you need to include a * for every type parameter the type has. We'll discuss the star projection in detail (including why it's called a projection) in section; for now, you can think of it as a type with unknown arguments (or an analog of Java's List<?>). In the previous example, you check whether a value is a List, and you don't get any information about its element type.

Note that you can still use normal generic types in as and as? casts. But the cast won't fail if the class has the correct base type and an incorrect type argument because the type argument isn't known at run time when the cast is performed. Because of that, the compiler will emit an "unchecked cast" warning on such a cast. It's only a warning, so you can later use the value as having the necessary type, as shown next.

Listing Using a type cast with a generic type

```
fun printSum(c: Collection<*>) {    val intList = c as? List<Int>                 ❶        ?: throw
IllegalArgumentException("List is expected")    println(intList.sum())

}
```

❶ Warning here: Unchecked cast: List<*> to List<Int>

Everything compiles fine: the compiler only issues a warning, which means this code is legitimate. If you call the printSum function on a list or a set of integers, it works as expected—it prints a sum in the first case and throws an IllegalArgumentException in the second case:

```
fun main() {    printSum(listOf(1, 2, 3))          ❶

  // 6

  printSum(setOf(1, 2, 3))               ❷
```

// IllegalArgumentException: List is expected }

❶ With lists, everything works as expected.

❷ The set isn't a list, so an exception is thrown.

But if you pass in a value of a wrong type, you'll get a ClassCastException at run time:

```
fun main() {    printSum(listOf("a", "b", "c"))                    ❶
    // ClassCastException: String cannot be cast to Number }
```

❶ the cast succeeds, but since strings cannot be summed, another exception is thrown later.

Let's discuss the exception that's thrown if you call the printSum function on a list of strings. You don't get an IllegalArgumentException because you can't check whether the argument is a List<Int>. Therefore, the cast succeeds, and the function sum is called on such a list anyway. During its execution, an exception is thrown. This happens because the function tries to get Number values from the list and add them together. An attempt to use a String as a Number results in a ClassCastException at run time.

Note that the Kotlin compiler is smart enough to allow is checks when the corresponding type information is already known at compile time.

Listing Using a type check with a known type argument

```
fun printSum(c: Collection<Int>) {                    ❶    when (c) {
    is List<Int> -> println("List sum: ${c.sum()}")    ❷        is Set<Int> -> println("Set sum: ${c.sum()}")
❷
    }
} fun main() {    printSum(listOf(1,2,3))
    // List sum: 6    printSum(setOf(3,4,5))
    // Set sum: 12
}
```

❶ Because the element type Int is known at compile time ...

❷ ... these checks are legitimate.

In listing, the check whether c has type List<Int> is possible because you know at compile time that this collection (no matter whether it's a list or another kind of collection) contains integer numbers—unlike the example you saw in listing, where no information about the type was available.

Generally, the Kotlin compiler takes care of letting you know which checks are dangerous (forbidding is checks and emitting warnings for as casts) and which are possible. You just have to know the meaning of those warnings and understand which operations are safe.

As we already mentioned, Kotlin does have a special construct that allows you to use specific type arguments in the body of a function, but that's only possible for inline functions. Let's look at this feature.

Functions with reified type parameters can refer to actual type arguments at run time

As we discussed earlier, Kotlin generics are erased at run time, which means if you have an instance of a generic class, you can't find out the type arguments used when the instance was created. The same holds for type arguments of a function. When you call a generic function, in its body, you can't determine the type arguments it was invoked with the following:

fun <T> isA(value: Any) = value is T

// Error: Cannot check for instance of erased type: T

This is true in general, but there's one case where this limitation can be avoided: inline functions. Type parameters of inline functions can be reified, which means you can refer to actual type arguments at run time.

We discussed inline functions in detail in section. As a reminder, if you mark a function with the inline keyword, the compiler will replace every call to the function with the actual code implementing the function. Making the function inline may improve performance if this function uses lambdas as arguments: the lambda code can be inlined as well, so no anonymous class will be created. This section shows another case when inline functions are helpful: their type arguments can be reified.

If you declare the previous isA function as inline and mark the type parameter as reified, you can check value to see whether it's an instance of T.

Listing Declaring a function with a reified type parameter

```
inline fun <reified T> isA(value: Any) = value is T    ❶
 fun main() {    println(isA<String>("abc"))
  // true    println(isA<String>(123))
  // false
}
```

❶ Now, this code compiles.

Let's look at some less trivial examples of the use of reified type parameters. One of the simplest examples where reified type parameters come into play is the filterIsInstance standard library function. The function takes a collection, selects instances of the specified class, and returns only those instances. Here's how it can be used.

Listing Using the filterIsInstance standard library function

```
fun main() {    val items = listOf("one", 2, "three")    println(items.filterIsInstance<String>())
  // [one, three]
}
```

You say that you're interested in strings only by specifying <String> as a type argument for the function. The return type of the function will, therefore, be List<String>. In this case, the type argument is known at run time, and filterIsInstance uses it to check which values in the list are instances of the class specified as the type argument.

Here's a simplified version of the declaration of filterIsInstance from the Kotlin standard library.

Listing A simplified implementation of filterIsInstance

```
inline fun <reified T>                    ❶        Iterable<*>.filterIsInstance(): List<T> {     val destination =
mutableListOf<T>()      for (element in this) {

    if (element is T) {                      ❷                destination.add(element)

    }

  }

  return destination

}
```

❶ reified declares that this type parameter will not be erased at run time.

❷ You can check whether the element is an instance of the class specified as a type argument.

Why reification works for inline functions only

How does this work? Why are you allowed to write element is T in an inline function, but not in a regular class or function?

As we discussed in section, the compiler inserts the bytecode implementing the inline function into every place where it's called. Every time you call the function with a reified type parameter; the compiler knows the exact type used as the type argument in that particular call. Therefore, the compiler can generate the bytecode that references the specific class used as a type argument. In effect, for the ilterIsInstance<String> call shown in listing, the generated code will be equivalent to the following:

```
for (element in this) {     if (element is String) {        ❶              destination.add(element)

  }

}
```

❶ References a specific class

Because the generated bytecode references a specific class, not a type parameter, it isn't affected by the type argument erasure that happens at run time.

Note that inline function with reified type parameters can't be called from Java code. Normal inline functions are accessible to Java as regular functions—they can be called but aren't inlined. Functions with reified type parameters require additional processing to substitute the type argument values into the bytecode; therefore, they must always be inlined. This makes it impossible to call them in a regular way, as the Java code does.

An inline function can have multiple reified type parameters, and it can have non-reified type parameters in addition to the reified ones. Note that the filterIsInstance function is marked as inline even though it doesn't expect any lambdas as arguments. In section, we discussed that marking a function as inline only has performance benefits when the function has function type parameters and the corresponding arguments— lambdas— are inlined together with the function. But in this case, you aren't marking the function as inline for performance reasons; instead, you're doing it to enable the use of reified type parameters.

To ensure good performance, you still need to keep track of the size of the function marked as inline. If the function becomes large, it's better to extract the code that doesn't depend on the reified type parameters into separate non-inline functions.

Avoiding java.lang.Class parameters by replacing class references with reified type parameters

One common use case for reified type parameters is building adapters for APIs that take parameters of type. An example of such an API is ServiceLoader from the JDK. It takes a representing an interface or an abstract class and returns an instance of a service class implementing that interface based on a previously provided configuration. Let's look at how you can use reified type parameters to make those APIs simpler to call.

To load a service using the standard Java API of ServiceLoader , you use the following call:

val serviceImpl = ServiceLoader.load(Service::class.java)

The ::class.java syntax shows how you can get a java.lang.Class corresponding to a Kotlin class. This is an exact equivalent of Service.class in Java. We'll cover this in much more detail in section, in our discussion of reflection.

Now, let's rewrite this example using a function with a reified type parameter, specifying the class of the service to load as a type argument of the loadService function:

val serviceImpl = loadService<Service>()

Much shorter, isn't it? Specifying a class as a type argument is easier to read because it's shorter than the ::class.java syntax you need to use otherwise.

Next, let's see how this loadService function can be defined:

inline fun <reified T> loadService() {　　❶　　return ServiceLoader.load(T::class.java) ❷ }

❶ The type parameter is marked as reified.

❷ Accesses the class of the type parameter as T::class

You can use the same ::class.java syntax on reified type parameters that you can use on regular classes. Using this syntax gives you the java.lang.Class corresponding to the class specified as the type parameter, which you can then use normally.

Simplifying the startActivity function on Android

If you're an Android developer, you may find another example to be more familiar: showing activities. Instead of passing the class of the activity as a java.lang.Class , you can also use a reified type parameter:

inline fun <reified T : Activity>

　　Context.startActivity() {　　　　❶　　val intent = Intent(this, T::class.java) ❷
startActivity(intent)

}

startActivity<DetailActivity>()　　　　　❸

❶ the type parameter is marked as reified.

❷ Accesses the class of the type parameter as T::class

❸ Invokes the method to show an activity

Declaring accessors with reified type parameters

Functions are not the only constructs in Kotlin that can be inlined and use reified type parameters. You already saw in section that property accessors can provide custom implementations for getters and setters. If a property accessor is defined on a generic type, marking the property as inline and the type parameter as reified allows you to reference the specific class used as the type argument.

In this example, you're providing an extension property canonical, which returns the canonical name of a generic class. Just like in section, this provides a more convenient way of accessing the canonicalName property, wrapping the call to T::class.java :

```
inline val <reified T> T.canonical: String    get() = T::class.java.canonicalName
fun main() {    println(listOf(1, 2, 3).canonical)
  // java.util.List
  println(1.canonical)    // java.lang.Integer
}
```

Reified type parameters come with restrictions

Even though reified type parameters are a handy tool, they have certain restrictions. Some are inherent to the concept, and others are determined by the current implementation and may be relaxed in future versions of Kotlin.

More specifically, here's how you can use a reified type parameter:

In type checks and casts (is , !is , as , as?)

To use the Kotlin reflection APIs, as we'll discuss in chapter 12 (::class)

To get the corresponding java.lang.Class (::class.java)

As a type argument to call other functions You can't do the following:

Create new instances of the class specified as a type parameter

Call methods on the companion object of the type parameter class

Use a non-reified type parameter as a type argument when calling a function with a reified type parameter Mark type parameters of classes or non-inline functions as reified.

The last constraint leads to an interesting consequence: because reified type parameters can only be used in inline functions, using a reified type parameter means the function along with all the lambdas passed to it are inlined. If the lambdas can't be inlined because of the way the inline function uses them or if you don't want them to be inlined for performance reasons, you can use the no inline modifier introduced in section to mark them as non inlineable.

Now, that we've discussed how generics work as a language feature, let's explore the concepts of subtyping and variance. We'll do so by taking a more detailed look at the most common generic types that come up in every Kotlin program: collections and their subclasses.

Variance describes the subtyping relationship between generic arguments

The concept of variance describes how types with the same base type and different type arguments relate to each other: for example, List<String> and List<Any>. First, we'll discuss why this relation is important in general, and then we'll look at how it's expressed in Kotlin. Understanding variance is essential when you write your own generic classes or functions: it helps you create APIs that don't restrict users in inconvenient ways and don't break their type-safety expectations.

Variance determines whether it is safe to pass an argument to a function

Imagine that you have a function that takes a List<Any> as an argument.

For example, let's consider a function that prints the contents of the list:

```
fun printContents(list: List<Any>) {    println(list.joinToString())
```

```
} fun main() {    printContents(listOf("abc", "bac"))

    // abc, bac

}
```

It looks like a list of strings works fine here. The function treats each element as Any, and because every string is Any, it's totally safe.

Now, let's look at another function, which modifies the list (and, therefore, takes MutableList as a parameter):

```
fun addAnswer(list: MutableList<Any>) {    list.add(42)

}
```

Can anything bad happen if you pass a list of strings to this function?

```
fun main() {

    val strings = mutableListOf("abc", "bac")

    addAnswer(strings)                    ❶        println(strings.maxBy { it.length })              ❷

    // ClassCastException: Integer cannot be cast to String

}
```

❶ If this line would compile ...

❷ ... you'd get an exception at run time.

You declare a variable strings of type MutableList<String>. Then you try to pass it to the function. If the compiler accepted it (which it doesn't), you'd be able to add an integer to a list of strings, which would then lead to a run-time exception when you tried to access the contents of the list as strings. For that reason, this call doesn't compile. This example shows that it's not safe to pass a MutableList<String> as an argument when a MutableList<Any> is expected; the Kotlin compiler correctly forbids that.

Now, you can answer the question of whether it's safe to pass a list of strings to a function that expects a list of Any objects. It's not safe if the function adds or replaces elements in the list because this creates the possibility of type inconsistencies. It's safe otherwise (we'll discuss why in more detail later in this section). In Kotlin, this can be easily controlled by choosing the right interface, depending on whether the list is mutable. If a function accepts a read-only list, you can pass a List with a more specific element type. If the list is mutable, you can't do that.

Later in this section, we'll generalize the same question for any generic class, not only List. You'll also see why the two interfaces List and MutableList are different with regard to their type argument. But before that, we need to discuss the concepts of type and subtype.

Understanding the differences between classes, types, and subtypes

As we discussed in section, the type of a variable specifies the possible values for this variable. We've sometimes used the terms type and class interchangeably, but they aren't—and now is the time to look at the difference.

In the simplest case, with a non-generic class, the name of the class can be used directly as a type. For example, if you write var x: String, you declare a variable that can hold instances of the String class. But note that the same class name can also be used to declare a nullable type: var x: String?. This means each Kotlin class can be used to construct at least two types.

The story becomes even more complicated with generic classes. To get a valid type, you have to substitute a specific type as a type argument for the class's type parameter. List isn't a type (it's a class), but all of the following substitutions are valid types: List<Int>, List<String?>, List<List<String>>, and so on. Each generic class produces a potentially infinite number of types.

In order for us to discuss the relation between types, you need to be familiar with the term subtype. A type B is a subtype of a type A if you can use the value of the type B whenever a value of the type A is required. For instance, Int is a subtype of Number, but Int isn't a subtype of String. This definition also indicates that a type is considered a subtype of itself. Figure illustrates this.

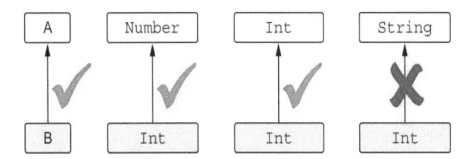

Figure B is a subtype of A if you can use it when A is expected. Since you can use an Int where a Number is expected, it is a subtype. Likewise, you can use an Int where an Int is expected; it is also a subtype of itself. Because you can't use an Int where a String is expected, it can't be considered a subtype.

The term supertype is the opposite of subtype. If A is a subtype of B, then B is a supertype of A.

Why is it important whether one type is a subtype of another? The compiler performs this check every time when you assign a value to a variable or pass an argument to a function. Consider the following example.

Listing Checking whether a type is a subtype of another

```
fun test(i: Int) {     val n: Number = i          ❶


    fun f(s: String) { /*...*/ }     f(i)                ❷
}
```

❶ Compiles because Int is a subtype of Number

❷ Doesn't compile because Int isn't a subtype of String

Storing a value in a variable is allowed only when the value type is a subtype of the variable type; for instance, the type Int of the variable initializer i is a subtype of the variable type Number, so the declaration of n is valid. Passing an expression to a function is allowed only when the type of the expression is a subtype of the function parameter type. In the example, the type Int of the argument i isn't a subtype of the function parameter String, so the invocation of the f function doesn't compile.

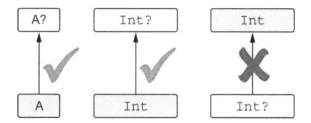

Figure A non-null type   A is a subtype of nullableA?, but not vice versa: you can use anInt where an Int? is expected, but you can't use anInt? where an Int is expected.

A non-null type is a subtype of its nullable version, but they both correspond to one class. You can always store the value of a non-nullable type in a variable of a nullable type, but not vice versa (null isn't an acceptable value for a variable of a non-nullable type). That makes the non-nullable type a subtype of the nullable type:

val s: String = "abc" val t: String? = s   **1**

1 This assignment is legal because String is a subtype of String?.

A generic class—for instance, MutableList —is called invariant on the type parameter if, for any two different types A and B, MutableList<A> isn't a subtype or a supertype of MutableList<B>. In Java, all classes are invariant (even though specific uses of those classes can be marked as non-invariant, as you'll see soon).

Covariance preserves the subtyping relation

A covariant class is a generic class (we'll use Producer<T> as an example) for which the following holds:

Producer<A> is a subtype of Producer<B> if A is a subtype of B. We say that the subtyping is preserved. For example, Producer<Cat> is a subtype of Producer <Animal> because Cat is a subtype of Animal.

In Kotlin, to declare the class to be covariant on a certain type parameter, you put the out keyword before the name of the type parameter:

interface Producer<out T> {   **1**   fun produce(): T

}

1 This class is declared as a covariant on T.

Marking a type parameter of a class as covariant makes it possible to pass values of that class as function arguments and return values when the type arguments don't exactly match the ones in the function definition. For example, imagine a function that takes care of feeding a group of animals, represented by the Herd class. The type parameter of the Herd class identifies the type of animal in the herd.

Listing Defining an invariant collection-like class

```
open class Animal {    fun feed() { /* ... */ }

}

class Herd<T : Animal> {         1     val size: Int get() = /* ... */    operator fun get(i: Int): T { /* ... */ }
} fun feedAll(animals: Herd<Animal>) {    for (i in 0..<animals.size) {        animals[i].feed()

    }

}
```

❶ the type parameter isn't declared as covariant.

Suppose a user of your code has a herd of cats and needs to take care of them.

Listing Using an invariant collection-like class

```
class Cat : Animal() {         ❶    fun cleanLitter() { /* ... */ }
}
fun takeCareOfCats(cats: Herd<Cat>) {    for (i in 0..<cats.size) {        cats[i].cleanLitter()
   }
   // feedAll(cats)              ❷
}
```

❶ A Cat is an Animal.

❷ Error: inferred type is Herd<Cat>, but Herd<Animal> was expected.

Unfortunately, the cats will remain hungry; if you tried to pass the herd to the feed All function, you'd get a type mismatch error during compilation. Because you don't use any variance modifier on the T type parameter in the Herd class, making it invariant, the herd of cats isn't a subclass of the herd of animals. You could use an explicit cast to work around the problem, but that approach is verbose, error prone, and almost never a correct way to deal with a type-mismatch problem.

Because the Herd class has an API similar to List and doesn't allow its clients to add or change the animals in the herd, you can make it covariant and change the calling code accordingly.

Listing Using a covariant collection-like class

```
class Herd<out T : Animal> {    ❶
  /* ... */
} fun takeCareOfCats(cats: Herd<Cat>) {    for (i in 0..<cats.size) {        cats[i].cleanLitter()
   }    feedAll(cats)              ❷
}
```


❶ The T parameter is now covariant.

❷ You don't need a cast.

You can't make any class covariant, as that would be unsafe. Making the class covariant on a certain type parameter constrains the possible uses of this type parameter in the class. To guarantee type safety, it can be used only in so-called out positions, meaning the class can produce values of type T but not consume them.

Uses of a type parameter in declarations of class members can be divided into in and out positions. Let's consider a class that declares a type parameter T and contains a function that uses T. We say that if T is used as the return type of a function, it's in the out position. In this case, the function produces values of type T. If T is used as the type of a function parameter, it's in the in position. Such a function consumes values of type T. Figure illustrates this.

```
interface Transformer<T> {
    fun transform(t: T): T
}
```

The in
position

The out
position

Figure Depending on where a generic parameter is used, its position is referred to differently. The function parameter type is called the in position, and the function return type is called the out position.

The out keyword on a type parameter of the class requires that all methods using T have T only in out positions and not in in positions. This keyword constrains possible use of T, which guarantees safety of the corresponding subtype relation.

Now, let's look at the List<T> interface. List is read-only in Kotlin, so it has a method get that returns an element of type T but doesn't define any methods that store a value of type T in the list. Therefore, it's also covariant.

interface List<out T> : Collection<T> {   operator fun get(index: Int): T   ❶   // ...

}

❶ Read-only interface that defines only methods that return T (so T is in the out position)

Note that a type parameter can be used not only as a parameter type or return type directly, but also as a type argument of another type. For example, the List interface contains a method subList that returns List<T> .

interface List<out T> : Collection<T> {   fun subList(fromIndex: Int, toIndex: Int): List<T> ❶   // ...

}

❶ Here, T is in the out position as well.

In this case, T in the function subList is used in the out position. We won't go deep into detail here; if you're interested in the exact algorithm that determines which position is out and which is in , you can find this information in the Kotlin language documentation.

Note that you can't declare MutableList<T> as covariant on its type parameter because it contains methods that take values of type T as parameters and return such values (therefore, T appears in both in and out positions). The compiler enforces this restriction. The following code, which attempts to declare the interface as covariant via the out keyword, reports an error, Type parameter T is declared as 'out' but occurs in the 'in' position:

interface MutableList<out T>   ❶   : List<T>, MutableCollection<T> {   override fun add(element: T): Boolean ❷ }

❶ MutableList can't be declared as covariant (via the out keyword) on T ...

❷ ... because T is used in the in position (T is used as the type of a function parameter).

Note that constructor parameters are in neither the in nor the out position. Even if a type parameter is declared as out, you can still use it in a constructor parameter declaration:

class Herd<out T: Animal>(vararg animals: T) { /* ... */ }

The variance protects the class instance from misuse if you're working with it as an instance of a more generic type: you just can't call the potentially dangerous methods. The constructor isn't a method that can be called later (after an instance creation); therefore, it can't be potentially dangerous.

If you use the val or var keyword with a constructor parameter, however, you also declare a getter and a setter (if the property is mutable). Therefore, the type parameter is used in the out position for a read-only property and in both out and in positions for a mutable property:

class Herd<T: Animal>(var leadAnimal: T, vararg animals: T) { /* ... */ }

In this case, T can't be marked as out because the class contains a setter for the leadAnimal property that uses T in the in position.

Also note that the position rules cover only the externally visible (public , protected , and internal) API of a class. Parameters of private methods are in neither the in nor the out position. The variance rules protect a class from misuse by external clients and don't come into play in the implementation of the class itself:

class Herd<out T: Animal>(private var leadAnimal: T,   vararg animals: T) { /* ... */ }

Now, it's safe to make Herd covariant on T because the leadAnimal property has been made private.

You may ask what happens with classes or interfaces where the type parameter is used only in an in position. In that case, the reverse relation holds. The next section presents the details.

Contravariance reverses the subtyping relation

The concept of contravariance can be thought of as a mirror to covariance: for a contravariant class, the subtyping relation is the opposite of the subtyping relations of classes used as its type arguments. Let's start with an example: the Comparator interface. This interface defines one method, compare, which compares two given objects:

```
interface Comparator<in T>  {
    fun compare(e1: T, e2: T): Int { /* ... */ }   ❶
}
```

❶ Uses T in in positions

You can see that the method of this interface only consumes values of type T. That means T is used only in in positions; therefore, its declaration can be preceded by the in keyword.

A comparator defined for values of a certain type can, of course, compare the values of any subtype of that type. For example, you might have a simple hierarchy of fruits—apples and oranges—that both share a common property, weight:

```
sealed class Fruit {    abstract val weight: Int
} data class Apple(    override val weight: Int,    val color: String,
): Fruit() data class Orange(    override val weight: Int,    val juicy: Boolean,
): Fruit()
```

If you now create a Comparator<Fruit> , you can use it to compare values of any specific type:

```
fun main() {    val weightComparator = Comparator<Fruit> { a, b ->
    a.weight - b.weight    }
```

```
val fruits: List<Fruit> = listOf(
    Orange(180, true),        Apple(100, "green")
)
val apples: List<Apple> = listOf(
    Apple(50, "red"),
    Apple(120, "green"),
    Apple(155, "yellow")
)
println(fruits.sortedWith(weightComparator))                    ❶
// [Apple(weight=100, color=green), Orange(weight=180, juicy=true)]
println(apples.sortedWith(weightComparator))
// [Apple(weight=50, color=red), Apple(weight=120, color=green),
    Apple(weight=155, color=yellow)] }
```

❶ You can use the weight comparator for any collection of objects that are a subtype of Fruit, such as apples and oranges.

The sorted with function expects a Comparator<String> (a comparator that can compare strings), and it's safe to pass one that can compare more general types. If you need to perform comparisons on objects of a certain type, you can use a comparator that handles either that type or any of its supertypes. This means

Comparator<Any> is a subtype of Comparator<String>, where Any is a supertype of String. The subtyping relation between comparators for two different types goes in the opposite direction of the subtyping relation between those types.

Now, you're ready for the full definition of contravariance. A class that is contravariant on the type parameter is a generic class (let's consider Consumer<T> as an example) for which the following hold Consumer<A> is a subtype of Consume<B> if B is a subtype of A. The type arguments A and B changed places, so we say the subtyping is reversed. For example, Consumer<Animal> is a subtype of Consumer<Cat>.

Figure shows the difference between the subtyping relation for classes that are covariant and contravariant on a type parameter. You can see that for the Producer class, the subtyping relation replicates the subtyping relation for its type arguments, whereas for the Consumer class, the relation is reversed.

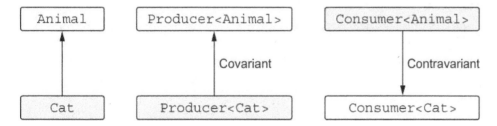

Figure For a covariant type Producer<T>, the subtyping is preserved, but for a contravariant type Consumer<T>, the subtyping is reversed.

The in keyword means values of the corresponding type are passed in to methods of this class and consumed by those methods. Similar to the covariant case, constraining use of the type parameter leads to the specific subtyping relation. The in keyword on the type parameter T means the subtyping is reversed and T can be used only in in positions. Table summarizes the differences between the possible variance choices.

A class or interface can be covariant on one type parameter and contravariant on another. The classic example is the Function interface. The following declaration shows a one-parameter Function:

```
interface Function1<in P, out R> {    operator fun invoke(p: P): R
}
```

The Kotlin notation (P) -> R is another, more readable form to express Function1 <P, R>. You can see that P (the parameter type) is used only in the in position and is marked with the in keyword, whereas R (the return type) is used only in the out position and is marked with the out keyword. That means the subtyping for the function type is reversed for its first type argument and preserved for the second. For example, if you have a higher order function that tries to enumerate your cats, you can pass a lambda accepting any animals:

```
fun enumerateCats(f: (Cat) -> Number) { /* ... */ } fun Animal.getIndex(): Int = /* ... */

fun main() {    enumerateCats(Animal::getIndex)    ❶
}
```

❶ This code is legal in Kotlin. Animal is a supertype of Cat, and Int is a subtype of Number.

Figure illustrates the subtyping relationships in the previous example.

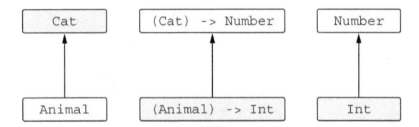

Figure The function (T) -> R is contravariant on its argument (reversing the subtyping) and covariant on its return type (preserving the subtyping).

Note that in all the examples so far, the variance of a class is specified directly in its declaration and applies to all places where the class is used. Java doesn't support that and instead uses wildcards to specify the variance for specific uses of a class. Let's look at the difference between the two approaches and see how you can use the second approach in Kotlin.

Specifying variance for type occurrences via use-site variance

The ability to specify variance modifiers on class declarations is convenient because the modifiers apply to all places where the class is used. This is called declaration-site variance. If you're familiar with Java's wildcard types (? extends and ? super), you'll realize that Java handles variance differently. In Java, every time you use a type with a type parameter, you can also specify whether this type parameter can be replaced with its subtypes or supertypes. This is called use-site variance.

Declaration-site variance in Kotlin vs. Java wildcards

Declaration-site variance allows for more concise code because you specify the variance modifiers once, and clients of your class don't have to think about them. In Java, to create APIs that behave according to users' expectations, the library writer must use wildcards all the time: Function<? super T, ? extends R> . If you examine the source code of the Java 8 standard library, you'll find wildcards on every use of the

Function interface. For example, here's how the Stream.map method is declared:

```java
/* Java */ public interface Stream<T> {
    <R> Stream<R> map(Function<? super T, ? extends R> mapper); }
```

Specifying the variance once on the declaration makes the code much more concise and elegant.

Kotlin supports use-site variance too, allowing you to specify the variance for a specific occurrence of a type parameter even when it can't be declared as covariant or contravariant in the class declaration. Let's see how that works.

You've seen that many interfaces, like MutableList, aren't covariant or contravariant in a general case because they can both produce and consume values of types specified by their type parameters. But it's common for a variable of that type in a particular function to be used in only one of those roles: a producer or consumer. For example, consider this simple function.

Listing A data copy function with invariant parameter types

```kotlin
fun <T> copyData(source: MutableList<T>,          destination: MutableList<T>) {    for (item in source) {        destination.add(item)
    }
}
```

This function copies elements from one collection to another. Even though both collections have an invariant type, the source collection is only used for reading, and the destination collection is only used for writing. In this situation, elements of a specific type can be copied into a collection that stores a supertype of these elements. For example, it's perfectly valid to copy a collection of strings into a collection with the generic type Any.

To make this function work with lists of different types, you can introduce the second generic parameter.

Listing A data copy function with two type parameters

```kotlin
fun <T: R, R> copyData(source: MutableList<T>,      ❶ destination: MutableList<R>) {    for (item in source) {        destination.add(item)
    } } fun main() {    val ints = mutableListOf(1, 2, 3)    val anyItems = mutableListOf<Any>()
    copyData(ints, anyItems)                ❷      println(anyItems)
    // [1, 2, 3]
}
```

❶ the source's element type should be a subtype of the destination's element type.

❷ You can call this function because Int is a subtype of Any.

You declare two generic parameters representing the element types in the source and destination lists. To be able to copy elements from one list to the other, the source element type should be a subtype of elements in the destination list, like Int is a subtype of Any in listing.

But Kotlin provides a more elegant way to express this. When the implementation of a function only calls methods that have the type parameter in the out (or only in the in) position, you can take advantage of it and add variance modifiers to the particular usages of the type parameter in the function definition.

Listing A data copy function with an out -projected type parameter

```
fun <T> copyData(source: MutableList<out T>,    ❶                    destination: MutableList<T>) {    for
(item in source) {        destination.add(item)

    }

}
```

❶ You can add the out keyword to the type usage: no methods with T in the in position are used.

You can specify a variance modifier on any usage of a type parameter in a type declaration, for a parameter type (as in listing), local variable type, function return type, and so on. What happens here is called type projection: we say that source isn't a regular MutableList but a projected (restricted) one. You can only call methods that return the generic type parameter or, strictly speaking, use it in the out position only. The compiler prohibits calling methods where this type parameter is used as an argument (in the in position):

```
fun main() {    val list: MutableList<out Number> = mutableListOf()    list.add(42)

    // Error: Out-projected type 'MutableList<out Number>' prohibits

    // the use of 'fun add(element: E): Boolean'

}
```

Don't be surprised that you can't call some of the methods if you're using a projected type. If you need to call them, you must use a regular type instead of a projection. This may require you to declare a second type parameter that depends on the one that was originally a projection, as in listing.

Of course, the right way to implement the function copy Data would be to use List<T> as a type of the source argument because we're only using the methods declared in List, not in MutableList, and the

variance of the List type parameter is specified in its declaration. But this example is still important for illustrating the concept, especially keeping in mind that most classes don't have a separate covariant read interface and an invariant read-write interface, such as List and MutableList.

There is no sense in having an out projection of a type parameter that already has out variance, such as List<out T>. That would mean the same as List<T> because List is declared as class List<out T>.

The Kotlin compiler will warn that such a projection is redundant.

In a similar way, you can use the in modifier on a type parameter to indicate that, in this location, the corresponding value acts as a consumer and the type parameter can be substituted with any of its supertypes. Here's how you can rewrite listing using an in projection.

Listing A data copy function with an in -projected type parameter

```
fun <T> copyData(source: MutableList<T>,

        destination: MutableList<in T>) {    ❶     for (item in source) {        destination.add(item)

    }

}
```

❶ Allows the destination element type to be a supertype of the source element type

Star projection: Using the * character to indicate a lack of information about a generic argument

While talking about type checks and casts earlier in this chapter, we mentioned the special star-projection syntax you can use to indicate that you have no information about a generic argument. For example, a list of elements of an unknown type is expressed using that syntax as List<*>. Let's explore the semantics of star projections in detail.

First, note that MutableList<*> isn't the same as MutableList<Any?> (it's important here that

MutableList<T> is invariant on T). A MutableList<Any?> is a list that you know can contain elements of any type. On the other hand, a MutableList<*> is a list that contains elements of a specific type you don't know.

The list was created as a list of elements of a specific type, such as String (you can't create a new

ArrayList<*>), and the code that created it expects it will only contain elements of that type. Because you don't know what the type is, you can't put anything into the list because any value you put there might violate the expectations of the calling code. But it's possible to get the elements from the list because you know for certain that all values stored there will match the type Any? , which is the supertype of all Kotlin types:

```
import kotlin.random.Random

fun main() {    val list: MutableList<Any?> = mutableListOf('a', 1, "qwe")    val chars = mutableListOf('a', 'b', 'c')

    val unknownElements: MutableList<*> =              ❶              if (Random.nextBoolean()) list else chars
    println(unknownElements.first())              ❷

    // a    unknownElements.add(42)              ❸

    // Error: Out-projected type 'MutableList<*>' prohibits

    // the use of 'fun add(element: E): Boolean' }
```

❶ MutableList<*> isn't the same as MutableList<Any?>.

❷ It's safe to get elements: first() returns an element of the Any? type.

❸ the compiler forbids you to call this method.

Why does the compiler refer to MutableList<*> as an out -projected type? In this context, MutableList<*> is projected to (acts as) MutableList<out Any?>: when you know nothing about the type of the element, it's safe to get elements of Any? type, but it's not safe to put elements into the list. Regarding Java wildcards, Kotlin's MyType<*> corresponds to Java's MyType<?>.

NOTE For contravariant type parameters such as Consumer<in T>, a star projection is equivalent to <in Nothing> . In effect, you can't call any methods that have T in the signature on such a star projection. If the type parameter is contravariant, it acts only as a consumer, and as we discussed earlier, you don't know exactly what it can consume. Therefore, you can't give it anything to consume.

You can use the star-projection syntax when the information about type arguments isn't important: you don't use any methods that refer to the type parameter in the signature, or you only read the data and you don't care about its specific type. For instance, you can implement the printFirst function taking List<*> as a parameter:

```
fun printFirst(list: List<*>) {    ❶    if (list.isNotEmpty()) {    ❷    println(list.first())    ❸    }
} fun main() {    printFirst(listOf("Sveta", "Seb", "Dima", "Roman"))

    // Sveta

}
```

❶ Every list is a possible argument.

❷ isNotEmpty() doesn't use the generic type parameter.

❸ first() now returns Any?, but in this case, that's enough.

As in the case with use-site variance, you have an alternative—to introduce a generic type parameter:

```
fun <T> printFirst(list: List<T>) {    ❶     if (list.isNotEmpty()) {        println(list.first())    ❷
    }
}
```

❶ Again, every list is a possible argument.

❷ first() now returns a value of T.

The syntax with star projection is more concise, but it works only if you aren't interested in the exact value of the generic type parameter: you use only methods that produce values, and you don't care about the types of those values.

Now, let's look at another example of using a type with a star projection and common traps you may fall into while using that approach. Let's say you need to validate user input, and you declare an interface FieldValidator. It contains its type parameter in the in position only, so it can be declared as contravariant. And indeed, it's correct to use the validator that can validate any elements when a validator of strings is expected (that's what declaring it as contravariant lets you do). You also declare two validators that handle String and Int inputs.

Listing Interfaces for input validation

```
interface FieldValidator<in T> {        ❶      fun validate(input: T): Boolean     ❷
} object DefaultStringValidator : FieldValidator<String> {    override fun validate(input: String) =
input.isNotEmpty()

} object DefaultIntValidator : FieldValidator<Int> {    override fun validate(input: Int) = input >= 0

}
```

❶ Interface declared as contravariant on T

❷ T is used only in the in position (this method consumes a value of T).

Now, imagine that you want to store all validators in the same container and get the right validator according to the type of input. Your first attempt might use a map to store them. You need to store validators for any types, so you declare a map from KClass (which represents a Kotlin class—chapter will cover KClass in detail) to FieldValidator<*> (which may refer to a validator of any type):

```
import kotlin.reflect.KClass

 fun main() {     val validators = mutableMapOf<KClass<*>, FieldValidator<*>>()
validators[String::class] = DefaultStringValidator     validators[Int::class] = DefaultIntValidator }
```

Once you do that, you may have difficulties when trying to use the validators. You can't validate a string with a validator of the type FieldValidator<*> . It's unsafe because the compiler doesn't know what kind of validator

it is:

```
validators[String::class]!!.validate("")                    ❶
// Error: Out-projected type 'FieldValidator<*>' prohibits
// the use of 'fun validate(input: T): Boolean'
```

❶ The value stored in the map has the type FieldValidator<*>.

You saw this error earlier when you tried to put an element into MutableList<*>. In this case, this error means it's unsafe to give a value of a specific type to a validator for an unknown type. One of the ways to fix that is to cast a validator explicitly to the type you need. It's not safe and isn't recommended, but we show it here as a fast trick to make your code compile so that you can refactor it afterward.

Listing Retrieving a validator using an explicit cast

```
val stringValidator = validators[String::class] as FieldValidator<String>  ❶
println(stringValidator.validate(""))
```

// false

❶ Warning: "unchecked cast"

The compiler emits a warning about the unchecked cast. Note, however, that this code will fail on validation only, not when you make the cast because, at run time, all the generic type information is erased.

Listing Incorrectly retrieving a validator

```
val stringValidator = validators[Int::class]          ❶                    as FieldValidator<String>     ❷
stringValidator.validate("")                    ❸ // java.lang.ClassCastException:
```

// java.lang.String cannot be cast to java.lang.Number

//   at DefaultIntValidator.validate

❶ You get an incorrect validator (possibly by mistake), but this code compiles.

❷ It's only a warning.

❸ the real error is hidden until you use the validator.

This incorrect code and listing are similar, in the sense that in both cases, only a warning is emitted. It becomes your responsibility to cast only values of the correct type.

This solution isn't type safe and is error prone. So, let's investigate what other options you have if you want to store validators for different types in one place.

The solution in listing uses the same validators map but encapsulates all the access to it into two generic methods responsible for having only correct validators registered and returned. This code also emits a warning about the unchecked cast (the same one), but here, the object Validators controls all access to the map, which guarantees no one will change the map incorrectly.

Listing Encapsulating access to the validator collection

```
object Validators {

    private val validators =                           ❶              mutableMapOf<KClass<*>,
FieldValidator<*>>()

    fun <T: Any> registerValidator(

        kClass: KClass<T>, fieldValidator: FieldValidator<T>) {        validators[kClass] = fieldValidator
❷

    }


    @Suppress("UNCHECKED_CAST")                                        ❸     operator fun <T: Any> get(kClass:
KClass<T>): FieldValidator<T> =        validators[kClass] as? FieldValidator<T>              ?: throw
IllegalArgumentException(
```

```
            "No validator for ${kClass.simpleName}")
}
fun main() {
    Validators.registerValidator(String::class, DefaultStringValidator)
    Validators.registerValidator(Int::class, DefaultIntValidator)
    println(Validators[String::class].validate("Kotlin"))
    // true    println(Validators[Int::class].validate(42))
    // true
}
```

❶ Uses the same map as before, but now, you can't access it outside

❷ Puts only the correct key-value pairs into the map, when a validator corresponds to a class

❸ Suppresses the warning about the unchecked cast to FieldValidator<T>

Now, you have a type-safe API. All the unsafe logic is hidden in the body of the class, and by localizing it, you guarantee it can't be used incorrectly. The compiler forbids you to use an incorrect validator because the Validators object always gives you the correct validator implementation:

```
println(Validators[String::class].validate(42))          ❶
```

// Error: The integer literal does not conform to the expected type String

❶ Now, the get method returns an instance of FieldValidator<String>.

This pattern can be easily extended to the storage of any custom generic classes. Localizing unsafe code in a separate place prevents misuse and makes use of a container safe. Note that the pattern described here isn't specific to Kotlin; you can use the same approach in Java as well.

Java generics and variance are generally considered the trickiest part of the language. In Kotlin, we've tried hard to come up with a design that is easier to understand and easier to work with, while remaining interoperable with Java.

Type aliases

When you're working with types that combine multiple generics, it can sometimes be cumbersome to keep track of the meaning behind a type signature. It may not immediately be obvious what the purpose of a collection with the type List<(String, Int) -> String> is, and you may want to avoid repeating the same complex combination of generic and functional types whenever you want to refer to it.

For cases like this, Kotlin allows you to define type aliases: alternative names for existing types. You introduce a type alias using the type alias keyword, followed by the alias. Then, after an = sign, specify the original, underlying type.

You may find type aliases specifically useful when looking to shorten long generic types. In this example, you declare a function to combine the names of the four authors of this book, combine Authors. The behavior of how the authors is combined can be passed in using a parameter of a functional type that takes four strings and returns a new, combined string. This is often convenient, since its type signature, (String, String, String, String) -> String, may be somewhat cumbersome to repeat for every use. Using a type alias, you can give this functional type a new name, NameCombiner. This alias can then be used wherever you would've previously used the underlying type:

```
typealias NameCombiner = (String, String, String, String) -> String          ❶
```

```kotlin
val authorsCombiner: NameCombiner = { a, b, c, d -> "$a et al." }     ❷  val bandCombiner:
NameCombiner = { a, b, c, d -> "$a, $b & The Gang" } ❷


fun combineAuthors(combiner: NameCombiner) {                    ❸     println(combiner("Sveta", "Seb",
"Dima", "Roman"))
}
fun main() {     combineAuthors(bandCombiner)                         ❹
   // Sveta, Seb & The Gang     combineAuthors(authorsCombiner)                         ❹     // Sveta et al.
   combineAuthors { a, b, c, d -> "$d, $c & Co."}               ❺     // Roman, Dima & Co.
}
```

❶ A type alias is defined using the typealias keyword, the alias, and the underlying type.

❷ Type aliases can be used wherever you would've used the underlying type, like variable declarations ...

❸ ... or function parameter declarations.

❹ The type alias resolves to the underlying type. So it's perfectly fine to pass a NameCombiner ...

❺ ... or a lambda taking four strings and returning a single string.

By introducing a type alias, you managed to imbue the functional type with additional context that may aid in reading the code. However, it's also worth keeping in mind that developers not familiar with your codebase might have to spend additional time mentally resolving the NameCombiner alias back to its underlying type when reading code or making changes. Determining when to introduce type aliases in your code base is ultimately a tradeoff you will have to decide for yourself.

It's also worth noting that from the perspective of the compiler, type aliases don't introduce any new constraints or changes—during compilation, aliases are expanded entirely to their underlying type. So, while they provide a useful shorthand, type aliases do not provide any additional type safety.

Inline classes and type aliases: When to use each

Type aliases provide a useful shorthand, but they do not provide any additional type safety. That means they can't be used for introducing additional safeguards that prevent accidentally using two types in each other's stead; the following example illustrates this. Introducing a typealias ValidatedInput for String helps make the signature of the save function clearer by signaling a validated input is expected; however, the compiler will accept any String without complaint:

```kotlin
typealias ValidatedInput = String
fun save(v: ValidatedInput): Unit = TODO()
fun main() {
   val rawInput = "needs validating!"     save(rawInput)                    ❶
}
```

❶ Type aliases introduce no extra compile-time guarantees.

If added type safety with minimized run-time overhead is your goal, make sure you use inline classes (as discussed in section). Since the types of inline classes are checked just like any other type, the preceding example would not compile because of a type mismatch between ValidatedInput and String, forcing the user of the save function to make the conversion from String to ValidatedInput explicit, thus catching potential bugs early:

```
@JvmInline value class ValidatedInput(val s: String)
fun save(v: ValidatedInput): Unit = TODO()
fun main() {
    val rawInput = "needs validating!"     save(rawInput)          ❶
}
```

❶ Won't compile because of the type mismatch between ValidatedInput and String

Annotations and reflection

Up to this point, you've seen many features for working with classes and functions, but they all require you to specify the exact names of classes and functions you're using as part of the program source code. To call a function, you need to know the class in which it was defined as well as its name and parameter types. Annotations and reflection give you the power to go beyond that and to write code that deals with arbitrary classes that aren't known in advance. You can use annotations to add additional metadata and semantics to declarations. For example, you could use them to indicate whether a declaration is deprecated (as you'll see in section), you could use them for integrations with the compiler, your IDE, and external tools (as you'll see in section), or you could use them to construct library-specific and custom semantics. Reflection allows you to analyze your declarations at run time.

Applying annotations is straightforward, but writing your own annotations, and especially writing the code that handles them, is less trivial. The syntax for using annotations is exactly the same as in Java, whereas the syntax for declaring your own annotation classes is a bit different. The general structure of the reflection APIs is also similar to Java, but the details differ.

As a demonstration of the use of annotations and reflection, we'll walk you through an implementation of a real-life project: a JSON serialization and deserialization library called JKid. The library uses reflection to access properties of arbitrary Kotlin objects at run time as well as to create objects based on data provided in JSON files. Annotations allow you to customize how specific classes and properties are serialized and deserialized by the library.

Declaring and applying annotations

Annotations allow you to associate additional metadata with a declaration. The metadata can then be accessed by tools that work with source code, with compiled class files, or at run time, depending on how the annotation is configured.

Applying annotations to mark declarations

In Kotlin, to apply an annotation, you put its name, prefixed with the @ character, at the beginning of the declaration you're annotating. You can annotate different declarations in your code, such as functions and classes.

For instance, if you're using the kotlin.test library together with the JUnit framework (https://junit.org/junit5/), you can mark a test method with the @Test annotation:

```
import kotlin.test.* class MyTest {
    @Test           ❶    fun testTrue() {       assertTrue(1 + 1 == 2)
    }
}
```

1 the @Test annotation instructs the framework to invoke this method as a test.

As a more interesting example, let's look at the @Deprecated annotation. It marks a declaration as deprecated, indicating it should no longer be used in code—usually because it has been replaced by a different declaration or the functionality it provides is no longer supported.

The @Deprecated annotation takes up to three parameters. First, a message explains the reason for the deprecation. An optional replaceWith parameter allows you to provide a replacement pattern to support a smooth transition to a new version of the API. You can also provide a level that helps with gradual deprecation— whereas WARNING serves as a mere notification to users of a declaration, ERROR and HIDDEN prevent new Kotlin code from being compiled against these APIs, with the latter only keeping binary compatibility for previously compiled code.

The following example shows how you can provide arguments for the annotation (specifically, a deprecation message and a replacement pattern). The arguments are passed in parentheses, just as in a regular function call.

Here, the remove function is annotated to indicate that removeAt(index) is the preferred replacement:

@Deprecated("Use removeAt(index) instead.", ReplaceWith("removeAt(index)")) fun remove(index: Int) { /* ... */ }

With this declaration, if someone uses the remove function, IntelliJ IDEA will not only show what function should be used instead (removeAt , in this case) but also offer a quick fix to replace it automatically (see figure).

```
4 ▷    fun main() {
5              remove( index: 1)
6        }
         'remove(Int): Unit' is deprecated. Use removeAt(index) instead.

           Replace with 'removeAt(index)'  ⌥⇧↵     More actions...  ⌥↵

           @Deprecated(message = "Use removeAt(index) instead.",
           public fun remove(
               index: Int
           ): Unit

           Deprecated:  Use removeAt(index) instead.
           Replace with: removeAt(index)
           Main.kt
           ⌂ ch12ex.main
```

Figure IntelliJ IDEA offers a quick fix to replace calls to functions that are annotated with @Deprecated.

Annotations can only have parameters of primitive types, strings, enums, class references, other annotation classes, and arrays thereof. The syntax for specifying annotation arguments looks as follows:

• Specifying a class as an annotation argument—Put ::class after the class name:

@MyAnnotation(MyClass::class) . For instance, a serialization library (as we will discuss later in this chapter) may provide an annotation that expects a class as an argument to establish the mapping between interfaces and the implementation used during the deserialization process:

@DeserializeInterface(CompanyImpl::class) .

- Specifying another annotation as an argument—Don't put the @ character before the annotation name. For instance, ReplaceWith in the previous example is an annotation, but you don't use @ when you specify it as an argument of the Deprecated annotation.

- Specifying an array as an argument—You can use brackets: @RequestMapping(path = ["/foo", "/bar"]) . Alternatively, you can also use the arrayOf function to specify the array. (If you are using an annotation class declared in Java, the value parameter is automatically converted to a var arg parameter if

necessary.)

Annotation arguments need to be known at compile time, so you can't refer to arbitrary properties as arguments. To use a property as an annotation argument, you need to mark it with a const modifier, which tells the compiler that the property is a compile-time constant. Here's an example of JUnit's @Timeout annotation that specifies the timeout for the test in seconds:

```
const val TEST_TIMEOUT = 10L     ❶
 class MyTest {
   @Test
   @Timeout(TEST_TIMEOUT)     ❷     fun testMethod() {        // ...
   }
}
```

❶ Omitting the const modifier ...

❷ ... results in the following compile-time error: "Only const val can be used in constant expressions."

Specifying the exact declaration an annotation refers to: Annotation targets

In many cases, a single declaration in the Kotlin source code produces multiple Java declarations, and each of them can carry annotations. For example, a Kotlin property corresponds to a Java field, a getter, and possibly a setter and its parameter. A property declared in the primary constructor has one more corresponding element: the constructor parameter. Therefore, it may be necessary to specify which of these elements needs to be annotated.

You specify the element to be annotated with a use-site target declaration. The use-site target is placed between the

@ sign and the annotation name and is separated from the name with a colon. The word get in figure causes the annotation @JvmName to be applied to the property getter.

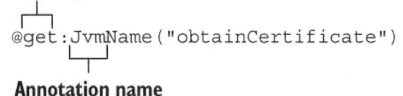

Figure The use-site target (like get or set) is placed between the @ sign and the annotation name, and is separated from the name with a colon.

If you want to change the way a function or property is accessed from Java, you can use the @JvmName annotation, which you briefly saw in section. Here, you use it to make the calculate function callable from Java code via performCalculation() :

```
@JvmName("performCalculation") fun calculate(): Int {     return (2 + 2) - 1

}
```

You can do the same with properties in Kotlin too; as you may remember from section 2.2.1, Kotlin properties automatically define a getter and setter. To explicitly apply the @JvmName annotation to the getter or setter of a property, use @get:JvmName() and @set:JvmName() , respectively:

```
class CertificateManager {

    @get:JvmName("obtainCertificate")                    ❶    @set:JvmName("putCertificate")
❷     var certificate: String = "-----BEGIN PRIVATE KEY-----" }
```

❶ Sets the JVM name for the getter

❷ Sets the JVM name for the setter

With these annotations in place, Java code can now access the certificate property using the renamed obtainCertificate and putCertificate functions:

```
class Foo {     public static void main(String[] args) {         var certManager = new CertificateManager();
var cert = certManager.obtainCertificate();         certManager.putCertificate("-----BEGIN CERTIFICATE-----
-");

    }

}
```

If the annotation you are using happens to be declared in Java, then it is applied to the corresponding field in Kotlin by default. For annotations defined in Kotlin, you can also declare them so that they can be directly applied to properties.

The full list of supported use-site targets is as follows:

property —Property (Java annotations can't be applied with this use-site target) field —Field generated for the property get —Property getter set —Property setter

receiver —Receiver parameter of an extension function or property param —Constructor parameter setparam —Property setter parameter

delegate —Field storing the delegate instance for a delegated property file —Class containing top-level functions and properties declared in the file

Any annotation with the file target needs to be placed at the top level of the file, before the package directive. One of the annotations commonly applied to files is @JvmName , which changes the name of the corresponding class. Section included an example: @file:JvmName("StringFunctions").

Kotlin allows you to apply annotations to arbitrary expressions, not only to class and function declarations or types. The most common example is the @Suppress annotation, which you can use to suppress a specific compiler warning in the context of the annotated expression. Here's an example that annotates a local variable declaration to suppress an unchecked cast warning:

```
fun test(list: List<*>) {     @Suppress("UNCHECKED_CAST")     val strings = list as List<String>     // ...

}
```

TIP Note that IntelliJ IDEA and Android studio offer "Suppress" as a quick fix when you press Alt-Enter on a compiler warning. Selecting this intention will insert the @Suppress annotation for you.

Controlling the Java API with annotations

Kotlin provides a variety of annotations to control how declarations written in Kotlin are compiled to Java bytecode and exposed to Java callers. Some of those annotations replace the corresponding keywords of the Java language (e.g., the @Volatile annotation serves as a direct replacement for Java's volatile keyword).

Others are used to change how Kotlin's declarations are visible to Java callers:

@JvmName changes the name of a Java method or field generated from a Kotlin declaration.

@JvmStatic can be applied to methods of an object declaration or a companion object to expose them as static Java methods.

@JvmOverloads, mentioned in section, instructs the Kotlin compiler to generate overloads for a function or constructor that has default parameter values.

@JvmField can be applied to a property to expose that property as a public Java field with no getters or setters.

@JvmRecord can be applied to a data class to declare a Java record class, as introduced in section.

You can find more details on the use of those annotations in their documentation comments and in the Java interop section of the online documentation.

Using annotations to customize JSON serialization

One of the classic use cases for annotations is customizing object serialization. Serialization is the process of converting an object to a binary or text representation that can then be stored or sent over the network. The reverse process, deserialization, converts such a representation back to an object. One of the most common formats used for serialization is JSON. There are several widely used Kotlin libraries for serializing Kotlin objects to JSON, including kotlinx.serialization which is developed by the Kotlin team at JetBrains. Additionally, libraries like and Gson that are designed to turn Java objects into JSON are also fully compatible with Kotlin.

Over the course of this chapter, we'll discuss the implementation of a pure Kotlin serialization library for this purpose, called JKid. It's small enough for you to read all of its source code easily, and we encourage you to do that while reading this chapter.

The library isn't as full-featured or flexible as kotlinx.serialization or other libraries, but provides a solid case study for how to perform annotation processing and reflection in Kotlin.

Because we will examine the most significant parts of a whole library, you may find it useful to keep the project open on your computer as you read this chapter. This gives you the opportunity to explore the structure and see how the individually discussed aspects of JKid fit together.

The JKid project features a series of exercises you can work through after you finish reading the chapter to ensure that you understand the concepts. You can find a description of the exercises in the project's README.md file or read it at the project page on GitHub.

Let's start with the simplest example to test the library: serializing and deserializing an instance of a class representing a Person. You pass the instance to the serialize function, and it returns a string containing its JSON representation:

```
data class Person(val name: String, val age: Int)

 fun main() {    val person = Person("Alice", 29)    println(serialize(person))    // {"age": 29, "name": "Alice"}
```

}

The JSON representation of an object consists of key-value pairs: pairs of property names and their values for the specific instance, such as "age": 29.

To get a Kotlin object back from the JSON representation, you call the deserialize function. When you create an instance from JSON data, you must specify the class explicitly as a type argument because JSON doesn't store object types. In this case, you pass the Person class:

fun main() {   val json = """{"name": "Alice", "age": 29}"""   println(deserialize<Person>(json))

    // Person(name=Alice, age=29)

}

Figure illustrates the equivalence between an object and its JSON representation. Note that the serialized class can contain not only values of primitive types or strings, as shown in the figure, but also collections and instances of other value object classes.

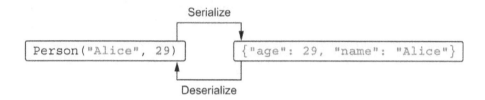

Figure Serialization and deserialization of the Person instance. Kotlin objects are converted into their textual JSON representation and back.

You can use annotations to customize the way objects are serialized and deserialized. When serializing an object to JSON, by default, the library tries to serialize all the properties and uses the property names as keys. The annotations allow you to change the defaults. In this section, we'll discuss two annotations, @JsonExclude and @JsonName, and you'll see their implementation later in the chapter:

 The @JsonExclude annotation is used to mark a property that should be excluded from serialization and deserialization.

 The @JsonName annotation allows you to specify that the key in the key-value pair representing the property should be the given string, not the name of the property.

Consider this example, in which you annotate the property firstName to change the key used to represent it in JSON. You also annotate the property age to exclude it from serialization and deserialization:

data class Person(

    @JsonName("alias") val firstName: String,

    @JsonExclude val age: Int? = null

)

Note that you must specify the default value of the property age. Otherwise, you wouldn't be able to create a new instance of Person during deserialization. Figure shows how the representation of an instance of the Person class changes.

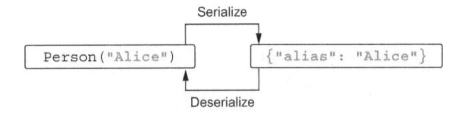

Figure Serialization and deserialization of the Person instance with annotations applied. The annotation changes the firstName field to be serialized to (and deserialized from) a field named alias, instead.

With that, you've seen most of the features available in JKid: serialize() , deserialize() , @JsonName , and @JsonExclude . Now, let's begin our investigation of its implementation, starting with the annotation declarations.

Creating your own annotation declarations

In this section, you'll learn how to declare annotations, using the annotations from JKid as an example. The

@JsonExclude annotation has the simplest form because it doesn't have any parameters. The syntax looks like a regular class declaration, with the added annotation modifier before the class keyword:

annotation class JsonExclude

Because annotation classes are only used to define the structure of metadata associated with declarations and expressions, they can't contain any code. Therefore, the compiler prohibits specifying a body for an annotation class.

For annotations that have parameters, the parameters are declared in the primary constructor of the class. You use the regular primary constructor declaration syntax, and mark all parameters as val (this is mandatory for parameters of an annotation class):

annotation class JsonName(val name: String)

Comparison with Java annotations

For comparison, here's how you would have declared the same annotation in Java:

/* Java */

public @interface JsonName {

   String value();

}

Note how the Java annotation has a method called value, whereas the Kotlin annotation has a name property. In Java, the value method is special: when you apply an annotation, you need to provide explicit names for all attributes you're specifying except value.

In Kotlin, on the other hand, applying an annotation is a regular constructor call. You can use the named-argument syntax to make the argument names explicit; you only specify the names for some arguments or omit the argument names entirely. In the case of the JsonName annotation, @JsonName(name = "first_name") is the same as @JsonName("first_name") in practice because name is the first parameter of the JsonName constructor. If you need to apply an annotation declared in Java to a Kotlin element, however, you're required to use the named argument syntax for all arguments except value , which Kotlin also recognizes as special.

Next, let's discuss how to control annotation usage and how you can apply annotations to other annotations.

Meta-annotations: Controlling how an annotation is processed

A Kotlin annotation class itself can be annotated. The annotations that can be applied to annotation classes are called meta-annotations. The standard library defines several of them, and they control how the compiler processes annotations. Other frameworks use meta-annotations as well—for example, many dependency-injection libraries use meta-annotations to mark annotations used to identify different injectable objects of the same type.

Of the meta-annotations defined in the standard library, the most common is @Target. The declarations of JsonExclude and JsonName in JKid use it to specify the valid targets for those annotations. Here's how it's applied:

@Target(AnnotationTarget.PROPERTY) annotation class JsonExclude

The @Target meta-annotation specifies the types of elements to which the annotation can be applied. If you don't use it, the annotation will be applicable to all declarations. That wouldn't make sense for JKid because the library processes only property annotations.

The list of values of the AnnotationTarget enum gives the full range of possible targets for an annotation. It includes classes, files, functions, properties, property accessors, types, all expressions, and so on. You can declare multiple targets if you need to: @Target(AnnotationTarget.CLASS, AnnotationTarget.METHOD) .

To declare your own meta-annotation, use ANNOTATION_CLASS as its target:

@Target(AnnotationTarget.ANNOTATION_CLASS) annotation class BindingAnnotation

@BindingAnnotation annotation class MyBinding

Note that you can't use annotations with a property target from Java code. To make such an annotation usable from Java, you can add the second target AnnotationTarget.FIELD. In this case, the annotation will be applied to properties in Kotlin and fields in Java.

The @Retention annotation

In Java, you may have seen another important meta-annotation: @Retention . You can use it to specify whether the annotation you declare will be stored in the .class file and whether it will be accessible at run time through reflection. Java by default retains annotations in .class files but doesn't make them accessible at run time. That means, by default, Java's annotations are only visible at compile time and for programs working directly on the .class files, such as bytecode analysis tools. Usually, most annotations

do need to be present at run time, so in Kotlin, the default is different: annotations have RUNTIME retention. That means even though the JKid annotations don't have an explicitly specified retention, you'll be able to access them for reflection, as you'll see in section.

Passing classes as annotation parameters to further control behavior

You've seen how to define an annotation that holds static data as its arguments, but sometimes, you need something different: the ability to refer to a class as declaration metadata. You can do so by declaring an annotation class that has a class reference as a parameter. In the JKid library, this comes up in the @DeserializeInterface annotation, which allows you to control the deserialization of properties that have an interface type. You can't create an instance of an interface directly, so you need to specify which class is used as the implementation created during deserialization.

Here's a simple example showing how the @DeserializeInterface annotation could be used to specify which class should be used to implement the interface:

interface Company {   val name: String

} data class CompanyImpl(override val name: String) : Company

```kotlin
data class Person(    val name: String,
@DeserializeInterface(CompanyImpl::class) val company: Company )
```

Upon deserialization, whenever JKid reads a nested company object for a Person instance, it creates and deserializes an instance of CompanyImpl and stores it in the company property. To specify this, you use CompanyImpl::class as an argument of the @DeserializeInterface annotation. In general, to refer to a class, you use its name followed by the ::class keyword.

Now, let's see how the annotation itself is declared. Its single argument is a class reference, as in @DeserializeInterface(CompanyImpl::class) :

```kotlin
annotation class DeserializeInterface(val targetClass: KClass<out Any>)
```

The KClass type is used to hold references to Kotlin classes; you'll see what it lets you do with those classes in section.

The type parameter of KClass specifies which Kotlin classes can be referred to by this reference. For instance, CompanyImpl::class has a type KClass<CompanyImpl> , which is a subtype of the annotation parameter type (see figure).

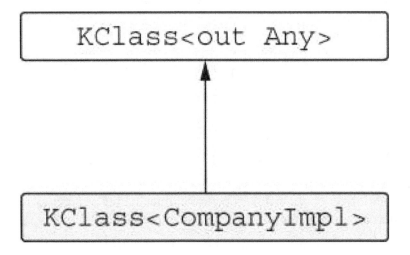

Figure The type of the annotation argument CompanyImpl::class (KClass<CompanyImpl>) is a subtype of the annotation parameter type (KClass<out Any>).

If you wrote KClass<Any> without the out modifier, you wouldn't be able to pass CompanyImpl::class as an argument; the only allowed argument would be Any::class . The out keyword specifies that you're allowed to refer to classes that extend Any, not just to Any itself. The next section shows one more annotation that takes a reference to generic class as a parameter.

Generic classes as annotation parameters

By default, JKid serializes properties of nonprimitive types as nested objects. But you can change this behavior and provide your own serialization logic for some values.

The @CustomSerializer annotation takes a reference to a custom serializer class as an argument. The serializer class should implement the ValueSerializer interface, providing a conversion from a Kotlin object to its JSON representation, and likewise, from a JSON value back to a Kotlin object:

```kotlin
interface ValueSerializer<T> {    fun toJsonValue(value: T): Any?
```

```
    fun fromJsonValue(jsonValue: Any?): T
}
```

Suppose you need to support serialization of dates, and you've created your own DateSerializer class for that, implementing the ValueSerializer<Date> interface. This class is provided as an example in the JKid source code (http://mng.bz/e1vQ). Here's how you apply it to the Person class:

```
data class Person(    val name: String,
    @CustomSerializer(DateSerializer::class) val birthDate: Date )
```

Now, let's see how the @CustomSerializer annotation is declared. The ValueSerializer class is generic and defines a type parameter, so you need to provide a type argument value whenever you refer to the type. Because you know nothing about the types of properties with which this annotation will be used, you can use a star projection (discussed in section) as the argument:

```
annotation class CustomSerializer(    val serializerClass: KClass<out ValueSerializer<*>> )
```

Figure examines the type of the serializerClass parameter and explains its different parts.

ValueSerializer interface.

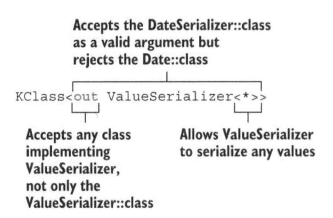

Figure The type of the serializerClass annotation parameter. Only class references to classes that extend ValueSerializer will be valid annotation arguments.

While this may seem tricky, the good news is that you can apply the same pattern every time you need to use a class as an annotation argument. You can write KClass<out YourClassName>, and if YourClassName has its own type arguments, replace them with *.

You've now seen all the important aspects of declaring and applying annotations in Kotlin. The next step is to find out how to access the data stored in the annotations. For this, you need to use reflection.

Reflection: Introspecting Kotlin objects at run time

Reflection is, simply put, a way to access properties and methods of objects dynamically at run time, without knowing in advance what those properties are. Normally, when you access a method or a property of an object, the source code of your program references a specific declaration, and the compiler statically resolves the reference and ensures the declaration exists. But sometimes, you need to write code that can work with objects of any type or where the names of methods and properties to be accessed are only known at run time. A serialization library is a great example of such code; it needs to be able to serialize any object to JSON, so it can't reference specific classes and properties. This is where reflection comes into play.

When working with reflection in Kotlin, you usually deal with the Kotlin reflection API. It's defined in the kotlin.reflect and kotlin.reflect.full packages. It gives you access to all Kotlin concepts, such as data classes, properties, and nullable types. An important note is that the Kotlin reflection API isn't restricted to Kotlin classes; you can use the same API to access classes written in any JVM language.

As a fallback, you can also use standard Java reflection, as defined in the java.lang.reflect package. Because Kotlin classes are compiled to regular Java bytecode, the Java reflection API supports them perfectly well. In particular, this means Java libraries that use the reflection API are fully compatible with Kotlin code.

NOTE To reduce the runtime library size on platforms where it matters, such as Android, the Kotlin reflection API is packaged into a separate JAR file, kotlin-reflect.jar, which isn't added to the dependencies of new projects by default. If you're using the Kotlin reflection API, you need to make sure the library is added as a dependency. The Maven group/artifact ID for the library is org.jetbrains.kotlin:kotlin-reflect .

In this section, you'll see how JKid uses the reflection API. We'll walk you through the serialization part first because it's more straightforward and easier for us to explain and then proceed to JSON parsing and deserialization.

But first, let's take a close look at the contents of the reflection API.

The Kotlin reflection API: KClass, KCallable, KFunction, and KProperty

The main entry point of the Kotlin reflection API is KClass, which represents a class. You can use it to enumerate and access all the declarations contained in the class, its superclasses, and so on. You get an instance of KClass by writing MyClass::class . Likewise, to get the class of an object myObject at run time, you write myObject::class :

```
import kotlin.reflect.full.*

class Person(val name: String, val age: Int)

fun main() {
    val person = Person("Alice", 29)    val kClass = person::class        ❶        println(kClass.simpleName)
    // Person    kClass.memberProperties.forEach { println(it.name) }
    // age
    // name
}
```

❶ Returns an instance of KClass<out Person>

This simple example prints the name of the class and the names of its properties and uses .memberProperties to collect all non-extension properties defined in the class as well as in all of its superclasses.

If you browse the declaration of KClass, you'll see that it contains a bunch of useful methods for accessing the contents of the class:

```
interface KClass<T : Any> {    val simpleName: String?    val qualifiedName: String?
val members: Collection<KCallable<*>>    val constructors: Collection<KFunction<T>>
val nestedClasses: Collection<KClass<*>>    // ...

}
```

Many other useful features of KClass, including memberProperties used in the previous example, are declared as extensions. You can see the full list of methods on KClass (including extensions) in the standard library reference.

NOTE You might expect the simpleName and qualifiedName properties to be non-nullable. However, recall that section showed you how to use object expressions to create anonymous objects. While these objects are still an instance of a class, that class is anonymous. As such, it has neither a nor a qualifiedName. Accessing those fields from a KClass instance will return.

You may have noticed that members, the list of all members for a class, is a collection of KCallable instances.

KCallable is a superinterface for functions and properties. It declares the call method, which allows you to call the corresponding function or the getter of the property:

```
interface KCallable<out R> {    fun call(vararg args: Any?): R    // ...
}
```

You provide the function arguments in a vararg list. The following code demonstrates how you can use call to call a function through reflection:

```
fun foo(x: Int) = println(x)

fun main() {
    val kFunction = ::foo    ❶    kFunction.call(42)    ❷
    // 42
}
```

❶ Obtains a reference of type KFunction1<Int, Unit> to foo

❷ Calls the function with the argument 42

You saw the::foo syntax in section, and now you can see that the value of this expression is an instance of the KFunction class from the reflection API. To call the referenced function, you use the KCallable.call method. In this case, you need to provide a single argument: 42. If you try to call the function with an incorrect number of arguments, such as kFunction.call(), it will throw a run-time exception:

"IllegalArgumentException: Callable expects 1 argument, but 0 were provided."

In this case, however, you can use a more specific method to call the function. The type of the::foo expression is KFunction1<Int, Unit>, which contains information about parameter and return types. KFunction1 denotes that this function takes one parameter. To call the function through this interface, you use the invoke method. It accepts a fixed number of arguments (one, in this case), and their types correspond to the type parameters of the KFunction1 interface. The parameter is of type Int, and the return type of the function is of type Unit. You can also call kFunction directly (section will explain the details of why it's possible to call kFunction without an explicit invoke):

```
import kotlin.reflect.KFunction2

fun sum(x: Int, y: Int) = x + y

fun main() {    val kFunction: KFunction2<Int, Int, Int> = ::sum    println(kFunction.invoke(1, 2) + kFunction(3, 4))
    // 10    kFunction(1)
    // ERROR: No value passed for parameter p2
```

}

Using invokes, rather than call, on kFunction prevents you from accidentally passing an incorrect number of arguments to the function—the code won't compile. Therefore, if you have a KFunction of a specific type with known parameters and return type, it's preferable to use it invoke method. The call method is a generic approach that works for all types of functions but doesn't provide type safety.

How and where are KFunctionN interfaces defined?

Types such as KFunction1 represent functions with different numbers of parameters. Each type extends

KFunction and adds one additional member invoke with the appropriate number of parameters. For example,

KFunction2 declares operator fun invoke(p1: P1, p2: P2): R , where P1 and P2 represent the function parameter types and R represents the return type.

These function types are synthetic compiler-generated types, and you won't find their declarations in the

kotlin.reflect package. That means you can use an interface for a function with any number of parameters, without artificial restrictions on the possible number of function type parameters.

You can invoke the call method on a KProperty instance as well, and it will call the getter of the property. But the property interface provides you with a better way to obtain the property value: the get method.

To access the get method, you need to use the correct interface for the property, depending on how it's declared.

Top-level read-only and mutable properties are represented by instances of the KProperty0 and

KMutableProperty0 interfaces, respectively—both of which have a no-argument get method:

var counter = 0

```
fun main() {
    val kProperty = ::counter    ❶    kProperty.setter.call(21)    ❷    println(kProperty.get())    ❸
    // 21
}
```

❶ kProperty is a reference to counter of type KMutableProperty0<Int>.

❷ Calls a setter through reflection, passing 21 as an argument

❸ Obtains a property value by calling get

A member property is represented by an instance of KProperty1 or KMutableProperty1, which both provide a one-argument get method. To access its value, you must provide the object instance for which you want to retrieve the value. The following example stores a reference to the property in a memberProperty variable; then, you call memberProperty.get(person) to obtain the value of this property for the specific person instance. So, if a memberProperty refers to the age property of the Person class, memberProperty.get(person) is a way to dynamically get the value of person.age . You previously encountered this concept in section:

class Person(val name: String, val age: Int)

```
fun main() {    val person = Person("Alice", 29)    val memberProperty = Person::age
    println(memberProperty.get(person))
    // 29
```

}

Note that KProperty1 is a generic class. The memberProperty variable has the type KProperty1<Person, Int>, where the first type parameter denotes the type of the receiver and the second type parameter stands for the property type. Thus, you can call it get method only with a receiver of the right type; the call memberProperty.get("Alice") won't compile.

Also note that you can only use reflection to access properties defined at the top level or in a class but not local variables of a function. If you define a local variable x and try to get a reference to it using::x , you'll get a compilation error saying, "References to variables aren't supported yet."

Figure shows a hierarchy of interfaces that you can use to access source code elements at run time. Because all declarations can be annotated, the interfaces that represent declaration at run time, such as KClass, KFunction, and KParameter, all extend KAnnotatedElement. KClass is used to represent both classes and objects.

KProperty can represent any property, whereas its subclass, KMutableProperty, represents a mutable property, which you declare with var. You can use the special interfaces Getter and Setter declared in

Property and KMutableProperty to work with property accessors as functions (e.g., if you need to retrieve their annotations). Both interfaces for accessors extend KFunction. For simplicity, we've omitted the specific interfaces for properties like KProperty0 in the figure.

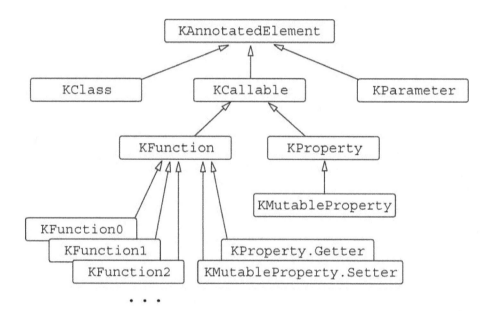

Figure Hierarchy of interfaces in the Kotlin reflection API

Now that you're acquainted with the basics of the Kotlin reflection API, let's investigate how the JKid library is implemented.

Implementing object serialization using reflection

First, let's recall the declaration of the serialization function in JKid:

fun serialize(obj: Any): String

This function takes an object and returns its JSON representation as a string. It'll build up the resulting JSON in a StringBuilder instance. As it serializes object properties and their values, it'll append them to this

StringBuilder object. To make the append calls more concise, let's put the implementation in an extension function to StringBuilder. That way, you can conveniently call the append method without a qualifier:

```kotlin
private fun StringBuilder.serializeObject(x: Any) {    append(/*...*/)
}
```

Converting a function parameter into an extension function receiver is a common pattern in Kotlin code, and we'll discuss it in detail in section. Note that serializeObject doesn't extend the StringBuilder API; it performs operations that make no sense outside of this context, so it's marked private to ensure it can't be used elsewhere. It's declared as an extension to emphasize a particular object as primary for this code block and to make it easier to work with that object.

Consequently, the serialize function delegates all the work to serializeObject:

```kotlin
fun serialize(obj: Any): String = buildString { serializeObject(obj) }
```

As you saw in section, buildString creates a StringBuilder and allows you to fill it with content in a lambda. In this case, the content is provided by the call to serializeObject(obj).

Now, let's discuss the behavior of the serialization function. By default, it will serialize all properties of the object.

Primitive types and strings will be serialized as JSON numbers, Booleans, and string values, as appropriate. Collections will be serialized as JSON arrays. Properties of other types will be serialized as nested objects. As we discussed in the previous section, this behavior can be customized through annotations.

Let's look at the implementation of serializeObject, where you can observe the reflection API in a real scenario.

NOTE In the repository, this function is called serializeObjectWithoutAnnotation —we'll rework this function, as you'll see later.

Listing Serializing an object

```kotlin
private fun StringBuilder.serializeObject(obj: Any) {    val kClass = obj::class as KClass<Any>          ❶
    val properties = kClass.memberProperties          ❷

    properties.joinToStringBuilder(
        this, prefix = "{", postfix = "}") { prop ->        serializeString(prop.name)          ❸
append(": ")          serializePropertyValue(prop.get(obj))          ❹
    }
}
```

❶ Gets the KClass for the object

❷ Gets all properties of the class

❸ Gets the property name

❹ Gets the property value

The implementation of this function should be clear: you serialize each property of the class, one after another. The resulting JSON will look like this: { "prop1": value1, "prop2": value2 }. The joinToStringBuilder function ensures that properties are separated with commas; the serializeString function escapes special characters, as required by the JSON format; and the serializePropertyValue function checks whether a value is a primitive value, string, collection, or nested object, serializing its content accordingly.

In the previous section, we discussed a way to obtain the value of the KProperty instance: the get method. In that case, you worked with the member reference Person::age of the type KProperty1<Person, Int> ,

which lets the compiler know the exact types of the receiver and the property value. In this example, however, the exact types are unknown because you enumerate all the properties of an object's class. Therefore, the prop variable has the type KProperty1<Any, *>, and prop.get(obj) returns a value of Any? type. You don't

get any compile-time checks for the receiver type, but because you're passing the same object from which you obtained the list of properties, the receiver type will be correct. Next, let's see how the annotations used to customize serialization are implemented.

Customizing serialization with annotations

Earlier in this chapter, you saw the definitions of annotations that let you customize the process of JSON serialization. In particular, we discussed the @JsonExclude, @JsonName, and @CustomSerializer annotations. Now, it's time to see how these annotations can be handled by the serializeObject function.

We'll start with @JsonExclude. This annotation allows you to exclude some properties from serialization. Let's investigate how the implementation of the serializeObject function needs to change to support that.

Recall that to get all member properties of the class, you use the extension property memberProperties on the KClass instance. But now, the task gets more complicated: properties annotated with @JsonExclude need to be filtered out. Let's see how this is done.

The KAnnotatedElement interface defines the property annotations, a collection of all annotation instances

(with run-time retention) that are applied to the element in the source code. Because KProperty extends KAnnotatedElement , you can access all annotations for a property via property.annotations .

But the code responsible for excluding properties actually needs to find a specific annotation. For this case, you can use the find Annotation function, which can be called on a KAnnotatedElement. This function returns an annotation of a type specified as an argument if such an annotation is present.

Combining with the filter standard library function, you can filter out the properties annotated with:

val properties = kClass.memberProperties

.filter { it.findAnnotation<JsonExclude>() == null }

The next annotation is @JsonName. As a reminder, we'll repeat its declaration and an example of its usage:

annotation class JsonName(val name: String)

 data class Person(

   @JsonName("alias") val firstName: String,
val age: Int

)

In this case, you're interested not only in its presence but also in its argument: the name that should be used for the annotated property in JSON. Once again, the findAnnotation function helps here:

val jsonNameAnn = prop.findAnnotation<JsonName>()   ❶ val propName = jsonNameAnn?.name ?: prop.name   ❷

❶ Gets an instance of the @JsonName annotation if it exists

❷ Gets its name argument or uses prop.name as a fallback

If a property isn't annotated with @JsonName, then jsonNameAnn is null and you still use prop.name as the name for the property in JSON. If the property is annotated, you use the specified name instead.

Let's look at the serialization of an instance of the Person class declared earlier. During the serialization of the firstName property, jsonNameAnn contains the corresponding instance of the annotation class JsonName.

Thus, jsonNameAnn?.name returns the non-null value "alias" , which is used as a key in JSON. When the age property is serialized, the annotation isn't found, so the property name age is used as a key. As such, the serialized JSON output for a Person("Alice", 35) object is { "alias": "Alice", "age": 35 }

Let's combine the changes discussed so far and look at the resulting implementation of the serialization logic in the following listing.

Listing Serializing an object with property filtering

```
private fun StringBuilder.serializeObject(obj: Any) {

    (obj::class as KClass<Any>)

        .memberProperties

        .filter { it.findAnnotation<JsonExclude>() == null }        .joinToStringBuilder(this, prefix = "{",
postfix = "}") {           serializeProperty(it, obj)

        }

}
```

Now, the properties annotated with @JsonExclude are filtered out. We've also extracted the logic responsible for property serialization into a separate serializeProperty function, as shown in the following listing.

Listing Serializing a single property

```
private fun StringBuilder.serializeProperty(        prop: KProperty1<Any, *>, obj: Any

) {    val jsonNameAnn = prop.findAnnotation<JsonName>()      val propName = jsonNameAnn?.name ?:
prop.name    serializeString(propName)     append(": ")

    serializePropertyValue(prop.get(obj))

}
```

The property name is processed according to the @JsonName annotation discussed earlier.

Next, let's implement the remaining annotation, @CustomSerializer. The implementation is based on the function getSerializer, which returns the ValueSerializer instance registered via the @CustomSerializer annotation. For example, if you declare the Person class, as shown next, and call getSerializer() when serializing the birthDate property, it will return an instance of DateSerializer:

```
import java.util.Date

 data class Person(    val name: String,

    @CustomSerializer(DateSerializer::class) val birthDate: Date )
```

Here's a reminder of how the @CustomSerializer annotation is declared to help you better understand the implementation of getSerializer :

annotation class CustomSerializer(val serializerClass: KClass<out ValueSerializer<*>>)

Here's how the getSerializer function is implemented.

Listing Retrieving the value serializer for a property

```
fun KProperty<*>.getSerializer(): ValueSerializer<Any?>? {    val customSerializerAnn =
findAnnotation<CustomSerializer>()
        ?: return null    val serializerClass = customSerializerAnn.serializerClass
    val valueSerializer = serializerClass.objectInstance
        ?: serializerClass.createInstance()
    @Suppress("UNCHECKED_CAST")    return valueSerializer as ValueSerializer<Any?>
}
```

getSerializer is an extension function to KProperty because the function operates on the property. It calls

the findAnnotation function to get an instance of the @CustomSerializer annotation if it exists. Its argument, serializerClass , specifies the class for which you need to obtain an instance.

The most interesting part here is the way you handle both classes and objects (Kotlin's singletons) as values of the @CustomSerializer annotation. They're both represented by the KClass class. The difference is that objects have a non-null value of the objectInstance property, which can be used to access the singleton instance created for the object. For example, DateSerializer is declared as an object, so it's objectInstance property stores the singleton DateSerializer instance. You'll use that instance to serialize all objects, and won't be called. If the KClass represents a regular class, you create a new instance by calling.

Finally, you can use getSerializer in the implementation of serializeProperty. The following listing shows the final version of the function.

Listing Serializing a property with custom serializer support

```
private fun StringBuilder.serializeProperty(

  prop: KProperty1<Any, *>, obj: Any
) {    val jsonNameAnn = prop.findAnnotation<JsonName>()    val propName = jsonNameAnn?.name ?:
prop.name    serializeString(propName)    append(": ")


    val value = prop.get(obj)    val jsonValue = prop.getSerializer()?.toJsonValue(value)  ❶        ?: value
  ❷      serializePropertyValue(jsonValue)
}
```

❶ Uses a custom serializer for the property if it exists ❷ Otherwise, uses the property value, as before uses the serializer to convert the property value to a JSON-compatible format by calling. If the property doesn't have a custom serializer, it uses the property value.

Now that you've seen an overview of the implementation of the JSON serialization part of the library, we'll move to parsing and deserialization. The deserialization part requires quite a bit more code, so we won't examine all of it, but we'll look at the structure of the implementation and explain how reflection is used to deserialize objects.

JSON parsing and object deserialization

Let's start with the second part of the story: implementing the deserialization logic. First, recall that the API, like the one used for serialization, consists of a single function. The function needs access to its type parameter at run time so that it is able to construct the correct resulting object during deserialization. As we previously discussed in section, this means its type parameter needs to be marked as reified, which also forces the function to be marked as inline:

inline fun <reified T: Any> deserialize(json: String): T

Here's an example of its use:

data class Author(val name: String) data class Book(val title: String, val author: Author)

 fun main() {

   val json = """{"title": "Catch-22", "author": {"name": "J. Heller"}}"""   val book = deserialize<Book>(json)   println(book)

   // Book(title=Catch-22, author=Author(name=J. Heller)) }

You pass the type of object to be deserialized as a reified type parameter to the deserialize function and get back a new object instance.

Deserializing JSON is a more difficult task than serializing because it involves parsing the JSON string input in addition to using reflection to access object internals. The JSON deserializer in JKid is implemented in a fairly conventional way and consists of three main stages: a lexical analyzer, usually referred to as a lexer; a syntax analyzer, or parser; and the deserialization component itself.

The lexical analysis splits an input string consisting of characters into a list of tokens. There are two kinds of tokens: character tokens, which represent characters with special meanings in the JSON syntax (comma, colon, braces, and brackets), and value tokens, which correspond to string, number, Boolean, and null constants. A left brace ({), a string value ("Catch-22"), and an integer value (42) are examples of different tokens.

The parser is generally responsible for converting a plain list of tokens into a structured representation. Its task in JKid is to understand the higher-level structure of JSON and to convert individual tokens into semantic elements supported in JSON: key-value pairs, objects, and arrays.

The JsonObject interface keeps track of the object or array currently being deserialized. The parser calls the corresponding methods when it discovers new properties of the current object (simple values, composite properties, or arrays).

Listing JSON parser callback interface

interface JsonObject {   fun setSimpleProperty(propertyName: String, value: Any?)

   fun createObject(propertyName: String): JsonObject

   fun createArray(propertyName: String): JsonObject

}

The propertyName parameter in these methods receives the JSON key. Thus, when the parser encounters an author property with an object as its value, the createObject("author") method is called. Simple value, with the actual token value passed as the value argument. The implementations are responsible for creating new objects for properties and storing references to them in the outer object.

Figure shows the input and output of each stage for lexical and syntactic analyses when deserializing a sample string. Once again, the lexical analysis divides an input string into a list of tokens; then, the syntactic analysis (the parser) processes this list of tokens and invokes an appropriate method of JSONObject on each new meaningful element.

```
{"title": "Catch-22", "author": {"name": "J.Heller"}}
```

   ↓ **Lexer:** Divides JSON into tokens

```
{ "title" : "Catch-22" , "author" : { "name" : "J.Heller" } }
```

   ↓ **Parser:** Handles different semantic elements

```
o1.setSimpleProperty("title", "Catch-22")
```
```
val o2 = o1.createObject("author")
```
```
o2.setSimpleProperty("name", "J.Heller")
```

   ↓ **Deserializer:** Creates and returns an instance of required class

```
Book("Catch-22", Author("J. Heller"))
```

Figure The process of parsing JSON: first, the lexer takes the input text and divides it into tokens. Then, the parser processes the different semantic elements. Finally, the deserializer turns them into the final Kotlin objects.

The deserializer then provides an implementation for JsonObject that gradually builds a new instance of the corresponding type. It needs to find the correspondence between class properties and JSON keys (title , author , and name in figure) and build nested object values (an instance of Author); only after that can it create a new instance of the required class (Book).

The JKid library is intended to be used with data classes, and, as such, it passes all the name-value pairs loaded from the JSON file as parameters to the constructor of the class being deserialized. It doesn't support setting properties on object instances after they've been created. This means it needs to store the data somewhere while reading it from JSON, before the construction of the actual object begins.

The requirement to save the components before creating the object looks similar to the traditional builder pattern, with the difference that builders are generally tailored to create a specific kind of object. In the case of deserialization, the solution needs to be completely generic. To avoid being boring, we use the term seed for the implementation. In JSON, you need to build different types of composite structures: objects, collections, and maps. The classes ObjectSeed , ObjectListSeed , and ValueListSeed are responsible for building objects and lists of composite objects or simple values appropriately. The construction of maps is left as an exercise for you.

The basic Seed interface extends JsonObject and provides an additional spawn method to get the resulting instance after the building process is finished. It also declares the createCompositeProperty method used to create both nested objects and nested lists (they use the same underlying logic to create instances through seeds).

Listing Interface for creating objects from JSON data

```
interface Seed: JsonObject {    fun spawn(): Any?

    fun createCompositeProperty(        propertyName: String,        isList: Boolean
    ): JsonObject

    override fun createObject(propertyName: String) =        createCompositeProperty(propertyName, false)

    override fun createArray(propertyName: String) =        createCompositeProperty(propertyName, true)
```

```
    // ...
}
```

You may think of spawn as an analogue of build —a method that returns the result value. It returns the constructed object for ObjectSeed and the resulting list for ObjectListSeed or ValueListSeed . We won't discuss in detail how lists are deserialized. Instead, we'll focus our attention on creating objects, which is more complicated and serves to demonstrate the general idea.

But before that, let's study the main deserialize function, shown in the following listing, which does all the work of deserializing a value.

Listing The top-level deserialization function

```
fun <T: Any> deserialize(json: Reader, targetClass: KClass<T>): T {    val seed = ObjectSeed(targetClass,
ClassInfoCache())    Parser(json, seed).parse()    return seed.spawn()
}
```

To start the parsing, you create an ObjectSeed to store the properties of the object being deserialized, and then you invoke the parser and pass the input stream reader json to it. Once you reach the end of the input data, you call the spawn function to build the resulting object.

Now, let's focus on the implementation of ObjectSeed , which stores the state of an object being constructed.

ObjectSeed takes a reference to the resulting class and a classInfoCache object containing cached information about the properties of the class. This cached information will be used later to create instances of that class. ClassInfoCache and ClassInfo are helper classes, which we'll discuss in the next section.

Listing Deserializing an object

```
class ObjectSeed<out T: Any>(    targetClass: KClass<T>,    override val classInfoCache:
ClassInfoCache
) : Seed {

    private val classInfo: ClassInfo<T> =                              ❶    classInfoCache[targetClass]
    private val valueArguments = mutableMapOf<KParameter, Any?>()    private val seedArguments =
mutableMapOf<KParameter, Seed>()

    private val arguments: Map<KParameter, Any?>                     ❷    get() = valueArguments +
seedArguments.mapValues { it.value.spawn() }
    override fun setSimpleProperty(propertyName: String, value: Any?) {    val param =
classInfo.getConstructorParameter(propertyName)    valueArguments[param] =
❸          classInfo.deserializeConstructorArgument(param, value)
    }    override fun createCompositeProperty(    propertyName: String, isList: Boolean
    ): Seed {
        val param = classInfo.getConstructorParameter(propertyName)    val deserializeAs =
❹
```

```
        classInfo.getDeserializeClass(propertyName)?.starProjectedType        val seed =
createSeedForType(                              ❺                    deserializeAs ?: param.type, isList
    )           return seed.apply { seedArguments[param] = this }              ❻

    override fun spawn(): T =                              ❼          classInfo.createInstance(arguments)

}
```

❶ Caches the information needed to create an instance of targetClass

❷ Builds a map from constructor parameters to their values

❸ Records a value for the constructor parameter if it's a simple value

❹ Loads the value of the DeserializeInterface annotation for the property, if any

❺ Creates an ObjectSeed or CollectionSeed according to the parameter type ...

❻ ... and records it in the seedArguments map

❼ Creates the resulting instance of targetClass, passing an arguments map

Note how calling arguments in the body of the spawn method launches the recursive building of composite (seed) arguments: the custom getter of arguments calls the spawn methods on each of the seedArguments. The createSeedForType function analyzes the type of the parameter and creates either ObjectSeed, ObjectListSeed , or ValueListSeed, depending on whether the parameter is some kind of collection. We'll leave the investigation into how it's implemented to you. Next, let's see how the ClassInfo.createInstance function creates an instance of targetClass.

The final step of deserialization: callBy() and creating objects using reflection

The last part you need to understand is the ClassInfo class, which builds the resulting instance and caches information about constructor parameters. It is used in ObjectSeed. But before we dive into the implementation details, let's look at the APIs that you use to create objects through reflection.

You've already seen the KCallable.call method, which calls a function or a constructor by taking a list of arguments. This method works great in many cases, but it has a restriction: it doesn't support default parameter values. In this case, if a user is trying to deserialize an object with a constructor that has default parameter values, you definitely don't want to require those arguments to be specified in the JSON.

Therefore, you need to use another method that does support default parameter values: KCallable.callBy:

```
interface KCallable<out R> {    fun callBy(args: Map<KParameter, Any?>): R    // ...
}
```

The method takes a map of parameters to their corresponding values that will be passed as arguments. If a parameter is missing from the map, its default value will be used if possible. This also provides the extra convenience that you don't have to put the parameters in the correct order; you can read the name-value pairs from JSON, find the parameter corresponding to each argument name, and put its value in the map.

However, you do need to take care of getting the types right. The type of the value in the args map needs to match the constructor parameter type; otherwise, you'll get an IllegalArgumentException at run time. This is particularly important for numeric types; you need to know whether the parameter takes an Int , a Long , a

Double, or another primitive type, and you need to convert the numeric value coming from JSON to the correct type. To do that, you use the KParameter.type property.

The type conversion works via the same interface used for custom serialization. If a property doesn't have an annotation, you retrieve a standard implementation based on its type.

To do so, you can provide a small function serializerForType that provides the mapping between a KType and the corresponding built-in ValueSerializer objects. To obtain a run-time representation of the types JKid knows about— Byte, Int, Boolean, and so on—you can use the typeOf<>() function to return their respective KType instances.

Listing Getting a serializer based on the type of the value

```
fun serializerForType(type: KType): ValueSerializer<out Any?>? =        when (type) {
typeOf<Byte>() -> ByteSerializer

        typeOf<Int>() -> IntSerializer            typeOf<Boolean>() -> BooleanSerializer            // ...

        else -> null

    }
```

The corresponding ValueSerializer implementations then perform the necessary type checking or conversion. As shown in the following example, the serializer for Boolean values checks that jsonValue is indeed a Boolean upon deserialization.

Listing Serializer for Boolean values

```
object BooleanSerializer : ValueSerializer<Boolean> {    override fun fromJsonValue(jsonValue: Any?):
Boolean {        if (jsonValue !is Boolean) throw JKidException("Boolean expected")        return jsonValue

    }      override fun toJsonValue(value: Boolean) = value

}
```

The callBy method gives you a way to invoke the primary constructor of an object, passing a map of parameters and corresponding values. The ValueSerializer mechanism ensures the values in the map have the right types.

Now, let's see how you invoke this API.

The ClassInfoCache class is intended to reduce the overhead of reflection operations. Recall that the annotations used to control the serialization and deserialization process (@JsonName and @CustomSerializer) are applied to properties, rather than parameters. When you're deserializing an object, you're dealing with constructor parameters, not properties. To retrieve the annotations, you need to find the corresponding property. Performing this search when reading every key-value pair would be exceedingly slow, so you do this once per class and cache the information. The following listing shows the entire implementation of ClassInfoCache.

Listing Storage of cached reflection data

```
class ClassInfoCache {
private val cacheData = mutableMapOf<KClass<*>, ClassInfo<*>>()

@Suppress("UNCHECKED_CAST")    operator fun <T : Any> get(cls: KClass<T>): ClassInfo<T> =
cacheData.getOrPut(cls) { ClassInfo(cls) } as ClassInfo<T>

}
```

The ClassInfo class is responsible for creating a new instance of the target class and caching the necessary information. To simplify the code, we've omitted some functions and trivial initializers. Also, you may notice that instead of !!, the actual JKid code in the repository throws an exception with an informative message (which is a good pattern for your own code, as well). Here, it is simply omitted for brevity.

Listing Cache of constructor parameter and annotation data

```
class ClassInfo<T : Any>(cls: KClass<T>) {    private val constructor = cls.primaryConstructor!!

    private val jsonNameToParamMap = hashMapOf<String, KParameter>()    private val
paramToSerializerMap =        hashMapOf<KParameter, ValueSerializer<out Any?>>()    private val
jsonNameToDeserializeClassMap =        hashMapOf<String, KClass<out Any>?>()

    init {        constructor.parameters.forEach { cacheDataForParameter(cls, it) }

    }    fun getConstructorParameter(propertyName: String): KParameter =
jsonNameToParam[propertyName]!!

    fun deserializeConstructorArgument(            param: KParameter, value: Any?): Any? {        val
serializer = paramToSerializer[param]        if (serializer != null) return serializer.fromJsonValue(value)

    validateArgumentType(param, value)        return value

    }    fun createInstance(arguments: Map<KParameter, Any?>): T {

    ensureAllParametersPresent(arguments)        return constructor.callBy(arguments)

    }


    // ...

}
```

On initialization, this code locates the property corresponding to each constructor parameter and retrieves its annotations. It stores the data in three maps: jsonNameToParam specifies the parameter corresponding to each key in the JSON file, paramToSerializer stores the serializer for each parameter, and

jsonNameToDeserializeClass stores the class specified as the @DeserializeInterface argument, if any.

ClassInfo can then provide a constructor parameter by the property name, and the calling code uses the parameter as a key for the parameter-to-argument map.

The cacheDataForParameter , validateArgumentType , and ensureAllParametersPresent functions are private functions in this class. The following listing shows the implementation of ensureAllParametersPresent ; you can browse the code of the others yourself.

Listing Validating that required parameters are provided

```
private fun ensureAllParametersPresent(arguments: Map<KParameter, Any?>) {    for (param in
constructor.parameters) {            if (arguments[param] == null &&

        !param.isOptional && !param.type.isMarkedNullable) {            throw JKidException("Missing
value for parameter ${param.name}")

    }

    }

}
```

This function checks that you provide all required values for parameters. Note how the reflection API helps you here. If a parameter has a default value, then param.isOptional is true and you can omit an argument for it; the default one will be used instead. If the parameter type is nullable (type.isMarkedNullable tells you that), null will be used as the default parameter value. For all other parameters, you must provide the corresponding arguments; otherwise, an exception will be thrown. The reflection cache ensures the search for annotations that customize the deserialization process is performed only once, rather than for every property you see in the JSON data.

This completes our discussion of the JKid library implementation. Over the course of this chapter, we've explored the implementation of a JSON serialization and deserialization library, implemented on top of the reflection APIs, and used annotations to customize its behavior. Of course, all the techniques and approaches demonstrated in this chapter can be used for your own frameworks as well.

Conclusion: Generics, Annotations, and Reflection in Kotlin

Embracing Kotlin's Elegance with Generics

Generics are a cornerstone of Kotlin's type-safe design, offering developers the ability to create flexible and reusable code while maintaining strong type safety. Kotlin's type inference, combined with powerful generic constructs like type bounds (<T : SomeType>), variance (out, in), and reified types in inline functions, takes the cumbersome boilerplate traditionally associated with generics and transforms it into a developer-friendly toolset.

With Kotlin 2025, the introduction of advanced tooling for generics has further refined its usage, making generic programming more accessible and efficient. Developers no longer need to rely on workarounds or extensions to handle complex type hierarchies, thanks to updated features like **typealias for generic types** and enhanced support for higher-order generics.

Generics also play a pivotal role in Kotlin's collection framework, enabling developers to handle data structures seamlessly. Whether managing mutable or immutable collections, or leveraging functions like filter, map, and fold, generics empower developers to write robust, scalable, and reusable solutions.

In summary, Kotlin's generics emphasize the principles of **type safety, reusability, and simplicity**. They encourage cleaner code while ensuring that type-related bugs are caught at compile time rather than runtime, aligning with Kotlin's philosophy of safer and more expressive programming.

Annotations: Building Metadata-Driven Applications

Annotations in Kotlin serve as powerful tools for adding metadata to your code, enabling interaction with frameworks, libraries, and the Kotlin compiler itself. Their importance lies in the ability to define behaviors, mark elements for specific purposes, or control runtime processes.

The capabilities of annotations have expanded significantly in Kotlin 2025. Custom annotations with **targeting and retention policies** (@Target, @Retention) remain essential for controlling where annotations can be applied and whether they are retained in the compiled class files or runtime. Meanwhile, Kotlin's seamless integration with Java annotations ensures that developers can work with legacy systems and third-party libraries without disruption.

Kotlin 2025 has brought advanced features such as **annotation parameters with lambdas**, **meta-annotations**, and better compiler support for processing annotations. These improvements make it easier to create domain-specific libraries or implement sophisticated systems such as dependency injection, serialization, and logging.

One notable highlight is Kotlin's growing role in **annotation processing tools (APT)** through Kotlin Symbol Processing (KSP). KSP has emerged as a more efficient and Kotlin-native alternative to Java's annotation processing framework (APT), giving developers the ability to process annotations with minimal overhead while adhering to Kotlin's design principles.

Annotations exemplify Kotlin's focus on expressiveness and extensibility. They streamline interaction between code and the systems that process it, reducing boilerplate and making development more intuitive.

In a world where modern development increasingly involves tools like Spring Boot, Hibernate, or Ktor, annotations ensure that Kotlin continues to thrive in metadata-driven ecosystems.

Reflection: The Window into Runtime Behavior

Reflection, a powerful mechanism for inspecting and interacting with the structure of your program at runtime, serves as a critical tool for dynamic behavior in Kotlin. While reflection is a complex and potentially performance-heavy feature, Kotlin ensures that it remains a practical and approachable tool through its concise and expressive syntax.

Kotlin's reflection API, encapsulated in the kotlin.reflect package, allows developers to query class structures (KClass), inspect properties, methods, and constructors, and even invoke functions dynamically. These capabilities are particularly useful in frameworks that rely on runtime configuration, such as serialization libraries, testing frameworks, or dependency injection systems.

One of the standout features in Kotlin is **reified generics**, which solve the problem of type erasure commonly faced in Java reflection. By using reified type parameters in inline functions, Kotlin enables developers to retain type information at runtime, eliminating the need for workarounds like passing Class<T> as an argument.

In Kotlin 2025, the reflection API has been further optimized for performance and usability. Developers can now leverage enhanced reflection capabilities such as:

1. **Improved efficiency**: Reflection operations are faster due to compiler optimizations and reduced overhead when retrieving metadata.

2. **Scoped reflection**: New APIs allow developers to limit the scope of reflection queries, reducing unnecessary runtime overhead.

3. **Support for sealed interfaces and records**: Reflection now fully supports inspecting these constructs, which were recently introduced to Kotlin.

Despite its immense power, reflection should be used judiciously. Its runtime nature can have performance implications, and over-reliance on reflection can lead to less maintainable code. That said, reflection remains an invaluable tool for scenarios where flexibility and adaptability are paramount.

The Synergy of Generics, Annotations, and Reflection

While each of these features—generics, annotations, and reflection—independently enhances Kotlin's capabilities, their true potential lies in their synergy. Together, they empower developers to build **dynamic, reusable, and scalable applications** with minimal effort.

For example:

- **Combining Generics and Annotations**: In libraries like Retrofit or Room, generic types are annotated to specify their behavior during runtime serialization or database interaction.

- **Annotations and Reflection**: Frameworks like Spring Boot or Ktor use annotations to define configurations and behaviors, while reflection processes these annotations at runtime to dynamically adapt application behavior.

- **Generics and Reflection**: Through reified generics, developers can safely inspect and manipulate generic types at runtime, reducing boilerplate and improving type safety.

These interactions make Kotlin not only a language for crafting efficient applications but also a preferred choice for building tools, libraries, and frameworks that serve diverse programming paradigms.

Looking Forward: Generics, Annotations, and Reflection in the Future of Kotlin

Kotlin's continual evolution ensures that these features will remain at the forefront of modern software development. Kotlin 2025 demonstrates JetBrains' commitment to enhancing developer productivity, reducing complexity, and enabling seamless integration with cutting-edge technologies.

As Kotlin continues to gain traction in areas like mobile development (Kotlin Multiplatform Mobile), backend development (Ktor), and data science (KotlinDL, Kotlin for Apache Spark), the importance of generics, annotations, and reflection will only grow. With advancements in **AI-driven development tools**, **cloud-native solutions**, and **serverless architectures**, these features will serve as the foundation for innovation in Kotlin-based projects.

Here's what the future holds:

1. **Better Tooling for Generics**: IDE enhancements to simplify working with advanced generics and detect misuse early.

2. **Expanded Annotation Capabilities**: Built-in support for advanced annotation uses cases, like asynchronous annotations or integration with AI-driven metadata analysis tools.

3. **Optimized Reflection**: Further improvements in performance, possibly leveraging AI to optimize runtime inspection and invocation dynamically.

Final Thoughts: Mastering the Trifecta

Mastering generics, annotations, and reflection in Kotlin unlocks a world of possibilities for developers. These features, while complex, exemplify Kotlin's philosophy of **pragmatic programming**—a balance between powerful abstractions and practical usability.

To fully harness their power, developers must embrace a mindset of experimentation, learn the nuances of each feature, and understand when and how to use them effectively. By doing so, you'll not only become a more proficient Kotlin developer but also contribute to crafting solutions that are both elegant and robust.

As Kotlin continues to evolve, its language features like generics, annotations, and reflection will remain indispensable tools for tackling the challenges of modern software development. Whether you're building a mobile app, designing a backend system, or exploring the frontiers of machine learning, these features ensure that Kotlin remains a top choice for developers worldwide.

In the journey of mastering Kotlin, **generics, annotations, and reflection** are not just tools—they're stepping stones to becoming a truly versatile and proficient developer.

8. Kotlin for Android and Web Development

Introduction

Kotlin, a versatile programming language, has gained significant traction in recent years, particularly in the realms of Android and web development. Initially developed by JetBrains, Kotlin offers a modern and concise syntax while maintaining compatibility with existing Java codebases. This flexibility has made it an attractive choice for developers looking to enhance productivity and streamline development workflows across different platforms.

Overview of Kotlin

Kotlin is a statically-typed programming language that runs on the Java Virtual Machine (JVM). It seamlessly interoperates with Java, allowing developers to leverage existing libraries and frameworks while benefiting from Kotlin's expressive syntax and robust features. Kotlin can also compile to JavaScript, enabling its use for frontend web development alongside traditional backend and mobile applications.

Kotlin for Android Development

Advantages of Kotlin on Android

Android developers have increasingly adopted Kotlin due to its enhanced safety features, null safety, and concise syntax, which reduce boilerplate code compared to Java. Kotlin's interoperability with Java ensures a smooth transition for developers familiar with Android's existing ecosystem. Key advantages include:

- **Null Safety:** Kotlin's type system helps eliminate null pointer exceptions, a common issue in Java development, by distinguishing between nullable and non-nullable types.

- **Conciseness:** Kotlin's expressive syntax allows developers to achieve more with less code, improving readability and maintainability.

- **Functional Programming:** Kotlin supports functional programming paradigms, such as higher-order functions, lambda expressions, and immutable data structures, enabling developers to write clean and modular code.

Getting Started with Kotlin on Android

To begin developing Android applications with Kotlin, developers can set up Android Studio, which provides seamless support for Kotlin out of the box. Kotlin's integration with Android's SDK simplifies tasks like UI development, network operations, and asynchronous programming.

Kotlin for Web Development

Kotlin/JS for Frontend Development

Kotlin's ability to compile to JavaScript makes it suitable for frontend web development. Kotlin/JS allows developers to write frontend code using Kotlin while leveraging existing JavaScript libraries and frameworks like React and Vue.js. Key features include:

- **Type Safety:** Kotlin's static typing ensures early detection of errors and improves code quality during development.

- **Interoperability:** Kotlin/JS seamlessly integrates with JavaScript, allowing developers to reuse JavaScript libraries and APIs within Kotlin codebases.

- **Tooling Support:** JetBrains provides excellent tooling support for Kotlin/JS, including integration with popular IDEs like IntelliJ IDEA and WebStorm.

Kotlin for Backend Development

In addition to frontend development, Kotlin also finds application in backend development through frameworks like Ktor. Ktor is a lightweight and asynchronous framework that allows developers to build scalable and high-performance web applications. Key features include:

- **Coroutines:** Kotlin's built-in coroutine support simplifies asynchronous programming on the backend, improving responsiveness and resource efficiency.
- **Routing and Middleware:** Ktor provides an intuitive API for defining routes, handling HTTP requests, and integrating middleware for tasks like authentication and logging.
- **Integration with Databases:** Kotlin's JDBC support and integration with ORM libraries like Exposed facilitate seamless database interactions, making it easier to develop data-driven applications.

Kotlin's Ecosystem and Community

Kotlin benefits from a vibrant ecosystem supported by JetBrains and a growing community of developers worldwide. The Kotlin standard library offers comprehensive APIs for common programming tasks, while third-party libraries and frameworks further extend Kotlin's capabilities across different domains. Community-driven initiatives, such as Kotlin User Groups and conferences like KotlinConf, foster collaboration and knowledge sharing among developers.

Let's begin,

Kotlin on Android

This chapter will explore building Android applications with Kotlin. It will detail why Kotlin is so popular for Android development and how it makes developers' lives easier.

We'll take a look at some of the tools being released by Google that make use of Kotlin, and how to create a new Android project, with Kotlin support, using Android Studio.

Finally, we'll explore the use of Android KTX and Kotlin Android Extensions in making Android development easier with Kotlin.

First class Kotlin for Android

Kotlin has become very popular in the Android development community. This has been an ongoing process over the past 4-5 years, and has seen Kotlin go from a small, community-driven niche to the primary development language for Android.

Adopting Kotlin for Android

This increase in popularity for Android development really started to take off in 2015, but it was two years later, in 2017, when Kotlin really came to the fore. That was when Google officially announced support for Kotlin as a development language for Android.

When Android Studio 3.0 was released in October 2017, there was no longer a major technical obstacle to the adoption of Kotlin in established projects. Organizations or teams that had been concerned about pre-release versions of plugins or IDEs could now try Kotlin with stable tools and the full, long-term support of Google. This allowed many teams to adopt the language, and thus began the surge in Kotlin's popularity that we see today.

This community support for Kotlin came about largely because of Android's dependency on Java 7 and Java 8. While newer versions of Java have much more modern functionality, Android was stuck with Java 7 and

8 for long-term compatibility. This meant that developers didn't have access to more modern features, such as lambdas, without additional plugins or updating their target language, which wasn't always feasible.

The adoption of Kotlin provided a more modern-feeling language that was still bytecode-compatible with the JVM versions that Android required. As prominent members of the Android development community began speaking out in favor of Kotlin, more and more developers started to give it a try. With official support from Google, pitching Kotlin to a team became a much easier sell, and teams could begin experimenting with Kotlin with minimal risk.

All of this has resulted in Kotlin becoming a major part of the Android ecosystem today.

Kotlin first

At Google I/O 2019, it was announced that Google would be taking a **Kotlin-first** approach to Android from now on. This means that new APIs will be built with Kotlin in mind first. And, in fact, some APIs will only be available in Kotlin.

Additionally, new courses, documentation, and samples are being created with Kotlin and generally default to Kotlin over Java when examples exist for both.

IntelliJ and Android Studio both make it incredibly easy to integrate Kotlin with existing Android projects, or to start new projects that are 100% Kotlin. Additionally, Google continues to invest in Kotlin with improved tooling and the Core-KTX Jetpack library, which makes building Android applications with Kotlin even more enjoyable.

The Android architecture components are now built with a Kotlin-first approach and include support for Kotlin features such as coroutines. To an even greater degree, the pre-alpha Jetpack Compose library from Google is an entirely new UI toolkit built with, and for, Kotlin.

As these tools mature and new ones are developed, Android will continue to become more and more Kotlin-first.

The future of Android

Google continues to invest heavily in Kotlin, and Kotlin appears to be the future of Android development. The combination of Kotlin's modern features, terrific tooling, and strong support from Google make it an incredibly appealing choice for Android developers moving forward.

Hello Android Kotlin

In this section, we're going to explore how to start building Android apps with Kotlin. We'll walk through how to create and set up a new Android Studio project with Kotlin support. Also, we'll then explore a few ways in which we can take advantage of Kotlin for Android development.

Creating an Android app with Kotlin support

Let's walk through the following steps to create an Android project with Kotlin support:

1. First, we need to open Android Studio on our development machine.
2. Select Start a new Android Studio project.
3. Select Empty Activity, and then click Next, shown as follows:

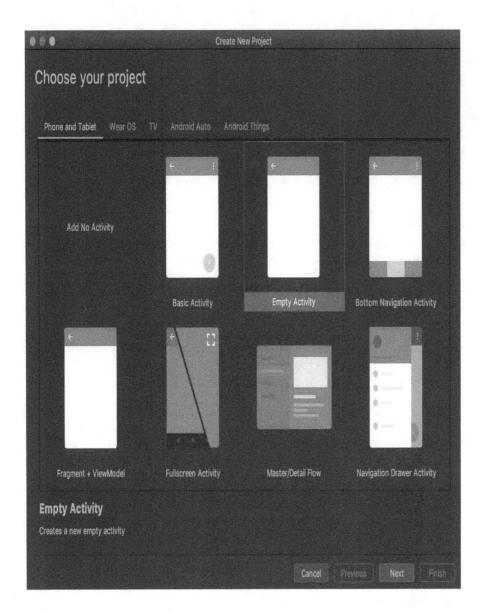

4. Update your project Name, package name, and Save location, as shown in the following screenshot:

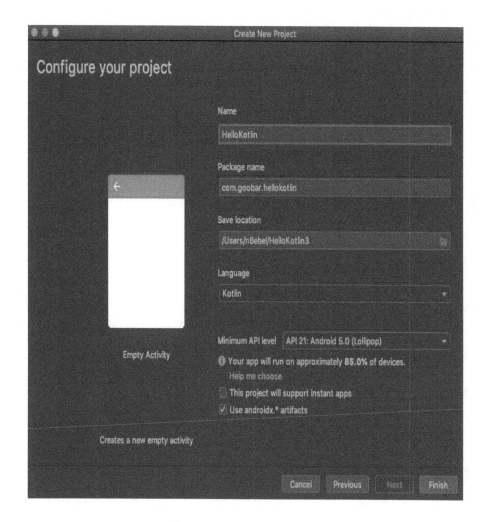

5. Ensure that Kotlin is selected in the Language drop-down menu, and then click Finish. This will ensure that

Kotlin is the default language for the project and that the IDE generates new code using Kotlin rather than Java:

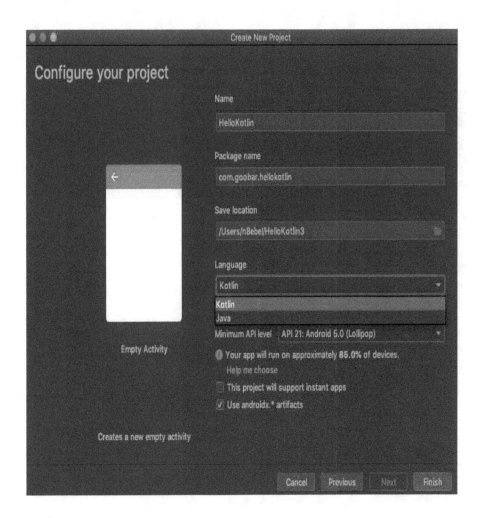

At this point, you will have a buildable Android project with Kotlin support, something similar to what is shown in the following screenshot:

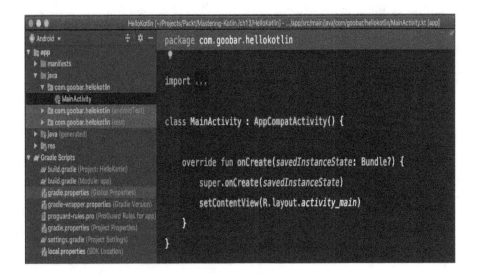

To see how Kotlin is configured for the project, open the root-level build.gradle file. In this case, it's the build.gradle file labeled Project: HelloKotlin. See the following screenshot:

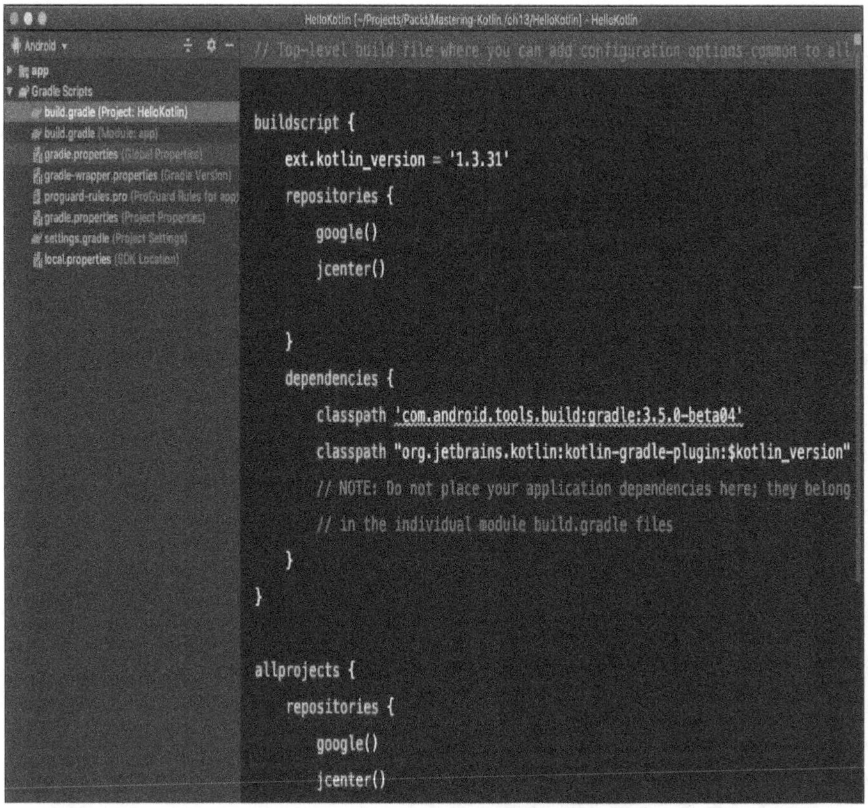

```
buildscript {

    ext.kotlin_version = '1.3.31'

    repositories {

        google()

        jcenter()


    }

    dependencies {

        classpath 'com.android.tools.build:gradle:3.5.0-beta04'

        classpath "org.jetbrains.kotlin:kotlin-gradle-plugin:$kotlin_version"

        // NOTE: Do not place your application dependencies here; they belong

        // in the individual module build.gradle files

    }

}


allprojects {

    repositories {

        google()

        jcenter()
```

This is the project-level build.gradle file.

There are two key things to be aware of in this build.gradle file:

The ext.kotlin_version variable defines the version of Kotlin used in the project, in this case, 1.3.31.

The Kotlin Gradle plugin has been added as a classpath dependency, allowing us to apply the plugin to our other Gradle modules, thereby making them Kotlin-aware.

Finally, if you open the build.gradle file labeled as Module: app, you'll notice three things:

The kotlin-android plugin has been applied.

The kotlin-android-extensions plugin has been applied.

The Kotlin standard library has been added as a dependency.

The following screenshot shows these elements:

```
                              HelloKotlin [~/Projects/Packt/Mastering-Kotlin/ch13/HelloKotlin] - app
  Android ▾              ÷ ☼ —     apply plugin: 'com.android.application'
▶ ▮ app
▼ ▮ Gradle Scripts                  apply plugin: 'kotlin-android'
   build.gradle (Project: HelloKotlin)
   build.gradle (Module: app)       apply plugin: 'kotlin-android-extensions'
   gradle.properties (Global Properties)
   gradle-wrapper.properties (Gradle Version)
   proguard-rules.pro (ProGuard Rules for app)
   gradle.properties (Project Properties)    dependencies {
   settings.gradle (Project Settings)
   local.properties (SDK Location)
                                        implementation"org.jetbrains.kotlin:kotlin-stdlib-jdk7:$kotlin_version"


                                        implementation fileTree(dir: 'libs', include: ['*.jar'])

                                        implementation 'androidx.appcompat:appcompat:1.0.2'

                                        implementation 'androidx.core:core-ktx:1.0.2'

                                        implementation 'androidx.constraintlayout:constraintlayout:1.1.3'

                                        testImplementation 'junit:junit:4.12'

                                        androidTestImplementation 'androidx.test.ext:junit:1.1.1'

                                        androidTestImplementation 'androidx.test.espresso:espresso-core:3.2.0'

                                    }


                                    android {

                                        compileSdkVersion 28

                                        defaultConfig {

                                            applicationId "com.goobar.hellokotlin"
```

At this point, you're now ready to start writing your Android app with Kotlin. In the next section, we'll explore how Kotlin can make that process easier.

Taking advantage of Kotlin on Android

Now that we have a working Android project that supports Kotlin, let's explore a few examples of common Android coding patterns that can be updated to take advantage of Kotlin.

Configuring a view reference

To get an immutable reference to a button, we could use something along the lines of the following code snippet:

val button = findViewById<Button>(R.id.button)

If we then wanted to configure multiple properties on that button, we could make use of the scoping function, apply:

val button = findViewById<Button>(R.id.button).apply {   text = "Hello Kotlin"   gravity = Gravity.START   setTextColor(resources.getColor(R.color.colorAccent)) }

The apply function provides us with a receiver, in this case, Button, which can then be referenced implicitly within the scope of the passed lambda. This can be a useful means of grouping related method calls or property updates.

Responding to click events

When writing Android View code with Kotlin, we can set click listeners on our Views using a lambda rather than an anonymous inner class, shown as follows:

button.setOnClickListener {

```
    // handle the event
}
```

The lack of parentheses here makes this easier to read and to write. Additionally, we could combine this click listener lambda with a functional property for responding to the click:

```
var clickHandler: (() -> Unit)? = null
```

```
... button.setOnClickListener {    // handle the event    clickHandler?.invoke() }
```

By exposing a public function property for responding to the click event, we can easily defer to that property within Button click listener and invoke the callback function only if it's non-null.

Creating factory methods for activities and fragments

A common pattern for the creation of new activities or fragments is to create static factory methods to start an activity, or to create an intent, or to create a new instance of Fragment. When using Kotlin, we can accomplish this using a companion object, which is shown in the following code block with the definition of Factory:

```
companion object Factory {    const val EXTRA_ID = "extra_id"
```

```
@JvmStatic
```

```
fun createIntent(context: Context, id: String) = Intent(context, DetailsActivity::class.java).apply {
putExtra(EXTRA_ID, id)
```

```
    }
}
```

Additionally, you could use a top-level function or extension function to achieve similar behavior, as follows:

```
fun createDetailsIntent(context: Context, id: String) =    Intent(context, DetailsActivity::class.java).apply {
putExtra(DetailsActivity.EXTRA_ID, id)
```

```
    }
```

```
fun Context.createDetailsIntent(id: String) =    Intent(this, DetailsActivity::class.java).apply {
putExtra(DetailsActivity.EXTRA_ID, id)    }
```

One possible drawback of using a top-level function is that it occupies the global namespace. If you're adding enough functions, it may become difficult for the IDE to autocomplete the function you're looking for. If this is the case for your project, using companion objects to scope your functions is likely the better choice.

Handling savedInstanceState

Kotlin allows us to perform null-safe method calls on variables that may, or may not, be null. One example of how this can reduce boilerplate in our code is in the handling of savedInstanceState.

A common pattern is to check whether savedInstanceState is non-null within onCreate(), and if it is, handle the restoration of that state. We can see an example of this in the following code snippet:

```
override fun onCreate(savedInstanceState: Bundle?) {    super.onCreate(savedInstanceState)
setContentView(R.layout.activity_details)
```

```
savedInstanceState?.let { it }
```

```
}
```

```
fun restoreSavedState(savedInstanceState: Bundle) {
```

```
    // restore state
}
```

Using a null-safe call to the let() function, we can safely restore our state only if savedInstanceState is non-null. And because of smart casting in Kotlin, we can define the restoreSavedState() function to only accept a non-null Bundle and then rely on the compiler to smart cast savedInstanceState for us. This helps us to enforce type safety and reduce NullPointerExceptions.

These have been just a couple of examples of how Kotlin can quickly make writing Android code safer and more concise. In the next section, we'll see how Kotlin can be applied to the build configuration of our project.

Building with Kotlin

Now that we've explored how we can write Kotlin code for our Android apps, we're going to examine how we can actually configure our Gradle build scripts using Kotlin rather than Groovy. This can provide several benefits, such as static type checking and improved refactoring.

The Gradle Kotlin DSL

The Gradle Kotlin DSL is an alternative method of configuring your Gradle build. Rather than relying on Groovy, you can leverage Kotlin to define your dependencies, build variants, and so on.

Moving your Gradle configuration to make use of the Gradle Kotlin DSL has several benefits:

Type-safe accessors allow you to reference Gradle/build entities by name.

Improved IDE support makes it easier to find and navigate to dependencies.

Migrating to the Kotlin buildscript

To explore the Gradle Kotlin DSL, we're going to migrate our existing Android project to make use of the DSL.

The first step will be to go through both of our build.gradle files and ensure that all string literals are using double quotes (") instead of single quotes (') and that all Gradle function calls are using parentheses.

In the case of the top-level build.gradle file, this means adding parentheses to the classpath() function calls. This is required because Groovy allows you to omit these parentheses, whereas Kotlin requires them to be used. The following code demonstrates what this update looks like in our project-level build.gradle file:

```
// root-level build.gradle buildscript {   ext.kotlin_version = "1.3.31"   repositories {     google()
jcenter()

    }

    dependencies {

      // addition of ( ) when using classpath function    classpath("com.android.tools.build:gradle:3.5.0-beta04")
classpath("org.jetbrains.kotlin:kotlin-gradle-plugin:$kotlin_version")

    }

}

...
```

The next step will be to rename each build.gradle file by adding .kts to the end so that the full filename is build.gradle.kts. This will indicate that the file is using the Kotlin Gradle DSL.

Once these filenames have been updated, we will have several errors to address. We will start by updating the rootlevel build.gradle.kts file.

First, we'll update the definition of the existing clean task as follows:

```
task(name = "clean", type = Delete::class) {    delete(rootProject.buildDir) }
```

Notice that we're able to make use of named parameters to define our invocation of the task function.

Next, we'll update our kotlin_version extension and its usage in declaring the Gradle Kotlin plugin. Consider the following code:

```
buildscript {    extensions.add("kotlin_version", "1.3.31")    repositories {    google()    jcenter()  }

 dependencies {    classpath("com.android.tools.build:gradle:3.5.0-beta04")

   // using extensions.get() to retrieve Kotlin version    classpath ("org.jetbrains.kotlin:kotlin-gradle plugin:${extensions.get("kotlin_version")}")

 }

}
```

We can define and retrieve extensions using extensions.add() or extensions.get(). Later on, we'll explore another means of defining our dependencies that doesn't rely on extensions.

Now, let's jump over to the app module's build.gradle.kts file. We'll start by updating the plugin declarations using the plugins block:

```
plugins {    id("com.android.application")    id("kotlin-android")

id("kotlin-android-extensions")

}
```

Next, we'll update our Android configuration block as follows:

```
android {    compileSdkVersion(28)    defaultConfig {    applicationId = "com.goobar.hellokotlin"
minSdkVersion(21)    targetSdkVersion(28)    versionCode = 1    versionName = "1.0"
testInstrumentationRunner =

      "androidx.test.runner.AndroidJUnitRunner"

 } buildTypes {    getByName("release") {    isMinifyEnabled = false

  proguardFiles(getDefaultProguardFile(

    "proguard-android-optimize.txt"), "proguard-rules.pro")

 }

 }

}
```

And lastly, we'll update our dependencies block:

```
dependencies {    implementation("org.jetbrains.kotlin:kotlin-stdlib-jdk7:1.3.31")

implementation("androidx.appcompat:appcompat:1.0.2")    implementation("androidx.core:core-ktx:1.0.2")
implementation("androidx.constraintlayout:constraintlayout:1.1.3")    testImplementation("junit:junit:4.12")
androidTestImplementation("androidx.test.ext:junit:1.1.1")

androidTestImplementation("androidx.test.espresso:espresso-core:3.2.0") }
```

At this point, our Gradle build is now using the Gradle Kotlin DSL. This gives us the familiar syntax and features of Kotlin when working with Gradle.

Simplifying dependency management with Kotlin

Now that we've migrated our build.gradle files to make use of the Kotlin Gradle DSL, let's improve the way in which we define dependencies and build constants. More specifically, we are going to use Kotlin object declarations to define our dependencies so they can be defined once and reused elsewhere. To do this, perform the following steps:

1. To start, create a new directory named buildSrc within the root project directory:

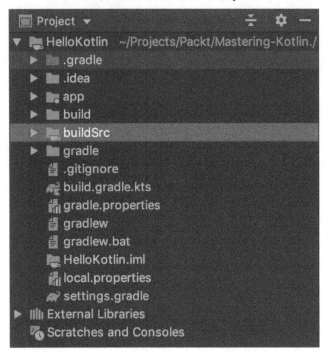

2. Next, we're going to create the following two files within the buildSrc directory:

buildSrc/build.gradle.kts buildSrc/src/main/kotlin/Dependencies.kt

This buildSrc directory is a special directory in which we can create constants and objects that Gradle will make available to us during the configuration and building of our project. To make this work, we first need to update buildSrc/build.gradle.kts with the following code:

```
repositories { jcenter() }

plugins {

 'kotlin-dsl'

}
```

By applying the 'kotlin-dsl' plugin, Gradle will use the objects and constants defined in this directory.

3. Now we can define some constants to use within our build. We'll define this within the newly created buildSrc/src/main/kotlin/Dependencies.kt file. To start, we'll define a String constant for the current version of Kotlin:

```
object Deps {    object Kotlin {       const val version = "1.3.31"

   }

}
```

Because we're working with a simple Kotlin file, we can define our constants as top-level properties or within an object declaration, as in the previous code snippet.

4. Once the constant is defined, we can make use of it from our other Gradle files like this:

```
// root/build.gradle.kts buildscript {

    extensions.add("kotlin_version", Deps.Kotlin.version)    repositories {        google()        jcenter()

    }    dependencies {        classpath("com.android.tools.build:gradle:3.5.0-beta04")        classpath
("org.jetbrains.kotlin:kotlin-gradle                plugin:${Deps.Kotlin.version}")

    }

}
```

We can access the defined constant as if it were any other type of Kotlin code that was referencing it. This approach can be used for more than just constants. We can define all of our dependencies within the buildSrc directory so they can be reused elsewhere in a consistent manner.

Let's examine how this works:

1. Let's start by updating Dependencies.kt with some additional dependency constants, as follows:

```
object Deps {    object Kotlin {        private const val version = "1.3.31"

const val gradlePlugin = "org.jetbrains.kotlin:kotlin gradle-plugin:$version"

    }

    object Android {        object Tools {            const val androidGradle = "com.android.tools.build:
gradle:3.5.0-beta04"

        }

    } }
```

2. Now, we can update build.gradle.kts to completely remove any reference to Kotlin version or plugin versions:

```
// root/build.gradle/kts buildscript {    repositories {        google()        jcenter()

    }    dependencies {

        classpath(Deps.Android.Tools.androidGradle)        classpath (Deps.Kotlin.gradlePlugin)

    }

}
```

This nicely encapsulates the available dependencies and their versions within the buildSrc directory. This makes your dependencies much easier to manage in larger, possibly multi-module, projects. This also makes it easier to navigate to dependencies from our build.gradle.kts files and to refactor dependencies across our project. Let's now move on to the tools used for this.

First-party tooling

As mentioned previously, Android is now Kotlin-first. With this approach comes a number of useful tools that help us take full advantage of Kotlin for Android development. In this section, we're going to explore several of these tools, including the following:

Android KTX

Kotlin Android Extensions

Architecture components

For each of these, we'll examine what it is, how it takes advantage of Kotlin, and why you might consider it for your Android projects.

Let's begin.

Exploring Android KTX

Android KTX is a set of different extensions for the Android framework and Jetpack. The Android KTX extensions are themselves a part of Jetpack and can be added to your project as a simple Gradle dependency. The functionality provided by Android KTX is aimed at making Android APIs more Kotlin idiomatic by taking advantage of features such as extension functions and higher-order functions.

To make the dependency more lightweight, Android KTX is broken up into several smaller dependencies, depending on the functionality they offer. Some of these are as follows:

Core KTX

Fragment KTX

SQLite KTX

ViewModel KTX

Navigation KTX

WorkManager KTX

The entirety of Android KTX provides a great deal of useful functionality. In the following sections, we're going to explore the functionality provided by two specific modules: Core KTX and Fragment KTX.

Adding Core KTX to your project

To start, we will update our project to make use of Core KTX. To do this, we'll first need to make sure we have the google() Maven repository added to our project. To add it, use the following code:

```
repositories {    google()
}
```

Next, we'll define a constant for core-ktx in our buildSrc directory:

```
object Android {    object Tools {        const val androidGradle = "com.android.tools.build:gradle:3.5.0-beta04"

    }      object Ktx {

        const val core = "androidx.core:core-ktx:1.0.1"      }

}
```

We'll then add the following dependency to app/build.gradle.kts:

```
dependencies {    ...
```

implementation(Deps.Android.Ktx.core) }

Now that Core KTX is added to our project, let's explore some of the ways in which it makes developers' lives easier.

Using Core KTX

Core KTX includes packages built around a variety of core Android framework libraries and APIs, including the following:

androidx.core.animation androidx.core.preference androidx.core.transition androidx.core.view

One of the best examples of using Android KTX to simplify platform APIs is in the use of SharedPreferences. With the functionality of Kotlin available to us, we can use a very fluent syntax for editing SharedPreferences that removes the need to explicitly call commit() or apply():

```
val preferences = getPreferences(Context.MODE_PRIVATE) preferences.edit {    putBoolean("key", false) putString("key2", "value") }
```

Another example of useful functionality provided by Android KTX is the View.onPreDraw() extension function:

```
button.doOnPreDraw {

// Perform an action when view is about to be drawn

}
```

This allows us to define a lambda containing logic that will be run when View is about to be drawn without having to create a new listener or having to unregister that listener.

Using Fragment KTX

Let's now explore the Fragment KTX module, which contains utility functions for working with fragments. First, we'll define our new dependency constant:

```
object Android {

    ...

    object Ktx {       const val core = "androidx.core:core-ktx:1.0.1"       const val fragment = "androidx.fragment:fragment-ktx:1.0.0"

    }

}
```

Now, we'll update app/build.gradle.kts:

```
dependencies {    ...

    implementation(Deps.Android.Ktx.core)     implementation(Deps.Android.Ktx.fragment) }
```

Once the dependency is added, we can define FragmentTransactions using the commit() extension function like this:

```
supportFragmentManager.commit {    addToBackStack("fragment name")    add(SampleFragment(), "tag") setCustomAnimations(R.anim.abc_fade_in, R.anim.abc_fade_out) }
```

This makes the addition of new FragmentTransaction feel more Kotlin idiomatic and removes some of the boilerplate around those operations.

As we've seen with Core KTX and Fragment KTX, these libraries can really improve the Android development experience. These types of extensions and additions are available across the Android KTX dependencies and can really help you take advantage of Kotlin for Android development.

In the next section, we'll take a look at the Kotlin Android Extensions plugin and how that provides additional functionality that makes Android development easier with Kotlin.

Using Kotlin Android Extensions

The Kotlin Android Extensions plugin provides a set of additional functionalities for working with Kotlin and Android. The two biggest examples of this are as follows:

Referencing Android views without findViewById()

Generating Parcelable implementations

To enable these features, we must enable the experimental features within the androidExtensions block of our app/build.gradle.kts file. The following code snippet demonstrates how to do this:

androidExtensions { isExperimental = true }

Once this configuration is added to our build.gradle.kts file, the features included with the Android Extensions plugin will be enabled. In the next section, we'll explore one of those features to help with building our Android views.

Binding views with Kotlin Android Extensions

Once the experimental features are turned on, we can reference synthetic view bindings to access our views. This means that the Android Extensions plugin will generate view bindings for us. In MainActivity, we can add the following import to reference the Button defined in our activity_main.xml file: import kotlinx.android.synthetic.main.activity_main.button

Once we've included the import, we can reference that view directly without any call to findViewById() or another variable declaration:

button.apply {   text = "Hello Kotlin"   gravity = Gravity.START
setTextColor(resources.getColor(R.color.colorAccent)) }

By default, the view will be named after the android:id attribute in the XML. In this case, our button had an ID of "@+id/button", so the binding generated was named button. However, if you want to use a different variable name, or have a conflict with another name, you can update the import statement and provide an alternative name using the following syntax: import kotlinx.android.synthetic.main.activity_main.button as theButton

After updating the import, we can now reference our button with the name theButton:

theButton.apply {   text = "Hello Kotlin"   gravity = Gravity.START
setTextColor(resources.getColor(R.color.colorAccent)) }

The synthetic view bindings will handle caching when used with activities and fragments and can be made to work with custom views as well. You can also control the caching strategy depending on your requirements by updating the androidExtensions block in your Gradle file:

androidExtensions {

// HASH_MAP, SPARSE_ARRAY, NONE   defaultCacheImplementation = "HASH_MAP" }

By using the Kotlin Android Extensions for your view references, you can avoid third-party libraries such as Butterknife or multiple findViewById() calls. Whether you should use these synthetic bindings—DataBinding, ViewBinding, or findViewById()—will largely depend on your project and preferences, and you should evaluate them on a project by - project basis.

Generating Parcelable implementations

Parcelable is a common interface within Android development aimed at providing a more performant serialization API. Generating implementations of the Parcelable interface can be a tedious and boilerplate-filled task involving the creation of a lot of simple and repetitive code. Thankfully, the Kotlin Android Extensions provide an annotation that can generate a Parcelable implementation for us. To make use of this functionality, we can add the @Parcelize annotation to any class that implements Parcelable:

```
@Parcelize data class Person(val firstName: String, val lastName: String): Parcelable
```

By adding the @Parcelize annotation to our model objects, the plugin will generate the required Parcelable implementations for us. This will allow you to skip the implementation, and maintenance of that Parcelable implementation. This reduces the amount of code required for your class and means you don't have to update your Parcelable implementation each time your class is modified; the plugin will do it for you when your code is compiled. This assists in protection from errors that can commonly arise from modifying a property, but forgetting to update the Parcelable implementation.

By making use of the Kotlin Android Extensions plugin, you can reduce the amount of code you must write and maintain, and allow the plugin to generate common boilerplate code for you.

Kotlin and Web Development

This chapter will explore the fundamentals of how Kotlin can be used for frontend web development. We will see how Kotlin can be compiled to a JavaScript target that can then be used in the development of backend services and web applications.

This chapter will help you to understand if Kotlin code can be written alongside existing JavaScript frameworks. It will also provide information of the limitations, if any, of compiling Kotlin to JavaScript and also how to build a web application that includes Kotlin.

Kotlin for the web

Kotlin's popularity can't be denied, and yet the vast majority of the attention given to Kotlin is within the realm of the JVM. Even more specifically, Kotlin is primarily used within the Android development community. However, one of the most interesting, ambitious, and potentially game-changing things about Kotlin is that it is becoming more and more useful beyond Android as new compilation targets become viable.

JetBrains continues to invest in support for multiple compilation targets for Kotlin. This means that it's possible to write Kotlin code that is compiled for targets other than the JVM. Currently, those targets include the following:

JavaScript

Native

Multiplatform

In this section, we're going to explore the ramifications of targeting JavaScript with Kotlin. We will also see how the compilation to JavaScript works, where we can apply the compiled JavaScript, and finally, why we might want to consider building with Kotlin for the web.

Compiling Kotlin to JavaScript

Let's start at the beginning. How is it that we can write Kotlin code that is then consumed as JavaScript? Throughout this book, we've seen many examples of how Kotlin is compiled down to JVM-compatible bytecode and how Kotlin interoperates so seamlessly with Java. With this in mind, it probably sounds a bit odd at first that we can take that same Kotlin code and use it in a JavaScript environment, so let's dive a bit deeper into how this is achieved.

Transpiling to JavaScript

The magic comes from the Kotlin compiler and your project target. In a standard JVM-targeted Kotlin project, the compiler generates JVM-compatible bytecode that runs on the JVM and is intrinsically compatible with other JVM code.

When creating a Kotlin project that targets JavaScript, all of the Kotlin code within that project will be transpiled to JavaScript when you build the project. If you're unfamiliar with the term transpile, it refers to the compilation of a programming language by converting it from one language to another. In a sense, the code is rewritten to match the target language. In this case, the Kotlin code you write is translated into compatible JavaScript that can then be consumed as if you had written any other JavaScript code. This includes any Kotlin code within your project, including the Kotlin standard library. However, this does not include any JVM-based code or libraries that are used. So, if you're consuming a Java library in your Kotlin code, you'll need to refactor that before it will be available in the transpiled JavaScript.

As with any programming language, there are often many ways to write functionally equivalent JavaScript code. When debugging or otherwise examining the JavaScript output of transpiled Kotlin, it's desirable to make that code as readable as possible. If the code looks like something a person would write, rather than something a compiler generates, it becomes easier to understand, debug, and reason about. To this end, JetBrains continues to work to ensure that the Kotlin compiler generates human-readable JavaScript during the transpiling phase.

Now that we understand that Kotlin is transpiled to JavaScript when a project is created that targets JavaScript, how do we actually target JavaScript when creating a new project? Let's see how this is done in the next section.

Targeting JavaScript

When we create a new Kotlin project, there are several ways to go about setting up that project and defining a compilation target. Throughout this book, we've primarily been working within IntelliJ IDEA to create new Kotlin projects and modules. Those projects have all targeted the JVM and have had minimal dependencies, so the actual project creation aspect hasn't been that interesting.

Now that we're considering how to create a Kotlin project that target's JavaScript, we can consider multiple means of creating a Kotlin project. In practice, there are the following four ways we could go about creating a new Kotlin project with a JavaScript target:

Building with Gradle

Building with Maven

Building within IntelliJ IDEA

Building from the command line

In the next section of this chapter, building a Hello Kotlin project, we will walk through how to set up a new Kotlin project using IntelliJ IDEA and make that project target JavaScript so that our Kotlin code can be consumed within a simple web app. Before continuing on to creating our own project, let's explore how and where we can integrate our transpiled Kotlin code.

Using the compiled JavaScript

A question that arises foremost is what we can do with our JavaScript once it's been transpiled from Kotlin. The simplest usage is to load the resulting script into an HTML page and execute whatever code we've defined in our main function.

For example, we can define a Kotlin main() function that prints to the console, as in the following example:

```
fun main(args: Array<String>) {   val message = "Hello Kotlin JavaScript"   println(message)
}
// outputs "Hello Kotlin JavaScript"
```

We can load the transpiled JavaScript equivalent of this code using a <script> tag with an HTML document to print out "Hello Kotlin JavaScript" to the console in our browser. We will see exactly how to do this in the very next section.

Beyond writing simple scripts, we could define model objects or business logic within Kotlin and then load those into our web app or server as well. Additionally, these scripts, functions, and models can be used in conjunction with other popular JavaScript frameworks, such as React. We'll discuss this in more detail in the Integrating with existing JavaScript section of this chapter.

Now, before diving into creating our own Kotlin project that targets JavaScript, let's explore why you might want to consider using Kotlin when targeting JavaScript.

Targeting JavaScript with Kotlin

You may be wondering why anyone would want to write Kotlin code that is then transpiled to Kotlin? Why go through the extra work? What are the benefits? These are perfectly reasonable questions, and ultimately, will depend a lot on your own experience and needs. However, we can explore some of the benefits to help inform your own investigation and decisions.

One benefit of using Kotlin for JavaScript is that it's statically typed. Many developers find JavaScript's lack of static typing to be disorienting and something to be desired. As such, there have been new languages that pop up, such as TypeScript, that aim to bring static typing to the JavaScript world. In this sense, Kotlin is similar to TypeScript. As a developer, you can work with static types provided by Kotlin and let the compiler work out how to translate that into proper JavaScript.

If you're an individual or team targeting multiple platforms for the same project, Kotlin could provide an avenue to achieve common code sharing. By defining common code, such as models or generic business logic, in Kotlin, that code can then be reused across multiple targets, including JavaScript, Native, and Android/JVM.

If you're a developer that is already familiar with Kotlin, targeting JavaScript can make both frontend and backend web development more approachable. Working with a familiar language can lower the barrier to entry for working in a new domain. With Kotlin for JavaScript, we can write simple JavaScript scripts, manipulate the DOM, or even write Node.js server-side code. This makes Kotlin a very powerful tool for a mobile developer, for example, who could theoretically use the same language, or even some of the same code, to write a mobile app, backend, and a web app.

With all of this in mind, let's start writing our own Kotlin project that targets JavaScript so that we can start to gain a first-hand understanding of how it works and what's possible.

Building a Hello Kotlin project

Now that we have an understanding of how the Kotlin to JavaScript compilation works, where you can make use of the compiled JavaScript, and why you might want to consider using Kotlin, let's walk through building a simple web app using Kotlin.

We're going to walk through the setup of a new Kotlin project with a JavaScript target. We'll then examine the output artifacts of the JavaScript compilation to understand what the compiler is actually producing when we build our project. And finally, we'll make use of those build artifacts to run a simple Kotlin function when our web page is loaded.

Creating a Kotlin project with a JavaScript target

To start a new Kotlin project that targets JavaScript, perform the following steps:

1. Open up IntelliJ IDEA and select Create New Project:

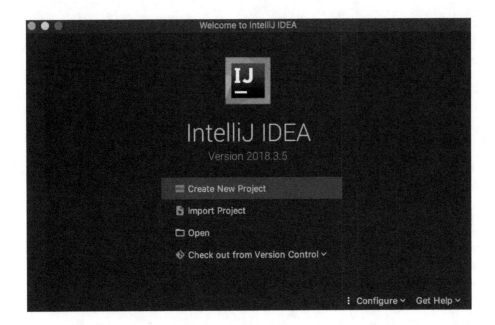

2. Navigate to the Kotlin project templates in the left-hand side of the dialog, select JS | IDEA, and then click NEXT. This will ensure that our newly created project is configured to target JavaScript using the IntelliJ IDEA build system:

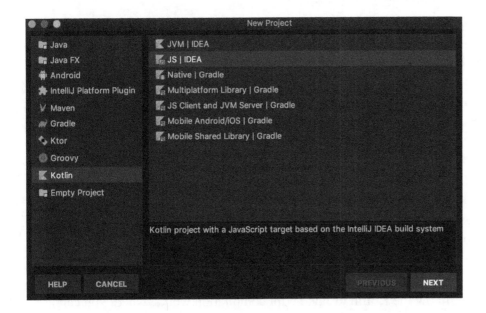

3. Next, we set our project name and project location. You can keep the Project SDK and Kotlin JS library fields as their default values unless you require a specific version of Kotlin. Once you've updated your name and project directory, click on FINISH:

At this point, we should now have an empty Kotlin project. Notice how the project is structured. There should be three elements in the root directory:

The .idea directory for IntelliJ configuration

An empty src directory

An .iml file with module configuration

In the next section, we'll add a Hello World example in Kotlin to understand how to start building Kotlin for JavaScript.

Writing Hello World for Kotlin JavaScript

To actually start transpiling some Kotlin into JavaScript, let's add a main.kt file to our project. To do so, we'll walk through the following steps:

1. Right-click on the src directory in the project pane and select New | Kotlin File/Class.

2. In the New Kotlin File/Class dialog, type main.kt and then click OK.

3. Navigate to main.kt and add the following code. This code will log a simple string message out to the console of the target environment:

```
fun main() {    val outputMessage = "Hello Kotlin JavaScript"    println(outputMessage) }
```

To this point, this should look very familiar. The Kotlin code we've written in main.kt is no different than what we would write if we were targeting the JVM. However, if we now build the project, we can see a difference in the resulting build artifacts, as shown in the following screenshot:

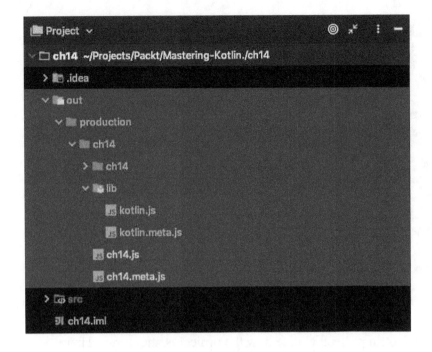

After building our project, the following four artifacts have been created:

lib/kotlin.js lib/kotlin.meta.js ch14.js ch14.meta/js

In the next section, we're going to look more closely at these outputs, and what they contain.

Examining the compiled JavaScript

As discussed previously in this chapter, when we build a Kotlin project that is targeting JavaScript, the compiler will transpile our Kotlin code into human-readable JavaScript for use in whatever web application we may be building. This includes the Kotlin standard library as well. The results of this compilation process can be seen in our output directory after a project build. The following screenshot depicts this:

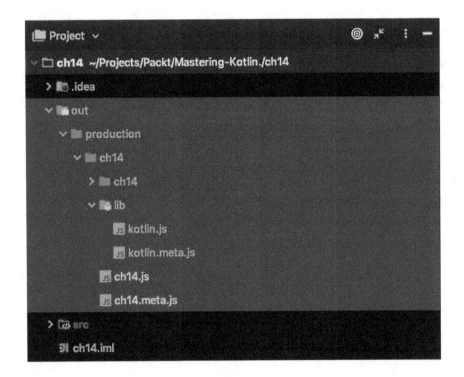

As mentioned in the last section, we have four outputs from the compilation of our current Hello World project:

lib/kotlin.js lib/kotlin.meta.js ch14.js ch14.meta/js

Notice the pattern with these outputs? We have ch14.js and lib/kotlin.js, as well as two examples of <file>.meta.js that correspond to the other two output files. For each module in our project, the compiler will create a <module>.js file. In our example, that is ch14.js.

At the project level, the compiler must generate JavaScript for the Kotlin standard library, which is output as kotlin.js. This kotlin.js file should be the same for any project using the same version of Kotlin.

For each transpiled .js file, the compiler also then generates a corresponding <file>.meta.js, which is used primarily for reflection. These files are generally of less concern to us as they are not generally human-readable. However, the .js files generated for the Kotlin standard library and each of our modules is designed to be human-readable, so we can understand what the transpiled JavaScript is doing.

If we open up ch14.js, we can see the JavaScript code equivalent of our Hello World Kotlin example, as shown here:

```
if (typeof kotlin === 'undefined') {   throw new Error("Error loading module 'ch14'. The dependency 'kotlin' was not found. Please, check whether 'kotlin' is loaded prior to 'ch14'.");
}
var ch14 = function (_, Kotlin) {
'use strict';
var println = Kotlin.kotlin.io.println_s8jyv4$;   function main() {     var outputMessage = 'Hello Kotlin JavaScript';     println(outputMessage);
  }
.main = main;   main();
Kotlin.defineModule('ch14', _);   return _;
}(typeof ch14 === 'undefined' ? {} : ch14, kotlin);
```

This JavaScript is the result of the compiler transpiling the Kotlin standard library, our own code, and then ensuring that all of the dependencies are still met. The result of this JavaScript is a variable assigned the result of a selfexecuting, anonymous function call. When that function is declared, it is executed, which, in turn, executes the transpiled version of our main() function from main.kt. In this case, this results in our "Hello Kotlin JavaScript" message being printed out to the console.

Now that we've seen how our Kotlin has been transpiled into usable JavaScript, let's look at how we can actually start consuming this code.

Consuming Kotlin through compiled JavaScript

Possibly the easiest way to start consuming our transpiled JavaScript is to load that JavaScript with a <script> tag within an HTML document. In doing this, we can run our main() function when the script is loaded and examine the output in the developer console.

To demonstrate this, let's walk through the following steps:

1. Add a new index.html file under the root directory, as in the following code snippet:

```
<!DOCTYPE html>
<html lang="en">
```

```html
<head>
    <meta charset="UTF-8">
    <title>HelloKotlinJS</title>
</head>
<body bgcolor="#E6E6FA">
    <!-- will load our JavaScript here -->
</body>
</html>
```

By adding this file, we give ourselves an entry point from which to load and run our JavaScript. If you then open this index.html file in your browser, you should see an empty page with a colored background. We will be updating this shortly.

2. Within the <body> tag, add two <script> tags, one for kotlin.js and one for ch13.js:

```html
<!DOCTYPE html>
<html lang="en">
    <head>
        <meta charset="UTF-8">
        <title>HelloKotlinJS</title>
    </head>
    <body bgcolor="#E6E6FA">
        <script type="text/javascript"
         src="out/production/ch14/lib/kotlin.js"></script>
        <script type="text/javascript"
         src="out/production/ch14/ch14.js"></script>
    </body>
</html>
```

By adding these <script> tags, we will load the Kotlin standard library and our module's JavaScript code. Note the order of these scripts. It's important that kotlin.js is loaded first because ch14.js relies on the Kotlin standard library. If ch14.js is loaded first, you'll receive an uncaught error when loading your script.

3.   Next, we'll save our index.html file, and then use IntelliJ to open index.html in Google Chrome. With index.html open, you should see several icons representing available web browsers that can be used to view the HTML page, as shown in the following screenshot:

```
<!DOCTYPE html>
<html lang="en">
    <head>
        <meta charset="UTF-8">
        <title>HelloKotlinJS</title>
    </head>
    <body bgcolor="#E6E6FA">
        <script type="text/javascript" src="out/production/ch14/lib/kotlin.js"></script>
        <script type="text/javascript" src="out/production/ch14/ch14.js"></script>
    </body>
</html>
```

Opening this into our browser will enable us to examine the results of running our JavaScript. Once index.html is open, you should see an empty web page.

4. To view the results of our JavaScript within Google Chrome, navigate to View | Developer | Developer Tools | Console:

This will allow us to view any console output from our web page. Once the Developer Tools pane has opened, reload your web page and you should then see "Hello Kotlin JavaScript" printed out to the console. This is the result of running our main() function that has been transpiled into ch14.js.

With that, we've completed the journey of creating a new Kotlin project, writing a simple Hello World function in Kotlin, and then consuming that code as JavaScript within a simple web page. While this is a very basic example, it covers the primary workflow of targeting JavaScript with Kotlin.

In the next section, we'll explore more about how to integrate Kotlin code with other JavaScript, and we'll build on our example to use Kotlin to actually manipulate the content of our web page.

Integrating with existing JavaScript

We've now seen how to set up a basic Kotlin project that targets JavaScript and can then be run in a simple web app. But how can we start to build something more interesting using Kotlin? These days, web development is largely dominated by different libraries and frameworks aimed at making the development process easier and more efficient.

How does Kotlin fit in with these frameworks? How can you build a scalable web application with Kotlin? In this section, we're going to start answering these questions. We'll start with an overview of popular frameworks that are compatible with Kotlin, and then we'll dive a bit deeper and explore manipulating the DOM from our Kotlin code.

Working with other JavaScript frameworks

As was mentioned previously, the landscape of JavaScript development today is filled with third-party frameworks such as React, Node.js, and Vue.js. They enable JavaScript developers to be more efficient and to build better applications and services. This begs the question: Can we use Kotlin in conjunction with popular third-party JavaScript libraries?

Thankfully, the answer is yes. We can leverage our Kotlin code alongside these frameworks in a few different ways:

Without direct interaction

By converting TypeScript definitions to work with strongly typed APIs

Interacting with non-strongly typed APIs directly using dynamic types

The most basic example of mixing Kotlin and JavaScript is writing Kotlin that doesn't rely on any direct interaction with other JavaScript frameworks. This is the approach we've seen so far in this chapter. Our Hello World code didn't know it was going to be run in a JavaScript environment. It didn't work with any framework, manipulate the DOM, or do other domain-specific tasks. This would be the same if we were simply writing our model objects in Kotlin so that they could be reused across multiple Kotlin projects. If we're working with simple data classes, there's a high likelihood they wouldn't need to be dependent on any specific JavaScript APIs.

What happens if we want to use a library that the Kotlin standard library doesn't provide JavaScript bindings for? Examples of this may include jQuery or react. In these cases, we have two options:

Our first option is to search for any available TypeScript headers for the library and convert them to Kotlin bindings using the conversion tool available at https://github.com/kotlin/ts2kt. The DefinitelyTyped project is a repository of static TypeScript bindings for JavaScript libraries and frameworks. The repository contains definitions for thousands of libraries. If you find definitions for a library you wish to use, you can convert those definitions to Kotlin using the freely available ts2kt tool. When using ts2kt, we can generate a Kotlin file containing strongly typed bindings for whichever library we want to use.

The second option is to use Kotlin's dynamic types to gain access to JavaScript functions that are available at runtime, but for which we don't have access to static bindings. By defining a variable as dynamic, we can call anything we would like on it, and it will not result in a compiler error. Take the following code snippet, for example:

```
// results in runtime error if invokeAnything() doesn't exist val someObject: dynamic = null
someObject.invokeAnything()
```

This code compiles, but unless the invokeAnything() function is defined somewhere at runtime, this code will result in an exception, as demonstrated in the following screenshot:

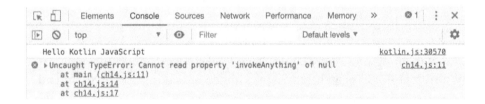

By using dynamic types, we have the flexibility to work with any JavaScript we need to, even if we don't have access to static bindings. As mentioned previously, we can find bindings for many popular libraries in the DefinitelyTyped repository that we can then make use of by converting them to Kotlin using ts2kt.

Additionally, JetBrains has provided its own repositories for several popular frameworks. Some of these are listed here:

Wrappers for popular libraries such as React and Redux—https://github.com/JetBrains/kotlin-wrappers.

A starter project for building a React app with Kotlin—https://github.com/JetBrains/create-react-kotlin-app.

Between available TypeScript definitions, the JetBrains-provided kotlin-wrappers repository, and dynamic types, Kotlin can potentially harness the full power and functionality of the JavaScript ecosystem.

To illustrate this, in the next section, we're going to generate jQuery bindings for Kotlin and use jQuery to manipulate our web page using Kotlin.

Manipulating the DOM via Kotlin

Let's walk through this concept of generating bindings to a third-party library to modify our web page using jQuery through our Kotlin code. To do this we're going to need to find TypeScript bindings for jQuery, convert those to Kotlin with ts2kt, and then use those bindings to manipulate our page from Kotlin.

By following these steps, we'll be able to add HTML elements to our web page programmatically from our Kotlin code:

1. First, install the ts2kt tool using the following npm command: npm -g install ts2kt.

2. Then, from the root directory of our project, install jQuery on your machine using npm install jquery. We'll need to test our project in our local development environment. This should result in a node_modules directory being added to the root level of the project. Within that folder, you should see a jquery directory.

3. Next, download the jquery.d.ts TypeScript definition file and save it to your root project directory.

4. We can then convert those headers into Kotlin with the following command: ts2kt -d src jquery.d.ts. This will generate a src/jquery.kt file under the root directory. This file will contain all the required Kotlin bindings for jQuery. If you open the file, you'll notice most of the bindings are implemented as external interface.

At this point, we're ready to start using jQuery within our Kotlin code. Let's start off by adding a basic header to our page. To do so, we can use the following code:

```
fun main() {    val outputMessage = "Hello Kotlin JavaScript"    println(outputMessage)
jQuery("body").append("<h1>We Added A Heading!!</h1>")

    ...

}
```

Running the code will append an <h1> tag to our <body> element when our script is loaded. Before we can see the results of this change, we need to include jquery.js as a script within index.html. This is what will allow our jQuery bindings to bind to the actual jQuery implementations. To include our local jQuery installation, add the following <script> tag to index.html:

```
<!DOCTYPE html>
<html lang="en">
  <head>
    <meta charset="UTF-8">
    <title>HelloKotlinJS</title>
  </head>
  <body bgcolor="#E6E6FA">
    <script src="node_modules/jquery/dist/jquery.js"></script>
    <script type="text/javascript"
    src="out/production/ch14/lib/kotlin.js"></script>
    <script type="text/javascript"
    src="out/production/ch14/ch14.js"></script>
```

```
    </body>
</html>
```

Now, we can rebuild our project and then reload ₍ᵢₙₐₑₓ.ₕₜₘₗ₎ in our browser. Once you do, your page should now look like this:

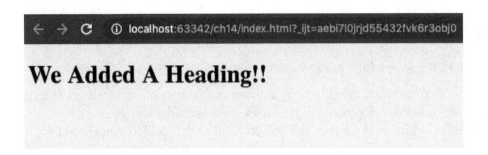

You can see that our <h1> element has been successfully added to our page. This is a small visual change, but a pretty large conceptual step. We were able to generate bindings for a popular JavaScript library, leverage those bindings from Kotlin, and use them to manipulate the content of our web page using a statically typed API.

Now, let's expand on this a bit by leveraging more Kotlin features to generate a more interesting web page. Here's how this is done:

1. Let's start by creating a ViewState data class that will contain the information to display on the page:

   data class ViewState(val title: String, val topics: List<String>)

2. Next, we'll create a PagePresenter class that will omit ViewState instances through a callback:

```
class PagePresenter(private val viewStateListener: (ViewState) -> Unit) {
    init {      viewStateListener(ViewState("Hello KotlinJS", headings))
    }
}
```

3. We'll also define a list of topics that can be passed to our ViewState:

   private val headings = listOf("Kotlin", "Programming", "JavaScript")

4. Now, within main.kt, we can create a new instance of PagePresenter. Within the callback lambda, we can use jQuery to bind our ViewState properties to our web page:

```
val presenter = PagePresenter() {   jQuery("body").append("<h1>${it.title}</h1>")   it.topics.forEach {
jQuery("body").append("<h2>${it}</h2>")
    }
}
```

Notice that within this callback, we're able to take advantage of Kotlin features such as String templates, and our Kotlin standard library functions such as forEach(). This makes it very easy to bind our ViewState to the UI by calling the appropriate jQuery functions.

If we rebuild this project and reload our web page, you should see that it now has a title and three subheadings:

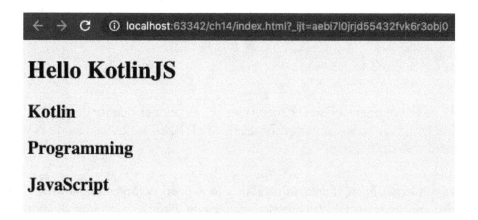

This example has shown how to start building for the web using JavaScript that is transpiled from type-safe Kotlin code. When writing in Kotlin, we can take advantage of familiar Kotlin features such as data classes and the Kotlin standard library and rely on the compiler to generate appropriate JavaScript for us. The ability to use existing, or generate new, JavaScript bindings for popular libraries means we aren't limited in how we can write JavaScript. Whether we want to use jQuery, React, Redux, Node.js, or other frameworks, the possibility of using Kotlin is available to us. In Chapter 15, Introducing Multiplatform Kotlin, we'll build on another, more interactive, example of using Kotlin for web development as we work within a multiplatform project.

Conclusion: Kotlin for Android and Web Development

Kotlin has firmly established itself as one of the most versatile and developer-friendly programming languages in modern software development. With its concise syntax, robust features, and seamless interoperability with Java, Kotlin provides an ideal balance of productivity and functionality. Its role in Android and web development is particularly significant, as it bridges the gap between mobile and web platforms, offering a cohesive experience for developers and users alike.

Kotlin's Impact on Android Development

Kotlin became the official language for Android development in 2017, endorsed by Google. Since then, it has redefined how developers approach mobile application development. Its concise syntax reduces boilerplate code, allowing developers to focus on core application logic rather than repetitive tasks. Features like null safety, extension functions, and coroutines simplify complex operations such as asynchronous programming, making apps more reliable and responsive.

The adoption of Kotlin has transformed the Android development landscape. Legacy Java codebases can gradually integrate Kotlin thanks to its full interoperability, ensuring a seamless transition for teams moving to a more modern development approach. Additionally, the Kotlin Multiplatform Mobile (KMM) framework extends its benefits by enabling developers to write shared code for Android and iOS, significantly reducing development time and effort.

Kotlin's Role in Web Development

While Kotlin's journey started with the JVM, its expansion into web development has been a game-changer. Kotlin/JS empowers developers to write type-safe, maintainable, and expressive code for the web, leveraging the strengths of Kotlin while integrating seamlessly with JavaScript libraries and frameworks. Whether you're building modern single-page applications with frameworks like React or creating interactive frontend components, Kotlin/JS ensures a streamlined development process with fewer runtime errors due to its static typing.

On the backend, Kotlin shines with frameworks like Ktor and Spring Boot. Ktor, in particular, is a Kotlin-native framework that takes advantage of coroutines for handling high-performance, asynchronous applications. With Kotlin's support for both frontend and backend development, it is possible to create full-stack applications entirely in Kotlin, reducing the cognitive load on developers and ensuring consistent coding standards across projects.

The Benefits of Kotlin for Developers

The reasons behind Kotlin's popularity go beyond its technical capabilities. Its developer-centric design prioritizes usability and productivity, making it an ideal language for teams of all sizes. Below are some key benefits that Kotlin offers to Android and web developers:

1. **Concise and Expressive Syntax**
   Writing code in Kotlin is a pleasant experience, thanks to its ability to express complex ideas with minimal verbosity. This not only improves readability but also reduces the likelihood of introducing errors.

2. **Null Safety**
   One of the most common causes of crashes in Java applications is the infamous NullPointerException. Kotlin's type system enforces null safety, ensuring that developers handle null values explicitly.

3. **Seamless Java Interoperability**
   Kotlin's ability to work alongside Java without friction makes it a practical choice for teams transitioning to modern practices while maintaining their legacy systems.

4. **Coroutines for Asynchronous Programming**
   Asynchronous programming is crucial for both mobile and web development. Kotlin's coroutines offer an elegant and efficient way to handle concurrency, resulting in responsive applications with fewer bugs.

5. **Cross-Platform Capabilities**
   Kotlin Multiplatform enables developers to share business logic across Android, iOS, and even web platforms. This approach significantly reduces the duplication of effort while maintaining native performance and user experiences.

6. **Tooling Support**
   Kotlin benefits from excellent IDE support, particularly in JetBrains' IntelliJ IDEA and Android Studio. Features like code completion, debugging tools, and refactoring make development faster and more reliable.

Challenges and How Kotlin Addresses Them

While Kotlin offers numerous benefits, adopting it does come with certain challenges, particularly for teams with existing Java codebases or those new to modern programming paradigms. However, Kotlin has made significant strides in addressing these issues:

- **Learning Curve:** Although Kotlin is easy to learn for developers familiar with Java, its advanced features, like coroutines and higher-order functions, may require some time to master. The wealth of documentation, tutorials, and a supportive community helps mitigate this challenge.

- **Build Times:** Initially, Kotlin build times were slower than Java, but continuous updates and optimizations have significantly improved performance, especially in the Android ecosystem.

- **Ecosystem Maturity:** While Kotlin's ecosystem is not as vast as JavaScript's, its rapid growth has brought high-quality libraries and frameworks to the forefront, making it a viable choice for both small and large projects.

Future Trends in Kotlin Development

Kotlin's growth shows no signs of slowing down. Its adoption in Android development is now the standard, and its expansion into other domains such as web development, backend services, and even data science is gaining momentum. The Kotlin Multiplatform project holds significant promise for unifying codebases across platforms, providing a compelling alternative to traditional cross-platform frameworks like Flutter or React Native.

In web development, Kotlin/JS continues to evolve, with increasing support for modern web frameworks and tools. Developers can look forward to a more mature ecosystem that allows them to build powerful, scalable, and maintainable web applications.

Why Choose Kotlin for Android and Web Development?

Kotlin is more than just a programming language—it's a tool that empowers developers to build better software. For Android development, it addresses long-standing pain points in Java and introduces features that enhance productivity and application stability. On the web, it brings type safety and a modern programming paradigm to JavaScript-based development, making it a strong contender in the full-stack development space.

Here are key reasons why developers and organizations should consider Kotlin:

- **Improved Developer Productivity:** Less code, fewer bugs, and better tooling translate to faster development cycles and lower maintenance costs.

- **Robust Community and Ecosystem:** With active support from JetBrains and Google, as well as a growing open-source community, Kotlin's ecosystem is constantly improving.

- **Scalability:** Whether building small hobby projects or large enterprise applications, Kotlin scales effectively to meet the demands of the project.

- **Future-Proof Technology:** Kotlin's momentum and widespread adoption ensure that it remains a relevant and valuable skill for developers in the coming years.

Final Thoughts

Kotlin's rise as a preferred language for Android and web development is a testament to its practical design and powerful features. It addresses the shortcomings of older languages while introducing modern capabilities that align with current development trends. From its seamless integration with Android Studio to its ability to build full-stack web applications, Kotlin provides developers with the tools they need to create innovative, high-quality software.

As more organizations adopt Kotlin for their projects, its ecosystem will continue to grow, bringing new opportunities and possibilities to developers worldwide. Whether you're an experienced developer or just starting your programming journey, Kotlin is a language worth mastering. Its versatility, productivity, and forward-thinking design make it an invaluable asset for anyone looking to build the future of mobile and web applications.

9. Testing in Kotlin

Introduction

Software testing is a vital part of application development that ensures code quality, reduces bugs, and improves reliability. Kotlin, as a modern and expressive programming language, offers robust support for writing testable code. From its concise syntax to its compatibility with existing Java testing frameworks, Kotlin has become a favored choice for developers aiming to enhance their testing strategies.

This guide dives deep into the world of testing in Kotlin, covering essential testing concepts, tools, frameworks, and best practices. By the end of this article, you will have a comprehensive understanding of how to design, write, and execute tests effectively in Kotlin.

Why Testing is Crucial

Testing is not just about identifying bugs; it plays a significant role in:

1. **Ensuring Code Reliability**: Verifies that the code behaves as expected under various scenarios.
2. **Facilitating Refactoring**: Allows developers to refactor code confidently, knowing tests will catch regressions.
3. **Improving Code Quality**: Encourages developers to write modular, maintainable, and readable code.
4. **Speeding Up Development**: Detects issues early, reducing debugging time during later stages.

Overview of Testing in Kotlin

Kotlin supports various types of testing, ranging from unit tests to end-to-end tests. Below is an overview of the main categories:

- **Unit Testing**: Testing individual components in isolation.
- **Integration Testing**: Verifying the interaction between different components or modules.
- **UI Testing**: Ensuring the correctness of the user interface.
- **Performance Testing**: Measuring and improving the application's performance.
- **End-to-End Testing**: Testing the entire application flow.

Key Features of Kotlin for Testing

1. **Interoperability**: Kotlin works seamlessly with existing Java testing frameworks like JUnit and TestNG.
2. **Extension Functions**: Simplify the creation of test utilities.
3. **Null Safety**: Prevents null pointer exceptions during tests.
4. **DSLs for Testing**: Kotlin's ability to create Domain-Specific Languages (DSLs) enables expressive and concise test definitions.
5. **Coroutines Support**: Testing asynchronous code becomes straightforward with Kotlin's coroutine capabilities.

Setting Up a Testing Environment in Kotlin

To get started with testing in Kotlin, you need to set up your development environment.

1. Adding Dependencies

Use Gradle or Maven to add testing libraries to your project. Here's an example of dependencies for a Kotlin project:

```
dependencies {
    // JUnit 5 for unit testing
    testImplementation("org.junit.jupiter:junit-jupiter:5.10.0")

    // MockK for mocking
    testImplementation("io.mockk:mockk:1.14.0")

    // AssertK for assertions
    testImplementation("com.willowtreeapps.assertk:assertk:0.25")

    // Kotlin Coroutines Test library
    testImplementation("org.jetbrains.kotlinx:kotlinx-coroutines-test:1.7.3")
}
```

2. Writing Your First Test

Here's a simple example of a unit test in Kotlin using JUnit 5:

```
import org.junit.jupiter.api.Assertions.assertEquals
import org.junit.jupiter.api.Test

class CalculatorTest {

    @Test
    fun `addition of two numbers`() {
        val calculator = Calculator()
        val result = calculator.add(2, 3)
        assertEquals(5, result)
    }
}

class Calculator {
    fun add(a: Int, b: Int): Int = a + b
}
```

Popular Testing Libraries and Tools in Kotlin

Kotlin integrates well with several testing libraries and tools, making it versatile for different testing needs.

1. JUnit 5

- **Description**: A widely used testing framework for Java and Kotlin.
- **Features**:
  - Annotations like @Test, @BeforeEach, and @AfterEach.
  - Parameterized tests for running a single test with different inputs.

2. MockK

- **Description**: A Kotlin-specific mocking library.
- **Features**:
  - Mocking classes and functions effortlessly.
  - Support for relaxed mocks to simplify testing.

Example:

```
import io.mockk.every
import io.mockk.mockk
import io.mockk.verify
import org.junit.jupiter.api.Test

class MockKExampleTest {

    @Test
    fun `mocking a service call`() {
        val mockService = mockk<Service>()
        every { mockService.getData() } returns "Mocked Data"

        val result = mockService.getData()

        assertEquals("Mocked Data", result)
        verify { mockService.getData() }
    }

    interface Service {
        fun getData(): String
    }
}
```

3. AssertK

- **Description**: A fluent assertion library for Kotlin.
- **Features**:
  - Easy-to-read assertions.

Example:

```kotlin
import assertk.assertThat
import assertk.assertions.isEqualTo
import org.junit.jupiter.api.Test

class AssertKExampleTest {

    @Test
    fun `testing with AssertK`() {
        val actual = 10
        assertThat(actual).isEqualTo(10)
    }
}
```

4. Kotlin Test

- **Description**: A testing library that comes with the Kotlin standard library.
- **Features**:
  - Supports test suites and assertions.

Example:

```kotlin
import kotlin.test.Test
import kotlin.test.assertEquals

class KotlinTestExample {

    @Test
    fun `Kotlin test example`() {
        val sum = 3 + 2
        assertEquals(5, sum)
    }
}
```

5. Spek Framework

- **Description**: A Kotlin DSL for writing specifications-based tests.
- **Features**:
  - Supports a structured and readable test layout.

Example:

```kotlin
import org.spekframework.spek2.Spek
import org.spekframework.spek2.style.specification.describe
import kotlin.test.assertEquals


object CalculatorSpec : Spek({

  describe("a calculator") {
    val calculator = Calculator()


    it("should return the sum of two numbers") {
      assertEquals(5, calculator.add(2, 3))
    }
  }


  class Calculator {
    fun add(a: Int, b: Int): Int = a + b
  }
})
```

Testing Asynchronous Code

Kotlin's coroutine library makes it simple to test asynchronous functions. Use the kotlinx-coroutines-test library to control and verify coroutine behavior.

Example:

```kotlin
import kotlinx.coroutines.test.runTest
import org.junit.jupiter.api.Test
import kotlin.test.assertEquals


class CoroutineTest {

  @Test
  fun `test async function`() = runTest {
    val result = asyncOperation()
    assertEquals("Success", result)
```

```
    }

    suspend fun asyncOperation(): String {
        // Simulate some asynchronous task
        return "Success"
    }
}
```

Test Best Practices in Kotlin

1. **Write Readable Tests**: Use meaningful names and structure tests logically.
2. **Isolate Unit Tests**: Ensure that unit tests focus on a single unit of functionality.
3. **Use Mocking Wisely**: Avoid overusing mocks; rely on real objects when possible.
4. **Adopt Parameterized Tests**: Test multiple scenarios with different inputs in a single test.
5. **Leverage Kotlin's Features**: Use extension functions, DSLs, and coroutines effectively in tests.
6. **Run Tests Regularly**: Automate test execution in your CI/CD pipeline.
7. **Measure Code Coverage**: Use tools like JaCoCo to monitor how much of your code is being tested.

Debugging and Profiling Tests

Kotlin's integration with IDEs like IntelliJ IDEA simplifies debugging and profiling test cases. Use breakpoints, watch expressions, and profiling tools to identify bottlenecks and issues in tests.

Let's begin,

Software testing serves as a critical part of the software development life cycle, acting as a safeguard against defects and enhancing the overall quality of software products. Certification from Quality Assurance (QA) is often used as the indicator of whether the software product is ready to go live.

We will discuss the role of QA and software testers in the industry. We will summarize the understanding of the role and how it might mean something different to different people.

We will explore several types of software testing and the testing pyramid. Additionally, we will discuss automated testing practices, which have gained popularity for their ability to enhance efficiency and ensure consistent test coverage.

We will also run an exercise of strict Test-Driven Development (TDD) using Kotest to gain insights into this methodology.

Unit testing

The bottom level of the pyramid is unit testing. Unit tests are the foundation of the testing pyramid. They focus on the smallest building blocks that can be tested in isolation. They often test the behaviors of functions, and they are executed as a part of the local project build.

Unit tests are comparatively easy to write and execute due to their small size and scope. Unit tests can be run inside the Integrated Development Environment (IDE), which provides the quickest feedback loop. Bugs can be found and reported by unit tests within minutes – if not seconds.

It is common for the local project build to fail if any unit tests are unsuccessful. Integrating automated unit tests into the build process helps identify bugs early in development. Testing and fixing bugs is most cost-effective during unit testing because the bugs are smaller in size, require less effort to address, and provide quicker feedback compared to other testing stages. Additionally, a system typically has more unit tests than any other type of test, as unit tests target the smallest components, resulting in a larger quantity compared to larger tests.

Unit Tests Should Be Meaningful

While unit tests are the smallest building blocks that can be tested, there are a few cases where a function is too small to be tested. If engineers struggle to explain what the test aims to verify, it is likely that the function is too small to be tested. A private function usually does not require a unit test, but a function that's called by other packages (i.e., a public function) should have a unit test. Functions extracted merely to avoid duplicated code are unlikely to form a meaning that requires testing. To summarize, unit tests should be meaningful.

Here is an example of a unit test in Kotlin powered by the Kotest framework:

```
class FindBiggestNumberKtTest : FunSpec({    test("Find the biggest out of positive numbers") {
findBiggestNumber(listOf(17, 18, 6)) shouldBe 18

    } })
```

The Kotest framework provides many test templates as specifications. **FunSpec** is the one used in the example. The test cases are passed in as lambda expressions. The **test** function takes the test name as an argument. A lambda expression under the scope of **TestScope** is passed in for the actual test. This unit test targets the **findBiggestNumber** function, which is given a list of integers: **17**, **18**, and **6**. The **shouldBe** infix function mimics the natural English language and validates whether the expected result is **18**.

Parameterized testing

You might question whether one test case is not enough to thoroughly test this function. The Kotest framework supports parameterized testing as follows:

```
class FindBiggestNumberParameterizedTest : FunSpec({    context("Find the biggest out of positive numbers") {

withData( emptyList<Int>() to null,       listOf(8) to 8,       listOf(99, 8) to 99,       listOf(17, 18, 6)
to 18,      listOf(944, 0, 633) to 944,       listOf(0, -32, 76) to 76,       listOf(-11, -32, -102) to -11,
listOf(-25, -57, 0) to 0,

        listOf(

          Integer.MAX_VALUE + 1,

          Integer.MAX_VALUE,

          0,

          Int.MIN_VALUE,

          -Int.MIN_VALUE - 1,

          -Int.MAX_VALUE,

          Int.MIN_VALUE - 1

        ) to Integer.MAX_VALUE,

      ) { (allNumbers, expectedMax) ->

        findBiggestNumber(allNumbers) shouldBe expectedMax
```

```
        }
    } })
```

For a function that takes a list of integers and returns the maximum number, there are many cases we can think of:

- Empty lists
- Lists of one integer
- Lists of two integers
- All positive integers
- All negative integers
- A mixture of zero, positive, and negative integers

Maximum, minimum, maximum plus one, minimum minus one, and the negation of these integers with parameterized testing, it is possible to test them all with code footprints smaller than if we had to duplicate them into separate test cases.

At this point, you might want to see the source code of the function being tested, to ensure that you have covered all cases, but do you need to? There is no right or wrong answer here because it represents two methods of software testing: blackbox testing and whitebox testing. Please note that these two testing styles are applicable to all levels of testing in the pyramid.

Before we discuss these two testing styles in detail, let us reveal the implementation: fun findBiggestNumber(numbers: List<Int>): Int? = numbers.maxOrNull()

It is a very simple implementation and uses the built-in **maxOrNull** Kotlin function to find the maximum number in the list or null for an empty list.

Blackbox testing

Blackbox testing evaluates the functionality being tested without any knowledge of the internal code or structure.

Testers focus merely on the inputs, expected outputs, and alleged functionality provided (known as the contract).

Whitebox testing

Whitebox testing goes in the opposite direction. It involves examining the internal implementation of the functionality being tested. Testers have knowledge of the code and internal logic, allowing them to design test cases based on the implementation details.

Comparing blackbox and whitebox testing

Blackbox testing focuses on the results and functionalities that would affect user experience. Not depending on implementation also enables testers to discover any discrepancies between actual and expected behaviors, revealing requirements that may not have been thoroughly defined. It may, however, miss some code branches in the test suite, which potentially hinders complete code coverage. Organizations that have independent QA teams, separated from the development teams, typically use blackbox testing as their default approach.

Whitebox testing enables comprehensive testing of internal logic, leading to the discovery of hidden bugs or vulnerabilities under specific circumstances. Knowing the code also helps testers identify security vulnerabilities and optimization opportunities that would help meet the non-functional requirements.

Knowing the code also brings bias in test cases to unknowingly omit test cases that can comprehensively cover external behaviors and user experience.

There are also human factors in play between the two styles. Once a tester has seen the internal implementation, it is difficult to pretend not to have seen it before and to write bias-free blackbox tests.

Both test styles have their merits and disadvantages. Due to the human factor mentioned, it is recommended to start writing blackbox tests without knowing the implementation first and to focus on testing the external behaviors. Afterward, check the implementation to write whitebox test cases and focus on code branches and non-functional requirements.

This will lead to a topic called TDD, which will be covered later in this chapter.

Component testing

Known as module testing, component testing is one level above unit testing in the pyramid. It focuses on testing the higher-order behaviors of self-contained modules. Component focuses on the behaviors emerging from the interactions of several units of code.

Component tests are also included as part of the local project build. So, if a component test has failed, the local project build fails. It is also often executed from IDE to provide a quick feedback loop.

However, component tests are bigger and require more effort to write. Each test usually involves setting a combination of states before the test. The test itself often involves multiple steps, and there are usually multiple places to verify the results. If there is a problem found, it is not immediately obvious where the problem is, and it would require some time to troubleshoot and debug. So, the cost of testing and fixing bugs is higher than unit testing.

One of the examples of component testing can be found in applications that use modular and layered architecture. For example, if we use the hexagonal architecture, component testing can be conducted at the core layer to verify the pure business logic without coupling technology choices. This is particularly useful if the bounded context of the application belongs to the Core domain.

The core layer of the Core domain is often perceived as the "crown jewel" of the entire system. It serves as the heartbeat around which everything else revolves. It makes the case to use component testing to ensure the central pure business behaviors are intact in every change made in the system.

Component testing the core layer of the Core domain with blackbox testing first would become the Behavior-Driven Development (BDD) approach, which will be discussed later in this chapter.

Mocking external resources

When writing component tests, it is almost inevitable to encounter situations when the code tries to integrate with external resources such as queues, files, databases, or other applications. These integration points put a burden on the testers to prepare the context and increase the effort of writing the test.

Mocking enables testers to isolate the component being tested from external dependencies. There are a few common mocking scenarios:

1. Verify whether the component has interacted with the external dependencies as expected, such as checking whether the correct API with expected parameters was called
2. Enable the component test to run without needing external dependencies to be available, for example, the database
3. Verify whether the component can handle the failures of external dependencies as expected
4. Maintain states that allow testing different conditions, such as returning different values based on the context of the tests

Here is an example of component testing with mocking, also using Kotest:

```
class ExerciseExecutorTest : BehaviorSpec({
    Given("Today is sunny") {
        val exerciseLog = mockk<ExerciseLog>()        val executor = ExerciseExecutor(exerciseLog)
every { exerciseLog.record(any(), any()) } returns Unit
        val weather = Weather.SUNNY        When("doing an exercise") {        val now = Instant.now()
            Then("running in the park") {
                executor.doExercise(weather, now) shouldBe Exercise.RunInThePark
            }
            And("the exercise is logged") {
                verify { exerciseLog.record(Exercise.RunInThePark, now) }
            }
        }
    } })
```

Firstly, this component test uses the **BehaviorSpec** from Kotest that follows the given-when-then format. It also matches the test pattern of Arrange, Act, Assert (3A).

The 3A Test Pattern

The 3A test pattern can be used in a unit test. It helps engineers and testers to organize tests by dividing them into three distinct sections. As a result, test scripts are easier to read, understand, reason, and maintain. Arrange is the initialization of preconditions and input data for the test. Act is the execution of the behaviors being tested. Assert is the verification of the actual outcome against the expected result.

Secondly, there is an external **ExerciseLog** dependency, which may involve persisting data in files or databases:

```
interface ExerciseLog {
    fun record(time: Instant, exercise: Exercise) }
```

The function record accepts an **Exercise** object and the corresponding time when the exercise was done:

```
enum class Weather {
    SUNNY,
    RAINY,
    CLOUDY,
    STORMY,
}
```

As the focus of the test is the logic of **ExerciseExecutor**, not **ExerciseLog**, we use the **mockk** function from the Mockk library to create a mock object that implements the **ExerciseLog** interface. We set up the mock object to accept the invocation of the **record** function with any parameters and to return a **Unit**.

The primary validation is that when the weather is sunny, the function returns **RunInThePark**, as defined by this sealed class:

```
sealed class Exercise {
    data object RunInThePark: Exercise()        data object GoToGym: Exercise()
```

}

The second validation is that **ExerciseExecutor** has passed the correct parameters to **ExerciseLog** to record this exercise. Here is the full implementation of **ExerciseExecutor**:

```
class ExerciseExecutor(    private val log: ExerciseLog
) {
    fun doExercise(        weather: Weather,        time: Instant
    ): Exercise {
        val exercise = when (weather) {
            Weather.SUNNY, Weather.CLOUDY -> Exercise.RunInThePark
            Weather.STORMY, Weather.RAINY -> Exercise.GoToGym
        }
        log.record(time, exercise)
        return exercise
    }
}
```

Mocks are one of the five types of test doubles used in software testing. Here is the full list:

Mocks: These are pre-programmed with expectations of how they should be used. They are used to verify whether the specific functions are invoked with the expected parameters

Stubs: These provide pre-defined responses to functions but do not verify interactions.

Spies: Spies log the parameters used and count the function calls. The actual function is still invoked.

Fakes: These allow for a simplified implementation of the external dependencies for testing purposes.

Dummies: A dummy is a simple object used just to satisfy parameter requirements without needing to implement any behavior.

Contract testing

Contract testing focuses on the interaction between API producers and consumers. It only aims at the communication protocol and the message content. It should not be used for business case testing because we already have component testing covering it in the lower level of the testing pyramid.

There are two types of contract testing:

Consumer testing: This focuses on the service that makes requests to another service. It defines the expectations of the interactions it will have with the producer, typically through a contract. It also verifies that the consumer service can handle all documented responses to the requests made. Consumer contract testing uses stubs or fakes to set up the target service to communicate with.

Producer testing: This focuses on the service that provides the functionality or data requested by another service. It aims to assert that the producer has fulfilled the API contract and met the expectations of its consumers. Producer tests may involve running the actual service, which makes it seem as though it should be higher up in the testing pyramid. It is also possible that producer testing mocks the business logic to produce the message and response defined in the contract. Producer testing is often used to ensure that updates and changes to contracts are backward compatible.

It is, however, important to have contract tests focus on the communication and message content only. For example, the OpenAPI specification document is a good target for writing contract tests. The contract tests ensure that both consumers and producers behave as specified in the **openapi.yaml** file. This leads to more reliable and maintainable systems, especially in microservices architectures.

Integration testing

Integration testing focuses on the interactions between different components or modules of the application. It is one level up from contract testing in the pyramid as integration tests do not use stubs or fakes. They identify issues when integrating various parts of the system and verify the parts work together as intended. Integration testing is also a part of the local project build.

Integration testing usually involves databases, file systems, external services, or APIs. The following are the common types of integration testing:

API integration testing: Use the exposed APIs to interact with the application for the given use case and to verify the result from the response.

Database integration testing: Confirm that data is correctly processed in the database. This is typically related to Create, Read, Update, Delete (CRUD) operations.

File system integration testing: Verify that the application can read from or write to files correctly, and verify the file reflects the result of the operations in the test.

Middleware or external service integration testing: Verify that the integration of middleware or external service connectivity is correctly configured, as well as that the application and middleware or external service can communicate as intended.

Integration tests are bigger than component and unit tests due to the required configuration and preparation. Integration tests are also more complex to write and reason about. Integration tests might involve various combinations of configurations, for instance, supporting multiple pluggable databases or message providers, while the business functionality remains the same.

Some tests may become uncertain due to how external resources or external services behave, especially if there is asynchronous processing external to the application.

Referring to component testing, if component testing focuses on the Core layer of a hexagonal architecture application, then integration testing focuses on the adapter layer.

Extending the exercise code example, we are going to write an integration test for an implementation of the **ExerciseLog** interface that appends a line to a file for each invocation. Each line starts with a local date-time using UTC, separated by a colon, and ends with the name of the exercise, as shown here:

2024-09-30T18:39:03.353250: GoToGym

An integration test can be written as follows:

```
class ExerciseExecutorIntegrationTest : StringSpec({
    "Gym when cloudy and run in the park when rainy as recorded in file log" {
        val file = File.createTempFile("Exer", "cise")
            .apply { deleteOnExit() }
        val exec = ExerciseExecutor(ExerciseFileLog(file))
        val now = Instant.now()
        val fourHoursLater = now.plus(4, HOURS)
        val utc = ZoneId.of("UTC")        exec.doExercise(RAINY, now)
```

```
    exec.doExercise(CLOUDY, fourHoursLater)
    FileReader(file).readLines() shouldBe listOf(
"${now.atZone(utc).toLocalDateTime()}: GoToGym",
"${fourHoursLater.atZone(utc).toLocalDateTime()}: RunInThePark",
    )
  } })
```

The test starts by creating a temporary file that will be deleted on exit. Then a list of two exercise entries is passed into the **ExerciseFileLog** object. The verification starts by reading the file line by line and asserts that each line contains the expected content.

The **ExerciseFileLog** class itself is straightforward:

```
class ExerciseFileLog(    private val file: File,
) : ExerciseLog {    val utc = ZoneId.of("UTC")    override fun record(        time: Instant,      exercise: Exercise,
  ) {      try {
        val utcDateTime = time.atZone(utc).toLocalDateTime()
        val text = "$utcDateTime: $exercise\n"
        file.appendText(text)      } catch (e: IOException) {
        println("error writing to the file: $file")
    }
  }
}
```

Test scripts should mostly be integration tests in the supporting and generic subdomain applications. This is because these subdomains usually do not contain a lot of business logic, or the combination of business cases is simple enough to be covered by integration tests.

End-to-end and automated GUI testing

So far, all the tests we have discussed have focused on either a single backend service or a specific group of software components. The next level is end-to-end automated testing, which includes graphical user interface (GUI) testing and contract testing. This type of testing evaluates system behavior across multiple services horizontally and across various tiers vertically. Additionally, it becomes more transparent to business stakeholders.

End-to-end and automated GUI testing focuses on a user journey that covers multiple services or components in the system. For example, an end-to-end test could involve creating two household records, and then having one household draft a contract with another household. Both households would then negotiate to reach an agreed contract, and finally, each of them would exercise the contract for the service described in the contract.

End-to-end testing uses APIs for communication with various parts of the system, while automated GUI testing simulates human interaction with the system.

Some systems have a suite of public APIs for integration with external Software-as-a-Service (SaaS) platforms (as discussed in Chapter 6). In this case, end-to-end testing should ensure that the user journey can be fulfilled by calling the exposed public APIs. The testing of this public API integration, known as headless integration, is as important as visual GUI testing.

The test script for one user journey is complex and fragile. It requires multiple services to be operational in an environment, which implies stable infrastructure as well. It is not practical to test all the variations of user journeys, as the test suite takes a long time to finish.

Tests at this level typically only cover the most crucial and user-facing features. They also usually only cover successful cases. The tests are run periodically, or on demand. If an error is found during the test, it would take a longer time to troubleshoot, and sometimes it could be caused by stability issues in the environment instead of actual bugs.

Manual and exploratory testing

Manual and exploratory testing is the highest level in the pyramid. It is not automated, so it is up to the QAs to manually run through the cases. This level of testing is the most time-consuming and laborious.

If a manual can be automated, QAs will aim to automate it as soon as possible to reduce the cost. There are a few cases where manual testing is necessary:

Usability testing: Evaluating user experience requires subjective analysis, involving elements such as visual layout, design, and overall satisfaction.

Short-lived features: Investment in automating tests may not be justified for short-lived features.

Context-heavy testing: Some tests heavily depend on complex workflows, interactions, or context understanding. Automating these tests to be reliable could outweigh the effort of testing them manually.

Security testing: Many security assessments, such as penetration testing, rely on the security expertise of humans to identify vulnerabilities that automated tests may not catch. Some tests require a quick pivot of the next step decided by security experts; these are difficult to automate.

Manual and exploratory testing is often executed on an ad hoc basis; however, some organizations allow QAs to timebox exploratory testing to discover hidden defects and usability issues.

Benefits of the testing pyramid

The testing pyramid serves as a guiding principle for structuring a testing strategy in software development. As testing and bug fixing become more expensive going up each level, it is natural to prioritize unit tests, followed by component tests, all the way up to manual tests, so the team can achieve a more efficient and cost-effective QA process.

By putting test cases at their appropriate level in the pyramid, the team not only enhances the overall quality of the software but also allows for a quick iterative feedback loop that incrementally improves software development practices.

So far, all the test case examples in this chapter have only used Kotest. However, there are a few other frameworks that can be considered as well:

Atrium
Kluent
Spek

Up next, we are going to discuss the TDD approach.

TDD

TDD has a history dating back to the 1970s, when the idea of "test-first" programming was discussed. It was not popular until TDD became a part of Extreme Programming (XP), which was introduced by Kent Beck in the 1990s.

"XP

XP is an agile software development methodology that aims to deliver high-quality software, meet evolving user requirements, and reduce risks due to uncertainties in the process. It has five core values — communication, simplicity, feedback, courage, and respect. It emphasizes short iterative development cycles and close collaboration between developers and stakeholders, encouraging frequent feedback to adapt to changing requirements. The key practices of XP include pair programming, TDD, continuous integration, and frequent releases of small and incremental changes."

In 2002, Beck published the book Test-Driven-Development: By Example, which provided detailed guidance on the TDD process and has since significantly influenced a lot of engineering practices, even today. TDD has even become a must-have interview coding practice in some organizations.

TDD uses a simple workflow of writing tests and production code, as shown in Figure:

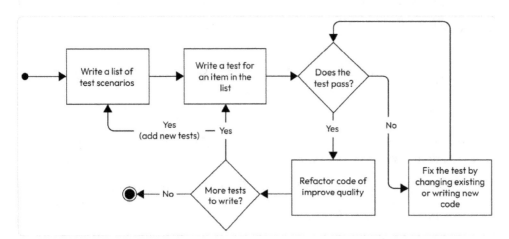

Figure– TDD workflow

The first step of TDD is to write a list of test scenarios. Test scenarios are written in business language that does not involve technical implementation. It describes what the expected behavior of the application is under certain conditions, without knowing how the application achieves it.

A test scenario is picked from the list, and we start writing the test. This part is interesting because the test case code usually does not compile due to requiring an enhancement of current APIs or a new API. This is normal because API contracts should be derived from the needs of the user, not the provider. Designing an API from users' perspectives naturally conforms to the Interface Segregation Principle (ISP). The test case should set up the preconditions, attempt to execute the steps, and verify the result.

At this moment, you are left with a test case that either does not pass (red) or does not even compile. The next step is to change the code so that the test passes (green). It is important to ensure that all other tests pass too. This is exactly what the influential advocator of TDD, Kent Beck, suggested when he said "fake it till you make it".

The test will now pass, but you might not be unsatisfied because the code can be optimized or organized better. This is your opportunity to improve quality by refactoring the code while ensuring all tests continue to pass. That is why TDD has another name: red-green-refactor.

There may be more test scenarios that need test cases written, or we may discover missed test scenarios. Nonetheless, the cycle repeats until there are no more test cases to write.

BDD

BDD evolved from TDD with the goal of addressing some of the limitations of TDD, such as test case classes filled with technical syntax that non-technical stakeholders would find difficult to read.

The concept of BDD was introduced by Dan North in 2003 during the discussions on improvement collaboration between technical and non-technical team members. This is also the year when he started the development of the JBehave framework as a replacement for the JUnit framework, emphasizing behaviors rather than tests.

The Gherkin language was created in the year after that, as a domain-specific language that is close to the natural English language. The language aims to bring non-technical stakeholders closer to technical team members.

The test scenario we have worked on during the TDD exercise can be expressed in the Gherkin language as follows:

Feature: Household creation
Scenario: Creation of households with non-empty surnames

Given the household surname is non-empty

When the user requests to create the household

Then the household is created

Gherkin uses a simple structured syntax to define test scenarios. The primary keywords include the following:

Feature: A feature of the application

Scenario: A specific situation or example

Given: Conditions before the test starts

When: Action or event that triggers behavior

Then: Expected outcome

And/But: Add additional steps, conditions, or expected outcome

A test scenario written in the Gherkin language needs to be translated into programming languages to be executed. Cucumber is the first major tool for BDD, and it was developed around 2005. It can translate test scenarios in Gherkin language to test scripts into multiple programming languages, such as Ruby, Rust, Java, Go, JavaScript, and Kotlin.

Specification by Example (SBE)

BDD has a close relationship with Specification by Example (SBE). The term SBE was made popular by Gojko Adzic in his book Specification by Example, which was published in 2011.

SBE advocates using concrete examples in real-world scenarios to clarify specifications and to communicate with non-technical stakeholders. This has influenced the conventional format of user stories as follows: "As a [user], I want to [feature], so that [business values]". This ensures clear and testable specifications based on real examples.

A user story is further expanded to have acceptance criteria to determine whether the feature is completed to the user's satisfaction. These acceptance criteria are reflected in the test scenarios, possibly in the Gherkin language as a BDD practice.

Adopting SBE and BDD has several implications. The test scenarios are written in Gherkin language and the vocabulary used should align with Ubiquitous Language, as discussed in Chapter 8. Secondly, human-readable test scenarios strongly suggest blackbox testing as the major approach.

Finally, many teams using Agile methodologies would even use SBE and BDD to improve their requirement gathering and testing processes. In a way, the concrete examples from SBE and test scenarios from BDD become the de facto agreement with non-technical stakeholders on the understanding of the feature.

BDD adoption in Kotlin

BDD is still actively adopted by many teams nowadays. Many Kotlin engineers are still using Cucumber as their BDD tool. However, there are reasons why some teams make a conscious decision not to use the Gherkin language to define test scenarios.

The Kotlin language is concise and less verbose than its predecessor, Java. Kotlin provides a lot of innate syntactic support and syntactic sugar to simplify the code for better readability.

With modern testing frameworks such as Kotest, Spek, and Kluent it is possible to have readable Kotlin-based test scripts that mimic the Gherkin format for test scenarios to a good extent.

It diminishes the need to introduce a translation layer, which can sometimes introduce bugs during testing. It is also a balanced act between the benefits of reading test scenarios and the cost of translating Gherkin test scripts to Kotlin.

However, having BDD and SBE in mind in the agile development process is always beneficial, as it elicits meaningful conversations with non-technical stakeholders in the endeavor of understanding user requirements.

There are a few types of testing that are conducted in production environments. There are justifications for why they need to run in customer-facing environments, and we are going to explore the reasons behind them.

Live testing, A/B testing, and segmentation

Live tests are no replacement for other types of tests conducted in lower environments. Each type of live testing serves a unique purpose in that it can only be executed in a live environment.

Post-release testing

Some systems integrate with external systems that do not provide a lower environment for testing. Engineers would normally mitigate this risk by having a simulator running in lower environments. The simulator is a fake component that runs simplified logic just to act like the target external system. Engineers rely on documentation or information from the third-party company to implement the simulator.

This approach is not ideal, but it is better than having nothing to detect defects in lower environments. Several risks come with this approach:

The simulator logic needs to closely follow the steps of external system changes. Otherwise, it creates a time gap of discrepancies.

The external system may release its changes without informing the team, resulting in malfunctioning of the system and requiring hotfixes.

Engineers must ensure that the simulator never runs in production environments to create false data. Data damage and remediation come at a huge cost.

Having all safety measures in place, the external system may simply be unavailable after release. Thus, the system is only partially operational.

Regardless of whether there is a test environment for external system integration, some mission-critical systems, such as financial trading systems, would perform a "test trade" with a minimal amount to ensure that the crucial features are operational and the corresponding data is correct.

A/B testing and seg mentation

Some tests are run in production for a longer period for reasons other than QA. A/B testing and segmentation are executed to discover needs and opportunities in the market.

Some organizations would segment their users into at least two groups. The segmentation can be done in the following ways:

A stateless algorithm

User data, such as demographics or preferences

Signed up voluntarily by users

Random and sticky assignments

Manually assigned to small groups

Each group has a different user experience, and metrics are in place to measure business metrics such as page landing counts, purchase statistics, and customer satisfaction. This is a typical segmentation setup:

Control group: The original experience; the baseline for comparisons

Variant groups: The modified experiences

By conducting A/B testing, the organization can gather useful information about users and the market. The data collected provides a quantitative perspective on which user experiences lead to a better outcome. This provides insights on real-user behaviors using empirical evidence, and it fosters a culture of hypothesis testing and data driven decision-making.

Some A/B tests could run only for a limited time just to collect enough data for analysis, while some could run for a very long time for continuous improvements. Some organizations would even run multiple A/B tests at the same time, but this comes at the cost of exponential complexity when performing statistical analysis.

Conclusion: Testing in Kotlin

Testing is a vital pillar of modern software development, ensuring that applications are reliable, maintainable, and scalable. Kotlin, with its concise and expressive syntax, has become a powerhouse for building robust applications, and its testing capabilities have grown to complement its role as a developer-friendly language. In this conclusion, we revisit the key elements of testing in Kotlin, reflect on its strengths, and outline best practices to leverage Kotlin's features effectively.

1. The Evolution of Testing in Kotlin

Kotlin's journey from a modern alternative to Java to a preferred language for developing Android and server-side applications has also brought significant advancements in its testing ecosystem. Over the years, Kotlin's compatibility with popular testing frameworks like JUnit, TestNG, and Mockito has ensured seamless adoption in projects. Moreover, the introduction of Kotlin-specific tools such as KotlinTest (now Kotest) and MockK has made writing, reading, and maintaining tests more intuitive.

As we stand in 2025, Kotlin testing frameworks and libraries have matured to include advanced features like property-based testing, coroutine support, and better DSLs for expressing test cases. These tools ensure that developers can write clean and expressive test code while maintaining a high standard of quality.

2. Key Advantages of Kotlin for Testing

Kotlin offers several advantages that make it a great choice for testing:

1. **Conciseness and Readability:** Kotlin's concise syntax reduces boilerplate code, which is especially beneficial when writing repetitive test cases. This clarity also makes tests easier to read and maintain.

2. **Null Safety:** With Kotlin's null safety features, developers can eliminate a large class of bugs caused by null pointer exceptions, reducing the need for excessive null checks in test cases.

3. **Coroutines Support:** Kotlin's first-class support for coroutines simplifies testing asynchronous code. Libraries like Kotest provide utilities to test suspending functions and coroutines effectively.

4. **Extension Functions:** Test-specific extension functions allow developers to create reusable utilities, enhancing test readability and reducing redundancy.

5. **Interoperability with Java:** Kotlin's 100% interoperability with Java ensures that existing Java-based testing frameworks and libraries can be used seamlessly in Kotlin projects.

6. **Custom DSLs:** Kotlin's ability to build custom domain-specific languages (DSLs) allows for intuitive and expressive testing syntax, as seen in Kotest.

3. Testing Best Practices in Kotlin

To fully harness Kotlin's potential for testing, it is crucial to follow best practices that align with both the language's strengths and general software engineering principles:

1. **Write Tests Early and Often:** Testing should be an integral part of the development process. Adopt test-driven development (TDD) to ensure that tests guide the implementation.

2. **Leverage Kotlin-Specific Libraries:** Use libraries like Kotest and MockK to take advantage of Kotlin's features. Kotest's DSL simplifies writing expressive tests, while MockK's coroutine-friendly mocking capabilities outperform traditional Java-based libraries.

3. **Use Parameterized Tests:** Parameterized testing helps reduce duplication by testing multiple input-output combinations in a single test case. Kotlin libraries support parameterized tests elegantly.

4. **Focus on Readability:** Ensure that your test cases are easy to understand. Favor descriptive naming, modularization, and clear assertions to communicate intent.

5. **Test Coroutines Properly:** Utilize libraries that provide coroutine test utilities, such as TestCoroutineDispatcher or Kotest's coroutine support, to ensure proper testing of asynchronous code.

6. **Mock Dependencies Wisely:** Use MockK's powerful mocking capabilities to mock dependencies effectively. Avoid over-mocking, as it can lead to brittle tests.

7. **Adopt Property-Based Testing:** Explore property-based testing for scenarios where testing multiple combinations of inputs is essential. Kotest's property-based testing module simplifies this process.

8. **Test Edge Cases and Error Scenarios:** While happy-path testing is important, ensure that you test for edge cases, boundary conditions, and error-handling scenarios to build resilient systems.

4. The Future of Testing in Kotlin

As the Kotlin ecosystem evolves, so does the landscape of testing. Emerging trends and tools indicate a promising future for Kotlin developers who prioritize testing:

1. **Increased Focus on Multiplatform Testing:** With the rise of Kotlin Multiplatform, developers can write shared business logic across platforms (iOS, Android, web) and test it using common testing libraries. This reduces duplication and enhances consistency across platforms.

2. **AI-Assisted Test Generation:** Artificial intelligence is being integrated into tools to assist with generating test cases, identifying edge cases, and even automating test maintenance.

3. **Improved IDE Support:** JetBrains, the creators of Kotlin, continue to enhance IntelliJ IDEA's capabilities for writing, running, and debugging tests, providing developers with a seamless experience.

4. **Stronger Integration with CI/CD Pipelines:** Modern development practices emphasize continuous integration and delivery. Kotlin's testing libraries are aligning with CI/CD tools to streamline test execution and reporting in automated pipelines.

5. **Advances in Performance Testing:** Kotlin's testing ecosystem is expanding to include more tools for performance and load testing, which are crucial for modern distributed systems.

5. Challenges and Overcoming Them

While Kotlin simplifies testing in many ways, developers may encounter some challenges:

1. **Learning Curve for New Libraries:** Developers transitioning from Java may find it challenging to learn Kotlin-specific libraries like Kotest or MockK. Overcoming this requires dedicated practice and exploration of documentation and tutorials.

2. **Managing Multiplatform Projects:** Testing shared logic in Kotlin Multiplatform projects requires understanding platform-specific nuances. Tools and frameworks are evolving to address these complexities.

3. **Maintaining Test Quality:** As with any language, poorly written tests can become a maintenance burden. Adhering to best practices, such as avoiding excessive mocking and ensuring proper test coverage, is essential.

4. **Tooling Limitations:** Although Kotlin's testing ecosystem is robust, some advanced testing needs (e.g., advanced property-based testing or niche integrations) may still require additional effort. Staying updated with new library releases helps mitigate these gaps.

6. Final Thoughts

Testing is not just about identifying bugs but also about building confidence in your codebase. Kotlin's rich feature set and growing ecosystem empower developers to write tests that are not only effective but also enjoyable to create. Whether you are testing a small utility function or a complex asynchronous workflow, Kotlin provides the tools and capabilities to simplify the process.

By embracing Kotlin's unique strengths, following best practices, and keeping up with emerging trends, you can ensure that your tests remain reliable and future-proof. In a world where software quality directly impacts user satisfaction and business success, mastering testing in Kotlin is a skill that will set you apart as a developer.

10. Kotlin/Native and Multiplatform

Introduction

Kotlin/Native and Kotlin Multiplatform have emerged as transformative technologies in the software development landscape. Designed to bridge the gap between different platforms while maintaining efficiency, scalability, and developer productivity, these tools empower developers to write robust and maintainable codebases for diverse ecosystems. This document provides a deep dive into the core concepts, features, and practical applications of Kotlin/Native and Kotlin Multiplatform as of 2025.

What is Kotlin/Native?

Definition

Kotlin/Native is an implementation of Kotlin that compiles to native binaries. Unlike Kotlin JVM, which relies on the Java Virtual Machine, Kotlin/Native enables developers to build applications that run without a virtual machine, making it ideal for environments where JVM isn't suitable.

Key Features

- **Platform Independence:** Supports platforms such as macOS, iOS, Windows, Linux, and embedded systems.
- **Interop with C and Objective-C:** Allows seamless integration with native code libraries.
- **No JVM Required:** Ideal for scenarios where JVM isn't available or desired.
- **Garbage Collection:** Uses Kotlin's memory management model or integrates with platform-specific memory management mechanisms.
- **Tooling and Ecosystem:** Integrated with IntelliJ IDEA and other JetBrains tools, ensuring a smooth development experience.

Use Cases

- Mobile development (iOS)
- Desktop applications
- Embedded systems
- Gaming (via libraries like SDL)
- High-performance scenarios where direct native execution is necessary

Kotlin Multiplatform Overview

Definition

Kotlin Multiplatform is a feature of Kotlin that enables code sharing across multiple platforms, such as Android, iOS, web, and desktop. It allows developers to write platform-independent business logic while maintaining platform-specific code for unique requirements.

Core Concepts

- **Shared Code:** Write once, reuse across platforms.
- **Expect/Actual Mechanism:** Define common code using expect keywords and provide platform-specific implementations using actual keywords.

- **Flexible Targets:** Supports JVM, JS, Native, and WASM (WebAssembly).
- **Gradle Multiplatform Plugin:** Simplifies project configuration.

Use Cases

- Cross-platform mobile apps (e.g., combining Android and iOS codebases)
- Cross-platform libraries
- Full-stack applications (e.g., using Ktor for backend and Kotlin/JS for frontend)
- Shared codebases for business logic in multi-platform systems

How Kotlin/Native Fits into Kotlin Multiplatform

Kotlin/Native is one of the key targets for Kotlin Multiplatform, providing the capability to execute shared Kotlin code on platforms that don't support JVM or JavaScript. This makes Kotlin/Native essential for targeting iOS and embedded systems in multiplatform projects.

4.1 Interoperability

Kotlin/Native's interoperability features allow:

- Access to native libraries via C interop.
- Smooth integration with platform-specific frameworks such as Swift/Objective-C on iOS.

Benefits

- Reduces duplication of business logic across platforms.
- Simplifies maintenance and feature rollouts for multi-platform projects.
- Enhances performance by leveraging native execution where required.

Advantages of Kotlin Multiplatform and Kotlin/Native

Productivity

- Write business logic once and share across platforms.
- Use familiar Kotlin language features and ecosystem tools.

Code Reusability

- Avoid duplicating effort for shared functionalities.
- Create libraries that can be consumed by different platform-specific modules.

Flexibility

- Opt-in to share only what makes sense (e.g., keep UI logic separate).
- Combine with existing platform-specific codebases incrementally.

Performance

- Native execution ensures optimized performance on target platforms.
- Lightweight binaries without JVM overhead.

Interoperability

- Easily interface with platform-specific libraries and APIs.
- Combine Kotlin/Native with platform-native languages like Swift, Objective-C, or C++.

Developing with Kotlin/Native

Setting Up the Development Environment

1. **Install Kotlin Multiplatform Plugin:** Available in IntelliJ IDEA.
2. **Configure Gradle:** Use Kotlin DSL to configure targets for your project.
3. **Use CocoaPods for iOS:** Integrate with iOS dependencies using CocoaPods support.
4. **Build and Debug:** Utilize debugging tools in IntelliJ IDEA or Xcode for native targets.

Writing Code

- Use shared modules for platform-independent logic.
- Define platform-specific modules for platform-dependent logic (e.g., UI).
- Leverage expect and actual keywords to provide platform-specific implementations.

Testing

- Write shared tests using Kotlin Test.
- Run platform-specific tests using tools like XCTest (iOS) or JUnit (JVM).

Kotlin Multiplatform in Action

Example Project Structure

```
project
├── shared (common module)
│   ├── src/commonMain/kotlin
│   └── src/commonTest/kotlin
├── androidApp (Android module)
│   ├── src/main/kotlin
│   └── src/test/kotlin
└── iosApp (iOS module)
    ├── src/main/kotlin
    └── src/test/kotlin
```

Sample Code

Shared Code (common module):

```
expect fun getPlatformName(): String
```

```
fun greet(): String = "Hello from ${getPlatformName()}!"
```

Android Implementation:

```
actual fun getPlatformName(): String = "Android"
```

iOS Implementation:

```
actual fun getPlatformName(): String = "iOS"
```

Tools and Frameworks

- **Ktor:** For creating cross-platform network layers.
- **SQLDelight:** For shared database layers.
- **Jetpack Compose + SwiftUI:** Combine Compose for Android and SwiftUI for iOS with shared business logic.

Challenges and Best Practices

Challenges

- **Learning Curve:** Requires familiarity with multiple platforms.
- **Platform-Specific Limitations:** Some features may not have direct equivalents across platforms.
- **Tooling Maturity:** While improving, some tools and plugins may still have rough edges.

Best Practices

- **Incremental Adoption:** Start with sharing business logic and gradually expand.
- **Use Expect/Actual Thoughtfully:** Avoid overcomplicating shared code.
- **Test Thoroughly:** Ensure platform-specific and shared code is well-tested.
- **Leverage Community Libraries:** Reuse existing multiplatform libraries.

The Future of Kotlin/Native and Multiplatform

As of 2025, Kotlin/Native and Kotlin Multiplatform continue to evolve rapidly:

- **WASM Support:** Expanding reach to WebAssembly environments.
- **Improved Performance:** Ongoing optimizations for compilation and runtime efficiency.
- **Enhanced Tooling:** Better IDE support and Gradle plugins.
- **Increased Adoption:** Growing adoption in enterprise applications and startups alike.

JetBrains' roadmap indicates a strong commitment to making Kotlin the go-to language for modern cross-platform development.

Let's begin,

While Kotlin began its existence focused on the JVM, it has since expanded in scope to include native and web development. In fact, as you'll see in the next chapter "Kotlin Multiplatform", alongside its popularity in Android development, you can even use Kotlin to assist in building iOS apps.

The technology used to bring Kotlin beyond the JVM is called **Kotlin/Native**. Kotlin/ Native allows you to compile Kotlin code outside of virtual machines, resulting in self-contained binaries that are native to the environment in which they're run. The Kotlin/Native compiler was announced in 2017, and in late 2018 reached version 1.0.

While this chapter looks at **Kotlin/Native** specifically, you can also use **Kotlin/JS** to compile Kotlin code to JavaScript.

In previous chapters, you've used IntelliJ IDEA to create and run Kotlin code. IntelliJ utilized the version of the Kotlin compiler for the JVM to build and run Java bytecode. In this chapter, you'll see how to install and use the Kotlin/Native compiler outside of IntelliJ in order to create native binaries that can be run outside the JVM.

Konan and LLVM

This diagram below shows the process through which Kotlin/Native takes Kotlin code and turns it into native code.

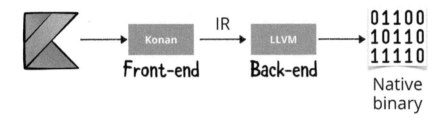

The Kotlin/Native compiler itself is named **Konan**. Konan handles the **front-end** of the process, compiling the Kotlin source code into an **Intermediate Representation (IR)** that is the input to the **back-end** of the process. Kotlin/Native leverages the **LLVM compiler** for the back-end.

If you're not familiar with LLVM, at one point it stood for "Low-Level Virtual Machine", but it actually has nothing to do with virtual machines as the term is used today. The name is now just a stand-alone acronym.

LLVM was created initially by a team led by Chris Lattner, who also led the team that created the Swift language at Apple. LLVM is a set of components that optimize IR code and compile it to machine-dependent binaries.

By combining Konan with LLVM, Kotlin/Native lets you produce native executables from your Kotlin code. In theory, Kotlin/Native can be used on any platform supported by LLVM.

You'll see another example of using the kotlin-jvm compiler in this chapter's challenges, but the rest of the chapter itself is focused on using Kotlin/Native.

In a terminal window, navigate to wherever you downloaded the compiler:

cd ~/Downloads/

Then, untar and unzip the file.

tar -xzvf kotlin-native-macos-1.4.20.tar.gz

Note: If you're directly copying the command from above, make sure the file name is correct for the version you downloaded. You may need to modify the command to match.

Then, move the resulting folder to a location in your home directory, for example, a **bin** folder.

For example:

mv kotlin-native-macos-1.4.20 /usr/local/bin

Next cd into that folder and take a look at what's inside using tree -L 2:

cd /usr/local/bin/kotlin-native-macos-1.4.20 tree -L 2

Note: If you're on macOS, you may need to install tree using brew install tree

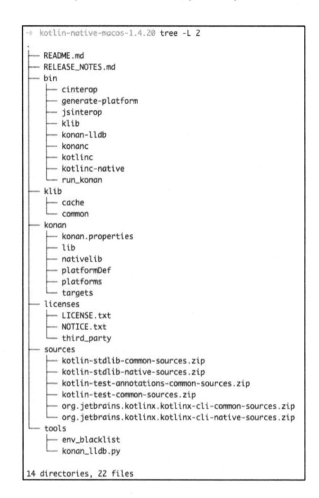

You see a few different items in the **bin** subfolder including **konanc** and **kotlinc**, the compilers you need for Kotlin/Native code. If you run a diff command on the two files, you see that they are in fact identical.

diff bin/kotlinc bin/konanc

Doing a less on either file, you can see that both reference a shell script named **run_konan**:

less bin/konanc

You'll want to add the **bin** subfolder of the Kotlin/Native distribution into your path by adding an export like this to your **.bashrc** file (or the equivalent for your shell):

export PATH="$PATH:/usr/local/bin/kotlin-native-macos-1.4.20/ bin"

Then run a source command on your **.bashrc** file to make the path update take effect in your current terminal session.

source ~/.bashrc

If you've also installed the kotlin-jvm compiler, for example, like in Chapter using SDKMan! or by using Homebrew on macOS, then you need to be careful to make sure you're using the right version of the Kotlin compiler when you want to compile code to native binaries and not to Java bytecode. If you stick to using

konanc and not **kotlinc**, then you'll be sure to be using the Kotlin/Native version and not the Kotlin jvm version.

Another important point to make is that when you use Kotlin/Native with IDEs such as **IntelliJ IDEA** and **Android Studio**, the build plugins you use with **Gradle** will install a separate version of the Kotlin/Native compiler than the one you just installed. So, in that case you don't need to associate the downloaded compiler with your IDE in any way; the IDE will use its own version of the compiler, based on settings in the build files.

Hello, Kotlin/Native

With a Kotlin/Native compiler in place, you can now proceed to write your first native program in Kotlin.

You can use IntelliJ IDEA to create and run Kotlin/Native code, or you can use a plain text editor. Creating a Kotlin/Native project in IntelliJ usually uses Gradle as the build system. In this chapter, you're working outside of Gradle and manually compiling the Kotlin code yourself.

Modern text editors will often have plugins for coding in languages like Kotlin, adding features such as syntax highlighting and code completion. For example, **Visual Studio Code** has a "Kotlin Language" extension. That extension does not provide code completion at this time, but does do syntax highlighting.

Create a new file in your text editor of choice and save it as **hello.kt**.

In the file, create a main function just like you have in previous chapters for code that ran on the JVM:

```
fun main() {

}
```

In earlier versions of Kotlin prior to 1.3, you had to supply main with an args parameter of type Array<String>, but now that's no longer necessary if you aren't going to use command-line arguments.

Add a single print statement to main(), and print the string "Hello, Kotlin/Native!".

```
println("Hello, Kotlin/Native!")
```

Save the file then switch to a terminal window and enter the command to compile the code into a native executable.

```
konanc -o hello hello.kt
```

The -o option lets you specify the name of the output executable. The command as written must be run in the same directory as the **hello.kt** file.

Go ahead and run the compiler command. The first time you compile a file with konanc, it's going to take a few minutes, since the Kotlin compiler will download the files, it needs to do the compilation, including the LLVM compiler. After your first run of konanc, compiles will take much less time.

When the command is done, do an ls -l command to see the output file, **hello.kexe**. The **kexe** extension denotes "Kotlin executable". Typically, you'll want to remove that extension since it's not a standard Unix convention.

If you don't use the -o option, the default output filename is **program.kexe**.

Next, run ./hello.kexe and see the native executable run:

```
Hello, Kotlin/Native!
```

The file **hello.kexe** is a native binary for macOS. The file was produced using Konan and LLVM. There is no Java bytecode to be found as far as the native binary is concerned, and you do not need the JVM to run the file.

Kotlin Standard Library

One thing you may notice is that, when compiled with v1.4.20 of Kotlin/Native, the executable file **hello.kexe** is about 945 KB on macOS, which is over 100 times larger than the executable for an equivalent program written in C would be. That large size is because the **Kotlin standard library** is statically linked in to the executable file. This means that you're free to use anything in the standard library in your program.

You can see that by adding something like a list into the program using the standard library listOf() function.

val numbers = listOf(1, 2, 3)

Then you can print out the size of the list.

println(numbers.size)

Go ahead and add that code and recompile the executable using the same command as before:

konanc -o hello hello.kt

Then run the executable file again. You'll see the size of the small list printed to the console.

Notice that, when including the standard library call to listOf(), you don't need to do any imports or do any special link command when you re-compile the file.

Kotlin Multiplatform

Swift and Kotlin have a multitude of similarities, including static typing, type safety, support for the functional and OOP paradigms, and safe-handling of null values. The languages are also syntactically very similar.

The advent of Kotlin/Native has opened up the possibility of integrating Kotlin code into your iOS projects. In fact, the **Kotlin Multiplatform (KMP)** approach is beginning to take off as a cross-platform toolset for iOS, Android, and beyond. In this chapter, you'll use **Android Studio** and **Xcode** to create a KMP project.

Note: Because KMP can also be used with JavaScript, in documentation you might also see reference to **KMM** which is Kotlin Multiplatform Mobile, KPM specifically used for Android and iOS.

The KMP Approach

Typical apps on iOS and Android pull down data from the Internet, parse the data into objects within the app code, and cache some of the network data locally in a database.

For iOS, you might use a library like **Alamofire** for networking and something like **JSONSerialization** to parse the data received from the network into objects. You'd use **Core Data** to store the data locally in a database.

You'd implement an architecture pattern like **MVVM** to structure your app code. You might use a library like **RxSwift** to make your code more declarative. And you'd have tests for the view models and other parts of the app. You'd show lists of data in a **UITableView** in a **UIViewController**.

On Android, you'd have analogs of all of that code. You might use **Retrofit** for networking, **Gson** or **Moshi** for parsing the JSON, **Room** for storing the data in a database, a pattern like **MVP** or **MVVM** for the architecture, and maybe use **RxJava** in the app. You'd repeat similar tests. And you'd show list data in a **RecyclerView** in an **Activity** or **Fragment** using an adapter.

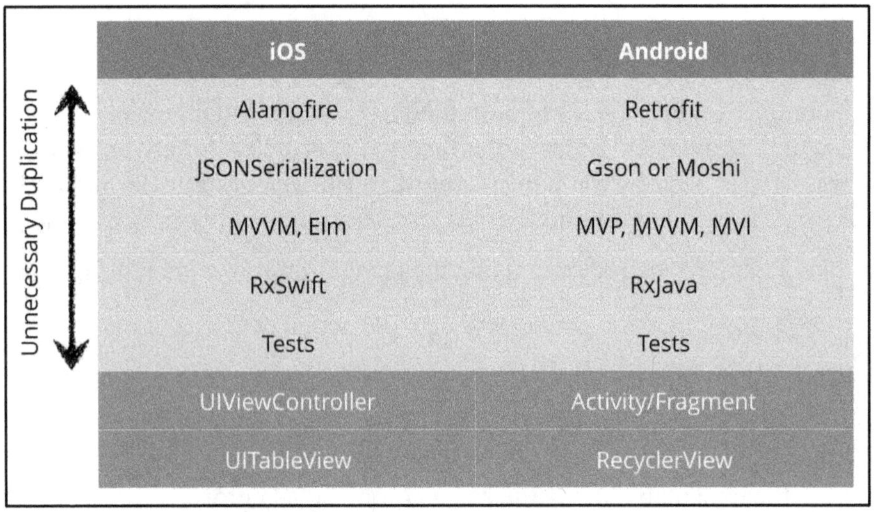

iOS	Android
Alamofire	Retrofit
JSONSerialization	Gson or Moshi
MVVM, Elm	MVP, MVVM, MVI
RxSwift	RxJava
Tests	Tests
UIViewController	Activity/Fragment
UITableView	RecyclerView

(left vertical label: Unnecessary Duplication)

That's a lot of duplication even for a simple app. Imagine that there were numerous screens in your app, with more data, networking calls, and local caching of the remote data, as there would be in a full-featured app. The amount of code duplication would grow essentially linearly with the size of the app, as would the amount of time and effort to first produce and then maintain the two apps for the two platforms.

Other Cross-Platform Frameworks

Reducing this duplication in targeting both iOS and Android has long been a vision of many developers and organizations in the mobile world. Early attempts included web frameworks such as **PhoneGap**.

Organizations like Microsoft have produced tools like **Xamarin**, which uses C# and .NET to target iOS and Android. **React Native**, a derivative of the **React** web framework from Facebook, has become a popular modern framework for mobile. Most recently, Google has released the cross-platform framework **Flutter**, which uses its own runtime to allow apps written in **Dart** to perform at native speeds on iOS and Android.

These and other cross-platform toolkits have had great promise, but none have truly taken hold in the mobile development world. There are many reasons for this, some technical, others, less technical. Just a few of the reasons are poor performance of the resulting apps, inconsistencies with the native user interfaces, an inability to stay up-to-date with the latest iOS and Android features, and developer loyalty to and expertise with the native SDKs.

This is where Kotlin Multiplatform comes in. It's not a cross-platform framework. In fact, it's not a framework at all. It's more of an approach to mobile app development that in some ways gives you the best of all possible worlds.

Kotlin Multiplatform has a number of distinct advantages over the other approaches:

   •   Android developers can leverage their Kotlin skills within shared code used by both the iOS and Android apps.

   •   iOS developers can use their knowledge of Swift to quickly get up to speed with Kotlin and contribute to the shared Kotlin code.

   •   The Android UI code remains Kotlin, and the iOS UI code remains in Swift, so the user interfaces can take advantage of the latest improvements on both platforms.

   •   Performance of both the iOS and Android apps matches the performance of purely platform-specific native apps.

Like the other approaches to cross-platform, Kotlin Multiplatform promises to cut down on the time and effort required to produce apps for both iOS and Android.

Sharing Code

With Kotlin Multiplatform, you reduce code duplication by putting code common to all front-end apps into one module or shared project. This includes business logic, and things like networking code, data parsing, data persistence, and more.

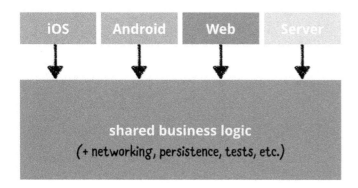

You can use various architectural patterns, and in a large app, you might consider something like **Clean Architecture**, where all the inner layers of the software are shared between front-ends, and only the outermost layer is unique to a given platform such as iOS, Android, Web, or Server. This significantly reduces the amount of duplication in the software, as most or all of the logic and functionality is only written in one place.

Another benefit of KMP, especially on a larger app development project, is that you can divide your team up into groups that work in different areas. You can have a group dedicated to the shared code, a group dedicated to the Android user interface, and a group dedicated to the iOS user interface. Each of these groups can have subgroups for a larger app.

An additional possible benefit, if your team's expertise is favored towards Kotlin, is that you can even write the iOS user interface code in Kotlin instead of Swift. This is not recommended in general, as it goes somewhat against the grain of what can be achieved with Kotlin Multiplatform. But it may be a good approach for an independent Android developer looking to create an iOS version of their app.

HelloKMP

You're going to build a simple app named **HelloKMP** that shares Kotlin code between iOS and Android apps. You'll start in Android Studio and first setup the Android app project and the project level build files for the entire KMP project.

You'll want to use Android Studio 4.1 or later with SDK 30 or later installed and Kotlin plugin 1.4.20 in order to follow along.

Open Android Studio and click the **Create New Project** link on the welcome screen.

Then choose **Empty Activity** and hit **Next**.

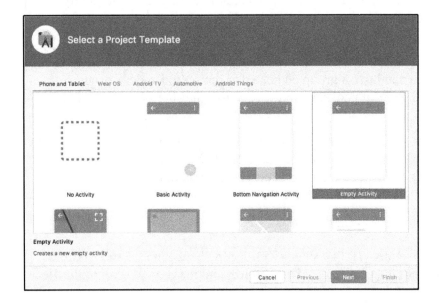

Name the project **HelloKMP**. The package name should be something like com.raywenderlich.hellokmp, and the language is Kotlin. Choose a location for the project and use API 21 for the minimum Android SDK level supported. Then click **Finish**.

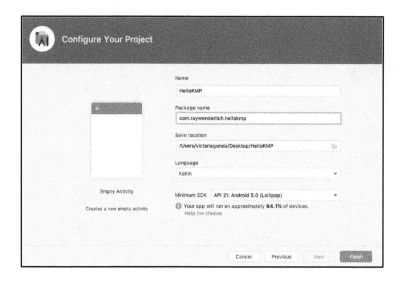

The project will open and a **Gradle** build will run.

In an Android emulator, run the initial Android app to make sure it builds and runs.

Renaming the app folder

The name of the android **app** folder is ideally something like **androidApp** instead of just the default **app**, in order to distinguish that part of the project as being the Android app.

To rename the folder, right click on the folder name and select **Refactor ▸ Rename**.

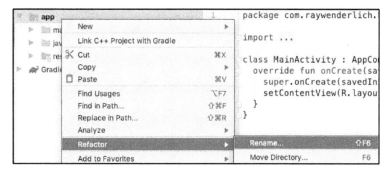

When prompted, select **Rename module**

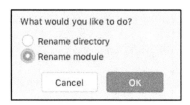

Then, enter **androidApp** as the name.

Finally, build and run the Android app in an emulator to make sure all is good after these changes.

Shared project

You're going to build up the shared project more or less by hand. That way, you'll see all that goes into creating the shared project.

In a terminal window and from the root of the HelloKMP project, first make directories for the shared project, using the -p option which creates parent directories as needed:

mkdir -p shared/src/androidMain/kotlin mkdir -p shared/src/commonMain/kotlin mkdir -p shared/src/iosMain/kotlin

You've made **commonMain**, **androidMain**, and **iosMain** folders.

Next, use the touch command to add the Kotlin source files you'll start with, along with a **build.gradle.kts** file for the shared project:

touch shared/src/commonMain/kotlin/common.kt touch shared/src/androidMain/kotlin/android.kt

touch shared/src/iosMain/kotlin/ios.kt touch shared/build.gradle.kts

Back in Android Studio, switch the **Project** panel to **Project** view to see the folder and file structure of the project, including the folders and files you just added.

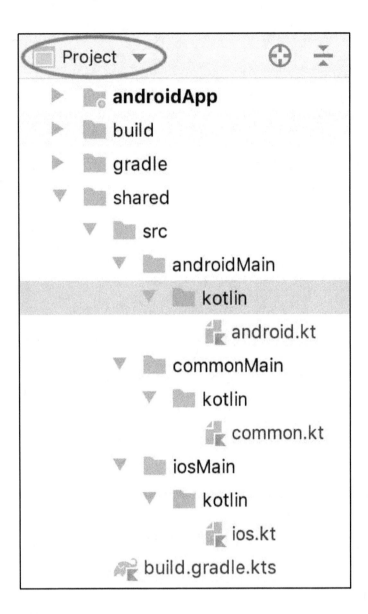

Configuring your environment

To work with Kotlin Multiplatform projects in Android Studio, you need to download the Kotlin Multiplatform Mobile plugin. Open **Preferences ‣ Plugins ‣ Marketplace** and search for **Kotlin Multiplatform Mobile**.

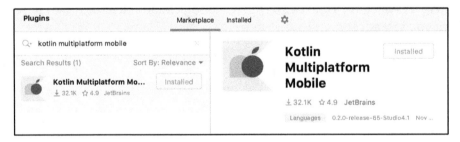

Install the plugin and restart Android Studio.

Note: There are generators to create Kotlin Multiplatform modules and apps included in this plugin. This chapter is not using them so you can learn the individual parts.

Shared code build file

The shared code will be turned into a **jar** file for running with the Android app, and an iOS **framework** for running with the iOS app. The shared project **build.gradle.kts** file is a Kotlin file where you will specify how that is done.

First, update the **settings.gradle** file at the project root to include building the shared code. Before the include for **androidApp**, add:

include ':shared'

Next, you turn to writing the build file for the shared project, **shared/ build.gradle.kts**.

First, set up the **multiplatform** plugin in order to pull in the compilers you need, such as the Kotlin/Native compiler.

```
plugins {
  kotlin("multiplatform")  id("com.android.library")
}
```

If you see a popup indicating that there is a new build context, be sure to accept the proposed change.

Add a kotlin section to define your targets:

```
kotlin {

}
```

Inside the kotlin section, first define some targets:

```
android() ios {  binaries {    framework {
    baseName = "shared"
  }
 }
}
```

This means you're targeting both iOS and Android.

Then, add sourceSets sections to the kotlin section, in which you define dependencies for the shared code:

```
sourceSets {
 val commonMain by getting  val androidMain by getting {
  dependencies {    implementation("com.google.android.material:material:
1.2.1")
  } }
 val iosMain by getting }
```

Having made changes to Gradle files in the project, you can finish up by syncing the project files to make sure there are no errors. The first sync will take a while, since Android Studio needs to pull down the Kotlin/Native compiler.

expect and actual

Compiling the entire shared project for all platforms is not the approach taken by Kotlin Multiplatform. Instead, a certain amount of code is common to all platforms, but some amount of the shared code is unique to each platform. Kotlin includes the **expect/actual** mechanism to allow for this.

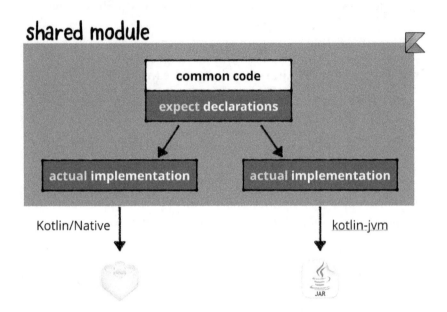

You can think of expect as defining something like an **interface** in Kotlin or a **protocol** in Swift. You use expect to say that the shared common code expects something to be available in the compiled code for all platforms. You then use actual to give the actual version of that something for each separate platform.

In the usage of expect and actual for HelloKMP, you're going to expect that each platform can tell the shared code what its name is as a string using a platformName() function. You can then use that platformName() function in other parts of the shared code.

You can use expect on entities such as functions, classes, or properties. Like a canonical interface, items tagged with expect do not include implementation code. That's where actual comes in.

In **iOSMain** and **androidMain**, you need to provide the actual version of the items specified with expect in the common code. The **androidMain** code will be compiled using kotlin-jvm, and the **iOSMain** code will be compiled by Kotlin/Native. Each will be combined with the compiled version of the common code for the respective platforms.

In **shared/src/commonMain/kotlin/common.kt**, add the package and an expect for the platformName() function:

package com.raywenderlich

expect fun platformName(): String

You'll see an error saying that there are no actual implementations for either JVM, which means Android, or Native, which means iOS.

Next, add a Greeting class to the same file in which you use the result of calling platformName():

class Greeting {

fun greeting(): String = "Hello, ${platformName()}" }

Since you don't use expect on this class, this is a Kotlin class that is the same for all platforms.

In **shared/src/androidMain/kotlin/android.kt**, add an actual version of platformName for Android.

```
package com.raywenderlich
 actual fun platformName(): String {
   return "Android"

 }
```

In **shared/src/iosMain/kotlin/ios.kt**, add an actual version of platformName for iOS.

```
package com.raywenderlich
import platform.UIKit.UIDevice
actual fun platformName(): String {
 return "${UIDevice.currentDevice.systemName()}"
}
```

Notice the platform package import of a **UIKit** class. There may be an unresolved reference error here. That's okay for now.

If you click on the **E** in the gutter of the Android Studio editor, you get taken to the corresponding expect definition. You see that the error you had before is gone now that you have actual versions of platformName() for both platforms.

Clicking the **A** in the gutter, you can choose to navigate to any of the actual implementations.

Building your projects

There are two small things you need to do before building:

1. Adding an Android manifest
2. Giving Gradle an SDK version for Android

First, right click on **shared/androidMain** and select **New File**. Name this file **AndroidManifest.xml**
Open the file and add these contents:

```
<?xml version="1.0" encoding="utf-8"?>
<manifest xmlns:android="http://schemas.android.com/apk/res/ android"
package="com.raywenderlich">

</manifest>
```

Then, Add this to the bottom of **shared/build.gradle.kts**:

```
android {
 compileSdkVersion(29)
 sourceSets["main"].manifest.srcFile("src/androidMain/
AndroidManifest.xml")  defaultConfig {   minSdkVersion(21)   targetSdkVersion(29)

 }
```

}

Now you have shared code that you can build.

Open the **Gradle** panel, find the **build** task folder under **shared/Tasks**, then doubleclick on **build**.

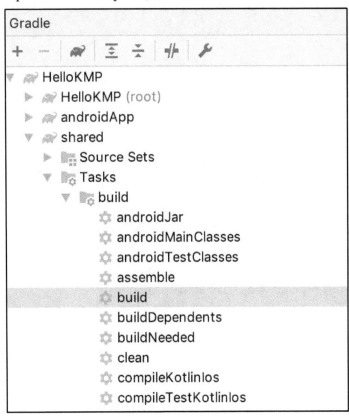

You can then watch the code build in the **Build** panel. You can see Gradle going through a number of build stages and tasks. This will typically take a bit of time to run, especially after a clean of the shared project.

You'll see a **BUILD SUCCESSFUL** message when it's done.

So now you've successfully built the shared project, in which you've defined a Greeting class that shows a greeting that's customized for the platform that you're running the app on.

Shared code from Android

Now it's time to use the shared library from the Android app.

In the **androidApp/build.gradle** file, add a packagingOptions call within the android block:

packagingOptions {

  exclude 'META-INF/*.kotlin_module'

}

This addresses a build error that might occur due to duplicated files in the build.

Then add a dependency of the Android project on the shared project to the dependencies block.

implementation fileTree(dir: 'libs', include: ['*.jar']) implementation project(':shared')

Sync the project Gradle files before you continue.

In **androidApp/src/main/res/layout/activity_main.xml**, add an id of greeting on the TextView that is included in the template android project:

android:id="@+id/greeting"

Then in **androidApp/src/main/java/com.raywenderlich.hellokmp/ MainActivity.kt** in the onCreate() function, set the text on the greeting TextView by calling into the shared code and using the Greeting class:

findViewById<TextView>(R.id.greeting).text =   Greeting().greeting()

You created a Greeting object and called it's greeting() method.

You should see an import for Greeting pulled in when you use the **option+return** keystroke, along with an import for TextView:

import android.widget.TextView import com.raywenderlich.Greeting

Build and run the Android app.

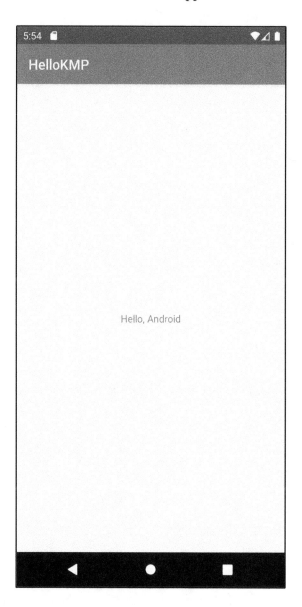

There is your greeting that displays "Hello, Android" as determined by the shared code.

The iOS app

Having used the shared project in an Android app, you now turn to using the shared code in an iOS app. But first you need to setup the iOS app project itself.

In a terminal window at the HelloKMP project root, create a directory for the iOS app:

mkdir iosApp

Then switch to Xcode version 11.3 or later, and choose **File ‣ New ‣ Project**, pick **Single View App**, and click **Next**.

The product name is **HelloKMP**, the organization identifier is com.raywenderlich, and make sure the language is Swift:

Choose options for your new project:

Product Name:	HelloKMP
Team:	Add account...
Organization Name:	Razeware
Organization Identifier:	com.raywenderlich
Bundle Identifier:	com.raywenderlich.HelloKMP
Language:	Swift

Use Core Data
Include Unit Tests
Include UI Tests

Cancel   Previous   Next

Click **Next**, and place the project in the new **iosApp** folder you just made.

Now build and run the app in the iOS Simulator just to make sure it builds correctly.

Packing the iOS framework

Next, back in Android Studio, you need to add a task to the Gradle build file **shared/ build.gradle.kts** for the shared project that will package the framework for Xcode.

Add this to the bottom of the file:

val packForXcode by tasks.creating(Sync::class) { }

Inside this block is where you'll build your task.

Start by adding the following:

group = "build"

/// selecting the right configuration for the iOS

/// framework depending on the environment

/// variables set by Xcode build

```
val mode = System.getenv("CONFIGURATION") ?: "DEBUG" val sdkName =
System.getenv("SDK_NAME") ?: "iphonesimulator" val targetName = "ios" + if
(sdkName.startsWith("iphoneos"))
```

```
"Arm64" else "X64"
```

```
val framework = kotlin.targets
```

```
  .getByName<KotlinNativeTarget>(targetName)
```

```
  .binaries
```

```
  .getFramework(mode) inputs.property("mode", mode) dependsOn(framework.linkTask)
}
```

This first section of the task sets a directory for the framework and determines the correct framework to build based on the selected target in the Xcode project, with a default of **DEBUG**.

Next, add this code to the bottom of the same block:

```
val targetDir = File(buildDir, "xcode-frameworks")
```

```
from({ framework.outputDirectory }) into(targetDir)
```

This section copies the file from the **build** directory into the **framework** directory:

Finally, add this to the block:

```
/// generate a helpful ./gradlew wrapper with embedded Java path
```

```
doLast {
```

```
  val gradlew = File(targetDir, "gradlew")   gradlew.writeText("#!/bin/bash\n"
```

```
    + "export 'JAVA_HOME=$
```

```
{System.getProperty("java.home")}'\n"
```

```
    + "cd '${rootProject.rootDir}'\n"
```

```
    + "./gradlew \$@\n")   gradlew.setExecutable(true)
}
```

Here, a bash script named **gradlew** is created in the framework directory that Xcode will call to build the shared framework.

The script uses the version of the JDK that is embedded in Android Studio.

At the bottom of the **build.gradle.kts** file, you need to specify that the shared code build task depends on the new packForXcode task:

```
tasks.getByName("build").dependsOn(packForXcode)
```

You then need to run a project Gradle sync due to the changes to **build.gradle.kts**

Now you can build the shared code into an iOS framework, using the Gradle panel in Android Studio like you did before.

When the build is done, check that the packaged Xcode framework is in the expected directory.

```
ls -l shared/build/xcode-frameworks
```

You should see the file **shared.framework** in the folder.

Go back to Xcode to finish the iOS app setup. Choose the app target and go to **General** settings.

In the **Embedded Binaries** section, click the plus and then select **Add Other** and **Add Files**. Navigate to and choose the shared framework **shared/build/xcodeframeworks/shared.framework**.

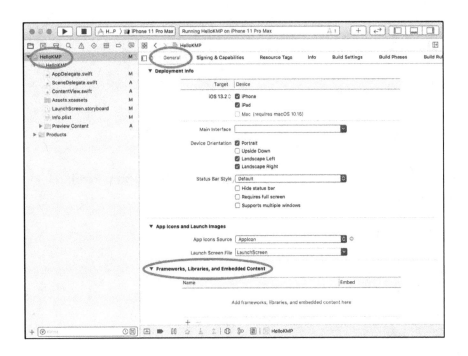

Since Kotlin/Native produces full native binaries, you need to disable the **Bitcode** feature for the project in **Build Settings**. Search on bitcode in the search box and choose **No** for **Enable Bitcode**.

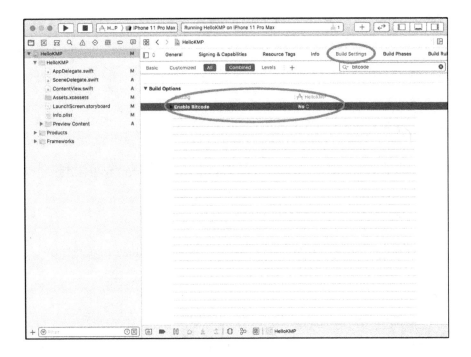

Now you need to update framework search paths for the iOS project.

In **Build Settings**, search for **Framework Search Paths**, and then add the framework directory you setup in the new Gradle task, using **$(SRCROOT)/../../ shared/build/xcode-frameworks**.

Xcode will then set the absolute path based on the **SRCROOT** value.

The last step you need for setting up the Xcode project is to add a new build phase to have Xcode build the shared code.

Switch to **Build Phases** and add a new **Run Script**.

In the run script, change the directory to the framework directory, and then call the bash script you created in the packForXcode task, passing in the Xcode configuration value.

cd "$SRCROOT/../../shared/build/xcode-frameworks"

./gradlew :shared:build -PXCODE_CONFIGURATION=${CONFIGURATION}

Then move the new run script to the top of the Build Phases, just below Dependencies.

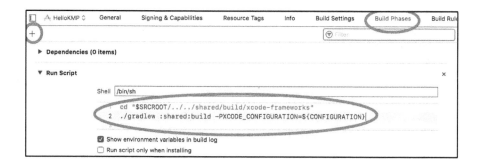

Now build and run the app to make sure there are no build errors due to any of these changes.

So you can run the iOS app from Android Studio, add the following line to **gradle.properties**:

xcodeproj=iosApp/HelloKMP

Sync Gradle. Then, select the iOS app to run.

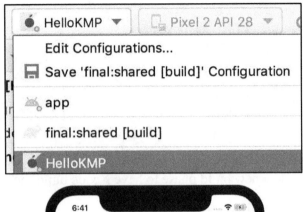

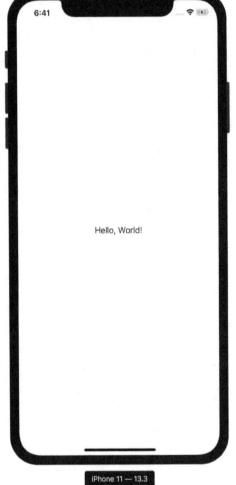

Note: To run this project in Xcode, you need to do additional configuration to inform Xcode how to build using the shared Kotlin code.

Shared code from iOS

With the iOS app project in place and linked up with the shared project, next you'll use the shared code in the iOS version of the HelloKMP app. The iOS app will consist primarily of user interface code, relying on the shared code to do most of the work.

Open **iosApp/HelloKMP/HelloKMP/ContentView.swift** and ddd an import for the **shared** code to the top of **ViewController.swift**:

import shared

This gives you access to the shared code in the Swift file. It might give you an error in Xcode without the extra Xcode configuration, and that's okay.

In the ContentView body, update the Text to call into the shared code:

Text(Greeting().greeting())

This simple Swift code is literally identical to the line in Kotlin that was used in the Android app. You create a Greeting object and then call its greeting() method.

You can now build and run the iOS app to see that everything is working.

When the app comes up in the simulator, there is your greeting that displays the iOS system name as determined in the shared code.

Conclusion: Kotlin/Native and Multiplatform

In the rapidly evolving world of software development, Kotlin/Native and Kotlin Multiplatform have emerged as key players in the drive for code reusability, cross-platform efficiency, and developer productivity. As we reflect on their progress and potential in 2025, it becomes evident that they are transforming the way developers approach application development for diverse platforms, ranging from mobile and web to desktop and embedded systems.

Strengths and Achievements

1. **Code Sharing and Reusability**: Kotlin Multiplatform (KMP) has become a robust solution for sharing code across platforms. Developers can now write shared business logic once and reuse it across Android, iOS, Web, and even server-side platforms. This capability significantly reduces development time and cost, enabling teams to focus on crafting platform-specific user experiences while maintaining a unified codebase for the application core.

2. **Native Performance**: Kotlin/Native allows developers to build performant applications by compiling Kotlin code directly into native binaries. This eliminates the need for a virtual machine and ensures that applications can take full advantage of platform-specific features and hardware. From iOS applications to embedded systems, Kotlin/Native's performance has proved comparable to traditional native languages like Swift, C, and C++.

3. **Seamless Interoperability**: Kotlin/Native's interoperability with C and Objective-C has simplified integrating Kotlin into existing native projects. Developers can use native libraries and frameworks without significant overhead, making Kotlin/Native an appealing option for teams with established native codebases.

4. **Ecosystem Maturity**: The Kotlin ecosystem has matured significantly by 2025. Tools like JetBrains' Compose Multiplatform simplify building shared UI components, while libraries like Ktor and SQLDelight offer powerful solutions for networking and database management. The active community and improved documentation further accelerate Kotlin's adoption.

5. **Support for Emerging Platforms**: Beyond mobile and desktop, Kotlin/Native has expanded into embedded systems, IoT, and even gaming, showcasing its versatility. With its lightweight runtime and ability to generate standalone executables, Kotlin/Native is well-suited for resource-constrained environments.

Addressing Challenges

Despite its progress, Kotlin/Native and Multiplatform have faced several challenges. Addressing these has been crucial for their continued success:

1. **Learning Curve**: Adopting Kotlin/Native and Multiplatform can be challenging for teams unfamiliar with Kotlin or cross-platform paradigms. However, initiatives such as improved onboarding resources, community-driven tutorials, and official training programs have reduced barriers to entry.

2. **Tooling and Debugging**: Early adopters often reported issues with debugging and tooling in Kotlin/Native projects. By 2025, advancements in IDE support, debuggers, and build tools like Gradle have mitigated many of these issues, making development smoother and more efficient.

3. **Platform Parity**: Achieving feature parity between platforms has been a complex task. Some platforms still lag behind in terms of library support or tooling. However, JetBrains and the open-source community have worked tirelessly to close these gaps, ensuring that developers can achieve near-parity in functionality across supported platforms.

4. **Performance Tuning**: While Kotlin/Native provides near-native performance, fine-tuning for specific platforms can be demanding. Efforts to provide more extensive documentation, profiling tools, and community-driven best practices have helped alleviate this challenge.

Competitive Landscape

Kotlin/Native and Multiplatform operate in a competitive landscape alongside frameworks like Flutter, React Native, and Xamarin. Each of these has its strengths, but Kotlin/Native's ability to compile directly to native binaries and Kotlin Multiplatform's unique code-sharing model provide distinct advantages.

Developers often choose Kotlin Multiplatform when:

- They prioritize sharing business logic while crafting platform-specific UIs.
- They require seamless interoperability with existing native code.
- They work in teams that already use Kotlin for Android or server-side development.

These differentiators make Kotlin/Native and Multiplatform a preferred choice for many organizations, particularly those looking for long-term maintainability and scalability.

The Future of Kotlin/Native and Multiplatform

1. **Wider Adoption**: By 2025, Kotlin/Native and Multiplatform have seen significant adoption across industries. Enterprises value their ability to streamline development processes and reduce duplication of effort. Small teams and startups appreciate the reduced overhead in maintaining separate codebases for multiple platforms.

2. **Enhanced Developer Experience**: JetBrains continues to prioritize improving developer experience. Enhanced IDE support, faster build times, and more intuitive APIs ensure that developers can focus on solving business problems rather than wrestling with tooling.

3. **Expanding Ecosystem**: The ecosystem surrounding Kotlin/Native and Multiplatform is growing steadily. Libraries, plugins, and frameworks designed specifically for Multiplatform projects are being developed at an unprecedented pace. This growth ensures that developers have access to modern solutions for everything from UI design to backend integration.

4. **Integration with Emerging Technologies**: Kotlin's adaptability makes it a natural fit for integrating with emerging technologies like AI, machine learning, and blockchain. The ability to write shared logic for applications leveraging these technologies positions Kotlin/Native and Multiplatform as forward-looking solutions for modern software challenges.

5. **Support for More Platforms**: As Kotlin/Native continues to evolve, support for additional platforms and architectures is becoming a reality. This includes advanced gaming consoles, AR/VR devices, and next-generation wearables, ensuring that Kotlin remains relevant in an ever-changing technological landscape.

Final Thoughts

In 2025, Kotlin/Native and Kotlin Multiplatform represent the forefront of cross-platform development. Their ability to combine the efficiency of shared codebases with the power and flexibility of native development is unmatched. While challenges remain, the consistent effort by JetBrains and the Kotlin community ensures that these technologies are well-positioned for the future.

For developers and organizations alike, Kotlin/Native and Multiplatform provide an opportunity to build high-quality, scalable, and maintainable applications for a diverse range of platforms. With their continued evolution, Kotlin's impact on the software development industry will only grow stronger in the years to come.

11. Future Trends and Case Studies

Introduction

Kotlin, introduced by JetBrains in 2011, has evolved into a versatile and widely-used programming language. Originally developed as a modern alternative to Java for the JVM ecosystem, Kotlin has since expanded its reach across various platforms, including Android, web development, server-side programming, and even multi-platform projects. As Kotlin matures, its future trends reveal exciting opportunities and challenges. This chapter explores key advancements anticipated for Kotlin in 2025, along with real-world case studies that highlight its applications.

Future Trends in Kotlin

1. Expansion of Multiplatform Development

One of Kotlin's standout features is its multiplatform capability, enabling developers to write shared code for various platforms such as Android, iOS, web, and desktop. In 2025, Kotlin Multiplatform (KMP) is expected to achieve greater stability and adoption.

- **Improved Tooling:** JetBrains is likely to enhance tools like Kotlin Multiplatform Mobile (KMM) for seamless development experiences.

- **Ecosystem Growth:** Libraries like Ktor and Compose Multiplatform will expand, enabling developers to write consistent and performant code across platforms.

- **Enterprise Adoption:** Businesses will increasingly adopt Kotlin's multiplatform features for cost-effective and efficient development.

2. AI and Machine Learning Integration

The rise of AI and machine learning (ML) across industries creates a demand for programming languages that facilitate such capabilities. Kotlin is poised to become a go-to choice for AI/ML development due to its interoperability with Java and Python libraries.

- **Kotlin for TensorFlow and PyTorch:** Tools and bindings for AI libraries will emerge, allowing Kotlin to directly integrate with TensorFlow and PyTorch.

- **Custom AI Frameworks:** Kotlin-based frameworks tailored for domain-specific AI applications are expected to flourish.

3. Enhanced Android Development

Kotlin has already established itself as the preferred language for Android development, thanks to Google's official endorsement in 2017. By 2025, Kotlin's dominance in this space will continue to grow.

- **Jetpack Compose Evolution:** Jetpack Compose, Google's modern UI toolkit, will see deeper Kotlin integration and feature enhancements.

- **Kotlin DSLs:** Domain-Specific Languages (DSLs) for Android-specific tasks will simplify configurations, navigation, and animations.

4. Server-Side and Cloud Computing

Kotlin's footprint in server-side development will expand, especially in microservices and cloud-native architectures.

- **Ktor Improvements:** Ktor, Kotlin's native asynchronous framework for building connected applications, will see increased adoption.

- **Serverless Kotlin:** Integration with serverless platforms such as AWS Lambda and Google Cloud Functions will improve.

- **Integration with Spring Boot:** Kotlin will solidify its role as a first-class citizen in Spring Boot applications, with better tooling and documentation.

5. Native Development with Kotlin/Native

Kotlin/Native, which allows Kotlin to compile directly into machine code, opens up opportunities for native applications beyond the JVM.

- **IoT and Embedded Systems:** Kotlin/Native will become a popular choice for Internet of Things (IoT) devices and embedded systems, thanks to its lightweight runtime.

- **Gaming Development:** With tools like libGDX and Unity integration, Kotlin will gain traction in game development.

6. Increased Focus on Performance and Compiler Enhancements

Performance optimizations and compiler improvements will continue to be a priority for Kotlin in 2025.

- **Faster Build Times:** Efforts to reduce build times will make Kotlin more attractive for large projects.

- **Improved Static Analysis:** Enhanced static analysis tools will help developers catch bugs earlier in the development lifecycle.

- **Better JVM and Native Interop:** Kotlin will offer seamless interop not only with the JVM but also with native platforms.

7. Community Growth and Open-Source Contributions

The Kotlin community plays a pivotal role in the language's success. In 2025, this community will continue to grow, contributing libraries, tools, and educational content.

- **Open-Source Libraries:** The number of high-quality Kotlin libraries will increase.

- **Educational Resources:** Platforms like JetBrains Academy will offer more courses and certifications.

Case Studies

Case Study 1: Revolutionizing Fintech with Kotlin

A leading fintech company migrated its backend systems from Java to Kotlin, leveraging the language's concise syntax and null safety features. This migration resulted in a 20% reduction in codebase size and a significant decrease in runtime errors.

- **Challenge:** The legacy Java system was prone to null pointer exceptions and verbose boilerplate code.

- **Solution:** By adopting Kotlin, the development team simplified the code and used coroutines for efficient asynchronous processing.

- **Outcome:** Improved developer productivity, faster feature delivery, and enhanced application reliability.

Case Study 2: Building Cross-Platform Apps with Kotlin Multiplatform Mobile

An e-commerce startup utilized Kotlin Multiplatform Mobile (KMM) to develop a single codebase for their Android and iOS applications. Shared business logic reduced duplication and accelerated development.

- **Challenge:** Maintaining separate codebases for Android and iOS was time-consuming and expensive.
- **Solution:** KMM enabled the team to write shared code for core features while using platform-specific APIs for UI.
- **Outcome:** The startup reduced development costs by 35% and launched their app two months ahead of schedule.

Case Study 3: Advancing AI Research with Kotlin

A research institution used Kotlin for their AI-powered predictive analytics project. By integrating Kotlin with TensorFlow, the team developed models for real-time data analysis.

- **Challenge:** The team needed a language that combined ease of use with compatibility with existing Java and Python libraries.
- **Solution:** Kotlin's interoperability allowed seamless integration with TensorFlow and Apache Spark.
- **Outcome:** The project achieved a 15% improvement in predictive accuracy and reduced training time by 25%.

Case Study 4: Scaling Microservices with Kotlin and Ktor

A SaaS company adopted Kotlin and Ktor to develop microservices for their cloud-native application.

- **Challenge:** The company's previous framework was difficult to scale and lacked flexibility.
- **Solution:** Ktor's lightweight architecture and Kotlin's concise syntax enabled rapid development and easy scalability.
- **Outcome:** The SaaS application now handles 40% more traffic with a 30% reduction in infrastructure costs.

Case Study 5: Game Development with Kotlin/Native

An indie game studio used Kotlin/Native to create a cross-platform game for desktop and mobile devices.

- **Challenge:** The studio needed a solution to deliver high performance across platforms without managing multiple codebases.
- **Solution:** Kotlin/Native provided a single codebase for core game logic, with platform-specific optimizations.
- **Outcome:** The game launched successfully on multiple platforms, receiving praise for its performance and smooth gameplay.

Let's begin,

The "Future Trends in Kotlin" module within "Kotlin Programming: Concise, Expressive, and Powerful" embarks on a forward-looking exploration, delving into the evolving landscape of Kotlin programming. As technology continues to advance, this module serves as a strategic guide for developers, architects, and technology enthusiasts, shedding light on the emerging trends, innovations, and transformations that will shape the future of Kotlin and its role in the dynamic world of software development.

Kotlin/Native and Multiplatform Development: Bridging Platforms Seamlessly

This segment kicks off the module by examining the future trajectory of Kotlin/Native and multiplatform development. Developers gain insights into Kotlin's expansion beyond the Java Virtual Machine (JVM) to native platforms, including iOS, Android, and even embedded systems. The module explores the potential of Kotlin's multiplatform capabilities, allowing developers to write shared code across different platforms, streamlining development and fostering code reuse. Real-world examples showcase the versatility of Kotlin in bridging the gap between diverse platforms seamlessly.

Kotlin for WebAssembly: Unlocking Web Development Possibilities

The module extends its exploration to the realm of web development, spotlighting Kotlin's potential for WebAssembly (Wasm). Developers gain insights into the growing trend of using Kotlin to target the web through Wasm, enabling the execution of Kotlin code in web browsers at near-native speeds. The module explores how Kotlin's strengths, such as conciseness and expressiveness, can be leveraged for building modern web applications, fostering a unified and efficient approach to full-stack development.

Kotlin for Cloud-Native Development: Orchestrating Microservices

As cloud-native development continues to gain prominence, this segment dives into Kotlin's role in orchestrating microservices and building scalable, resilient, and cloud-native applications. Developers gain practical insights into using Kotlin to develop microservices architecture, leveraging frameworks and tools that align with cloud-native principles. Real-world examples illustrate how Kotlin's features contribute to the development of distributed systems, enabling developers to navigate the complexities of modern cloud environments with ease.

Kotlin and Machine Learning Integration: Shaping Intelligent Applications

Machine learning is at the forefront of technological innovation, and this part of the module explores Kotlin's integration with machine learning frameworks and libraries. Developers gain insights into the emerging trend of using Kotlin for building intelligent applications that leverage machine learning models. The module showcases how Kotlin's versatility and expressive syntax contribute to the development of applications that harness the power of artificial intelligence, paving the way for innovative solutions in various domains.

Kotlin and Quantum Computing: Pioneering the Future Frontier

Quantum computing represents the next frontier in computational power, and this segment peers into the future of Kotlin in the realm of quantum computing. Developers gain insights into Kotlin's potential role in quantum computing development, exploring the challenges and opportunities presented by this cutting-edge technology. The module underscores the significance of Kotlin's adaptability in pioneering the future of computing, positioning developers to embrace quantum computing paradigms as they become increasingly accessible.

Kotlin for Augmented and Virtual Reality: Crafting Immersive Experiences

The module explores the immersive realms of augmented and virtual reality, highlighting Kotlin's potential in crafting applications that redefine user experiences. Developers gain practical insights into using Kotlin for AR and VR development, leveraging its strengths to create interactive and immersive applications. Real-world examples showcase Kotlin's role in shaping the future of augmented and virtual reality, opening up possibilities for creating engaging and innovative experiences in diverse industries.

Kotlin for Internet of Things (IoT): Powering Connected Devices

As the Internet of Things (IoT) ecosystem expands, this segment delves into Kotlin's role in powering connected devices. Developers gain insights into using Kotlin to develop IoT applications, addressing the unique challenges of the IoT landscape. The module explores how Kotlin's concise syntax and robust features contribute to building efficient and scalable IoT solutions, paving the way for the integration of Kotlin into the fabric of the interconnected devices that define the IoT era.

Quantum Computing and Blockchain Integration: Securing the Future

This part of the module explores the convergence of quantum computing and blockchain technology, showcasing how Kotlin can play a role in securing the future of decentralized and secure systems. Developers gain insights into the potential synergy between quantum-resistant algorithms and Kotlin-powered smart contracts, addressing the evolving landscape of blockchain security. Real-world examples illustrate how Kotlin's adaptability positions it at the forefront of developing blockchain solutions that can withstand the challenges posed by quantum computing advancements.

Beyond Syntax: Kotlin's Contribution to Developer Well-Being

The module concludes by exploring the overarching theme of Kotlin's contribution to developer well-being. As the programming landscape evolves, the importance of a language that prioritizes developer experience, mental health, and work-life balance becomes increasingly crucial. The module highlights Kotlin's commitment to providing a concise, expressive, and powerful language that not only enables developers to tackle complex challenges but also enhances their overall well-being, contributing to a positive and sustainable future for the developer community.

The "Future Trends in Kotlin" module stands as a beacon guiding developers through the evolving landscape of Kotlin programming. By examining Kotlin's expansion into native platforms, its role in web development, cloud native architectures, machine learning integration, quantum computing, augmented and virtual reality, IoT, quantum computing and blockchain integration, and its commitment to developer well-being, this module equips developers with the knowledge and insights needed to navigate the future of Kotlin confidently. As Kotlin continues to shape the technological landscape, developers are empowered to embrace emerging trends and contribute to the ongoing evolution of software development in the years to come.

Kotlin 2.0 Features and Improvements

The "Future Trends in Kotlin" module within the book "Kotlin Programming: Concise, Expressive, and Powerful" delves into the anticipated advancements in the Kotlin programming language, with a particular focus on the "Kotlin 2.0 Features and Improvements" section. This segment explores the evolving landscape of Kotlin, shedding light on the latest enhancements, features, and improvements that developers can expect in the next major version of the language.

Conciseness and Readability Enhancements

In the pursuit of maintaining its reputation for conciseness and readability, Kotlin 2.0 introduces further language enhancements. The section emphasizes the language's commitment to reducing boilerplate code and improving expressiveness, allowing developers to write more efficient and clear code. New syntax features are anticipated to enhance the overall readability of Kotlin code.

```
// Example: Kotlin 2.0 Enhanced Syntax data class Person(val name: String, val age: Int)
```

```kotlin
fun main() { val person = Person("Alice", 30)
println("Name: ${person.name}, Age: ${person.age}") }
```

Extension Function Improvements

The "Kotlin 2.0 Features and Improvements" section highlights enhancements to extension functions, a powerful feature in Kotlin. Developers can expect improved functionality and more flexibility in defining extension functions, enabling them to augment existing classes with additional methods seamlessly.

```kotlin
// Example: Kotlin 2.0 Extension Function Improvement fun String.isPalindrome(): Boolean { val
cleanString = this.replace("\\s+".toRegex(), "").toLowerCase() return cleanString == cleanString.reversed()
}
```

```kotlin
fun main() { val phrase = "A man a plan a canal Panama"
println("Is palindrome: ${phrase.isPalindrome()}") }
```

Improved Null Safety Features

Null safety has been a cornerstone of Kotlin's design, and Kotlin 2.0 aims to enhance this aspect even further. The section explores additional features and improvements related to null safety, offering developers more tools to handle nullable and non-nullable types effectively.

```kotlin
// Example: Kotlin 2.0 Null Safety Improvement fun calculateStringLength(text: String?): Int {
// New null check syntax
return text?.length ?: 0
}
```

```kotlin
fun main() { val message: String? = "Hello, Kotlin 2.0!"
println("Message length: ${calculateStringLength(message)}") }
```

Concurrency and Multiplatform Enhancements

As the demand for concurrent and multiplatform development continues to rise, Kotlin 2.0 is expected to introduce improvements in these areas. The section underscores how developers can benefit from enhancements in coroutine support, making it even more efficient to write concurrent code. Additionally, multiplatform projects are anticipated to see advancements, allowing developers to share more code across different platforms seamlessly.

```kotlin
// Example: Kotlin 2.0 Coroutine Enhancement import kotlinx.coroutines.*
```

```kotlin
fun main() = runBlocking { val job = launch {
// Improved coroutine functionality delay(1000L)
println("Task completed after 1 second.")
}
println("Main function is not blocked.")
job.join() }
```

The "Kotlin 2.0 Features and Improvements" section of the "Future Trends in Kotlin" module provides a glimpse into the evolving nature of the Kotlin programming language. From enhanced conciseness and readability to improvements in extension functions, null safety, and concurrency, Kotlin 2.0 promises to bring forth a set of features that will further solidify its position as a concise, expressive, and powerful programming language.

Industry Adoption and Trends

The "Future Trends in Kotlin" module within the book "Kotlin Programming: Concise, Expressive, and Powerful" anticipates the trajectory of Kotlin in terms of industry adoption and emerging trends. The "Industry Adoption and Trends" section delves into the evolving landscape of Kotlin in the professional sphere, shedding light on its increasing popularity and the trends that developers and organizations are likely to witness in the coming years.

Widespread Adoption in Android Development

Kotlin's ascent to prominence in the world of Android development has been remarkable. The "Industry Adoption and Trends" section underscores the increasing preference for Kotlin over Java in Android app development. As more organizations recognize the benefits of Kotlin's concise syntax and enhanced features, the language is expected to continue its dominance in the Android ecosystem.

```kotlin
// Example: Kotlin in Android Development class MainActivity : AppCompatActivity() { override fun onCreate(savedInstanceState: Bundle?) { super.onCreate(savedInstanceState)
setContentView(R.layout.activity_main)

// Kotlin code for Android development

val textView: TextView = findViewById(R.id.textView)

textView.text = "Hello, Kotlin!"

}

}
```

Expansion into Backend and Server-Side Development

Beyond its stronghold in mobile app development, Kotlin is steadily making inroads into backend and server-side development. The section emphasizes the growing trend of using Kotlin to build robust and scalable server applications. As developers recognize the advantages of a unified language stack, Kotlin's seamless interoperability with existing Java codebases becomes a significant driver for its adoption in backend development.

```kotlin
// Example: Kotlin in Backend Development fun main() {

// Kotlin code for server-side application val server = embeddedServer(Netty, port = 8080) { routing { get("/") { call.respondText("Hello, Kotlin!")

}

}

}

server.start(wait = true)

}
```

Integration with Spring Framework and Microservices

The "Industry Adoption and Trends" section explores the trend of integrating Kotlin with the Spring Framework for building robust and scalable enterprise applications. Kotlin's expressive syntax and null safety features complement the Spring ecosystem, providing developers with a modern and efficient toolset for building microservices and other distributed systems.

```kotlin
// Example: Kotlin with Spring Boot @SpringBootApplication class MyApplication
```

```kotlin
fun main() {
// Kotlin code for Spring Boot application runApplication<MyApplication>()
}
```

Increased Demand for Kotlin Multiplatform Projects

As the need for cross-platform development rises, the module anticipates an increased demand for Kotlin Multiplatform Projects (KMP). The "Industry Adoption and Trends" section emphasizes how KMP allows developers to write shared code that can be utilized across multiple platforms, including iOS and Android, reducing development time and effort.

```kotlin
// Example: Kotlin Multiplatform Project expect fun platformSpecificFunction(): String
fun commonFunction(): String { return "This is common code."
}
fun main() {
// Shared Kotlin code in a multiplatform project
println(commonFunction()) println(platformSpecificFunction()) }
```

The "Industry Adoption and Trends" section anticipates a bright future for Kotlin as it continues to gain traction across various domains of software development. From Android app development to backend services, Spring integration, and multiplatform projects, Kotlin's versatility positions it as a language that resonates with the evolving needs of the industry.

Kotlin in Emerging Technologies

Kotlin, a modern programming language developed by JetBrains, has rapidly gained traction in the ever-evolving landscape of emerging technologies. As organizations seek more efficient and expressive ways to build software, Kotlin has emerged as a language of choice, offering conciseness, expressiveness, and power. In the module "Future Trends in Kotlin" from the book "Kotlin Programming: Concise, Expressive, and Powerful," the authors delve into how Kotlin is seamlessly integrating into cutting-edge technologies, shaping the future of software development.

1. Mobile App Development:

One of the foremost areas where Kotlin is making significant strides is in mobile app development. With its interoperability with Java and concise syntax, Kotlin has become the preferred language for Android app development. The module explores Kotlin's role in enhancing the development experience for Android applications, showcasing examples of how its features contribute to cleaner and more maintainable code.

```kotlin
// Example of Kotlin in Android development class MainActivity: AppCompatActivity() { override fun
onCreate(savedInstanceState: Bundle?) { super.onCreate(savedInstanceState)
setContentView(R.layout.activity_main)
// Kotlin's concise syntax for handling click events
button.setOnClickListener { showToast("Button clicked!")
}
}
private fun showToast(message: String) {
Toast.makeText(this, message, Toast.LENGTH_SHORT).show() }
```

```
}
```

2. Server-Side Development:

As server-side development continues to evolve, Kotlin has found its place in this domain as well. The module explores how Kotlin's conciseness and expressiveness shine in server-side applications, enabling developers to write robust and scalable code. It delves into examples illustrating Kotlin's compatibility with frameworks like Spring, showcasing its versatility beyond client-side applications.

```
// Example of Kotlin in Spring Boot application

@RestController class ExampleController {

@GetMapping("/hello") fun hello(): String { return "Hello, Kotlin in Spring Boot!"

}

}
```

3. Kotlin in Data Science:

Surprisingly, Kotlin is making inroads into the realm of data science, traditionally dominated by languages like Python and R. The module explores Kotlin's potential in this field, highlighting its capabilities in handling data processing and analysis. Detailed examples demonstrate how Kotlin's expressive syntax can streamline data science workflows.

```
// Example of Kotlin in data processing fun processData(data: List<Double>): Double { // Kotlin's concise syntax for calculating the average return data.average()

}
```

The module on "Future Trends in Kotlin" within the book "Kotlin Programming: Concise, Expressive, and Powerful" sheds light on how Kotlin is seamlessly adapting to and driving emerging technologies. Whether in mobile app development, server-side applications, or data science, Kotlin's concise and expressive nature positions it as a language with a promising future in the ever-evolving world of programming.

Community Predictions and Contributions

The module on "Future Trends in Kotlin" from the book "Kotlin Programming: Concise, Expressive, and Powerful" goes beyond the technical aspects of the language and delves into the vibrant ecosystem created by the Kotlin community. One key aspect explored is the community's predictions regarding Kotlin's trajectory and the valuable contributions that enthusiasts bring to the language's evolution.

1. Community-Driven Innovation:

A standout feature of Kotlin's success lies in its open-source nature and the active involvement of a passionate community. This section of the module sheds light on the community's predictions for the language, exploring how Kotlin enthusiasts actively contribute to its growth. The authors discuss the collaborative spirit that has led to the emergence of various libraries, frameworks, and tools that enhance the Kotlin development experience.

```
// Example of a community-contributed Kotlin library dependencies {
implementation("io.github.kotlinx:kotlinx-coroutines-core:1.5.2") }
```

2. Predictions for Language Evolution:

As the module looks towards the future, it examines the community's predictions regarding Kotlin's evolution. This includes discussions on potential language features, improvements, and adaptations to emerging trends. The authors detail how the community plays a pivotal role in shaping the language's roadmap, fostering a dynamic and responsive development environment.

```
// Hypothetical example of a community-suggested language feature inline fun <reified T>
List<T>.customFilter(predicate: (T) -> Boolean): List<T> { return filter { item -> predicate(item) }
}
```

3. Community Initiatives and Events:

Beyond code contributions, the module explores how the Kotlin community engages in various initiatives and events. This includes hackathons, conferences, and collaborative projects aimed at advancing Kotlin's presence in diverse domains. The authors emphasize the importance of these communal efforts in not only fostering a sense of belonging but also in propelling Kotlin to new heights.

```
// Example of a community-driven Kotlin conference fun main() { val conference = KotlinConf(year =
2023, location = "Virtual") conference.registerParticipant("John Doe") conference.start() }
```

The "Community Predictions and Contributions" section within the "Future Trends in Kotlin" module provides readers with insights into the dynamic and collaborative nature of the Kotlin community. From predicting the language's future trajectory to actively contributing code and participating in events, the community's involvement is integral to Kotlin's success and ensures its continued relevance in the ever-evolving landscape of programming languages.

Kotlin Case Studies

The "Kotlin Case Studies" module within "Kotlin Programming: Concise, Expressive, and Powerful" embarks on a captivating journey into the practical realm of Kotlin, exploring real-world case studies that illustrate the language's versatility, efficiency, and impact across diverse industries. This module serves as a comprehensive guide for developers, architects, and technology enthusiasts, offering a deep dive into the success stories and lessons learned from Kotlin implementations in various domains.

Healthcare Innovations: Kotlin in Medical Imaging Applications

This segment delves into the intersection of Kotlin and healthcare, showcasing case studies where Kotlin has played a pivotal role in developing innovative medical imaging applications. Developers gain insights into the challenges and solutions encountered in the healthcare industry, exploring how Kotlin's expressive syntax, safety features, and scalability contribute to the creation of robust and efficient medical imaging solutions. Real-world examples highlight Kotlin's role in advancing healthcare technologies, improving diagnostics, and enhancing patient care.

E-Commerce Optimization: Kotlin-Powered Scalability

The module extends its exploration to the realm of e-commerce, highlighting case studies that demonstrate Kotlin's prowess in optimizing and scaling e-commerce platforms. Developers gain practical insights into how Kotlin has been leveraged to address the complexities of large-scale e-commerce systems, from enhancing backend performance to streamlining frontend development. Real-world examples illustrate how Kotlin's conciseness and versatility contribute to creating seamless and efficient online shopping experiences for users around the globe.

Financial Sector Solutions: Kotlin for Fintech Innovation

As the financial sector undergoes digital transformation, this part of the module explores case studies showcasing Kotlin's role in driving fintech innovation. Developers gain insights into how Kotlin has been employed to develop financial applications, trading platforms, and secure payment systems. The module addresses the challenges of the financial sector and illustrates how Kotlin's features contribute to the creation of robust, secure, and scalable solutions that meet the evolving needs of the fintech industry.

Educational Technology: Enhancing Learning Experiences with Kotlin

The module turns its attention to the realm of educational technology, exploring case studies that highlight Kotlin's contribution to enhancing learning experiences. Developers gain insights into how Kotlin has been utilized to build educational platforms, interactive learning applications, and tools that facilitate remote and personalized learning. Real-world examples illustrate Kotlin's adaptability in creating engaging and effective educational solutions that cater to the diverse needs of students and educators.

Automotive Innovation: Kotlin in Connected Vehicles

As the automotive industry embraces digital transformation, this segment examines case studies demonstrating Kotlin's role in connected vehicle technologies. Developers gain practical insights into how Kotlin has been employed to develop software for in-car infotainment systems, telematics, and connected vehicle platforms. The module explores the challenges of automotive software development and showcases how Kotlin's features contribute to building efficient, reliable, and user-friendly solutions that redefine the driving experience.

Travel and Hospitality: Kotlin for Seamless Customer Experiences

The module extends its exploration to the travel and hospitality sector, unveiling case studies that showcase Kotlin's impact on creating seamless customer experiences. Developers gain insights into how Kotlin has been harnessed to build booking platforms, travel apps, and hospitality management systems. Real-world examples illustrate Kotlin's role in streamlining operations, enhancing user interfaces, and providing travelers with intuitive and feature-rich applications that elevate their overall journey.

Media and Entertainment: Kotlin-Powered Content Delivery

As the media and entertainment landscape evolves, this part of the module explores case studies highlighting Kotlin's contribution to content delivery platforms, streaming services, and digital entertainment solutions. Developers gain insights into the challenges of delivering high-quality media experiences and discover how Kotlin's features contribute to building scalable, performant, and immersive applications. Real-world examples illustrate Kotlin's adaptability in meeting the demands of modern consumers in the dynamic media and entertainment industry.

Government and Public Services: Kotlin for Efficient Governance

The module delves into case studies in the government and public services sector, showcasing Kotlin's role in developing solutions that contribute to efficient governance. Developers gain insights into how Kotlin has been utilized to create citizen-centric applications, e-government platforms, and public service innovations. Real-world examples illustrate how Kotlin's features enable the development of secure, accessible, and citizen-friendly solutions that enhance government services and foster transparency.

Startup Success Stories: Kotlin as the Catalyst for Innovation

This segment explores the startup landscape, unveiling case studies that highlight Kotlin as the catalyst for innovation and success. Developers gain practical insights into how Kotlin has been embraced by startups across various industries, propelling them to achieve milestones and disrupt traditional markets. The module examines the agility, productivity, and scalability that Kotlin provides to startups, contributing to their journey from ideation to market impact.

Lessons Learned and Best Practices: Extracting Wisdom from Kotlin Case Studies

The module concludes by extracting valuable lessons learned and best practices from the showcased Kotlin case studies. Developers gain insights into common challenges, innovative solutions, and the strategic decisions that contributed to the success of Kotlin implementations in diverse industries. The module emphasizes the importance of adaptability, collaboration, and continuous learning, offering a wealth of practical knowledge that developers can apply to their own Kotlin projects.

The "Kotlin Case Studies" module stands as a testament to the real-world impact of Kotlin across diverse industries. By exploring case studies in healthcare, e-commerce, finance, education, automotive, travel, media, government, startups, and distilling lessons learned and best practices, this module equips developers with a deep understanding of Kotlin's versatility and effectiveness in solving complex challenges. As developers draw inspiration from these case studies, they gain valuable insights into how Kotlin can be harnessed to drive innovation, efficiency, and success in their own projects and industries.

Success Stories of Kotlin Adoption

The module on "Kotlin Case Studies" within the book "Kotlin Programming: Concise, Expressive, and Powerful" dives into real-world applications of Kotlin, highlighting success stories that illuminate the language's impact in various industries. This section explores how Kotlin has been adopted across diverse domains, showcasing instances where its concise and expressive nature has resulted in tangible benefits.

1. Android Development at Airbnb:

One compelling case study featured in the module is the adoption of Kotlin in Android development at Airbnb. The authors detail how Kotlin's interoperability with Java and its concise syntax proved instrumental in streamlining the development process. The case study presents snippets of code that demonstrate Kotlin's readability and conciseness, emphasizing its role in enhancing the overall codebase.

```
// Example of Kotlin code in Airbnb's Android app class MainActivity: AppCompatActivity() { override fun onCreate(savedInstanceState: Bundle?) { super.onCreate(savedInstanceState)
setContentView(R.layout.activity_main)
```

```
// Kotlin's concise syntax for handling click events
```

```
button.setOnClickListener { showToast("Welcome to Airbnb!")
```

```
}
```

```
}
```

```
private fun showToast(message: String) {
```

```
Toast.makeText(this, message, Toast.LENGTH_SHORT).show() }
```

```
}
```

2. Server-Side Transition at Netflix:

Another noteworthy success story discussed in the module is Netflix's transition to using Kotlin on the server side. The authors provide insights into how Kotlin's expressive features, such as extension functions and data classes, contributed to the development of robust and maintainable server-side applications. Code snippets showcase Kotlin's versatility in server-side scenarios.

```
// Example of Kotlin code in Netflix's server-side application data class Movie(val title: String, val genre: String)
```

```
// Kotlin's concise syntax for defining extension functions fun Movie.displayDetails() { println("Title: $title, Genre: $genre")
```

```
}
```

3. Financial Modeling at Square:

The module delves into Square's success story, emphasizing how Kotlin has been leveraged in the realm of financial modeling. The concise syntax of Kotlin is highlighted as a key factor that facilitates the creation and maintenance of complex financial algorithms. The authors provide snippets of Kotlin code that illustrate its readability and suitability for mathematical computations.

// Example of Kotlin code in Square's financial modeling fun calculateCompoundInterest(principal: Double, rate: Double, time: Double

): Double {

// Kotlin's concise syntax for mathematical calculations return principal * (1 + rate).pow(time) }

The "Success Stories of Kotlin Adoption" section within the "Kotlin Case Studies" module showcases the real-world impact of Kotlin in diverse industries. From enhancing Android development at Airbnb to facilitating server-side transitions at Netflix and powering financial modeling at Square, these case studies provide concrete examples of how Kotlin's concise, expressive, and powerful features contribute to success in various application domains. The detailed code snippets further underscore the language's practicality and effectiveness in real-world scenarios.

Challenges Faced and Solutions

Within the module "Kotlin Case Studies" of the book "Kotlin Programming: Concise, Expressive, and Powerful," an insightful exploration into the challenges encountered during Kotlin adoption is presented, alongside innovative solutions that organizations have implemented to overcome these hurdles. This section sheds light on the pragmatic aspects of incorporating Kotlin into existing projects and workflows.

1. Integration with Legacy Code at Uber:

One notable challenge discussed in the module is the integration of Kotlin with legacy codebases, illustrated by the experiences at Uber. The authors delve into the complexities faced during the transition and how Kotlin's interoperability with Java played a pivotal role. Code snippets showcase how seamless integration was achieved, maintaining compatibility with existing Java code.

// Example of Kotlin-Java interoperability at Uber

class LegacyJavaClass { fun performLegacyOperation() { println("Performing legacy operation in Java")

}

}

// Utilizing Java class in Kotlin

fun main() { val legacyInstance = LegacyJavaClass() legacyInstance.performLegacyOperation()

}

2. Transitioning at Expedia:

The module explores the transition process undertaken by Expedia and the challenges faced when migrating from Java to Kotlin. It emphasizes the need for thorough training and the adaptation of development workflows. Kotlin's succinct syntax is highlighted as a solution, reducing boilerplate code and easing the learning curve for developers.

// Example of Kotlin's concise syntax at Expedia data class Booking(val id: String, val status: String)

// Kotlin's concise syntax for data class instantiation fun createBooking(id: String): Booking { return Booking(id, "Confirmed")

}

3. Team Adoption at Spotify:

Spotify's case study introduces the challenge of team-wide adoption and the strategies employed to ensure a smooth transition. The authors discuss the importance of documentation and collaborative learning within teams. Code examples showcase how well-documented Kotlin code can facilitate the onboarding process for new team members.

```
// Example of well-documented Kotlin code at Spotify
/**
    *    Calculates the Fibonacci sequence up to the specified limit.
    *    @param limit The upper limit for the sequence.
    *    @return The Fibonacci sequence as a list.
*/
fun generateFibonacciSequence(limit: Int): List<Int> { // Implementation details omitted for brevity
// ...
}
```

The "Challenges Faced and Solutions" section within the "Kotlin Case Studies" module provides a comprehensive view of the practical obstacles encountered during Kotlin adoption and the effective solutions implemented by organizations. From integrating with legacy code at Uber to transitioning at Expedia and ensuring team adoption at Spotify, these case studies offer valuable insights into overcoming challenges with thoughtful strategies and leveraging Kotlin's features to their fullest extent. The included code snippets serve to illustrate the pragmatic application of Kotlin's capabilities in addressing real-world development hurdles.

Lessons Learned from Kotlin Projects

Within the module "Kotlin Case Studies" of the book "Kotlin Programming: Concise, Expressive, and Powerful," the section on "Lessons Learned from Kotlin Projects" encapsulates valuable insights gleaned from real-world experiences of adopting Kotlin. This section provides a reflective examination of the challenges faced, solutions applied, and the broader lessons that can guide developers and organizations in their Kotlin journey.

1. Prioritizing Comprehensive Testing at Pinterest:

One prominent lesson explored in this module is the importance of comprehensive testing, as highlighted by the experiences at Pinterest. The authors emphasize the need for robust testing practices to ensure the stability of Kotlin projects. Code snippets showcase how Kotlin's expressive syntax contributes to writing concise and readable test cases.

```
// Example of a Kotlin test case at Pinterest class MathUtilsTest {
@Test
fun `adding two numbers should return the sum`() {
val result = MathUtils.add(2, 3) assertEquals(5, result)
}
}
```

2. Maintaining Code Consistency at Google:

The module delves into Google's experiences, emphasizing the lesson of maintaining code consistency within Kotlin projects. The authors discuss the establishment of coding conventions and the use of tools to enforce a consistent code style. Code examples illustrate how Kotlin's readability contributes to adhering to these conventions.

// Example of enforcing code style in Kotlin at Google class User(val id: String, val name: String)

// Kotlin's consistent naming conventions val newUser = User(id = "123", name = "John Doe")

3. Continuous Learning and Adaptation at Square:

Square's case study introduces the lesson of continuous learning and adaptation. The module details how Square embraced the evolving Kotlin ecosystem and encouraged developers to stay abreast of new language features. Code snippets highlight the adoption of Kotlin's coroutine functionality as an example of adapting to emerging language capabilities.

// Example of using Kotlin coroutines at Square suspend fun fetchData(): String {

// Coroutine implementation details omitted for brevity

// ...

return "Data fetched successfully"

}

4. Community Engagement at JetBrains:

The importance of community engagement surfaces as a crucial lesson, drawing on JetBrains' experiences. The authors discuss the significance of active participation in the Kotlin community, leveraging shared knowledge, and contributing to the language's growth. Code snippets showcase community-driven enhancements.

// Example of a community-contributed Kotlin extension function fun String.customExtensionFunction(): String { // Implementation details omitted for brevity

// ...

return "Custom extension function result"

}

The "Lessons Learned from Kotlin Projects" section within the "Kotlin Case Studies" module provides a reflective examination of key takeaways from real-world Kotlin adoption experiences. From prioritizing comprehensive testing and maintaining code consistency to embracing continuous learning and community engagement, these lessons offer practical guidance for developers and organizations navigating Kotlin projects. The included code snippets underscore the application of these lessons in the context of Kotlin's concise, expressive, and powerful features.

Case Studies from Various Industries

The module "Kotlin Case Studies" within the book "Kotlin Programming: Concise, Expressive, and Powerful" delves into diverse case studies from various industries, showcasing the versatility of Kotlin in addressing unique challenges and contributing to innovative solutions. This section explores how Kotlin's features are applied across domains, providing readers with a holistic understanding of the language's applicability.

1. E-commerce at Shopify:

The case study from Shopify highlights Kotlin's role in e-commerce applications. The authors illustrate how Kotlin's concise syntax and robust type system contribute to the development of scalable and maintainable codebases. Code snippets showcase Kotlin's readability, a crucial factor in the complex world of e-commerce application logic.

```kotlin
// Example of Kotlin in e-commerce at Shopify

data class Product(val id: String, val name: String, val price: Double)

// Kotlin's concise syntax for processing product data fun calculateTotalPrice(products: List<Product>): Double { return products.sumByDouble { it.price }

}
```

2. Healthcare Solutions at Siemens Healthineers:

The module explores Kotlin's applications in healthcare solutions at Siemens Healthineers. The authors discuss how Kotlin's safety features, such as null safety, contribute to the reliability of healthcare software. Code snippets demonstrate Kotlin's capability to prevent null pointer exceptions, crucial in applications where precision and reliability are paramount.

```kotlin
// Example of null safety in Kotlin at Siemens Healthineers data class Patient(val id: String, val name: String?, val age: Int)

// Kotlin's null safety in usage val patient = Patient(id = "123", name = null, age = 30) val patientNameLength = patient.name?.length ?: 0
```

3. Automotive Systems at Ford:

Ford's case study presents Kotlin's role in developing automotive systems. The authors delve into how

Kotlin's expressive features aid in modeling complex automotive logic. Code snippets highlight the use of Kotlin to create readable and maintainable code for intricate systems within the automotive industry.

```kotlin
// Example of Kotlin in automotive systems at Ford

data class Vehicle(val model: String, val year: Int, val mileage: Double)

// Kotlin's expressive syntax for filtering vehicles fun findNewVehicles(vehicles: List<Vehicle>): List<Vehicle> { return vehicles.filter { it.year >= 2022 }

}
```

4. Entertainment Platforms at Netflix:

Netflix's case study showcases Kotlin's applications in entertainment platforms. The authors discuss how Kotlin's conciseness is leveraged to develop user-friendly interfaces and efficient backend services. Code snippets highlight Kotlin's adaptability in creating seamless and responsive experiences within the entertainment industry.

```kotlin
// Example of Kotlin in entertainment platforms at Netflix class Movie(val title: String, val genre: String)

// Kotlin's concise syntax for defining movie details val actionMovie = Movie(title = "Inception", genre = "Action")
```

The "Case Studies from Various Industries" section within the "Kotlin Case Studies" module offers a panoramic view of Kotlin's applications across different sectors. From e-commerce and healthcare to automotive systems and entertainment platforms, these case studies exemplify Kotlin's versatility and effectiveness in addressing industry-specific challenges. The inclusion of detailed code snippets enhances the understanding of how Kotlin's features are practically applied in diverse real-world scenarios.

Conclusion: The Road Ahead for Kotlin

The future of Kotlin is brighter than ever, driven by its continuous evolution, developer-centric innovations, and the robust ecosystem surrounding it. This conclusion delves into the key takeaways from recent trends, the impact of Kotlin's versatility across industries, and its potential to shape the software development landscape in the coming years.

1. Kotlin's Role in the Evolving Development Landscape

Kotlin has transitioned from being a secondary JVM language to becoming a principal choice for modern development. The trends of 2025 emphasize Kotlin's adaptability to new paradigms:

- **Multiplatform Development**: Kotlin Multiplatform has gained immense traction, allowing developers to write shared code across platforms like Android, iOS, web, and desktop. The efficiency of shared business logic has redefined cross-platform development, saving time and resources while maintaining native-level performance.

- **AI and Machine Learning**: With Kotlin's seamless Java interoperability, it is increasingly being adopted for AI and ML projects. Libraries like KotlinDL are empowering developers to build powerful neural networks with Kotlin's concise syntax.

- **Emerging Backend Frameworks**: Frameworks like Ktor continue to simplify server-side development. Kotlin's capabilities for asynchronous programming, coupled with frameworks tailored for microservices, have made it a go-to choice for scalable backend solutions.

2. Industry Adoption and Case Studies

The growing adoption of Kotlin across industries underpins its rising prominence. Here are a few notable case studies that showcase Kotlin's versatility:

- **Finance and Banking**: Kotlin has revolutionized app development in the finance sector. Companies like Square have harnessed Kotlin for creating secure, scalable payment systems, leveraging its null-safety features and concise syntax to reduce bugs.

- **Healthcare**: Telemedicine and health-tech solutions are increasingly turning to Kotlin Multiplatform for cross-platform applications. For example, a leading telehealth provider used Kotlin to reduce time-to-market for its multi-platform app while maintaining robust performance.

- **E-commerce**: Major e-commerce platforms like Flipkart and Netflix have migrated significant portions of their codebases to Kotlin to enhance development efficiency and app responsiveness.

- **Game Development**: Kotlin's growing use in game development, particularly for Android and cross-platform games, highlights its adaptability to diverse domains.

3. Kotlin's Innovations in Developer Productivity

One of Kotlin's standout features is its dedication to improving developer experience. The productivity-centric features introduced in 2025 include:

- **Kotlin Symbol Processing (KSP)**: KSP has streamlined annotation processing, enabling faster builds and a smoother developer experience compared to Java-based tools.

- **Better Tooling and IDE Support**: JetBrains has consistently enhanced Kotlin's integration with IntelliJ IDEA, introducing intelligent suggestions, debugging tools, and real-time linting to minimize errors during development.

- **Coroutines and Flow Enhancements**: Asynchronous programming with coroutines has become even more powerful in 2025, enabling better scalability and simplifying complex workflows.

4. Sustainability and Kotlin's Role in Green Computing

With sustainability becoming a critical focus in tech, Kotlin is contributing to green computing by:

- **Optimizing Resource Usage**: Kotlin's lightweight syntax and efficient compiler help reduce build times, lowering energy consumption in large-scale projects.
- **Enabling Cloud Efficiency**: Kotlin is increasingly being used to write serverless applications, optimizing cloud resources and reducing unnecessary infrastructure usage.

5. Kotlin's Future Potential

Looking ahead, Kotlin is poised to make waves in several emerging domains:

- **WebAssembly (WASM)**: Kotlin/WASM is opening doors for Kotlin's use in web development. As WASM becomes more mainstream, Kotlin could challenge JavaScript in delivering highly performant web applications.
- **Quantum Computing**: While still nascent, Kotlin's simplicity and interop capabilities make it a promising candidate for future quantum programming tools.
- **DevOps and CI/CD Pipelines**: Kotlin scripting is streamlining automation in DevOps, with increased adoption in CI/CD pipelines for tasks like build automation and deployment.
- **Custom DSLs**: Kotlin's ability to create custom domain-specific languages (DSLs) is finding new applications in complex business logic modeling and infrastructure as code.

6. Challenges and the Path Forward

Despite its successes, Kotlin faces challenges that need to be addressed for sustained growth:

- **Learning Curve**: Although Kotlin is easier to learn for Java developers, the growing feature set may intimidate beginners. Efforts to streamline learning resources and community support will be crucial.
- **Ecosystem Maturity**: While Kotlin Multiplatform is promising, its ecosystem and tooling need further maturity to compete with established frameworks like Flutter.
- **Competition**: With languages like Dart, Rust, and Swift competing in specific domains, Kotlin must continue to innovate to maintain its edge.

7. Building a Robust Developer Community

Kotlin's vibrant developer community has been a cornerstone of its growth. Efforts to sustain and expand this community include:

- **Open-Source Contributions**: Kotlin's open-source nature encourages community-driven innovations, with JetBrains actively collaborating with developers.
- **Education and Upskilling**: Organizations and institutions are increasingly offering Kotlin-specific courses, fostering a new generation of developers.
- **Conferences and Meetups**: Events like KotlinConf have become hubs for knowledge sharing, enabling developers to explore new trends and connect with peers.

8. Kotlin and the Vision

As we look to 2025 and beyond, Kotlin embodies the principles of innovation, simplicity, and efficiency. Its journey from a JVM language to a global phenomenon underscores its potential to adapt to and shape the future of technology.

Key focus areas for Kotlin in 2025 include:

- Strengthening its ecosystem for Multiplatform development.
- Expanding its use in emerging domains like AI, blockchain, and quantum computing.
- Building more tools and resources to empower developers.

Final Thoughts

Kotlin is more than just a programming language—it's a mindset of innovation and adaptability. As industries evolve and technologies transform, Kotlin will remain at the forefront, driving change and enabling developers to build smarter, faster, and more efficient solutions. Whether you are an aspiring developer or an experienced technologist, Kotlin's journey is one worth being a part of, as it shapes the future of software development.

Final Note

Congratulations on reaching the end of **Kotlin Bootstrapped: Learn, Code, and Build Like a Pro**! By now, you've built a strong foundation in Kotlin, explored its powerful features, and learned how to apply them in real-world development. From mastering Kotlin's syntax to leveraging its advanced capabilities for modern applications, you are now equipped to take on any challenge.

Kotlin is constantly evolving, and the best way to stay ahead is to keep experimenting, building, and contributing to the community. Whether you're developing Android apps, backend services, or multi-platform applications, Kotlin's versatility will empower you to write efficient, expressive, and maintainable code.

This book may be ending, but your Kotlin journey is just beginning. Keep coding, stay curious, and continue refining your skills. If you found this book helpful, consider sharing your thoughts through reviews or discussions with fellow developers. Your feedback not only helps others but also inspires more in-depth Kotlin explorations in the future.

Happy coding!

Mike Zephalon

www.ingramcontent.com/pod-product-compliance
Lightning Source LLC
LaVergne TN
LVHW082125070326
832902LV00041B/3044

9798309014224